Lonely Planet Publications
Melbourne | Oakland | London

W9-AUO-438

Neil Wilson

Prague

The Top Five

1 Charles Bridge
Stroll the bridge as dusk gilds the rooftops of the Old Town (p68)

2 Vltava River
Enjoy dinner with a view over Prague's finest feature (p121)

3 Obecní dům
Feast your eyes on Art Nouveau extravagance (p77)

4 Prague Castle
Explore the world's biggest castle, seat of Czech power (p53)

5 Josefov
Discover the historic heart of Prague's former Jewish district (p73)

Contents

Published by Lonely Planet Publications Pty Ltd
ABN 36 005 607 983

Australia Head Office, Locked Bag 1, Footscray,
Victoria 3011, ☎ 03 8379 8000, fax 03 8379 8111,
talk2us@lonelyplanet.com.au

USA 150 Linden St, Oakland, CA 94607,
☎ 510 893 8555, toll free 800 275 8555,
fax 510 893 8572, info@lonelyplanet.com

UK 72–82 Rosebery Ave, Clerkenwell, London,
EC1R 4RW, ☎ 020 7841 9000, fax 020 7841 9001,
go@lonelyplanet.co.uk

Printed by SNP SPrint (S) Pte Ltd, Singapore

The Author

NEIL WILSON

Neil first succumbed to the pleasures of Prague back in 1995, beguiled, like everyone else, by its ethereal beauty, but also drawn to the darker side of its hidden history. He has returned regularly for a fix of the world's finest beers, and the chance to track down yet another obscure monument. In recent years Neil has been working on Lonely Planet's *Eastern Europe, Czech & Slovak Republics* and *Prague* guides. A full-time freelance writer since 1988, Neil has travelled in five continents and written around 40 travel and walking guides for various publishers. He is based in Edinburgh, Scotland.

PHOTOGRAPHER

Richard Nebeský was not born with a camera in his hand; however, not long after, his father (an avid photo enthusiast) gave him his first happy-snap unit. Ever since, the camera has always been by Richard's side while skiing, cycling or researching Lonely Planet travel guidebooks around the globe. Work for various magazines, travel guidebook publishers and plenty of social photography followed. He has been commissioned to photograph Prague twice for the respective Lonely Planet city guides.

Introducing Prague

The Czechs call it *matička Praha* – 'little mother Prague' – their national capital, the cradle of Czech culture, and one of the most beautiful and fascinating cities in Europe. Kidnapped by communism for 40 years until it was freed by the Velvet Revolution of 1989, Prague has since become one of Europe's most popular tourist destinations.

Largely undamaged by the ravages of WWII, the cityscape offers a smorgasbord of stunning architecture, from the soaring verticals of Gothic and the buxom exuberance of baroque, to the sensuous elegance of Art Nouveau and the chiselled cheekbones of Cubist façades. Also on offer is an equally wide-ranging menu of musical delights, from the Prague Spring festival of classical music and opera, through countless jazz and rock venues, to some of Central Europe's top dance clubs.

In recent years Prague has seen its traditional pubs and eateries augmented by a wave of gourmet restaurants, cocktail bars and trendy cafés – though if you like, you can still feast on pork and dumplings, washed down with a beer, for just over 100Kč. And what beer! The Czechs have been brewing since at least the 9th century, and invented Pilsner – the world's first clear, golden beer – in 1842. Czech breweries still produce some of the world's finest beers.

Above all Prague is a place to be explored at leisure, whether venturing along the medieval lanes and hidden passages of the Staré Město (Old Town), strolling through the city's many wooded parks or taking a leisurely cruise along the Vltava River. Everywhere you go you will uncover some aspect of the city's multi-layered history – in its time Prague has been the capital of the Holy Roman Empire, the Habsburg Empire, the first Czechoslovak Republic (1918–38), the Nazi Protectorate of Bohemia and Moravia, the Communist Republic of Czechoslovakia, and the modern, democratic Czech Republic.

It is a city that rewards patient exploration and demands many return visits. Beware, though – Prague is a city that gets under your skin, and many people end up staying longer than they mean to. As Kafka once wrote, '…this little mother has claws'.

Lowdown

Population 1,378,700

Time zone GMT + 1hr

Cappuccino 35Kč

3-star double room 4000Kč

Essential accessory A novel by Kafka or Kundera conspicuously poking from pocket or handbag

Metro/tram ticket 12Kč

No-no Pouring the dregs of your first glass of beer into your freshly froth-topped second glass. Philistine!

Portrait by Charles Bridge caricaturist 200Kč

Annual beer consumption 160L per head

Number of bars in Prague Over 11,000

Number of churches in Prague Around 150

NEIL'S TOP PRAGUE DAY

I'd start the day by buying the *Prague Post* and the *Guardian* from a kiosk on Na příkopě and heading to Ebel Coffee House (p126) in Týnský dvůr to read the papers over a giant cappuccino. Then, after browsing the bookshelves at Anagram (p167) and Big Ben (p168) bookshops, I'd cross the river and spend the rest of the morning wandering through the gardens of Malá Strana (p102), stopping to read for a while on a park bench in either the Valdštejnská zahrada (p64) or Palácové zahrady pod Pražským hradem (p64).

For lunch I'd plump for some succulent grilled *candát* (pikeperch) at a riverside table at Rybářský klub (p119), and then take the funicular railway up Petřín (p66). A climb up the lookout tower would be followed by a stroll through the gardens to Strahovský klášter (p61) for yet another look at the gob-smacking library, and then a wander through Prague Castle (p53), by which time I'd be more than ready for a beer or two. I'd round of the day with dinner-with-a-view at U zlaté studně (p120) followed by live jazz (and more beer) at U malého Glena (p150 and p159).

Essential Prague

- Prague Castle (p53)
- Muzeum hlavního města Prahy (p81)
- Palác Lucerna (p85)
- Veletržní palác (p93)
- Vyšehrad (p89)

City Life

City Life

PRAGUE TODAY

As the 21st century gets into its stride, Prague has almost completely recovered from its communist hangover and is fast becoming like any other big capitalist European city, with all the freedoms and pitfalls that entails. Among the states that recently joined the EU, the Czech Republic had the highest GDP and highest inward investment, and its capital city has them in spades. Financially Prague operates on a level above that of the rest of the country.

The rapid transition from communism to capitalism has brought plenty of problems, though. The gap between rich and poor grows wider, and the growth of car culture has led to an increasing gridlock on the city's streets. Plans to build a ring road have been floating around for years, but lack of funds – plus objections from the council of every district the road would pass through – means that construction has not yet begun.

In recent years the city has suffered from a huge increase in the number of British and Irish stag parties attracted by cheap flights, cheap beer and not-so-cheap sex clubs; there are even travel agencies in the UK that specialise in 'Prague piss-ups'. As a result, the city centre is occasionally disrupted by large gangs of noisy lads surfing from pub to pub on a tidal wave of beer and testosterone. You'll see plenty of signs on pub doors requesting 'Please, no groups of drunken British men allowed'.

> ### Hot Conversation Topics
>
> - Apart from that, what has the European Union ever done for us?
> - So, who is the Czech national ice-hockey team going to beat in next year's World Championship final?
> - Staropramen beer – has it gone downhill since it was taken over by a multinational brewery?
> - Do you think Prague's ring-road will ever get built?
> - Whom did you vote for in *Česko hledá SuperStar* (the Czech version of *Pop Idol/American Idol*)?

CITY CALENDAR

Prague caters for visitors all year round, and there's no bad time to visit. The city is at its prettiest in spring, when the many parks begin to bloom with flowers, and the budding leaves on the trees are a glowing green.

Periods when the tourist crush is especially oppressive include the holidays at Easter and Christmas–New Year, as well as May (during the Prague Spring festival), June and September. Many Czechs go on holiday in July and August, during which time the supply of budget accommodation actually increases, as student hostels are opened to visitors.

If you can put up with the cold and the periodic smog alerts during weather inversions, hotel space is plentiful in winter (outside Christmas–New Year), and the city looks both gorgeous and mysterious under a mantle of snow.

Old Town Square (p67), Staré Město

JANUARY

SVÁTEK TŘÍ KRÁLŮ (THREE KINGS' DAY)
Three Kings' Day marks the formal end of the Christmas season on 6 January; it is celebrated with carol singing, bell ringing and gifts to the poor.

ANNIVERSARY OF JAN PALACH'S DEATH
A gathering on 19 January in Wenceslas Square in memory of the Charles University student who burned himself to death in 1969 in protest against the Soviet occupation (see p86).

MARCH

MATĚJSKÁ POUT' (ST MATTHEW FAIR)
From the Feast of St Matthew (24 February) up to and including Easter weekend, the exhibition grounds at Výstaviště (p92) fill up with roller coasters, fairground rides, ghost trains, shooting galleries and stalls selling candyfloss and traditional heart-shaped cookies. The fair is open 2pm to 10pm Tuesday to Friday, 10am to 10pm Saturday and Sunday.

PRAGUE WRITERS' FESTIVAL
www.pwf.pragonet.cz
International meeting of writers from around the world, with public readings, lectures, discussions and bookshop events.

BIRTHDAY OF TOMÁŠ G MASARYK
Commemoration of Czechoslovakia's father figure and first president on 7 March.

PONDĚLÍ VELIKONOČNÍ (EASTER MONDAY)
The city collapses in a mirthful rite of spring – Czech males of all ages chase their favourite girls and swat them on the legs with beribboned willow switches (you'll see them on sale all over the place); the girls respond with gifts of hand-painted eggs (likewise), then everyone gets down to some serious partying. This is the culmination of several days of serious spring-cleaning, cooking and visiting.

FEBIOFEST
www.febiofest.cz
This international festival of film, television and video features new works by international filmmakers. Shown throughout the Czech Republic and Slovakia.

APRIL

JEDEN SVĚT (ONE WORLD)
www.oneworld.cz
This week-long film festival is dedicated to documentaries on the subject of human rights, with screenings held at various small cinemas including Kino Aero and Kino Perštýn (see p162).

PÁLENÍ ČARODĚJNIC (BURNING OF THE WITCHES)
This is the Czech version of a pre-Christian (Pagan) festival for warding off evil, featuring burning brooms at Výstaviště (see p86), and all-night, end-of-winter bonfire parties on Kampa island (p65) and in suburban backyards. It's held on 30 April.

MAY

SVÁTEK PRÁCE (LABOUR DAY)
Once sacred to the communists, the 1 May holiday is now just a chance for a picnic or a day in the country. To celebrate the arrival of spring, many couples lay flowers at the statue of the 19th-century romantic poet, Karel Hynek Mácha (Map pp250–1), author of *Máj* (May), a poem about unrequited love. Ex-president Havel has been known to pay homage here.

SVĚT KNIHY (BOOKWORLD PRAGUE)
www.bookworld.cz
This major international book festival is held at the Výstaviště exhibition grounds in Holešovice (p86). Though primarily an industry event, it's open to the general public and has author readings, book launches, exhibits, seminars and lectures, mostly in English.

PRAŽSKÉ JARO (PRAGUE SPRING)
Running from 12 May to 3 June, this international music festival is Prague's most prestigious event, with classical-music concerts in theatres, churches and historic buildings. See the boxed text on p157.

KHAMORO
www.khamoro.cz
This is a festival of Roma culture, with performances of traditional music and dance, exhibitions of art and photography, and a parade through Staré Město, usually held in late May.

JUNE

TANEC PRAHA (DANCE PRAGUE)

www.tanecpha.cz

This is an international festival of modern dance held at various theatres around Prague throughout June.

JULY

DEN JANA HUSA (JAN HUS DAY)

To mark the occasion celebrations are held on 6 July to commemorate the burning at the stake of the great Bohemian religious reformer Jan Hus in 1415. The day is kicked off with low-key gatherings and bell-ringing at Prague's Betlémská kaple (Bethlehem Chapel; p79) the evening before.

AUGUST

VERDI FESTIVAL

www.sop.cz/en

Beginning in August and extending into September, this festival features the works of Verdi performed at the Státní opera Praha (Prague State Opera; p157); it provides a chance to see quality productions outside the main opera season.

SEPTEMBER

PRAŽSKÝ PODZIM (PRAGUE AUTUMN)

www.prazskypodzim.cz

This international classical music festival is the autumn version of Prague Spring. Most performances are held at the Rudolfinum (p73).

OCTOBER

MEZINÁRODNÍ JAZZOVÝ FESTIVAL (INTERNATIONAL JAZZ FESTIVAL)

www.jazzfestivalpraha.cz/jazz

Established in 1964, and based at the Reduta Jazz Club (p159), this two-week jazz festival stretches from late October into early November, and presents a mix of Czech musicians and star performers from around the world.

DECEMBER

VÁNOCE-NOVÝ ROK (CHRISTMAS–NEW YEAR)

From 24 December to 1 January many celebrate an extended holiday, stuffing themselves with carp (sold live from big tubs in the streets). Prague is engulfed by revellers from all over Europe as the tourist season is on again. A Christmas market is held in Old Town Square in the shadow of a huge Christmas tree.

CULTURE

IDENTITY

Despite increasing immigration and a thriving expat community, the Czech capital is still pretty homogeneous – Praguers are almost all Czechs. In addition to Slovak and Roma minorities, there are significant numbers of expatriates – especially Americans and Germans – living and working in Prague. Based on work-permit statistics and educated guesses about the ratio of legal to illegal workers, it's thought there are between 20,000 and 60,000 expatriates living in the city.

The ugly side of the Czech population's homogeneity is an often vicious racism directed at the Roma minority. The Roma community in Prague is small compared with other parts of the country – many live in the poorer parts of town, including Karlín and western Smíchov. For more on the Czech Republic's Roma community check out www.romove.cz/en.

LIFESTYLE

Prague is an expensive city and much more so for Czechs than for foreigners. The average monthly salary in Prague is around 29,000Kč (that's about £600, or US$1100),

Top Five Books about Prague

- *Prague In Black and Gold*, Peter Demetz (1997) – a personal view of Prague's history and its people
- *The Coasts of Bohemia*, Derek Sayer (2000) – draws on an array of literary, musical, visual and documentary sources to create a sense of Czech society and identity
- *Magic Prague*, Angelo Ripellino (1995) – a literary and cultural odyssey through the history of Prague
- *The Spirit of Prague*, Ivan Klima (1998) – a collection of essays charting five critical decades of the city's history
- *Prague Tales*, Jan Neruda (2000) – a collection of Neruda's wry, bittersweet stories of life among the inhabitants of 19th-century Prague

At the Weird & the Wonderful

One of the most distinctive features of Prague's street scene is the colourful and often unusual house signs that adorn the façades of many of the older buildings. Before 1770 (when house signs were banned by Josef II in favour of street numbers) merchants, tradesmen and other notable citizens would have their initials, a symbol of their trade, or some other distinctive device carved on the front of their house which served in place of an address.

Nerudova (see p63) in Malá Strana is particularly rich in surviving examples. Here you will find U bílé labutí (At the White Swan; No 49), U dvou sluncû (At the Two Suns; No 47), U zeleného raka (At the Green Lobster; No 43), U zlaté podkovy (At the Golden Horseshoe; No 34), U tří houslíček (At the Three Fiddles; No 12) and U červeného orla (At the Red Eagle; No 6).

Old Town Square (see p67) is graced by U kamenného zvonu (At the Stone Bell; No 13), U kamenného beránka (At the Stone Lamb; No 17), on the corner with U bílého koníčká (At the Little White Horse), U zlatého jednorožce (At the Golden Unicorn; No 20) and U modré hvězdy (At the Blue Star; No 25), while nearby Karlova has U zlatého hada (At the Golden Snake) at No 18.

The tradition is carried on today in the naming of many of Prague's pubs and restaurants, with unusual and inventive names ranging from U modré kachičky (At the Blue Duckling; see p120) to U vystřeleného oka (At the Shot-Out Eye; see p153).

and it's common for at least half of that to go on rent. So all those fancy restaurants and stylish bars are out of reach of the majority of Praguers, their custom confined to expats, gangsters, and a small elite of monied entrepreneurs (or corporate thieves, depending on your point of view).

Despite the everyday difficulties of making ends meet, Praguers remain for the most part mild-mannered people with a good sense of humour, and an attachment to old-fashioned values. On the tram, even the roughest-looking skinhead will often give up a seat for an elderly passenger and holding open a door for a lady is still considered the right thing to do. It's customary to say *dobrý den* (good day) to all and sundry when entering a shop, café or quiet bar, and to say *na shledanou* (goodbye) when you leave. If you're invited to someone's home, bring flowers or some other small gift for your host, and remember to remove your shoes when you enter the house.

Financial hardship is never considered an excuse for slackness when it comes to looking your best for a night on the town. When attending a classical concert, opera or play in one of the traditional theatres, men typically wear a suit and tie, and women an evening dress – it's only foreigners who don't. Casual dress is considered OK at performances of modern music, avant-garde plays and so on.

One legacy of the communist era that continues to plague the lives of ordinary Praguers is the petty corruption that riddles many areas of public life, from the city council to health care. It's not unusual to bring a small 'gift' when you visit your doctor, just to make sure that any tests or referrals you may need are given the priority they deserve.

Nepotism and cronyism are also rife in business and politics. There's a Czech saying, *'Já na bráchu, brácha na mí'*, which translates literally as 'I help my brother, my brother helps me', but is used in the wider sense of 'You scratch my back, and I'll scratch yours'. So prevalent is this philosophy in everyday life that the original phrase has evolved into a single word, *jánabráchismus*, which means 'mutual back-scratching, cronyism, corruption'.

The love of beer is just one of several traits that the Czechs share with the British, and it's not unusual to see workers downing a glass at breakfast time on the way to the building site or office. Another shared characteristic is a dark, satirical and often surrealist sense of humour – Monty Python is a big favourite here. Another is a love of dogs; the city's parks are filled with dog-walkers and dog poop, despite a determined effort by the city council to get owners to clean up after their canine companions. The annual dog-licence fee was increased in January 2004 from 1000Kč to 1550Kč in order to help finance a team of Parisian-style 'pooper scoopers' with moped-mounted vacuum cleaners. Whatever; watch your feet when strolling in the park.

Paneláky

Prague's outer suburbs consist mainly of huge 1970s and '80s housing estates characterised by serried ranks of high-rise apartment blocks, known in Czech as *paneláky* (singular *panelák*) because they were built using prefabricated, reinforced concrete panels. Each block contains hundreds of identical flats, and each estate contains dozens of identical blocks.

Western visitors often assume that these concrete suburbs must be sink estates, filled with the city's poor and riddled with crime and drugs. Nothing could be further from the truth. The *panelák* suburbs are home to a broad spectrum of Czech society, from students to surgeons, from lawyers to street sweepers. Local services and public transport are good, there is plenty of open parkland, and there is a surprisingly strong sense of community. Since the fall of communism, the few who can afford it have moved away from the concrete suburbs to detached houses and villas on the edge of the city. But as Prague property prices have boomed in anticipation of a rising market following EU admission, rent-controlled *panelák* flats continue to offer affordable accommodation within reasonable commuting distance of the city centre. Many tenants have ripped out the flimsy partition walls, laid laminate floors and installed new kitchens and bathrooms to create more attractive, open-plan living spaces. There is even a magazine called *Panel Story* which is devoted to DIY *paneláky* projects.

Although perhaps lacking in aesthetic appeal, Prague's *paneláky* were neither particularly cheap nor quick to build, in contrast to the often shoddy residential blocks of similar vintage that blight many Russian cities. Rather, the prime motive for their construction was ideological. Their very uniformity was the antithesis of bourgeois individuality and spoke of a new order where all were to be equal.

The biggest conglomeration of *paneláky* is in Jižní Město (Map pp242–3) on the southeastern edge of the city, comprising the suburbs of Háje, Opatov and Chodov. Take the metro to Háje at the end of line C for a stroll among the concrete canyons.

FOOD & DRINK

Czech cuisine is typical of Central Europe, with German, Austrian, Polish and Hungarian influences. It's very filling, often meat, dumplings, and potato or rice topped with a heavy sauce, and is usually served with a vegetable or sauerkraut.

The standard meal, which is offered in just about every Czech restaurant, is '*knedlo, zelo, vepřo*' (bread dumpling, sauerkraut and roast pork). Caraway seed, salt and bacon are the most common flavourings – most Czech chefs are rather generous with salt. Everything is washed down with alcohol, mainly beer. Diet food it isn't.

Breakfast

A typical Czech *snídaně* (breakfast) consists of *chléb* (bread) or *rohlík* (bread roll) with butter, cheese, eggs, ham or sausage, jam or yogurt, and tea or coffee. Some Czechs eat breakfast at self-service *bufety*, which are open between 6am and 8am – these serve up soup or hot dogs, which are washed down with coffee or beer.

A hotel breakfast is typically a cold plate or buffet with cheese, sausage or meat, bread, butter, jam, yogurt, and coffee or tea. Some also offer cereal and milk, pastries, fruit and cakes. Only at top-end hotels and a few restaurants can you get an American- or English-style fried breakfast. Some eateries serving Western-style breakfasts are noted in the boxed text on p130.

You can also go to a *pekárna* or *pekařství* (bakery), or to one of the French or Viennese bakeries, for *loupáčky*, like croissants but smaller and heavier. Czech bread, especially rye, is excellent and varied.

Lunch & Dinner

Oběd (lunch) is the main meal and, Sunday excepted, it's a hurried affair. Because Czechs are early risers they may sit down to lunch as early as 11.30am, though latecomers can still find leftovers in many restaurants at 3pm. Even some of the grungiest spots are nonsmoking until lunch is over. *Večeře* (dinner) might only be a cold platter with bread.

Bufet, jídelna and/or *samoobsluha* are self-service buffets, sit-down or stand-up, for lunch on the run. Common items are *buřt* (mild pork sausages), *chlebíčky* (open sandwiches), *párky* (hot dogs), *klobásy* (spicy sausages), *guláš* (goulash) and the good old *knedlo, zelo, vepřo*.

Most *hospoda* and *hostinec* (pubs), *vinárny* (wine bars) and *restaurace* (restaurants) serve sit-down meals with several courses until at least 8pm or 9pm. Some stay open until midnight.

Czechs tend to start their main meals with *polévka* (soup). Other common starters are sausage, the famous *Pražská šunka* (Prague ham) and open sandwiches. Salads and condiments may cost extra. The most common main meal is *knedlíky* (dumplings), made from *bramborové knedlíky* (potato) or *houskové knedlíky* (bread), served with pork and sauerkraut. Beef may be served with dumplings and comes with a sauce – usually goulash, *koprová omáčka* (dill cream sauce) or *houbová omáčka* (mushroom sauce). A delicious Czech speciality is *svíčková na smetaně* – roast beef and bread dumplings covered in sour-cream sauce, served with lemon and cranberries. Another Czech speciality is *ovocné knedlíky* (fruit dumplings). Unfortunately, the bread-and-potato dumplings you get in most restaurants are factory-produced and pale in comparison to homemade ones.

Fish is plentiful, and is usually *kapr* (carp) or *pstruh* (trout). *Štika* (pike) and *úhoř* (eel) are found on more specialised menus. Seafood – not surprisingly – is found only in a handful of expensive restaurants. Note that the price on the menu is usually not for the whole fish but per 100g. Ask how much the trout weighs before you order it!

Poultry is also common, either roasted or as *kuře na paprice* (chicken in spicy paprika cream sauce). *Kachna* (duck), *husa* (goose) and *krůta* (turkey) usually come roasted with dumplings and sauerkraut. Turkey is the traditional Christmas Day lunch.

A few restaurants specialise in game. Most common are *jelení* (venison), *bažant* (pheasant), *zajíc* (hare) and *kanec* (boar) – fried or roasted and served in a mushroom sauce or as goulash.

Dessert
Most Czech restaurants have little in the way of *moučník* (dessert). For cakes and pastries it is better to go to a *kavárna* (café) or *cukrárna* (cake shop). Most desserts consist of *kompot* (canned/preserved fruit), either on its own or *pohár* – in a cup with *zmrzlina* (ice cream) and whipped cream. *Palačinky* or *lívance* (pancakes) are also very common. Other desserts include *jablkový závin* (apple strudel), *makový koláč* (poppy-seed cake) and *ovocné koláče* (fruit slices).

Patrons sitting at outdoor tables, Old Town Square (p67), Staré Město

Vegetarian Meals

Bezmasá jídla ('meatless' dishes) are advertised on most menus, but some of these may be cooked in animal fat or even with pieces of ham or bacon! If you ask, most chefs can whip up something genuinely vegetarian.

Useful phrases include the following.

I'm a vegetarian.	*Jsem vegetarián/ka.* (m/f)	ysem ve-ge-ta-ri-aan/-ka
I don't eat meat.	*Nejím maso.*	ne-yeem ma-so
I don't eat fish/chicken/ham.	*Nejím rybu/kuře/šunku.*	ne-yeem ri-bu/ku-rzhe/shun-ku

Some common meatless dishes:

knedlíky s vejci	kned-lee-ki s-vey-tse	fried dumplings with egg
omeleta se sýrem a bramborem	o-me-le-ta se seer-em a bram-bo-rem	cheese and potato omelette
smažené žampiony	sma-zhe-ne zham-pi-o-nee	fried mushrooms
smažený květák	sma-zhe-nee kvye-taak	fried cauliflower with egg and onion
smažený sýr	sma-zhe-nee seer	fried cheese with potatoes and tartar sauce

Fortunately, there are several good vegetarian restaurants in Prague – see the boxed text on p127.

Snacks

The most popular Czech snacks are *buřt* or *vuřt* (thick sausages, usually pork) and *klobásy* (spicy pork or beef sausages), fried or boiled, served with mustard on rye bread or a roll. Other snacks are *párky*, *bramborák* (a potato cake made from strips of potato and garlic) and *hranolky* (chips or French fries).

Locally produced *bílý jogurt* (natural white yogurt) is a popular product that is much better than the imported versions. Also good is *Kostka – tvarohový krém*, a frozen yogurt ice cream on a stick and covered in chocolate. In autumn, street vendors offer *kaštany* (roasted chestnuts).

Coffee & Tea

Káva (coffee) and *čaj* (tea) are very popular. Homemade Czech coffee is the strong *turecká* (Turkish) – hot water poured over ground beans that end up as sludge at the bottom of your cup. *Espreso* means 'black coffee', and is sometimes a fair equivalent of the Italian version; *espreso s mlékem* is coffee with milk. *Vídeňská káva* (Viennese coffee) is topped with whipped cream.

Many hotels – even expensive ones – dish up thermos flasks of dismal instant coffee at breakfast. Fortunately, there are lots of cafés which serve excellent coffee, including caffè latte and cappuccino.

Tea tends to be weak and is usually served with a slice of lemon; if you want it with milk, ask for *čaj s mlékem*. *Čajovná* (tea houses) have proliferated in recent years; they serve a wide range of Indian, Sri Lankan, Chinese and herbal teas.

Nonalcoholic Drinks

In Prague it is very hard to find *limonády* (soft drinks) other than Western imports. One Czech energy drink – which is clearly not being marketed just to track and field stars – is Erektus. Another is Semtex, which is in honour of the infamous plastic explosive made in the former Czechoslovakia. Locally bottled mineral water is widely available, as many Czechs don't like the taste of their tap water. Fruit drinks labelled 'juice' aren't always 100% juice.

Beer

Czech *pivo* (beer) is among the best beer in the world, with a pedigree that goes back to the 9th century; see the boxed text on p154. The world's first lager was brewed in Plzeň (Pilsen) in West Bohemia. The Czech Republic has for some years been the world's No 1 beer-drinking nation, with an annual per capita consumption of some 160L. Beer is served almost everywhere; even cafeterias and breakfast *bufety* have a tap. Most pubs close at 10pm or 11pm, but some bars and nightclubs are open until 6am.

Most Czech beers are lagers, naturally brewed from malt and flavoured with hand-picked hops. Czechs like their beer at cellar temperature with a creamy, tall head. Americans and Australians may find the beer a bit warm. When ordering draught beer, ask for a *malé pivo* (0.3L) or *pivo* (0.5L).

Most beer is either light or dark, and either *dvanáctka* (12°) or *desítka* (10°). This indicator of specific gravity depends on factors such as texture and malt content, and doesn't directly indicate alcohol content. Most beers are between 3% and 6% alcohol, regardless of their specific gravity.

The best-known Czech beer is Plzeňský Prazdroj (Plzeň's Pilsner Urquell), which is exported worldwide. Many Czechs also like another Plzeň brew, Gambrinus. Sharp marketing (and a tasty brew) has seen Krušovice (from Central Bohemia, west of Prague) rise to national prominence. The most widely exported Czech beer is Budvar (Budweiser in German), the name of which is also used by an unrelated American brew. The Czech Budvar's mild, slightly bitter taste is popular in Austria, Germany and Scandinavia. A newish beer from Prague breweries, with a fine and very smooth taste, is Velvet, in light form, or Kelt, as a dark beer. Other Prague brands are Smíchovský Staropramen and Braník.

Some pubs brew their own beer; best known are the strong, dark beer served at U Fleků (p152) in Nové Město, and a light beer made by its near neighbour, Novoměstský pivovar (p152).

Most glass bottles can be returned to the point of purchase for a refund of about 3Kč to 10Kč, a small boost for your beer budget.

Wine

Although not as popular as beer, *víno* (wine) is widely available in *vinárny* (wine bars), restaurants and pubs – but not in many beer halls. *Suché víno* is dry wine and *sladké* is sweet.

Reasonable local wines are available in Prague shops, but the best ones are bought straight from the vineyards. Bohemia's largest wine-producing area, around Mělník (p199), produces good whites (such as Ludmila bílá or Mělnické zámecké), though its reds don't measure up to Moravia's. The

There's No Beer Like Beer

Není pivo jako pivo (there's no beer like beer) – trust the Czechs to come up with a near nonsensical proverb extolling the virtues of their national drink.

Even in these times of encroaching coffee culture, *pivo* (beer; see the boxed text on p154) remains the life-blood of Prague. Czechs drink more beer per head of population than anywhere else in the world, and the local *hospoda* or *pivnice* (pub or small beer hall) remains the social hub of the neighbourhood. Many people drink at least one glass of beer every day – local nicknames for beer include *tekutý chleb* (liquid bread) and *živá voda* (life-giving water) – and it's not unusual to see people stopping off for a glass of *desítka* (10° beer, lower in alcohol than the stronger 12° *dvanáctka*) on their way to work in the morning. Rather than a drink to accompany your meal, Prague pubs offer *pivní chuťovky* (snacks to accompany your beer).

There's an etiquette to be observed if you want to sample the atmosphere in a traditional *hospoda* without drawing disapproving stares and grumbles from the regulars. First off, don't barge in and start rearranging chairs and tables – if you want to share a table or take a spare seat, ask *je tu volno?* (is this free?) first. Take a coaster from the rack and place it in front of you, and wait for the bar-staff to come to you; waving for service is guaranteed to get you ignored.

You can order without saying a single thing – it's automatically assumed that you're here for the beer. Just raise your thumb for one beer, thumb and index finger for two, etc – providing you want a 0.5L glass of the pub's main draught ale. Even just a nod will do. The waiter will keep track of your order by marking a slip of paper that stays on your table; whatever you do, don't write on it or lose it. When you want to pay up and go, just say *zaplatím* (I'll pay).

And on your way out, reflect on another Czech proverb – *Kde se pivo vaří, tam se dobře daří* (where beer is brewed, life is good).

Burgundy-like Ludmila is the most popular. The best Moravian label is Vavřinec, a red from the southeast; another good red is Frankovka. A good dry white is Tramín. Rulandské bílé is a semi-dry white, and Rulandské červené a medium red. Czech champagnes are excellent for the price – try Bohemia Sekt Brut or Demi-Sekt.

A popular summer drink is *vinný střik*, white wine and soda water with ice. In winter mulled wine is popular.

Burčak is a wine-based beverage and is only available for about three weeks each year from the end of September to mid-October. It is a new wine in the passing stage of the fermentation process when it is transforming from grape juice to a full-bodied wine and its taste changes daily. The delicious and sweet taste of Burčak is more reminiscent of cider than wine and contains around 3% to 5% alcohol.

Spirits

Probably the most unique of Czech *lihoviny* (spirits) is Becherovka, with its 'cough-medicine' taste, from the spa town of Karlovy Vary. Another bitter spirit is Fernet. A good brandy-type spirit is Myslivecká.

The fiery and potent *slivovice* (plum brandy) is said to have originated in Moravia, where the best brands still come from. The best commercially produced *slivovice* is R Jelínek from Vizovice. Other regional spirits include Meruňkovice apricot brandy and juniper-flavoured Borovička. If you have a sweet tooth, try Griotka cherry liqueur.

The deadliest locally produced spirit is Hills Liquere absinthe from Jindřichův Hradec. While it's illegal in many countries, in part because of its high alcohol content, absinthe is legal in the Czech Republic. Unfortunately, connoisseurs of absinthe consider Hills little better than highly alcoholic mouthwash.

Spirits are drunk neat and usually cold (an exception is *grog*, a popular year-round hot drink: half rum, half hot water or tea, and lemon). Spirits, including Western brands, are available in all restaurants and most pubs and wine bars.

FASHION

It must be something in the tap water; spend any time people-watching in Prague and you'll soon notice that there are a lot of gorgeous women here. All those sharp Slavic cheekbones, slim silhouettes and seductive, Mucha-maiden eyes were just made for showing off designer clothes. It's hardly surprising that Czech names litter any list of supermodels – Eva Herzigová, Karolina Kurková, Daniela Peštová, Hana Soukupová and latest hot property Linda Vojtova.

In recent years Czech names have been popping up on the other side of the catwalk, with Prague fashion designers making names for themselves in Western Europe, and opening boutiques across Prague. Names to look out for include Klara Nademlýnská (p169), Helena Fejková (p173), Hana Stocklassa (p168), Martina Nevarilová, Tatiana Kovariková and Lucie Blazková.

Although there is a small Czech contingent that plumps for the nylon tracksuit and socks-with-sandals look, most Praguers are pretty style-conscious and take pleasure in looking good. Folk here still dress up for dinner, and as for going to the opera in anything but your best, well, you must be a tourist.

SPORT

Football (Soccer)

Football is a national passion in the Czech Republic. The national team performs well in international competitions, having won the European Championship in 1976 (as Czechoslovakia), reaching the final in 1996, and the semifinal in 2004. Pavel Nedvěd, who currently plays for Italian club Juventus, is the country's top player, and was named European Footballer of the Year in 2003. He played for Sparta Praha in the early 1990s.

Prague has three teams that play in the Czech First Division – Sparta Praha, Slavia Praha and Viktoria Žižkov (see p162 for details of home stadiums). Sparta is the most successful team, frequently qualifying for the European Champions League and taking second place in the 16-team Czech league in 2004; its main rival, Slavia, was fourth and Viktoria 15th. The football season runs from August to December and February to June.

Ice Hockey

It's a toss-up whether football or ice hockey inspires more passion in the hearts of Prague sports fans, but hockey probably wins. The Czech national team has been rampant in recent years, winning the World Championship three years running (1999–2001) and taking Olympic gold in 1998 by defeating the mighty Russians in the final.

Prague's two big hockey teams are HC Sparta Praha and HC Slavia Praha (see p163), both of which compete in the 14-team national league. Promising young players are often lured away by the promise of big money in North America's National Hockey League, and there is a sizeable Czech contingent in the NHL.

Sparta plays at the huge, modern T-Mobile Aréna (p163) at Výstaviště in Holešovice; games are fast and furious, and the atmosphere can be electrifying – it's well worth making the effort to see a game. The season runs from September to early April.

Tennis

Tennis is another sport that the Czechs do well in, having produced world-class players such as Jan Kodeš, Ivan Lendl, Petr Korda, Hana Mandlikova, Jana Novotna, Cyril Suk, and probably the finest woman tennis player ever, Martina Navratilova.

In May the Český Lawn Tennis Klub on Ostrov Štvanice (Hunt Island; p164) hosts the Prague Open, a relatively recent competition that was established in 2001 in the hope of luring international tennis talent back to the Czech capital (Prague no longer hosts the Czech Open, which is now held at Prostějov). In 2005 the Prague Open will be joined by a women's WTA tournament, which will run concurrently.

Ice-hockey match of premier league teams, T-Mobile Aréna (see p163), Holešovice

MEDIA

The Czechs are newspaper junkies, and you'll see people with their noses buried in the latest rag in bars, on trams, on park benches, and even walking along the street. Sadly, though, the overall quality of newspaper journalism is low, any lingering tradition of quality investigative reporting having been thoroughly stamped out during the communist era.

There are five national daily newspapers; most are now in the hands of German and Swiss media magnates. The biggest seller is the lurid tabloid *Blesk*, with sales of almost half a million. Second favourite is the centre-right *Mlada Fronta Dnes* (circulation 361,000), followed by the left-leaning *Právo* (circulation 190,000), the only national paper still in Czech ownership.

The weekly, English-language *Prague Post* (www.praguepost.cz; 65Kč) is good for local news and features, and has a useful 'Night & Day' arts and entertainment section, with travel tips, and concert, film and restaurant reviews.

The *New Presence* (subtitled Prague Journal of Central European Affairs; www.new-presence.cz; 80Kč) is a quarterly English translation of the Czech *Nová Přítomnost*, with features and essays on current affairs, politics and business. And look out for the bilingual (Czech/English) monthly magazine *Think* (www.think.cz; free), a youth-oriented mag with an alternative take on music, fashion and art.

LANGUAGE

Naturally enough for the capital of the Czech Republic, the dominant language in Prague is Czech, although you will find that many older Czechs speak some German. Under communism everybody learned Russian at school, but this has now been replaced by English. While you'll have little trouble finding English speakers in central Prague, they're scarce in the suburbs and beyond, as are translated menus.

For more information on Czech and a list of useful words and phrases, see p226–30.

ECONOMY & COSTS

Prague's economy is largely a service one, and an estimated 60% of the city's cash comes from the pockets of visiting tourists. Although it was once an industrial powerhouse, only about 9% of Prague's population is now employed in manufacturing (major industries are textiles, machinery, brewing and food processing); even so, it is still the largest industrial centre in the republic. Although the nationwide unemployment rate is more than 10%, in Prague it is only 3%.

The average monthly wage in Prague is about 29,000Kč (£600), enough for a reasonably comfortable life if you live in its outer suburbs; for Prague residents living in the central tourist zones, however, costs have gone through the roof. And the average wage for the whole country is only 18,700Kč (£400) a month, making the capital prohibitively expensive for most Czech citizens.

Prague is not a cheap destination for visitors either, unless you're on the backpacker trail. You can expect to pay around 4000Kč to 4500Kč a night for a double room in an attractive central hotel, and budget 500Kč a head for lunch and 1500Kč a head for dinner (without wine) if you plan to sample the best of Prague's restaurants.

How Much?

1L of petrol 25Kč

Bottled water (1.5L) 15Kč

Guardian newspaper 85Kč

Beer (0.5L) in tourist/nontourist pub 60Kč plus/25Kč

Pork & dumplings 80Kč

Souvenir T-shirt 300Kč

Ticket to Laterna Magika 690Kč

Tour of Obecní dům 150Kč

Cinema ticket 90-170Kč

Vintage car tour 800Kč

GOVERNMENT & POLITICS

Prague is the capital of the Czech Republic and the seat of government, parliament and the president. The city itself is governed separately from other regions of the country by the Local Government of the Capital City of Prague, headed by a council and a mayor. The acting body of this government is the municipal office together with the council. Prague is divided into 10 districts and 57 suburbs, governed by district and local governments.

Since 1989 Prague citizens have voted heavily (typically about 60%) for right-of-centre parties. Václav Klaus (whose constituency included Prague) and his Civic Democratic Party (ODS) collected more than 40% of the city's popular vote in the 1998 and 2002 elections, while the two other right-leaning parties together polled another 20%. Prague was in fact the only place in the country where the ODS polled at the top.

But country-wide the ODS is in opposition to the left-of-centre Social Democrats (ČSSD), led by Vladimir Spidla, prime minister from 2002 to 2004. Klaus, prime minister from 1992 to 1997 and the force behind many of the country's post-1989 reforms, was widely regarded as a Thatcherite, though others saw his policies as a practical mix of market reforms and socialism. Spidla, a historian and former labour and social affairs minister, is committed to expanding the welfare state, a policy at odds with the country's mounting budget deficit.

The Czech Communist Party (KSČM) is one of the few left in the world that still adheres to Marxist-Stalinist doctrine; it has a solid core of mostly elderly followers. In the 2002 elections it won 41 seats, up from 24 in 1998.

Despite an overwhelming referendum vote in favour of joining the European Union, the Czechs displayed a degree of apathy in relation to European Parliament elections in 2004; it is said that more Czechs voted for their favourite candidates in the TV programme *Česko hledá SuperStar* (the Czech equivalent of *Pop Idol* in the UK, or *American Idol* in the USA) than turned out in the European elections.

ENVIRONMENT

During most of the year Prague's air is fairly breathable, but in mid-winter the air can become foul with vehicle emissions, particularly during temperature inversions. If you're here for just a few days, there's little to worry about, though Prague residents have high rates of respiratory ailments. Radio and TV stations provide bulletins about pollution levels, and the Pražská informační služba (PIS; Prague information service; p222) should be able to tell you if there's a risk.

THE LAND

Central Prague sits in a sweeping bend of the Vltava, the longest river in the Czech Republic. Low, rocky hills rise immediately above the west bank, while on the east bank is a low-lying basin bounded by the long ridge of Vítkov (or Žižkov Hill; see p94) in the north, the riverside crags of Vyšehrad in the south, and the high ground of Vinohrady to the east. North of Vítkov is another low-lying plain, now occupied by the suburbs of Karlín and Libeň.

This geography defined the city's layout, with Prague Castle and the fortress of Vyšehrad founded on the hills to the northwest and southeast respectively, and the original settlements of Malá Strana and Staré Město growing up on the river banks on either side of the only possible fording place.

The Vltava rises in the Šumava hills near the Czech Republic's southern border with Austria and, along with its tributary the Berounka (which joins the Vltava a short distance upstream from Prague), drains most of southern and western Bohemia. Because of this huge drainage basin, Prague has found itself prone to severe flooding since its earliest days.

A flood washed away the Judith Bridge in 1342 (the Charles Bridge was built as its replacement), and in recent centuries there have been serious floods in 1784, 1827, 1845 and 1890. A carved stone head set into the embankment near the east end of Charles Bridge (on the downstream side, close to the modern flood gauge) marks the height reached by the 1890 flood, as do several metal plaques around Kampa island in Malá Strana (see p102).

The construction of the Slapy Dam 20km south of the city in the 1950s was intended to bring the Vltava under human control, but the flood that hit the city in August 2002 proved that the river was still untamed. The flood killed 19 people and caused about €2.4 billion of damage; 18 metro stations were flooded, and the metro remained out of operation for more than six months. The catastrophe was caused by unusually heavy rainfall from thunderstorms in southwestern Bohemia – about 9.7 cubic kilometres of rain fell in the space of just nine days.

GREEN PRAGUE

Czechs have been recycling waste for a long time; you'll find large bins for glass, plastics and paper all over Prague. Most bottles are recyclable, and the price of most bottled drinks includes a deposit of between 3Kč and 10Kč, refundable at supermarkets and food shops (some beer bottles only have a 0.40Kč deposit).

When it comes to large-scale recycling, sustainable energy and organic farming, the Czech Republic still lags a long way behind Germany, the UK and Scandinavia. All the same, Czech industry has cleaned up its act considerably since the fall of communism, with the annual production of greenhouse gases falling to one-thirtieth of pre-1989 levels.

Meanwhile, two new commercial developments on opposite sides of the city – the Park, next to Chodov metro station in the south, and River City in Karlín, in the north – are being touted as Prague's first 'green' buildings. Both have been designed to minimise energy consumption, using the sun's warmth to heat the offices in winter and river water to cool them in summer; recycled rainwater feeds the fountains and irrigates gardens.

One of the more unusual of Prague's new wave of environmentally aware businesses is František Maška Construction, which provides the red clay used for surfacing clay tennis courts. Its raw material? Recycled roof tiles which would otherwise be dumped in landfill sites. So successful is this small family firm that it now supplies 45% of the Czech Republic's tennis courts, and is planning to start exporting to Poland and Austria.

URBAN PLANNING & DEVELOPMENT

Prague city council's plans for the future are focussed on easing the pressure on the already overcrowded centre by moving development into the inner suburbs, notably Karlín, Smíchov, Pankrác and Holešovice. The vast Nový Smíchov shopping and entertainment mall (p175) opened in 2003; other new developments include the Palác Flora shopping centre in Vinohrady (p175) and the huge exhibition centre in Letňany (p92).

One of Prague's flagship developments is the River City complex in Karlín, whose first phase of office blocks opened in 2002, and which will eventually create a whole new district of offices, shops, hotels, restaurants and a riverside park. Situated just east of the Hilton Hotel, it will be linked by pedestrian footbridges to Ostrov Štvanice and the Pražská tržnice (city market) across the river in Holešovice.

Plans for a ring-road remain stalled and the city's main traffic routes are descending into gridlock, as anyone who has ever tried to drive across the city (or walk across the freeway at the top of Wenceslas Square) can testify. It has been estimated that car ownership in Prague has increased by more than 75% in the last decade, yet the city still suffers from the communist-era legacy of a poorly planned and hastily executed traffic system that feeds major highways through the congested city centre. Plans for inner and outer ring roads have languished on paper for years, but by some estimates the proposals could cost upwards of US$3 billion and the city just doesn't have that kind of money.

Meanwhile, Prague's metro system continues to grow, with line C (which used to end at Nádraží Holešovice) now extending northeast across the river to a new terminus at Ládví. More ambitiously the city council has finally agreed a US$760 million plan to extend metro line A from Dejvická to Ruzyně airport; work on this project could begin as early as 2006.

Arts

Arts

Art is everywhere in Prague, and not only in its many galleries – there are countless sculptures in the streets and squares; sgraffito, mosaic and painted decoration on buildings; bookshops boasting poetry readings; and always, somewhere, the strains of a piano sonata wafting through an open window.

MUSIC

Prague enjoys a rich and varied musical life, and its concert halls, churches, jazz clubs and rock bars provide an almost unceasing choice of musical entertainment that you can dip into as you choose. Praguers have eclectic musical tastes, and are interested in all kinds of music, ranging from Mozart, who conducted the premiere of *Don Giovanni* here in 1787, to the Rolling Stones, who played to No 1 fan ex-president Václav Havel in 2003.

The winner of best female artist in the Czech music industry's 2004 annual awards was 30-year-old Prague singer-songwriter Radůza, who first shot to fame in 1993 when she shared a stage at the Lucerna Music Bar with Suzanne Vega. But cast aside your preconceptions – Radůza's instrument of choice is…the accordion. Her songs are modern and lyrical, but firmly rooted in Czech folk music and the Bohemian beer-hall tradition.

Alfons Mucha

Alfons Mucha (1660–1939) is probably the most internationally famous visual artist to come out of the Czech lands, although his reputation within the Czech Republic is less exalted than it is abroad.

He was born in the small town of Ivančice, 40km southwest of Brno, and grew up in the heart of rural Moravia, a region steeped in the traditional Czech folklore that would later play such an important part in his art. Rejected by Prague's Academy of Fine Arts, he worked in Vienna as a scenery painter in the theatre and studied art in Munich before ending up in Paris as a penniless artist. Here he eked out a living producing commercial illustrations for magazines, posters and calendars, and became friends with Paul Gauguin, with whom he shared a studio for a few months.

But the publication of a single poster saw his life and career change almost overnight. A chance meeting in a print shop led to him designing a poster for the famous actress Sarah Bernhardt, promoting her new play *Giselda* (you can see the original lithograph in the Muchovo Muzeum (p81). The poster, with its tall narrow format, muted colours, rich decoration and sensual beauty created a sensation.

Mucha quickly became the most talked about and sought-after artist in Paris. He signed a six-year contract with Bernhardt during which time he created nine superb posters for her in the style that became known as 'le style Mucha'. He also designed jewellery, costumes and stage sets, and went on to produce many more famous posters promoting, among other things, Job cigarette papers, Möet & Chandon champagne and tourism in Monaco and Monte Carlo.

Although firmly associated in the public mind with Art Nouveau, Mucha himself claimed that he did not belong to any artistic movement, and saw his own work as a natural evolution of traditional Czech art. His commitment to the culture and tradition of his native land was expressed in the second half of his career, when he worked without payment on the decoration of the Primatorský sál (Lord Mayor's Hall) in Prague's Obecní dům (p77), designed new stamps, banknotes and police uniforms, and devoted 18 years (1910–28) to creating his *Slovanské epopej* (Slav Epic), which he then gifted to the Czech nation.

The 20 monumental canvasses of Mucha's *Slav Epic* encompass a total area of around 0.5 sq km and depict events from Slavic history and myth. Although very different in style from his famous Paris posters, they retain the same mythic, romanticised quality, full of wild-eyed priests, medieval pageantry and battlefield carnage, all rendered in symbolic tints – in the artist's own words: 'Black is the colour of bondage, blue is the past, yellow the joyous present, orange the glorious future'. (The *Slav Epic* is on display in the town of Moravský Krumlov, near Brno, 200km southeast of Prague.)

When the Nazis occupied Czechoslovakia at the beginning of WWII, Mucha was one of the first people to be arrested and interrogated by the Gestapo. He was released, but died a few days later shortly before his 79th birthday. He is buried in the Slavín at Vyšehrad Cemetery (p91).

(Mucha's granddaughter, Jarmila Plockova, uses elements of his paintings in her work – those interested can check out Art Décoratif [see p168] in Staré Město.)

David Černý – Artist-Provocateur

Czech artist David Černý (1967–) first made international headlines in 1991 when he painted Prague's memorial to WWII Soviet tank crews bright pink (see p95). Since then he has cultivated a reputation as the *enfant terrible* of the Prague arts scene – his works often turn into major media events, occasionally with police involved. He strongly supported the Czech Republic's entry into the EU, and is virulently anti-communist – when the Rolling Stones played Prague in 2003, Keith Richards wore a T-shirt designed by Černý with the slogan 'Fuck the KSČM' (KSČM is the Communist Party of Bohemia and Moravia). He also incurred the wrath of older-generation Czechs by describing them as 'an unmixed, uninteresting, slightly dumplingish, untanned mass'.

Since the 'pink tank' episode Cerny has become internationally famous. He lived for a time in the USA and his art has been exhibited in New York, Chicago, Berlin, Dresden, Stockholm and London. Many of his works are on display throughout Prague, including the statue of St Wenceslas astride a dead horse in the Palác Lucerna (p85), the creepy, crawling babies of Miminka (p96), the Quo Vadis (the Trabant on legs in the German Embassy gardens (p102) and Viselec (the 'hanging man' suspended above Husova street in Staré Město).

His latest installation caused great consternation in some circles and great amusement in others when it was unveiled at the Futura Gallery in Smíchov (p97) in 2003. It consists of two huge, naked human figures, bent over at the waist with their heads buried in a blank wall. A ladder allows viewers to climb up and place their head – and there's really no polite way to say this – up one figure's arse, where they can watch a video of Czech president Václav Klaus and the director of Prague's National Gallery spooning mush into each other's mouths. Richly metaphorical, to say the least.

You can find more details of Černý's work on his website at www.davidcerny.cz.

CLASSICAL

Classical music is hugely popular in Prague, and not only with the crowds of aficionados who flock to the Prague Spring (p157) and Prague Autumn (p10) festivals – the Czechs themselves have always been keen fans of classical music. Both locals and visitors can choose from a rich programme of concerts, performed by Prague's three main resident orchestras – the Symfonický orchestr hlavního města Prahy (Prague Symphony Orchestra; www.fok.cz), the Česká filharmonie (Czech Philharmonic Orchestra; www.czechphilharmonic.cz) and the world-renowned Český národní symfonický orchestr (Czech National Symphony Orchestra; www.cnso.cz).

Czech classical music arose in the mid-19th century, when the National Revival saw the emergence of several great composers who drew inspiration from traditional Czech folk music in their work. Prior to that period, the Counter-Reformation had suppressed Czech musical culture.

Bedřich Smetana (1824–84), the first great Czech composer, incorporated folk melodies into his classical compositions. His best-known works are *Prodaná nevěsta* (The Bartered Bride), *Dalibor a Libuše* (Dalibor & Libuše) and the patriotic *Má Vlast* (My Homeland), which opens the Prague Spring festival each year.

Antonín Dvořák (1841–1904) is probably the best-known Czech composer internationally. He spent four years in the USA where he lectured on music and composed the symphony *From the New World*. Among his other well-known works are the two *Slovanské tance* (Slavonic Dances; 1878 and 1881), the operas *Rusalka* and *Čert a Káča* (The Devil & Kate) and his religious masterpiece *Stabat Mater*.

Moravian-born Leoš Janáček (1854–1928), who also incorporated folk elements into his heavier music, was a leading 20th-century

Violin display

Czech composer. Never as popular as Smetana or Dvořák in his native country, his better-known compositions include the opera *Jenůfa*, the *Glagolská mše* (Glagolitic Mass) and *Taras Bulba*, while one of his finest pieces is *Stories of Liška Bystrouška*.

Other well-known Czech composers include Josef Suk (1874–1935), Dvořák's son-in-law, whose best known works include *Serenade for Strings* and the *Asrael Symphony*; and Bohuslav Martinů (1890–1959), famed for his opera *Julietta* and his Symphony No 6 *(Fantaisies Symphoniques)*.

JAZZ

Jazz was already being played in Prague in the mid-1930s, and has retained a grip on Czech cultural life that is unmatched almost anywhere else in Europe. Czech musicians remained at the forefront of the European jazz scene until the communist takeover in 1948 when controls were imposed on the performance and publication of jazz music, considered to be a corrupting product of the capitalist system. Even so, in the late 1950s Prague Radio still had a permanent jazz orchestra led by Karel Krautgartner.

Restrictions were gradually lifted in the 1960s. One of the top bands in this period was the SH Quartet, which played for three years at Reduta (p159), the city's first professional jazz club. Another leading band was the Junior Trio, with Jan Hamr and the brothers Miroslav and Allan Vitouš, who all left for the USA after 1968. Jan Hamr (keyboards) became prominent in 1970s American jazz-rock as Jan Hammer, while Miroslav Vitouš (bass) rose to fame in several American jazz-rock bands.

One of the most outstanding musicians in today's jazz scene is Jiří Stivín who in the 1970s produced two excellent albums with the band System Tandem and has since been regarded as one of the most original jazz musicians in Europe. Another is Milan Viklický who still performs in many of Prague's jazz clubs. Milan Svoboda, as well as being an accomplished pianist, is best known for his conducting abilities.

ROCK & POP

Rock, known as *bigbít* (Big Beat) in Czech, was often banned by communist authorities because of its 'corrupting influence', although certain local bands and innocuous Western groups such as Abba were allowed.

Sputnici, the pioneers of Czech rock, were the best known of several 1960s bands recycling American hits – Malostranská beseda (p160) in Malá Strana (Little Quarter) was a popular venue – but serious rock remained an underground movement enjoyed by small audiences in obscure pubs and country houses; devotees included many political dissidents such as Václav Havel. Raids and arrests were common – the Czech rock band Plastic People of the Universe achieved international fame after being imprisoned following a 1970s show trial intended to discourage underground music.

Since 1989 rock has really taken off. When Václav Havel – a long-standing rock fan – became president, one of his first acts was to invite Frank Zappa to come and play in Prague. Havel even wanted to appoint Zappa as his special ambassador to the US, but had to settle for the post of unofficial cultural attaché. (Zappa died in 1993, but when the surviving members of his band, the Mothers of Invention, played in Prague in 2004, the gig sold out several times over.)

Popular bands on the home front include pop-oriented Buty; hard-rock bands Lucie and the less-refined Alice; and even a country-and-western rock band Žlutý Pes (Yellow Dog). More alternative are several veteran outfits, including the grunge band Support Lesbiens, and Visací Zámek (Padlock). Lucie Bílá, the diva of 1990s Czech pop, started out sounding like a toned-down Nina Hagen, but has lately turned to rock musicals and Czech versions of American and British hits. Newer talent includes Patti Smith–like Načeva, and avant-garde violinist and vocalist Iva Bittová, who has made first-rate classical and modern recordings.

Although Prague has a lively club scene, many of the city's best rock venues (especially those in city-owned properties) have shut down as a result of court actions against noise.

LITERATURE

The earliest literary works in Bohemia were hymns and religious texts in Old Church Slavonic, replaced by Latin in the late 11th century. The 14th and 15th centuries saw the appearance of reformist theological texts, mostly in Czech, by Jan Hus and others.

With the imposition of the German language after the Thirty Years' War, Czech literature entered a dark age, re-emerging only in the early 19th century in the Czech-language works of the linguists Josef Dobrovský and Josef Jungmann. In the mid-19th century František Palacký published a five-volume history of Bohemia and Moravia.

Karel Hynek Mácha, possibly the greatest of all Czech poets, was the leading representative of Romanticism in the early 19th century; his most famous lyrical work is *Máj* (May). Mid-19th-century romanticism produced outstanding pieces about life in the country, especially *Grandmother* by Božena Němcová (the first major female Czech writer), and *Flowers* by Karel Erben.

The radical political journalist Karel Havlíček Borovský criticised the Habsburg elite and wrote excellent satirical poems. Two poets of the time who took much inspiration from Czech history were Jan Neruda (who also wrote *Povídky malostranské*, or Prague Tales, a collection of stories about daily life in Malá Strana) and Svatopluk Čech.

At the end of the 19th century Alois Jirásek wrote *Staré pověsti české* (Old Czech Legends), a compendium of stories from the arrival of the Czechs in Bohemia to the Middle Ages, as well as nationalistic historical novels, his best being *Temno* (Darkness). A major political philosopher and writer of his time was Tomáš Garrigue Masaryk, who later became Czechoslovakia's first president.

One of the best-known Czech writers of all is Franz Kafka. Along with a circle of other German-speaking Jewish writers in Prague, he played a major role in the literary scene at the beginning of the 20th century (see the boxed text on p26). His two complex and claustrophobic masterpieces are *The Trial* and *The Castle*. Others in the same circle were critic Max Brod and journalist Egon Erwin Kisch.

Among their Czech-speaking contemporaries was Jaroslav Hašek, now best known for *Dobrý voják Švejk* (The Good Soldier Švejk), which is full of good, low-brow WWI humour about the trials of Czechoslovakia's literary mascot, written in instalments from Prague's pubs.

The post-WWI Czech author Karel Čapek is famous for a science-fiction drama, *RUR* (Rossum's Universal Robots), from which the word 'robot' first entered the English language. Well-known poets of the interwar years are Jaroslav Seifert (awarded the Nobel Prize for Literature in 1984) and Vítěslav Nezval.

Top Five Reads

- *Mendelssohn Is on the Roof,* Jiří Weil (1960) – a moving and often wryly humorous memoir of Jewish life in Prague during WWII
- *City Sister Silver,* Jáchym Topol (1994) – a postmodern stream-of-consciousness novel that takes the reader on an exhilarating exploration of post-communist Prague
- *I Served the King of England,* Bohumil Hrabal (1974) –a humorous and deceptively simple tale of one man's rise to riches and ultimate fall into poverty, mirroring Czech history from 1918 to the communist era
- *The Trial,* Franz Kafka (1915) – perhaps Kafka's most famous story: a man is put on trial by an incomprehensible bureaucracy, not even knowing what crime he has been accused of
- *The Widow Killer,* Pavel Kohout (2000) – a gripping thriller set in Nazi-occupied Prague, in which a Czech detective and a Gestapo agent combine forces to track down a serial killer

The early communist period produced little of literary value, although the 1960s saw a resurgence of writing as controls were relaxed. Writers such as Václav Havel, Josef Škvorecký, Milan Kundera and Ivan Klíma produced their first works in the years preceding the 1968 Soviet-led invasion. Klíma's best-known novel is *A Ship Named Hope*.

After the invasion some, including Havel, stayed and wrote for the *samizdat* (underground press) or had manuscripts smuggled to the West. Others left, producing their best work in exile. Kundera's best novel is probably *The Joke*; two other well-known works are *The Unbearable Lightness of Being* and *The Book of Laughter and Forgetting*. Two good

Kafka's Prague

Literary Prague at the onset of the 20th century was a unique melting pot of Czechs, Germans and Jews. Although he wrote in German, Franz Kafka is a son of the Czech capital. He lived in Prague all his life, haunting the city and being haunted by it, needing it and hating it. One could look at *The Trial* as a metaphysical geography of Staré Město (Old Town), whose Byzantine alleys and passages break down the usual boundaries between outer streets and inner courtyards, between public and private, new and old, real and imaginary.

Most of Kafka's life was lived around Josefov and Old Town Square (Staroměstské náměstí). He was born on 3 July 1883 in an apartment beside kostel sv Mikuláše (St Nicholas Church); only the stone portal remains of the original building. As a boy he lived at Celetná 2 (1888–89); dům U minuty, the Renaissance corner building that's now part of the Staroměstská radnice (Old Town Hall; 1889–96); and Celetná 3 (1896–1907), where his bedroom window looked into kostel Panny Marie Před Týnem (Týn Church). He took classes between 1893 and 1901 at the Old Town State Gymnasium in palác Kinských (Goltz-Kinský Palace) on the square, and for a time his father ran a clothing shop on the ground floor there.

On the southern side of the square, at No 17, Berta Fanta ran an intellectual salon in the early part of the 20th century to which she invited fashionable European thinkers of the time, including Kafka and fellow writers Max Brod (Kafka's friend and biographer), Franz Werfel and Egon Erwin Kisch.

After earning a law degree from the Karolinum in 1906, Kafka took his first job from 1907 to 1908, an unhappy one as an insurance clerk with the Italian firm Assicurazioni Generali, at Wenceslas Square (Václavské náměstí 19), on the corner of Jindřišská. At Na poříčí 7 in northern Nové Město (New Town) is the former headquarters of the Workers' Accident Insurance Co, where he toiled on the 5th floor from 1908 until his retirement in 1922.

The last place Kafka lived with his parents (1913–14) – and the setting for his horrific parable *Metamorphosis* – was a top-floor flat across Pařížská from kostel sv Mikuláše, facing Old Town Square. At the age of 33 he finally moved into a place of his own at Dlouhá 16 (at the narrow corner with Masná), where he lived from 1915 to 1917, during which time he also spent a productive winter (1916–17) at a cottage rented by his sister at Zlatá ulička 22(Golden Lane), inside the Prague Castle (Pražský hrad) grounds. By this time, ill with tuberculosis, he took a flat for a few months in 1917 at the Schönborn Palace at Tržiště 15 (now the US embassy) in Malá Strana (Little Quarter).

Kafka died in Vienna on 3 June 1924 and is buried in the Jewish Cemetery at Žižkov (see p96 for details).

reads by Škvorecký are *Cowards* and *The Bride of Texas*. Other important figures of this time are philosopher Jan Patočka and poet Jiří Kolář.

Until his accidental death – in traditional Czech fashion, he died after falling from a window – the Czech Republic's leading contemporary novelist was Bohumil Hrabal (1914–97). One of his most notable novels *The Little Town Where Time Stood Still* is a humorous portrayal of the interactions of a small, close-knit community. Another popular Hrabal work is *Closely Watched Trains*, which was made into an Oscar-winning film in 1966.

Among the emerging generation of Prague writers, one of the most interesting (and commercially successful) is poet and rock lyricist turned novelist Jáchym Topol (1962–). Son of a playwright, Topol signed the dissident manifesto Charta 77 at the tender age of 15. His 1994 novel *Sestra* (translated into English as *City Sister Silver*) is an exhilarating exploration of post-communist Prague, a stream-of-consciousness odyssey that vividly captures the sense of chaos and social dislocation that swept over the city in the wake of the Velvet Revolution.

Bookshop shelf display

VISUAL ARTS

Think visual arts in Prague and most visitors will be thinking of Alfons Mucha (p22), but the city has much more to offer than Mucha's sultry maidens. Prague has a rich tradition of public sculpture ranging from the baroque period to the present day – David Černý (p23) is still creating controversy – and there is always something new and fascinating to see in the Veletržní palác (p93) and the recently opened Futura (p97).

PAINTING

The luminously realistic, 14th-century paintings of Magister Theodoricus (Master Theodoric), whose work hangs in the kaple sv Kříže (Chapel of the Holy Cross) at Karlštejn Castle and in the kaple sv Václava (Chapel of St Wenceslas) in chrám sv Víta, influenced art throughout Central Europe.

Another gem of Czech Gothic art is a late-14th-century altar panel by an artist known only as the Master of the Třeboň Altar; what remains of it is in the klášter sv Jiří (Convent of St George) in Prague Castle.

The Czech National Revival in the late 18th and early 19th centuries witnessed the appearance of a Czech style of realism, in particular by Mikuláš Aleš and father and son Antonín and Josef Mánes. Alfons Mucha is well known for his late-19th-century Art Nouveau posters. Czech landscape art developed in the works of Anton Kosárek, followed by a wave of Impressionism and Symbolism at the hands of Antonín Slavíček, Max Švabinský and others. The earliest notable woman painter, Zdenka Braunerová, concentrated on painting and sketching Prague and the Czech countryside.

> ### Top Five Galleries
>
> - **Dům U zlatého prstenu** (House at the Golden Ring; p70)
> - **Galerie Mánes** (p86)
> - **Klášter sv Anežky** (Convent of St Agnes; p73)
> - **Šternberský palác** (Sternberg Palace; p60)
> - **Veletržní palác** (Centre for Modern & Contemporary Art; p93)

In the early 20th century, Prague developed as a centre of avant-garde art, concentrated in a group of artists called Osma (The Eight). Prague was also a focus for Cubist painters, including Josef Čapek. The functionalist movement flourished between WWI and WWII in a group called Devětsil, led by the adaptable Karel Teige. Surrealists followed, including Zdeněk Rykr and Josef Šíma.

Forty years of communism brought little art of interest, at least through official channels. Underground painters of the time included Mikuláš Medek (whose abstract, Surrealist art was exhibited in out-of-the-way galleries) and Jiří Kolář, an outstanding graphic artist and poet. Some of the works of art that were not exhibited by artists of the postwar years have surfaced since 1989.

SCULPTURE

Public sculpture has always played prominent role in Prague, from the baroque saints that line the parapets of Charles Bridge (Karlův most; p68) to the monumental statue of Stalin that once stood on Letná terrace. And, more often than not, that role has been a political one (p94).

In the baroque era, religious sculpture sprouted in public places, including 'Marian columns' erected in gratitude to the Virgin for protection against the plague or victory over anti-Catholic enemies; one such Marian column stood in Old Town Square from 1650 until 1918 (see p94). The placing of the statue of sv Jan Nepomucký (St John of Nepomuk) on Charles Bridge in 1683 was a conscious act of propaganda designed to create a new – and Catholic – Czech national hero who would displace the Protestant reformer Jan Hus from popular memory. As such it was successful – Jan Nepomucký was canonised in 1729 and the Nepomuk legend, invented by the Jesuits, passed into the collective memory.

The period of the Czech National Revival saw Prague sculpture take a different tack – to raise public awareness of Czech tradition and culture. One of the most prolific sculptors of this period was Josef Václav Myslbek, whose famous statue of St Wenceslas (p82), the

Czech patron saint, dominates the upper end of Wenceslas Square. He also created the four huge statues of the mythical Czech characters Libuše, Přemysl, Šárka and Ctirad that now grace the gardens in Vyšehrad fortress (p90).

The Art Nouveau sculptor Ladislav Šaloun was responsible for one of Prague's most iconic sculptures, the monument to Jan Hus (p67) that was unveiled in the Old Town Square in 1915. The figure of Hus – standing firm and unmoving, while the events of history swirl around him – symbolised the Czech nation which, three years later, would be independent for the first time in its history. For three short years he stared across the square at a statue of the Virgin Mary – symbol of the Habsburg victory over the Czechs – until a mob toppled her soon after independence was declared in 1918 (see p94). Šaloun's works grace the façade of the Obecní dům (p77), the Grand Hotel Evropa (see the boxed text on p83) and City Hall (p107), and he also created the bust of Antonín Dvořák that adorns the composer's tomb in Vyšehrad cemetery (p91).

Probably the most imposing and most visible sculpture in Prague is the huge, mounted figure of Hussite hero Jan Žižka – reputedly the biggest equestrian statue in the world – that dominates the skyline above Žižkov (the district was named after him). Created by sculptor Bohumil Kafka (no relation to the writer) in 1950, it was originally intended to form part of the Národní památník (National Monument; p89) in memory of the Czechoslovak legions who had fought in WWI. But it was hijacked by the communist government and made to serve instead as a political symbol of Czech peasants and workers.

The city's long tradition of politically charged sculpture continues today with the controversial and often wryly amusing works of David Černý (see the boxed text on p23).

CINEMA

The pioneer of Czech cinema was the architect Jan Kříženecký who made three comedies in American-slapstick style that were shown at the 1898 Exhibition of Architecture and Engineering.

The domestic film industry took off in the early years of this century and Czechs were leading innovators. The first film ever to show full-frontal nudity was Gustaf Machatý's *Extase* (Ecstasy; 1932). It was a hit (and a scandal) at the 1934 Venice Film Festival. Revealing all was one Hedvige Kiesler, who went on to Hollywood as Hedy Lamarr. Hugo Haas directed a fine adaptation of Karel Čapek's anti-Nazi science-fiction novel *Bílá nemoc* (White Death) in 1937. Fear of persecution drove him to Hollywood, where he made and starred in many films.

The Nazis limited the movie industry to nationalistic comedies, while under communism the focus was on low-quality propaganda films. A 'new wave' of Czech cinema rose between 1963 and the Soviet-led invasion in 1968. Its young directors escaped censorship because they were among the first graduates of the communist-supervised Academy of Film. It was from this time that Czech films began to win international awards.

Cinema poster

Among the earliest outstanding works was *Černý Petr* (Black Peter, known in the USA as *Peter & Paula*; 1963) by Miloš Forman, who fled the country after 1968 and became a successful Hollywood director with films such as *One Flew over the Cuckoo's Nest* (1975) and

Amadeus (1984). Other prominent directors were Jiří Menzel, Věra Chytilová and Ivan Passer.

Some post-1968 films critical of the regime were banned or production was stopped. Probably the best film of the following two decades was Menzel's internationally screened 1985 comedy *Vesničko má středisková* (My Sweet Little Village), a subtle look at the workings and failings of socialism in a village cooperative.

Directors in the post-communist era are struggling to compete with Hollywood films, as well as the good Czech films of

Arts – Theatre

the 1960s. So far the only one who has succeeded is Jan Svěrák, whose 1994 hit *Akumulátor* was the most expensive Czech film produced to date. In 1996 it was surpassed at the box office by the internationally acclaimed *Kolja* (Kolya), about a Russian boy raised by a Czech bachelor (played by the director's father). A year later *Kolja* won the award of best foreign film at the Cannes Film Festival and the US Academy Awards.

Věra Chytilová continues to produce good films and win prizes at film festivals. In 2000 another brilliant young director David Ondříček released *Samotáři*, the story of a group of seven people trying to find love and a partner in the 1990s.

More recently, Jan Hřejbek's superb black comedy *Musíme Si Pomáhat* (Divided We Fall; 2000), exploring the conflicting loyalties of small-town Czechs during WWII, won an Oscar nomination for best foreign film. In 2001 Jan Svěrák, director of *Kolja*, produced another potential Oscar-winner with *Dark Blue World*, a story of two Czech fighter pilots who return home after WWII only to be sent to labour camps by the communist authorities.

The Czech film studios at Barrandov in southwestern Prague are known for their world-class animated and puppet films, many of which were made from the 1950s to the 1980s. *A Midsummer Night's Dream* (1959) was the best of the puppet films, and was produced by the talented Jiří Trnka.

THEATRE

Czech-language theatre did not develop fully until the 16th century. Themes were mostly biblical and the intent was to moralise. At Prague's Karolinum, Latin drama was used for teaching. The best plays were written by Jan Ámos Komenský (John Comenius) in the years before the Thirty Years' War, after which plays in Czech were banned. German drama and Italian opera were popular during the 17th and 18th centuries, when many theatres were built.

In 1785 Czech drama reappeared at the Nostitz Theatre (now Stavovské divadlo, Estates Theatre; p157), and Prague became the centre of Czech-language theatre. Major 19th-century playwrights were Josef Kajetán Tyl and Ján Kolář. Drama, historical plays and fairy tales flourished as part of the Czech National Revival. In 1862 the first independent Czech theatre, the Prozatímní divadlo (Temporary Theatre), opened in Prague.

Marionettes on display

Drama in the early years of Czechoslovakia was led by the brothers Karel and Josef Čapek, and also František Langer. Actor and playwright EF Burian later became known for his experimental dramas.

Under communism classical theatrical performances were of a high quality, but the modern scene was stifled. Exceptions included the pantomime of the Černé divadlo (Black Theatre) and the ultramodern Laterna Magika (Magic Lantern), founded by Alfréd Radok.

Many fine plays, including those by Václav Havel, were not performed locally as a result of their anti-government tone, but appeared in the West. In the mid-1960s free expression was explored in Prague's divadlo na Zábradlí (Theatre on the Balustrade; p160), with works by Havel, Ladislav Fialka and Milan Uhde, and performances by the comedy duo of Jiří Suchý and Jiří Šlitr.

Marionette performances have been popular in Prague since the 16th century. A major figure of this art form was Matěj Kopecký (1775–1847).

Marionette theatres opened in Prague and Plzeň in the early 20th century. Josef Skupa's legendary Spejbl & Hurvínek (the Czech Punch and Judy) attracted large crowds, and still does.

Even during communism, puppet and marionette theatre was officially approved and popular, and Czech performances were ranked among the best in the world, especially in the films of Jiří Trnka.

Architecture

Architecture

Prague is a living textbook of 1000 years of European architecture. The city's historic core is unparalleled in Europe, having escaped damage in WWII and avoided large-scale redevelopment. It records a millennium of continuous urban development, with baroque façades encasing Gothic houses perched on top of Romanesque cellars, all following a street plan that emerged in the 11th century. Malá Strana (Little Quarter), Staré Město (Old Town) and Nové Město (New Town) were given Unesco World Heritage status in 1992; of more than 3500 buildings, over 1500 are designated cultural monuments.

ROMANESQUE

The oldest surviving buildings in Prague date back to the era of the Přemysl dynasty, which began with the founding of Prague Castle by Prince Bořivoj in 870. In the crypt of chrám sv Víta (St Vitus Cathedral; p57) you can see the sparse remains of the Rotunda of St Vitus, built for Duke Wenceslas (Václav; the 'Good King Wenceslas' of the Christmas carol) in the early 10th century.

Several of these stone-built Romanesque rotundas (circular churches dating from the 10th and 11th centuries) survive intact in Prague, though most have since been incorporated into larger churches. Examples include the rotunda sv Longina (Rotunda of St Longinus; early 12th century; p87) in Nové Město, the kaple sv Kříže (Rotunda of the Holy Cross; mid-12th century; p80) in Staré Město, and the rotunda sv Martina (St Martin's Rotunda; late 11th century; p90) at Vyšehrad.

Prague's finest Romanesque structure, however, is the Bazilika sv Jiří (Basilica of St George; p58) at Prague Castle. Although its exterior is hidden behind an elaborate 17th-century baroque façade, the interior exhibits the heavy walls and plain columns, barrel-vaulted ceilings, and small doors and windows with semicircular arches that typify the Romanesque style.

GOTHIC

The Gothic style, which flourished in Prague from the 13th to the 16th centuries, represented not just a new aesthetic but also a revolution in architectural design that allowed architects to build thinner walls and higher vaults. Gothic architecture is characterised by tall, pointed arches, ribbed vaults and columns, external flying buttresses (to support the weight transmitted from the ribbed vaults) and tall, narrow windows with intricate tracery supporting great expanses of stained glass. As time went by Gothic designs became ever taller, pointier and more elaborately decorated.

Czech Gothic architecture thrived during the rule of Charles IV, especially in the hands of German architect Petr Parler (Peter Parléř), best known for the eastern part of chrám sv Víta (St Vitus Cathedral; p57) at Prague Castle. Begun by Matyáš z Arrasu (Matthias of Arras) in 1344, work on the cathedral continued under Parler, the most influential mason in Prague at that time, until his death in 1399. His bold experiments with the design of the cathedral's vaults – note the dazzling star-, fan- and diamond-shaped formations of the ribbed vaults in the choir – laid the foundations for the even more impressive achievements of German architects in the 15th century, while the open-work staircase that Parler installed on the outside of the Great Tower was later copied in the cathedrals of Strasbourg and Ulm.

Top Five Notable Buildings

- chrám sv Víta (St Vitus Cathedral; p57)
- dům U černé Matky Boží (House of the Black Madonna; p77)
- Národní divadlo (National Theatre; p85)
- Obecní dům (Municipal House; p77)
- Tančící dům (Dancing Building; p86)

Parler was also responsible for the Gothic design of Charles Bridge (Karlův most; see the boxed text on p68), the Staroměstská mostecká věž (Old Town Bridge Tower; p72), the kostel Panny Marie Sněžné (Church of Our Lady of the Snows; p83) and the chrám sv Barbora (Cathedral of St Barbara; p206) in Kutná Hora.

Another master builder of the Gothic period was Benedikt Rejt, who was summoned to Prague Castle to improve the fortifications and the royal living quarters. His finest legacy to the city is the petal-shaped vaulting of the Vladislavský sál (Vladislav Hall; 1487–1500; p58) in the Old Royal Palace. Its flowing, intertwined ribs are a beautiful example of late-Gothic craftsmanship, while the huge windows on the south wall are considered to be the earliest example of Renaissance style in Bohemia.

Other fine Gothic buildings in the city include the klášter sv Anežky (Convent of St Agnes; 1234–1380; p73), and the late-Gothic Prašná brána (Powder Gate; 1475; p78) by Matěj Rejsek.

chrám sv Víta (p57), Prague Castle

Architecture – Renaissance

RENAISSANCE

When the Habsburgs took over the Bohemian throne in the early 16th century (p42) they invited Italian designers and architects to Prague to help create a royal city worthy of their status. The Italians brought a new enthusiasm for classical forms, an obsession with grace and symmetry and a taste for exuberant decoration.

The mixture of local and Italian styles gave rise to a distinctive 'Bohemian Renaissance' style, featuring heavy ornamental stucco decorations and paintings of historical or mythical scenes. The technique of sgraffito – from the Italian word meaning 'to scrape' – was much used, creating patterns and pictures by scraping through an outer layer of pale plaster to reveal a darker surface underneath.

The rebuilding of Hradčany and Malá Strana after a devastating fire in 1541 (see p42 for details) was undertaken almost entirely in Renaissance style, with the emphasis firmly on luxurious palaces, pleasure gardens and merchant houses rather than on churches and religious buildings.

The Letohrádek (Summer Palace, or Belvedere; 1538–60; p56) in the gardens to the north of Prague Castle was built for Queen Anna, the consort of Ferdinand I, Prague's first Habsburg ruler. It is almost pure Italian Renaissance in style, with features that will strike a chord with anyone familiar with the buildings of Brunelleschi in Florence.

Other fine examples of Renaissance buildings are the Míčovna (Ball-Game House; 1569; p56) in Prague Castle, the Schwarzenberský palác (Schwarzenberg Palace; 1546–67; p60) in Hradčany, with its striking, Venetian-style sgraffito decoration, the dům U minuty (House at the Minute; 1564–1610; p72) in Staré Město, and the Letohrádek Hvězda (Star Summer Palace; 1556; p100).

BAROQUE

In the aftermath of the Thirty Years' War (1618–48; p43), the triumphant Habsburg empire embarked on a campaign of reconstruction and re-Catholicisation of the Czech lands. The baroque style of architecture, with its marble columns, florid sculpture, trompe l'oeil paintings, frescoed ceilings and rich, gilded ornamentation full of curves and ovals, was consciously used by the Catholic Church as an instrument of propaganda – the extravagant and awe-inspiring interiors of baroque churches were designed to impress the faithful with the splendour of the divine, while the elaborate façades were visual symbols of the Church's triumph over the Protestant reformers.

This was the grandest period in Prague's architectural development, responsible for the largely baroque face that you see in Prague today. Not only were churches built in the baroque style, but also palaces, villas, town houses, ornamental gardens and country chateaux. From the early 17th century onwards, noble families such as Schwarzenberg, Nostitz, Liechtenstein, Kolovrat and Czernin decided that they needed a base in the city, and began building their palaces and gardens close to the castle in Hradčany and Malá Strana.

By the early 18th century a distinctively Czech baroque style had emerged. Its best-known practitioners were the Bavarian father and son Kristof and Kilian Ignatz Dientzenhofer (see the boxed text on p34), the Italian Giovanni Santini and the Bohemian František Kaňka.

The most impressive example of Prague baroque is the Dientzenhofers' kostel sv Mikuláše (Church of St Nicholas; 1704–55; p63) in Malá Strana, one of the finest baroque buildings in central Europe. Its massive green dome dominates Malá Strana in a fitting symbol of the Catholic Church's dominance over 18th-century Prague. You enter through the western door at the foot of an undulating, tripartite façade decorated with the figures of saints, into a fantasy palace of pale pink, green and gold, where a profusion of pilasters, sinuous arches and saintly statues leads your eye ever upward towards the luminous glow of the dome. The magnificent fresco that adorns the ceiling of the nave – at 1500 sq m it is one of the biggest in Europe – depicts the Apotheosis of St Nicholas, and portrays the saint (among other things) rescuing shipwrecked sailors, saving three unjustly condemned men from the death sentence, and saving women from prostitution by throwing them bags of gold.

The Dientzenhofer Dynasty

No two men did more to give Prague its overwhelmingly baroque face than the Bavarian architects Kristof Dientzenhofer (1655–1722) and his son Kilian Ignatz Dientzenhofer (1689–1751). Born into a large family of German builders and architects from Aibling on the borders of Bavaria and Austria, Dientzenhofer senior arrived in Prague at the age of 23 in the hope of making his fortune amid the spate of building activity that accompanied the Counter-Reformation.

He married a German widow and moved into a house at No 2 Nosticova in Malá Strana, where his son Kilian was born in 1689, but he also made several study trips to Austria, Italy and France in his quest to become one of the leading architects of his time. His son attended Malá Strana's Jesuit school and went on to read mathematics and philosophy at Charles University, before spending nine years studying architecture in Vienna under the famous Austrian architect Johann Lukas von Hildebrandts.

Working in collaboration with his father until the latter's death, and later on his own, Kilian Dientzenhofer created more than 250 superb buildings, not only in Prague but also elsewhere in Bohemia, Austria, Italy, France and Hungary. His religious buildings are characterised by undulating façades, an interplay of convex and concave surfaces, and a soaring and harmonious composition which both impresses and inspires, conveying both the spiritual and the material power of the Catholic Church. But despite being a favourite architect of the imperial court, he was often paid poorly or not at all, and when he died his family was left in poverty.

The most prominent Dientzenhofer contributions to Prague's cityscape:

- **kostel sv Mikuláše** (Church of St Nicholas; 1704–55; p63), Malá Strana
- **bazilika sv Markéty, Břevnov** (Church of St Margaret; 1720; p100)
- **Loreta** (1711–51; p61)
- **Vila Amerika** (1717–20; p88)
- **kostel sv Jan Nepomucký** (Church of St John Nepomuk; 1720–29; p106)
- **kostel sv Mikuláše, Staré Město** (Church of St Nicholas; 1732–35; p71)
- **Palác Sylva-Taroucca** (Sylva-Taroucca Palace; 1751; see the boxed text on p84)
- **palác Kinských** (Goltz-Kinský Palace; 1755–65; p72)

The final flourish of the late baroque period was the rococo style, a sort of 'super-baroque' with even more (and even more elaborate) decoration. The palác Kinských (Goltz-Kinský Palace; 1755–65; p72), overlooking Old Town Square, has a rococo façade.

CZECH NATIONAL REVIVAL

The success of the Czech National Revival (p43) in the second half of the 19th century, when Prague gained a measure of self-government within the Habsburg empire and Czech political parties won control of the city council, saw the commissioning of many public buildings whose designs evoked the elegance and grandeur of the Renaissance era.

The architecture of this period sought to achieve a distinctively Czech style that would reflect the reviving confidence of Czech culture and stand in contrast to the baroque which had come to symbolise, for many Czechs, the domination of the Habsburg empire.

Buildings in this so-called neo-Renaissance style include the Národní muzeum (National Museum; 1891; p84) on Wenceslas Square, the Rudolfinum (1876–84; p73) on náměstí Jana Palacha, and, most impressive of all, the Národní divadlo (National Theatre; 1883; p85) on Národní třída, all designed by Josef Zítek and Josef Schulz.

The Národní divadlo in particular was deeply tied up with the National Revival. A group of Czech patriots, led by historian František Palacký, petitioned the Habsburg emperor to be allowed to build an independent Czech-language theatre, which was to be funded entirely by public donation, and designed and decorated by all the leading Czech artists of the period. So strongly did these plans fire the Czech imagination that when the theatre was seriously damaged by a fire before it had even opened, it took only six weeks to raise enough money to rebuild it. The theatre opened officially in 1883 with a performance of Smetana's patriotic opera *Libuše*.

ART NOUVEAU

As the 19th century drew to a close Czech architecture came under the spell of Art Nouveau, with its sinuous, botanical lines and colourful renderings of flowers and (mostly female) human figures. The term came from the French *l'art nouveau* (New Art) and was known as *secese* in Bohemia, *Sezessionstil* in Austria and *Jugendstil* in Germany.

The building of the Průmuslový palác (Palace of Industry; p92), for the Jubilee Exhibition of 1891, saw the first arrival of Art Nouveau in Prague, and over the next two decades it became the favoured style of the city's middle classes.

When the Jewish ghetto of Josefov was cleared in the late 19th century and the broad boulevard of Pařížská was driven through the former slums, fashionable new apartment blocks in Art Nouveau style were built along its length. Similar blocks were built in the expanding middle-class suburb of Vinohrady, notably along the desirable streets just to the east of Riegrovy sady.

The Art Nouveau style was also applied to upmarket hotels, including the Hotel Central (1899–1901; undergoing restoration at the time of writing, and reopened as a hotel in summer 2004) on Hybernská in Nové Město (Map pp252–3), whose façade is decorated with stuccoed foliage, ornate lamps and a glass cornice beneath a decorated gable. The more famous Grand Hotel Europa (1906; see the boxed text on p83), on Wenceslas Square, is even grander and more ornate (on the outside, at least; its accommodation leaves a lot to be desired), while the Hotel Paříž (1904; p184) has retained its interior as well as exterior splendour.

Architect Josef Fanta was responsible for the old, Art Nouveau section of Praha hlavní nádraží (Prague Main Train Station; 1901–09; p82), whose dome and twin towers rise above the busy freeway of Wilsonova, and also for the pretty House of the Hlahol Choir (1906; p86), on the banks of the Vltava.

But the city's finest expression of Art Nouveau architecture is the magnificent Obecní dům (Municipal House; 1906–12; p77). Like the Národní divadlo before it, it was envisaged as a symbol of resurgent Czech culture, with every aspect of the building's decoration designed by the leading Czech artists of the time, most famously the Primatorský sál (Lord Mayor's Hall), which was decorated by Alfons Mucha (also see the boxed text on p22 for more information on Mucha).

CUBIST

In a period of just 10 years (1910–20), barely half a dozen architects bequeathed to Prague a unique legacy of buildings – mostly private homes and apartment blocks – that were influenced by the Cubist movement in art.

The Cubist style spurned both the regular lines of traditional architecture and the sinuous forms of Art Nouveau in favour of triangular, polygonal and pyramidal forms, emphasising diagonals rather than horizontals and verticals, and achieving a jagged, faceted, almost crystalline effect, whose appearance changes as the angle of the sun moves through the day.

Some of Prague's finest Cubist façades were designed by Josef Chochol between 1912 and 1914, and can be seen in the neighbourhood below the Vyšehrad fortress; check out the buildings at the corner of Vnislavova and Rašínovo nábřeží, Rašínovo nábřeží 6–10 and Neklanova 30 (see the boxed text on p91). Other appealing examples include the dům U černé Matky Boží (House of the Black Madonna; 1912; p77) in Staré Město, and the twin houses on Tychonova in Dejvice (p105), all by Josef Gočár, and a 1921 apartment building at Elišky Krasnohorské 10–14 in Staré Mesto, created by Otakar Novotný.

Less well known, but still showing strong Cubist influences, are the early-20th-century apartment blocks along and around Křížkovského (Map pp258–9), on the border between Žižkov and Vinohrady, just east of Riegrovy sady.

After WWI Cubism evolved into another unique Prague architectural style as architects such as Pavel Janák and Josef Gočár added colour and decorative elements to their angular façades in another attempt to define a Czech national style. The more rounded forms that characterise these buildings led to the name rondocubism. This short-lived style is seen in Janák's monumental Adria Palace (1922–25; p84), on Národní třída, and in the tall, narrow apartment building at No 4 Jungmannovo náměstí, but its finest expression is seen in Gočár's Legiobank (Bank of the Czechoslovak Legions; 1921–23) at Na poříčí 24, with its hypnotic alternation of rounded and right-angled features.

The latter is a celebration of the achievements of the Czechoslovak Legions, who fought against the German and Austrian armies in WWI. The façade, which contrasts strongly with the smooth, Functionalist façade (1937–39) to its left, is enlivened by four muscular sculptures topping the street-level pillars and representing, from left to right, the Legions in the Trenches; Defiance and Courage; Waiting and Yearning for Home; and Throwing Grenades and Defence Against Gas Attack. The frieze above, by Otto Gutfreund, illustrates the Legions' victorious homecoming.

During this period Cubist designs were extended into the field of decorative arts – examples of Cubist furniture, ceramics, and glassware can be seen in the Umělecko-průmyslové muzeum (Museum of Decorative Arts; see p74) and the muzeum Českého Kubismu (Museum of Czech Cubism; p77) – and the more mundane domain of street furniture: Prague must be the only city in the world with a Cubist lamppost (p104). Even Franz Kafka's tombstone (p96), designed by Leopold Ehrmann in 1924, evokes the Cubist style in its crystal-like prismatic pillar.

MODERNIST

The creation of an independent Czechoslovakia in 1918 was followed by a wave of excitement and creativity. The architecture of this period was influenced by new technology and materials, and by the streamlined forms of modern transportation such as cars, steam locomotives and ocean liners. Form and purpose were merged dramatically in a new movement that became known as Functionalism.

Functionalist buildings were typified by extreme geometric simplicity, clean lines, and modern materials such as reinforced concrete, plate glass and steel. A classic example is the Baťa shoe store (1929; see the boxed text on p83) on Wenceslas Square, which was the city's first concrete-framed building. Its seven-storey façade consists almost entirely of glass, and there are few structural members to impede the open sales areas on each floor.

The city's first Functionalist building was the vast Veletržní palác (Trade Fair Palace; 1926–28; p93), built as an exhibition space and now home to Prague's main gallery of modern art. The huge central space, overlooked by six levels of galleries lined with stainless steel guardrails, has the feel of a cruise liner's decks.

Other Functionalist masterpieces include the Galerie Mánes (Mánes Gallery; 1927–30; p86) in Nové Město and the Müllerova vila (Müller Villa; 1930; p99) in Střešovice.

One of the more idiosyncratic architects to leave his mark on Prague during this period was the Slovenian Joze Plečnik, a friend of President Tomáš Masaryk, who was commissioned to update and renovate parts of Prague Castle. He also designed the remarkable kostel Nejsvětějšího Srdce Páně (Church of the Most Sacred Heart of Our Lord; 1928–32; p97), a building inspired by the forms of early Christian basilicas and Egyptian temples, and one which still defies classification.

The architectural legacy of the communist era consists mostly of concrete monstrosities, such as the Kongresové centrum (Congress Centre; 1981; see p112) in Vyšehrad, and the serried ranks of mass-produced apartment blocks that comprise the city's outer suburbs (see the boxed text on p12). More imposing monuments to communism include the Stalinist tower of the Hotel Crowne Plaza (1954; see p98), the extraordinary Hotel Praha (1981; see p193) and Žižkov's space-age Televizní vysílač (TV Tower; 1985–92; see p96).

POST-1989

Prague's post-1989 architecture is a mixed bag, some quite out of keeping with its surroundings, some simply ugly and some surprisingly attractive.

One of Prague's most idiosyncratic and appealing examples of new architecture is the Tančící dům (Dancing Building; 1992–96; p87) on Rašínovo nábřeží in Nové Město, designed by the Prague architect Vlado Milunič and the American Frank O Gehry. Built on a gap site left by a stray WWII American bomb, it drew much criticism from the older generation of Czechs. In contrast to the bland, mass-produced, functional architecture of the communist era, and the spate of historic renovations that characterised post-1989 Prague, this was a bold, innovative and individualistic project.

The building's striking resemblance to a pair of dancers soon saw it acquire the nickname 'Fred and Ginger', after the legendary dancing duo Astaire and Rogers. Some critics, however, have likened the wasp-waisted Ginger to 'a crushed Coke can', while some have compared the building's effect on the Prague cityscape to a second American bomb. But Prague's younger generation are more positive, seeing the Dancing Building as an expression of personal freedom. A poll found that 68% of Praguers liked Fred and Ginger, with only 16% actively disliking it.

The architect Milunič claims that his original idea for the building back in the early 1990s was to create a symbol of the new Czechoslovakia – a dialogue between old and new, static and dynamic, the past dancing with the future. Despite its boldly modern lines, the Dancing Building somehow blends in perfectly with its surroundings.

By contrast, the bland, glass-and-metal façade of the Mýslbek Building (1996), designed by the French firm Caisse des Dépots et Consignations in collaboration with local architects, clashes unpleasantly with its *fin-de-siècle* neighbours on Na příkopě. On the other hand, the building's rear façade, on Ovocný trh, blends in masterfully.

Tančící dům (p87), Nové Město

The building boom that began in the mid-1990s continues apace, with new shopping centres, office buildings and apartment blocks appearing all over the city. Most are undistinguished but a few stand out, notably the swooping glass façade of the Anděl Center (by French architect Jean Nouvel) and the huge Nový Smíchov shopping mall (see p175; by local design agency D3A), both in Smíchov.

The latest architectural story to hit the headlines is the controversial proposal to build a huge, seven-storey Palace of Art, which will house a permanent collection of around 1500 works by Spanish surrealist Salvador Dalí. The building, which will occupy a site on the banks of the Vltava at the north end of Revoluční, has been designed by Polish-born architect Daniel Libeskind, famous for the Jewish Museum in Berlin and the design for the Freedom Tower that is to be built on the site of the World Trade Center in New York.

History

History

THE RECENT PAST

Despite the city's turbulent history, Prague's progress in recent years has been more stately than revolutionary. The booming tourism sector and a solid industrial base have left its citizens in better economic shape than the rest of the country. Unemployment is minimal, the shops are full, and façades that were crumbling a decade ago have been given face-lifts. Big new shopping malls and multiplex cinemas are popping up all over the place, there's a huge new sporting and events arena (see p163), the metro system is being extended and – in the tourist parts of town at least – visible damage from the massive floods that struck in 2002 has been pretty much cleared up.

There are downsides, of course. Rumours of corruption in City Hall are rife, affordable housing remains in short supply, the health system is under strain, and traffic congestion and crime rates are up. Despite this, the mood of the city remains buoyant.

Václav Havel's 13 years as president came to an end in February 2003, when his place was taken by hard-nosed, right-wing economist Václav Klaus. More change was to come: the decision on whether the Czech Republic should join the European Union was settled by a referendum – with 77% voting in favour – and on 1 May 2004 the Czech Republic became a member of the EU.

The wobbly coalition between the Social Democratic Party (ČSSD) and the Christian Democrat Coalition (Koalice), formed after the 2002 elections, finally collapsed in June 2004, and Prime Minister Vladimir Spidla resigned. After much haggling, a new government was formed with new ČSSD leader Stanislav Gross as prime minister – at 34 years of age, Europe's youngest premier. This coalition government – made up of the same parties as before, with the same paper-thin, one-seat majority – narrowly survived a vote of confidence in August 2004, amid allegations of bribery and corruption. Czech politics in the period leading up to the general election in 2006 looks set to be just as unstable as before.

FROM THE BEGINNING

The oldest evidence of human habitation in the Prague valley dates from 600,000 BC, but more numerous clues were left by hunters during the last ice age, about 25,000 years ago. Permanent communities were established around 4000 BC in the northwestern parts of Prague, and the area was inhabited continuously by various Germanic and Celtic tribes before the arrival of the Slavs. It was from a Celtic tribe called Boii that Bohemia got its name, a name still used today for the western part of the Czech Republic.

THE COMING OF THE SLAVS

In the 6th century, two Slav tribes settled on opposite sides of a particularly appealing stretch of the Vltava River. The Czechs built a wooden fortress where the residential area Hradčany stands today, and the Zličani built theirs upstream at what is now Vyšehrad. They had barely dug in when nomadic Avars thundered in, to rule until the Frankish trader Samo united the Slav tribes and drove the Avars out. Samo held on for 35 years before the Slavs reverted to squabbling.

TIMELINE	6th century	863	870s
	First settlement on Vyšehrad hill	SS Cyril and Methodius bring Christianity to the Czech lands	Founding of Prague Castle

In the 9th century Prague was part of the short-lived Great Moravian Empire. Under its second ruler, Rastislav (r 846–70), emissaries were invited to come from Constantinople, and Christianity took root in the region. The Moravians (the ancient lands of Moravia now form the eastern part of the Czech Republic) were ultimately undone by internal conflicts, especially with the Czechs, who finally broke away from the empire.

THE PŘEMYSL DYNASTY

Prague Castle (Pražský hrad, or just *hrad* to the Czechs) was built in the 870s by Prince Bořivoj as the main seat of the Přemysl dynasty. Vyšehrad sometimes served as an alternative in the 10th and 11th centuries (see p89).

Christianity became the state religion under the rule of the pious Wenceslas (Václav in Czech), duke of Bohemia (r c 925–29), now the chief patron saint of the Czech people. Wenceslas was the 'Good King Wenceslas' of the well-known Christmas carol written in 1853 by English clergyman John Mason Neale. Neale, a scholar of eastern European church history, had read about St Wenceslas' legendary piety, and based his carol on the story of the duke's page finding strength and warmth by following in the footsteps of his master as they carried food, wine and firewood to a poor peasant on a freezing cold Boxing Day. The unfortunate Wenceslas was murdered by his owned brother, Boleslav; the Chapel of St Wenceslas (see p58) in chrám sv Víta (St Vitus Cathedral) is decorated with scenes from the saint's life.

In 950 the German king Otto I conquered Bohemia and incorporated it into the Holy Roman Empire. By 993 Přemysl princes had forged a genuine Slav alliance, and ruled Bohemia on the Germans' behalf until 1212, when the pope granted Otakar I the right to rule as a king. Otakar bestowed royal privileges on the Staré Město (Old Town), and Malá Strana (Little Quarter) was established in 1257 by Otakar II.

Přemysl lands stretched at one point from modern-day Silesia (a region on the Czech-Polish border) to the Mediterranean Sea. Their Austrian and Slovenian domains, however, were lost when Otakar II died and his army was thrashed at the 1278 Battle of Moravské Pole (fought near modern-day Dürnkrut in Austria) by the Austrian Habsburgs.

PRAGUE'S GOLDEN AGE

The murder of Wenceslas III in 1306 left no male heir to the Přemysl throne. Two Habsburg monarchs briefly ruled Bohemia until the Holy Roman emperor John of Luxembourg (Jan Lucemburský to the Czechs) also became king of Bohemia by marrying Wenceslas III's daughter Elyška in 1310. Under the rule of John's son Charles (Karel) IV (r 1346–78), as king and Holy Roman emperor, Prague grew into one of the continent's largest and most prosperous cities, acquiring its fine Gothic face, and landmarks including the Karolinum (Charles University), Charles Bridge (Karlův most) and chrám sv Víta.

THE HUSSITE REVOLUTION

The late 14th and early 15th centuries witnessed the Church-reform movement led by Jan Hus (see the boxed text on p42). Hus' eventual conviction for heresy and his death at the stake in 1415 sparked a nationalist rebellion in Bohemia led by the Hussite preacher Jan Želivský. In 1419 several Catholic councillors were flung from the windows of Prague's Novoměstská radnice (New Town Hall) by Želivský's followers, thus introducing the word 'defenestration' (the act of throwing someone or something out of a window) to the political lexicon.

After the death in 1419 of Holy Roman emperor and king of Bohemia Wenceslas IV, Prague was ruled by various Hussite committees. In 1420 combined Hussite forces led

929	1338	1357	1415
Wenceslas (Václav), duke of Bohemia, is murdered	Staroměstská radnice is established in Staré Město	Charles IV commissions building of Charles Bridge	Jan Hus burned at the stake

Jan Hus

Jan Hus was the Czech lands' foremost, and one of Europe's earliest, Christian reformers, anticipating Martin Luther and the Lutheran Reformation by a century.

He was born into a poor family in southern Bohemia in 1372. At the age of 18 he enrolled at the Karolinum (Charles University) and two years after graduating he started work as a teacher there. Five years later he was made dean of the philosophy faculty, at a time when the university was caught up in a struggle against German influence.

Like many of his Czech colleagues, Hus was inspired by the English philosopher and radical reformist theologian John Wycliffe. The latter's ideas on reform of the Roman Catholic clergy meshed nicely with growing Czech resentment at the wealth and corruptness of the higher clergy, who together owned about half of all Bohemia, and its heavy taxation of the peasantry.

Prague reformers had in 1391 founded the Betlémská kaple (Bethlehem Chapel; see p79), where sermons were given in Czech rather than Latin. Hus preached here for about 10 years, while continuing his duties at the university.

Because German masters at the university enjoyed three votes to the Czech masters' one, antireform attitudes officially prevailed there. In 1403 the masters declared many of Wycliffe's writings to be heresy. During the Great Schism (1378–1417), when Roman Catholics had two popes, the masters opposed the 1409 Council of Pisa that was called to sort things out. This so infuriated Wenceslas IV that he abrogated the university constitution and gave the Czech masters three votes to the Germans' one, leading to a mass exodus of Germans from Prague.

In the chaos surrounding the Great Schism, one pope was persuaded to prohibit preaching in private chapels such as Betlémská kaple. Hus refused to obey, and was excommunicated, though he continued to preach at the chapel and teach at the university. A disagreement with Wenceslas IV over the sale of indulgences cost him the king's support. The Council of Constance, called to put a final end to the Great Schism, convicted Hus of heresy, and Hus was burned at the stake in 1415.

by the military commander Jan Žižka successfully defended Prague against the first anti-Hussite crusade during the Battle of Vítkov Hill, launched by Sigismund, the Holy Roman emperor.

In the 1420s a split developed in the Hussite ranks between radical Taborites, who advocated total war on Catholics, and moderate Utraquists, who consisted mainly of nobles who were more concerned with transforming the Church.

In 1434 the Utraquists agreed to accept Sigismund's rule in return for religious tolerance; the Taborites kept fighting, only to be defeated in the same year at the Battle of Lipany.

Following Sigismund's death, George of Poděbrady (Jiří z Poděbrad) ruled as Bohemia's one and only Hussite king, from 1452 to 1471, with the backing of Utraquist forces. He was centuries ahead of his time in suggesting a European council to solve international problems by diplomacy rather than war, but he couldn't convince the major European rulers or the pope. After George's death two weak kings from the Polish Jagiellonian dynasty ruled Bohemia, though real power lay with the Utraquist nobles, the so-called Bohemian Estates.

HABSBURG RULE

In 1526 the Austrian Catholic Habsburgs were again asked by the Czech nobility to rule Bohemia. In the second half of the century the city enjoyed great prosperity under Emperor Rudolf II, and was made the seat of the Habsburg empire. Rudolf established great art collections, and renowned artists and scholars were invited to his court.

A huge fire in 1541 laid waste many sections of Malá Strana and Hradčany. The fire started on Hradčanské náměstí, on the site now occupied by the Šternberský palác (see p60), and swept through the largely wooden houses of merchants and artisans, destroying

1419	1420	1618	1620
First Defenestration of Prague; Catholic councillors thrown from Novoměstská radnice	Hussites prevail at Battle of Vítkov Hill	Second Defenestration of Prague kicks off the Thirty Years' War	Habsburg victory at Battle of Bílá Hora

most of the district. The rebuilding that took place following the fire gave Hradčany and Malá Strana much of the beautiful Renaissance and baroque architecture that still graces their streets.

An ill-fated uprising of the Bohemian Estates in 1618, which began when two Habsburg councillors and their secretary were flung from an upper window in Prague Castle, dealt a blow to Czech fortunes for the next 300 years. This 'Second Defenestration of Prague' sparked off the Thirty Years' War, devastating much of Europe, and Bohemia in particular – a quarter of the Bohemian population perished.

The following year the Bohemian Estates elected Frederick of the Palatinate as their ruler. But because of ineffective leadership, low morale among their heavily mercenary army, and limited international support, the crucial Battle of Bílá Hora (White Mountain) on 8 November 1620 was lost by the Protestants to the Habsburgs almost before the first shots were fired. The 'Winter King' (so-called because he ruled Bohemia for just one winter) fled and, in 1621, the 27 nobles who had instigated the revolt were executed in Old Town Square (Staroměstské náměstí); for those with a stomach for these things, the sword of the executioner, Jan Mydlář, is displayed in the Lobkovický palác (p59).

The defeat slammed the door on Czech independence for almost three centuries. Czechs lost their privileges, rights and property, and almost their national identity due to forced Catholicisation and Germanisation (part of the wider Counter-Reformation movement). During the Thirty Years' War, Saxons occupied Prague from 1631 to 1632, and Swedes seized Hradčany and Malá Strana in 1648. Staré Město, though unconquered, suffered months of bombardment. Prague's population declined from 60,000 in 1620 to 24,600 in 1648. The Habsburgs moved their throne back to Vienna, reducing Prague to a provincial town, although it did get a major baroque face-lift over the next century, particularly after a great fire in 1689.

In the 18th century the city was again on the move, economically and architecturally. The four towns of Prague – Staré Město, Nové Město, Malá Strana and Hradčany – were joined into a single, strong unit by imperial decree in 1784.

THE CZECH NATIONAL REVIVAL

In the 19th century Prague became the centre of the so-called Czech National Revival (České národní obrození), which found its initial expression not in politics – political activity was forbidden by the Habsburgs – but in Czech-language journalism, literature and drama. Important figures included linguists Josef Jungmann and Josef Dobrovský, and František Palacký, author of *Dějiny národu českého* (History of the Czech Nation). A distinctive architecture also took form (p35); Prague landmarks of this period include the Národní divadlo (National Theatre; p157), Národní muzeum (National Museum; p84) and Novoměstská radnice (New Town Hall; p89).

While many of the countries in post-Napoleonic Europe were swept up by similar nationalist sentiments, social and economic factors gave the Czech revival particular strength. Educational reforms by Empress Maria Theresa (r 1740–80) had given even the poorest Czechs access to schooling, and a vocal middle class was emerging with the Industrial Revolution. Austrian economic reforms, plus changes in industrial production, were forcing Czech labourers into the bigger towns, cancelling out the influence of large German minorities there.

Prague also joined in the 1848 democratic revolutions that swept Europe, and the city was the first in the Austrian empire to rise in favour of reform. Yet like most of the others, Prague's uprising was soon crushed. In 1861, however, Czechs defeated Germans in Prague council elections and edged them out of power forever, though the shrinking German minority still wielded substantial influence well into the 1880s.

1621	1648	1784	1787
27 Protestant nobles executed in Old Town Square	Swedish army occupies Prague Castle; end of Thirty Years' War	Prague's four towns united as a single city	Mozart conducts premiere of *Don Giovanni* at Prague's Stavovské divaldo

WWI & INDEPENDENCE

Czechs had no interest in fighting for their Austrian masters in WWI, and neighbouring Slovaks felt the same about their Hungarian rulers. Many defected to renegade legions fighting against the Germans and Austrians.

Meanwhile, Tomáš Garrigue Masaryk, Edvard Beneš and the Slovak Milan Štefánik began to argue the case – especially in the USA with President Wilson – for the Czechs' and Slovaks' long-cherished dream of independence. Wilson's interest was in keeping with his own goal of closer ties with Europe under the aegis of the League of Nations (the unsuccessful precursor to the UN). The most workable solution appeared to be a single federal state of two equal republics, and this was spelled out in agreements signed in Cleveland in 1915 and then in Pittsburgh in 1918.

As WWI drew to a close Czechoslovakia declared its independence, with Allied support, on 28 October 1918. Prague became the capital, and the popular Masaryk, a writer and political philosopher, became the republic's first president.

On 1 January 1922 Greater Prague was established by the absorption of several surrounding towns and villages, growing to a city of 677,000. Like the rest of the country, Prague experienced an industrial boom until the Great Depression of the 1930s. By 1938 the population had grown to one million.

WWII

Unfortunately the new country was not left to live in peace. Most of Bohemia's and Moravia's three million German speakers wished to join Greater Germany, and in October 1938 the Nazis occupied the Sudetenland (the border regions with Germany and Austria), with the acquiescence of Britain and France in the infamous Munich Agreement. On 15 March 1939 Germany occupied all of Bohemia and Moravia, declaring the region a 'protectorate', while Slovakia proclaimed independence as a Nazi puppet state.

The Jews of Prague

Prague's Jewish community was first moved into a walled ghetto in about the 13th century, in response to directives from Rome that Jews and Christians should live separately. Subsequent centuries of pogroms and official repression culminated in Ferdinand I's (r 1526–64) threat, only grudgingly withdrawn, to throw all Jews out of Bohemia.

The reign of Rudolf II saw honour bestowed on Prague's Jews, a flowering of Jewish intellectual life, and prosperity in the ghetto. Mordechai Maisel (or Maisl), mayor of the ghetto, Rudolf's finance minister and Prague's wealthiest citizen, bankrolled some lavish redevelopment. Another major figure was Judah Löw ben Bezalel (Rabbi Löw) prominent theologian, chief rabbi, student of the mystical teachings of the cabbala, and nowadays best known as the creator of the mythical golem – a kind of proto-robot made from the mud of the Vltava River.

When they helped to repel the Swedes on Charles Bridge in 1648, Prague's Jews won the favour of Ferdinand III, to the extent that he had the ghetto enlarged. But a century later they were driven out of the city for over three years, to be welcomed back only because Praguers missed their business.

In the 1780s Emperor Joseph II outlawed many forms of discrimination, and in 1848 the ghetto walls were torn down and the Jewish quarter – named Josefov in honour of Joseph II – was made a borough of Prague.

The demise of the quarter (which had slid into squalor as its population fell) came between 1893 and 1910 when it was cleared, ostensibly for public-health reasons, split down the middle by Pařížská třída (Paris Ave) and lined with Art Nouveau apartment buildings.

The community itself was all but eliminated by the Nazis and the communist regime slowly strangled what remained of Jewish cultural life. Thousands emigrated. Today only about 6000 Jews live in Prague.

1881	1893–1910	28 October 1918	1938
Národní divadlo opens, is burnt down, then rebuilt	The Jewish ghetto of Josefov is cleared and redeveloped	Republic of Czechoslovakia proclaimed in Prague's Obecní dům	Nazis occupy the Sudetenland

Star of David above main entrance to Staronová synagóga (p74), Josefov

Prague suffered little physical damage during the war, although the Germans destroyed the Czech resistance – and hundreds of innocent Czech villagers – in retaliation for the assassination in Prague of SS General and Reichsprotektor Reinhard Heydrich (see the boxed text on p46).

Prague's pre-WWII community of some 120,000 Jews was all but wiped out by the Nazis. Almost three-quarters of them – and some 90% of all the Jews in Bohemia and Moravia – died of starvation or were exterminated in camps from 1941.

On 5 May 1945 the population of Prague rose against the German forces as the Red Army approached from the east. US troops had reached Plzeň, but held back in deference to their Soviet allies. The only help for Prague's lightly armed citizens came from Russian soldiers of the so-called Vlasov units, former POWs who had defected to the German side and now defected in turn to the Czech cause (they subsequently retreated to western Bohemia and surrendered to the Americans). Many people died before the Germans began pulling out on 8 May, having been granted free passage out of the city by the Czech resistance movement (in return for which the Germans left without destroying any more buildings or bridges).

Most of Prague was thus liberated by its own residents before Soviet forces arrived the following day. Liberation Day is now celebrated on 8 May; under communism it was 9 May.

EXPULSION OF SUDETEN GERMANS

In 1945 Czechoslovakia was re-established as an independent state. One of the government's first acts was the expulsion of Sudeten Germans from the borderlands. By 1947 nearly 2.5 million Sudetenlanders had been stripped of their Czechoslovak citizenship and their land, and forcibly expelled to Germany (mainly Bavaria) and Austria. Thousands died during forced marches.

1939	27 May 1942	5–8 May 1945	9 May 1945
Nazis invade Czech lands; Prague becomes capital of Protectorate of Bohemia and Moravia	Assassination of Reichsprotektor Reinhard Heydrich	Prague Uprising sees citizens rise up against Nazi occupiers	Red Army enters Prague

The Assassination of Heydrich

In 1941, in response to strikes and sabotage by the increasingly well organised Czech underground movement, the German government replaced its Reichsprotektor in Bohemia and Moravia with the SS general and antisubversion specialist Reinhard Heydrich, who cracked down on resistance activities with a vengeance.

In a clandestine operation, Britain trained a number of Czechoslovak paratroopers for an attempt to assassinate Heydrich. Astonishingly, it succeeded. Two paratroopers, Jan Kubiš and Jozef Gabčík, managed, on 27 May 1942, to bomb and shoot Heydrich as he rode in his official car in the city's Libeň district. He later died of his wounds. The assassins and five co-conspirators fled but were betrayed in their hiding place in the kostel sv Cyril a Metoděj (Church of SS Cyril & Methodius); in the ensuing siege all were killed or committed suicide.

The Nazis reacted with a frenzied wave of terror, including the annihilation a month later of two entire Czech villages, Lidice and Ležáky (see p201 for more on the grim fate of Lidice), and the shattering of the underground movement.

Despite a 1997 declaration of mutual apology for wartime misdeeds by the Czech Republic and Germany, the issue still brings emotions to the boil. Most Sudeten survivors feel their Czech citizenship and property were taken illegally. Many Czechs, on the other hand, remain convinced that Sudetenlanders forfeited their rights when they sought help from Nazi Germany, and that a formal apology by President Václav Havel in January 1990 was unwarranted.

COMMUNISM

In the 1946 elections the Communist Party of Czechoslovakia (KSČ) became the republic's dominant party with 36% of the popular vote, and formed a coalition government with other socialist parties.

Tension grew between democrats and communists, and in February 1948 the communists staged a coup d'état with the backing of the Soviet Union. A new constitution established the KSČ's dominance, and government was organised along Soviet lines. Thousands of noncommunists fled the country.

The 1950s were an era of harsh repression and decline, as communist economic policies nearly bankrupted the country. Many people were imprisoned. Hundreds were executed and thousands died in labour camps, often for little more than a belief in democracy. In a series of Stalin-style purges organised by the KSČ, many people, including top members of the party itself, were executed.

THE 'PRAGUE SPRING' & CHARTA 77

In the late 1960s, Czechoslovakia enjoyed a gradual liberalisation under Alexander Dubček, the reformist general secretary of the KSČ. These reforms reflected a popular desire for full democracy and an end to censorship – 'socialism with a human face', as the party called it in its April 1968 'Action Programme'.

But Soviet leaders grew alarmed at the prospect of a democratic society within the Soviet bloc, and its certain domino effect in Poland and Hungary. The brief 'Prague Spring' was crushed by a Soviet-led Warsaw Pact invasion on the night of 20–21 August 1968. Prague was the major objective; Soviet special forces with help from the Czechoslovak secret service, the StB (Státní bezpečnost, or State Security), secured Ruzyně airport for Soviet transport planes. At the end of the first day, 58 people had died. Passive resistance followed; street signs and numbers were removed from buildings throughout the country to disorient the invaders.

In 1969 Dubček was replaced by the orthodox Gustav Husák and exiled to the Slovak forestry department. Around 14,000 party functionaries and 280,000 members who refused to

1948	1955	1962	1968
Communist Party takes control of government in putsch known as 'Victorious February'	World's largest statue of Stalin erected on Prague's Letná Terása	World's largest statue of Stalin blown up	Alexander Dubček ushers in reforms known as Prague Spring

renounce their belief in 'socialism with a human face' were expelled from the party and lost their jobs. Many other educated professionals became street cleaners and manual labourers.

In January 1977 a group of 243 writers, artists and other intellectuals signed a public demand for basic human rights, Charta 77 (Charter 77), which became a focus for opponents of the regime. Prominent among them was the poet and playwright Václav Havel (see the boxed text below).

THE VELVET REVOLUTION

The communist regime remained in control until the breaching of the Berlin Wall in November 1989. On 17 November Prague's communist youth movement organised an officially sanctioned demonstration in memory of nine students who were executed by the Nazis in 1939 (see the boxed text on p86). But the peaceful crowd of 50,000 was cornered in Národní třída, where hundreds were beaten by police and about 100 were arrested.

Czechs were electrified by this wanton official violence, and the following days saw nonstop demonstrations by students, artists and finally most of the populace, peaking in a rally on Letná plain by some 750,000 people. Leading dissidents, with Havel at the forefront, formed an anticommunist coalition, which negotiated the government's resignation on 3 December. A 'Government of National Understanding' was formed, with the communists as a minority group. Havel was elected president of the republic by the federal assembly on 29 December.

The days following the 17 November demonstration have become known as the 'Velvet Revolution' (Sametová revoluce) because of its almost totally nonviolent character.

THE VELVET DIVORCE

Free elections to the federal assembly in 1990 were won by Civic Forum (OH) and its Slovak counterpart, People Against Violence (VPN). But the OH soon split, over economic policy, into the right-of-centre ODS led by Václav Klaus, and the left-of-centre OH led by Jiří Dienstbier. Klaus forced through tough economic policies, and their success gave the ODS a slim victory in the 1992 elections.

Meanwhile, separatists headed by Vladimír Mečiar won the 1992 elections in Slovakia, depriving the ODS of a parliamentary majority. The very different economic positions of

Václav Havel

Václav Havel was born in October 1936, the son of a wealthy Prague restaurateur. His family's property was confiscated after the communist coup of 1948, and as the child of bourgeois parents he was denied easy access to education. He nevertheless finished high school and studied for a time at university before landing a job at the age of 23 as a stagehand at the divadlo na Zábradlí (Theatre on the Balustrade). Nine years later he was its resident playwright.

His enthusiasm over the liberal reforms of the 'Prague Spring', and his signature on the Charta 77 (Charter 77) declaration, made him an enemy of the Husák government. His works – typically focussing on the absurdities and dehumanisation of totalitarian bureaucracy – were banned, his passport was seized and altogether he spent some four years in jail for his activities on behalf of human rights in Czechoslovakia.

The massive demonstrations of November 1989 thrust Havel into the limelight as a leading organiser of the noncommunist Civic Forum movement, which pressed for democratic reforms and ultimately negotiated a new government of national reconciliation. Havel himself was elected president of the country the following month, and the first president of the new Czech Republic in 1993.

In 2003, after two terms as president, Havel was replaced by former prime minister Václav Klaus. The lack of a credible successor to Havel was emphasised by the fact that it took three attempts before the Czechs were able to elect a new president, and the uncharismatic Klaus is far from being the popular leader that Havel once was.

20–21 August 1968	16 January 1969	1977	3 December 1989
Soviet-led Warsaw Pact troops and tanks invade Prague	Student Jan Palach burns himself to death in protest at Soviet invasion	Dissidents sign Charta 77, a demand for basic human rights	Velvet Revolution marks the end of communist rule

Mečiar and Klaus made compromise almost impossible, with Mečiar favouring gradual transformation and independence for Slovakia. The two leaders decided that splitting the country was the best solution, and on 1 January 1993, Czechoslovakia ceased to exist for the second time in that century.

Prague became the capital of the new Czech Republic, and Havel was elected as its first president.

AFTER THE DIVORCE

Since 1993 Czech politics have been plagued by instability – no election since the Velvet Divorce has produced a government with a majority of more than a single seat. The decade leading up to 2002 was characterised by an unlikely coalition between the nominally right-wing ODS of Václav Klaus (Czech president since 2003), and the supposedly left-wing ČSSD – the equivalent of an alliance between the Conservative and Labour parties in the UK, or between Republicans and Democrats in the USA.

In January 1998 Václav Havel was re-elected as president, by a margin of just one vote. He described the unholy coalition of right and left in the Czech parliament as a deal struck between 'a left-wing party that has for years fought against a government of embezzlers, and a right-wing party that has called for mobilisation against a left allegedly attempting a return to communism'.

The 2002 elections did nothing to improve the situation. The ČSSD remained the largest party with an increased share of the vote (30.2%) but only 70 seats, headed by Prime Minister Vladimir Spidla. The ODS was second with 24.5% and 58 seats – their worst ever showing. The centrist Koalice (14.3%, 31 seats) slipped to fourth, but the big surprise was the Czech Communist Party (KSČM), which moved up to third place with 18.5% and 41 seats – up from 24 seats in 1998.

After several weeks of negotiations, Spidla formed a coalition government with Koalice and together the parties wielded a wafer-thin majority of 101 seats in the 200-seat parliament. Havel's term in office finally came to an end in 2003, when he was replaced by ODS leader Václav Klaus. Then in June 2004 the coalition collapsed and Spidla resigned. Czech politics looks set to lurch from crisis to crisis for some time to come.

In the international arena the Czech Republic has joined the big league: along with Poland and Hungary it became a member of NATO in 1999. The Lower House of the Czech parliament voted 154 to 38 in favour of NATO membership, though there was little public debate on the subject and no public referendum, as was held in Hungary (where 85% voted in favour). Even more momentously, the Czech Republic became one of ten nations to join the European Union on 1 May 2004.

Relations with Germany and Austria have in recent years been strained by the Czechs' refusal to decommission the ageing Temelin nuclear power station in southern Bohemia, and their continued upholding of the Beneš Decree, which saw the forced expulsion of Sudeten Germans from postwar Czechoslovakia.

1993	2002	2003	1 May 2004
Czech and Slovak republics part company in Velvet Divorce	August sees the worst floods to hit Prague in 200 years	Václav Klaus replaces Václav Havel as Czech president	Czech Republic joins the European Union

Districts

Districts

The Vltava River insinuates itself through the middle of Prague like a giant question mark, with the city centre nestling snugly in its curve. There is little method in Prague's haphazard sprawl – it's a city that has grown organically from its medieval roots, snagging villages and swallowing suburbs as its tendrils spread out into the wooded hills of central Bohemia.

The oldest parts of the city cluster tightly beside the river bend – **Hradčany**, the medieval castle district, and **Malá Strana** (Little Quarter) on the western bank; **Staré Město** (Old Town), **Nové Město** (New Town) and the ancient citadel of **Vyšehrad** on the eastern bank.

Around this core lie the mostly 19th- and 20th-century suburbs, just a 10-minute tram ride away – elegant **Vinohrady** and grungy **Žižkov** and **Karlín** to the east, **Holešovice** and **Bubeneč** and **Dejvice** to the north and northwest, and formerly industrial **Smíchov** to the south. We have also gathered the more outlying districts, such as Troja, Střešovice and Zbraslav together under this heading. You can find details of public transport under each district heading and on p211.

ITINERARIES
One Day

Prague in a day? Ambitious. Get up early and take a wander through Prague Castle's courtyards before the main sights open, then spend the morning visiting **chrám sv Víta** (St Vitus Cathedral; p57), the **Starý královský palác** (Old Royal Palace; p58), and the **bazilika sv Jiří** (Basilica of St George; p58), timing things to catch the **Changing of the Guard** (p55) at noon. Descend to Malá Strana through

Top Five Viewpoints

- **Great Tower**, chrám sv Víta (St Vitus Cathedral; p57)
- **Letenské sady** (Letná Gardens; p92)
- **Petřínská rozhledna** (Petřín Tower; p66)
- **Televizní vysílač** (TV Tower; p96)
- **Vyšehrad Citadel** (p90)

Buildings lining the banks of the Vltava River

the **Palácové zahrady pod Pražským hradem** (Palace Gardens Beneath Prague Castle; p64), and walk through the **Valdštenská zahrada** (Wallenstein Garden; p64) on your way to lunch on the riverside terrace at **Hergetova Cihelna** (p119). In the afternoon, stroll across **Charles Bridge** (Karlův most; p68) and continue along Karlova to the **Old Town Square** (Staroměstské náměstí; p67); after watching the **Astronomical Clock** (p71) do its thing, head to the **Obecní dům** (Municipal House; p77) and have a coffee while you admire the Art Nouveau décor. Choose somewhere special for dinner – **U Zlaté Studně** (p120) or **La Perle de Prague** (p128).

Three Days

Much better – you can devote a day each to Malá Strana, Staré Město, and Nové Město. Spend your first morning at the **castle** (p53), and after lunch with a view at **U Zlaté Studně** (p120) enjoy a leisurely afternoon exploring the sights of **Malá Strana** (p62) before rounding off the day with a romantic dinner at **Kampa Park** (p119) and an evening stroll across **Charles Bridge** (Karlův most; p68).

On day two, kick off with a wander round the **Old Town Square** (Staroměstské náměstí; p67), then devote an hour or two for the various sights that make up the **Židovské muzeum Praha** (Prague Jewish Museum; p74). Have lunch at a swanky Pařížská restaurant – **Pravda** (p123) would be good – then go on the guided tour of the **Obecní dům** (Municipal House; p77) that you booked in the morning, followed by a look around the **Mucha Museum** (p81). Have dinner at **V zátiší** (p125) then head for an Old Town **jazz club** (p159).

Your final day is for **shopping** (p165), exploring the passages and arcades around **Wenceslas Square** (Václavské náměstí; p166), and taking a metro ride out to **Vyšehrad** (p89). Round off a memorable three days with a **classical concert** (p157) and dinner at **La Perle de Prague** (p128).

One Week

Cover the sights mentioned in the three-day itinerary, but spend more time on the places that take your fancy. Add in visits to the **Veletržní palác** (Trade Fair Palace; p93) and the **Muzeum hlavního města Prahy** (Prague City Museum; p81), and set aside a day to do the **walking tour** (p109) from Letná to Troja; get the boat back into town (see p52 for details). You'll have time for a day trip to **Kutná Hora** (p204), and for more of that essential Prague activity of just sitting around in cafés and pubs, soaking up the atmosphere.

ORGANISED TOURS

Pragotur (p52) and various private companies operating from kiosks along Na příkopě (Map pp256–7) offer three-hour city bus tours for around 600Kč per person. These are OK if your time is short, but the castle and other sights get so crowded that you often can't enjoy the tour; we suggest taking one of the walking tours (see p53) instead.

Bicycle

CITY BIKE Map pp246-7 ☎ 776 180 284;
Králodvorská 5, Staré Město; ☻ 9am-7pm
Two-hour tours start at 450Kč. Much better value is the four-hour tour plus two-hour free ride for 500Kč. Nine hours of free riding is 700Kč.

PRAHA BIKE Map pp246-7
☎ 732 388 880; www.prahabike.cz; Dlouhá 24, Staré Město; tour 2hr 420Kč; ☻ 9am-7pm; metro Náměstí Republiky

Take a two-hour guided cycling tour through the city, or an easy evening pedal through the parks. Tours depart from the Praha Bike office at 2.30pm from mid-March to October, and also at 11.30am and 5.30pm from May to mid-September. Trips outside the city can also be arranged. Helmets and locks are provided, and bikes are also available for private rental (p209).

Boat

EVROPSKÁ VODNÍ DOPRAVA
EVD; ☎ 224 810 030; www.evd.cz; Čechův most, Staré Město; tram 17
EVD operates large cruise boats based at the quay beside Čechův most (Bohemia Bridge, which is near Hotel Inter-Continental). EVD offers a one-hour return cruise departing hourly from 10am to 6pm (220/110Kč per adult/child); a two-hour return cruise including lunch and music, departing at noon (640/380Kč per adult/child); a two-hour return cruise to Vyšehrad (350/270Kč), departing at 3pm; and a three-hour evening

return cruise with dinner and music (740/500Kč), departing at 7pm. All run year-round.

PRAGUE VENICE Map pp246-7

☎ 603 819 947; www.prague-venice.cz; Charles Bridge; adult/child 270/135Kč; ☼ 10.30am-11pm Jul & Aug, to 8pm Mar-Jun, Sep & Oct

Operates entertaining 30-minute cruises in small boats from under the hidden arches of Charles Bridge and along the Čertovka mill stream in Kampa. Jetties are at the Staré Město end of Charles Bridge (entry from Křížovnické náměstí; Map pp246–7), on the Čertovka stream in Malá Strana (Map pp244–5), and at the western end of Mánesův most (Mánes Bridge; Map pp244–5), near Malostranská metro station.

PRAŽSKÁ PAROPLAVEBNÍ SPOLEČNOST Map pp252-3

Prague Passenger Shipping, PPS; ☎ 224 930 017; www.paroplavba.cz; Rašínovo nábřeží 2, Nové Město; metro Karlovo Náměstí

From April to October PPS runs cruise boats along the Vltava, departing from the central quay on Rašínovo nábřeží (Map pp252–3). Most photogenic is a two-hour jaunt to Štvanice island and then to Vyšehrad, departing at 3.30pm from April to October (250Kč). A one-hour cruise between the Národní divadlo and Vyšehrad costs 170Kč per person and departs hourly from 11am to 6pm April to October.

At 9am Friday to Sunday in July and August, a boat goes 37km south (upstream) through a wild, green landscape to the Slapy Dam at Třebrenice. This fine, all-day escape costs 300Kč return, arriving back in the city at 6.30pm.

Boats making the 1¼-hour trip to Troja (near the zoo; 80Kč one way) depart 8.30am (weekdays in May and June only), 9.30am, 12.30pm and 3.30pm daily May to August, and at weekends and hols September and October. Returning boats depart Troja 11am, 2pm and 5pm.

Other more expensive trips go up and down the river while you lunch, snack, dine and dance to disco or country-and-western music.

Bus & Tram

NOSTALGIC TRAM NO 91

☎ 233 343 349; www.dpp.cz; Muzeum MHD (Public Transport Museum), Patočkova 4, Střešovice; adult/child 25/10Kč; ☼ departs hourly noon-6pm Sat, Sun & hols Apr–mid-Nov

Vintage tram cars dating from 1908 to 1924 trundle back and forth along a special sightseeing route, starting at the muzeum MHD (Pub-

lic Transport Museum) and going via stops at Prague Castle, Malostranské náměstí, Národní divadlo, Wenceslas Square, náměstí Republiky and Štefánikův most to finish at Výstaviště. You can get on and off at any stop, and buy tickets on board; ordinary public transport tickets and passes cannot be used on this line.

PRAGUE SIGHTSEEING TOURS

☎ 222 314 661; www.pstours.cz; Klimentská 22, Nové Město; 'Informative Prague' 2hr adult/child 390/300Kč, 'Grand City' 3½hr 650/350Kč

Offers a whole range of tours. The 'Informative Prague' bus tour (departing 11am and 1.30pm April to October) takes in all the important historical sites, and the 'Grand City' tour (departing 10am Friday and Saturday April to October) combines a bus tour of the main sites with a walk through Prague Castle (p53).

Jewish-Interest
PRECIOUS LEGACY TOURS

☎ 222 321 951; www.legacytours.cz; Maiselova 16, Staré Město; per person 630Kč; ☼ tours begin 10.30am Sun-Fri, also at 2pm by arrangement

Offers guided tours of places of interest to Jewish visitors, including a three-hour walking tour of Prague's Josefov district (fee includes admission to four synagogues, but not the Staronová Synagogue – this is 200Kč extra). There's also a daily six-hour excursion to Terezín (1160Kč per person; departs 10am); for more information on Terezín see p201. All revenue goes towards supporting the activities of Prague's small Jewish community, including social work and the reconstruction of property returned after 1989.

WITTMANN TOURS Map pp252-3

☎ 222 252 472; www.wittmann-tours.com; Mánesova 8, Vinohrady; adult/student 630/500Kč; ☼ tours begin 10.30am & 2pm Sun-Fri May-Oct, 10.30am Apr, Nov & Dec

This outfit's three-hour walking tour of Josefov has been recommended by readers; it starts from the square in front of the Hotel Inter-Continental on Pařížská. Wittmann also runs seven-hour day trips to Terezín (see p201) for 1150/1000Kč per adult/student.

Personal Guides
PRAGOTUR Map pp246-7

☎ 224 482 562; guides@pis.cz; Old Town Hall, Staroměstské náměstí 1; 3hr tour per person 1000Kč, per 2 persons 1200Kč plus 300Kč per additional person; ☼ 9am-6pm Mon-Fri, 9am-4pm Sat & Sun

An affiliate of the Prague Information Service (PIS), Pragotur can arrange personal guides fluent in all major European languages. Its desk is in the PIS office in the Staroměstská radnice (Old Town Hall; p72).

Vintage Car

A couple of businesses offer tours around the city in genuine vintage Czech cars dating from the late 1920s and early 1930s. There are pick-up points at various city centre locations; tours depart as available, or whenever you ask, if it's quiet.

3 VETERANS

☎ 603 767 987; www.3veterani.cz; 1-2 persons 900Kč, 3-4 persons 1200Kč; ☺ 9am-6pm

This operation has a small fleet of Praga Piccolos and early Škodas, all from the early 1930s. Try to get driver Robert Dzyben, better known as Crocodile Dundee – you won't learn much about history and architecture, but his running commentary on Prague policemen, wheel clamps, traffic lights and tourist crowds is hilarious. Pick-up points in Staré Město (Map pp246–7) are on Rytířská, in Malé náměstí, and at the junction of Pařížská and Staroměstské náměstí; and on Malostranské náměstí in Malá Strana (Map pp244–5).

OLD TIMER HISTORY TRIP

☎ 607 112 559; www.historytrip.cz; 1-2 persons 800Kč, 3-6 persons 1200Kč; ☺ 9am-6pm

Rattle along the city's cobble-stone streets in a 1928 Praga Piccolo, or a larger 1929 Praga Alfa. Pick-up points in Staré Město (Map pp246–7) are at the corner of Melantrichova and Rytířská, in Malé náměstí, on Karlova and at the junction of Pařížská and Staroměstské náměstí; and on Malostranská náměstí in Malá Strana (Map pp244–5).

Walking

The corner of Old Town Square outside the Staroměstská radnice is usually clogged with dozens of people touting for business as walking guides; quality varies, but the best are listed here. Most operators don't have an office – you can join a walk by just turning up at the starting point and paying your money, though it's best to phone ahead to be sure of a place. Most walks begin at the Astronomical Clock (Map pp246–7); prices range from 300Kč to 1000Kč per person.

CITY WALKS

☎ 608 200 912; www.praguewalkingtours.com; per person 300-450Kč

Offers a long list of guided walks ranging from 90-minute Prague Intro (begins at the Astronomical Clock at 12.30pm) to the four-hour Insider Tour (departing 9.45am from the statue of St Wenceslas in Wenceslas Square), as well as a Revolution Walk detailing the events of 1968 and 1989, and an evening Ghost Trail.

PRAGUEMASTER/GEORGE'S GUIDED WALKS

☎ 607 820 158; www.praguemaster.com; per 2 persons €30-60, per additional person €10-20

Travellers have raved about George, whose intimate, personalised tours include a four-hour History Walk, a two-hour Iron Curtain Walk, and a five-hour pub crawl, including dinner in a Czech pub. George will meet you at your hotel, or anywhere else that's convenient.

PRAGUE WALKS

☎ 603 271 911; www.praguewalks.com; per person 300-390Kč

Interesting walks with themes ranging from Prague architecture to everyday life, from Žižkov pubs to the Velvet Revolution.

Districts – Prague Castle

PRAGUE CASTLE

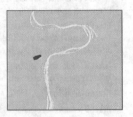

Prague Castle (Pražský hrad, or just *hrad* to Czechs) – almost a small town in itself – is Prague's most popular attraction. According to *Guinness World Records*, it's the largest ancient castle in the world – 570m long, an average of 128m wide and covering a total area bigger than seven football fields.

Its history starts in the 9th century when Prince Bořivoj founded a fortified settlement here. It grew as rulers made their own additions, which explains its mixture of styles. The castle has always been the seat of Czech rulers as well as the official residence of the head of state, although the Czech Republic's first president, Václav Havel, chose to live in his own house on the outskirts of the city.

Prague Castle has had four major reconstructions, from that of Prince Soběslav in the 12th century to a classical face-lift under Empress Maria Theresa (r 1740–80). In the 1920s President Masaryk hired a Slovene architect, Jože Plečník, to renovate the castle.

Orientation

We've organised the castle information starting with the main entrance at the western end, and following through with the various courtyards before exiting at the eastern end.

The castle grounds are open 5am to midnight, and the gardens 10am to 6pm April to October. The cathedral and other historic buildings accessible by ticket are open 9am to 5pm. From November to March the grounds open 6am to 11pm, and the historic buildings open from 9am to 4pm; the gardens are closed.

There's a **post office** (⊠ 8am-7pm Mon-Fri, 10am-7pm Sat) and currency exchange is available at **Chequepoint** (⊠ 8.10am-6.10pm), which is next to the castle's own **information centre** (☎ 224 373 368, 224 372 434; www.hrad.cz; ☎ 9am-5pm Apr-Oct, to 4pm Nov-Mar). The centre is in the Third Courtyard, opposite the main entrance to chrám sv Víta (St Vitus Cathedral). Here you'll also find an ATM, and you can get a free castle map, buy admission tickets, rent an audio-guide and organise a guided tour.

One-hour guided tours are available in Czech (200Kč for up to five people, plus 40Kč per additional person), and in English, French, German, Italian, Russian and Spanish (450Kč, plus 90Kč per additional person) Tuesday to Sunday. Alternatively you can rent an audio-guide (cassette player and headphones) for 145/180Kč for two/three hours.

The following areas are wheelchair-accessible: the main entrance to chrám sv Víta, the Starý Královský palác (Old Royal Palace, Vladislav Hall), bazilika sv Jiří (Basilica of St George), Míčovna (Ball-Game House), obrazárna Pražského hradu (Prague Castle Gallery) and the castle gardens. There's a wheelchair-accessible toilet to the right of the cathedral entrance.

Transport

Metro The nearest metro station is Malostranská, but from here it's a stiff climb up the Old Castle Steps to the eastern end of the castle. Hradčanská is about 10 minutes' walk from the castle, but it's an easy, level walk.

Tram Take tram No 22 or 23 from Národní třída on the southern edge of Staré Město, Malostranská náměstí in Malá Strana, or Malostranská metro station to the Pražský hrad stop. If you want to explore Hradčany first, stay on the tram until Pohořelec, the next stop but one.

Tickets

Entry is free to the castle courtyards and gardens, and to the nave of chrám sv Víta. There are four different tickets, which allow entry to various combinations of sights. You can buy tickets at the information centre in the Third Courtyard, or at the entrance to each of the main sights (chrám sv Víta, Starý Královský palác and bazilika sv Jiří).

You can buy tickets for concerts and other special events at the **box office** (☎ 1080; ⊠ 9am-5pm Apr-Oct, to 4pm Nov-Mar) in the kaple sv Kříže (Chapel of the Holy Cross) in the Second Courtyard.

The tickets listed here do not include admission to the other art galleries and museums within the castle grounds (those admission costs are listed in the individual reviews). The tickets here are valid for one day only.

Ticket A (adult/concession/family 350/175/520Kč) Includes entry to chrám sv Víta (St Vitus Cathedral, including Great Tower), Starý Královský palác (Old Royal Palace, including the Story of Prague Castle exhibit), bazilika sv Jiří (Basilica of St George), Prašná věž (Powder Tower), Zlatá ulička (Golden Lane) and Daliborka.

Ticket B (adult/concession/family 220/110/330Kč) Includes entry to chrám sv Víta (including Great Tower), Starý Královský palác, Zlatá ulička and Daliborka Tower.

Ticket C (adult/family 50/100Kč) Allows admission to Zlatá ulička and Daliborka Tower.

Ticket D (adult/concession/family 50/25/100Kč) Admission for bazilika sv Jiří.

Concession prices are for those aged seven to 16, students and disabled visitors; children aged six or under get in free. The family ticket is valid for two adults and any children aged 16 or under.

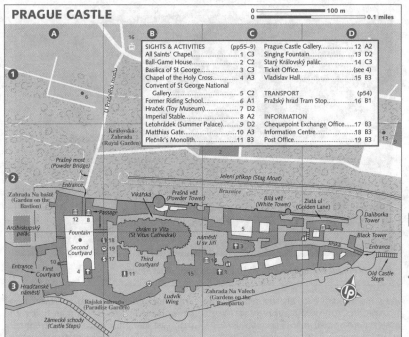

PRAGUE CASTLE

SIGHTS & ACTIVITIES	(pp55–9)
All Saints' Chapel...................................1	C3
Ball-Game House....................................2	C2
Basilica of St George...............................3	C3
Chapel of the Holy Cross........................4	A3
Convent of St George National Gallery...5	C2
Former Riding School.............................6	A1
Hraček (Toy Museum)............................7	D2
Imperial Stable......................................8	A2
Letohrádek (Summer Palace).................9	D2
Matthias Gate......................................10	A3
Plečník's Monolith...............................11	B3

Prague Castle Gallery.........................12	A2
Singing Fountain.................................13	D2
Starý Královský palác..........................14	C3
Ticket Office.....................................(see 4)
Vladislav Hall.....................................15	B3

TRANSPORT	(p54)
Pražský hrad Tram Stop.......................16	B1

INFORMATION
Chequepoint Exchange Office.............17	B3
Information Centre..............................18	B3
Post Office...19	B3

FIRST COURTYARD

The castle's main gate, on Hradčanské náměstí, is flanked by huge, baroque statues of **battling Titans** (1767–70), which dwarf the castle guards who stand beneath them. After the fall of communism in 1989, then-president Václav Havel hired Theodor Pistek, the Czech costume designer from the film *Amadeus* (1984), to replace their communist-era khaki uniforms with the stylish pale-blue kit they now wear, which harks back to the army of the first Czechoslovak Republic of 1918–38.

The **changing of the guard** takes place every hour on the hour, but the longest and most impressive display is at noon, when banners are exchanged while a brass band plays a fanfare from the windows of the **Plečníkova síň** (Plečník Hall), which overlooks the First Courtyard.

This impressive hall, which opens off the left side of the baroque **Matyášova brána** (Matthias Gate; 1614), was created by Slovenian architect Jože Plečník as part of the 1920s restoration of the castle; the pointy flagpoles in the First Courtyard are also Plečník's. As you pass through the gate, note the contrast between the gilded baroque staircase to your right and the Doric simplicity of Plečník's stair to the left.

SECOND COURTYARD

You pass through the Matyášova brána into the Second Courtyard, centred on a baroque fountain and a 17th-century well with beautiful Renaissance lattice work. On the right the **kaple sv Kříže** (Chapel of the Holy Cross; 1763) was once the treasury of chrám sv Víta; today it houses the castle's box office and souvenir shop (for more information see the boxed text opposite).

The magnificent **Španělský sál** (Spanish Hall) and **Rudolfova galerie** (Rudolph Gallery) in the northern wing of the courtyard are reserved for state receptions and special concerts (open to the public just one or two days a year, on special occasions).

OBRAZÁRNA PRAŽSKÉHO HRADU

Map above
Prague Castle Gallery; ☎ 224 373 368; Pražský hrad, II. nád-voří; adult/concession 100/50Kč; ☽ 10am-6pm; metro Malostranská

Views of Prague Castle from Vrtbovská zahrada (p66), Malá Strana

The same Swedish army that looted the famous bronzes in the Valdštejnská zahrada (Wallenstein Garden; p64) in 1648 also took Rudolf II's art collection. This gallery, housed in the beautiful Renaissance stables at the northern end of the Second Courtyard, is based on the Habsburg collection that was begun in 1650 to replace the lost paintings. The display of 16th- to 18th-century European art includes works by Rubens, Tintoretto and Titian.

KRÁLOVSKÁ ZAHRADA

The gate on the northern side of the Second Courtyard leads to the **Prašný most** (Powder Bridge; 1540), which spans the **Jelení příkop** (Stag Moat) and leads to the **Královská zahrada** (Royal Garden), which started life as a Renaissance garden built by Ferdinand I in 1534. The most beautiful of the garden's buildings is the **Míčovna** (Ball-Game House; 1569), a masterpiece of Renaissance *sgraffito* where the Habsburgs once played a primitive version of badminton. To the east is the **Letohrádek** (Summer Palace, or Belvedere; 1538–60), the most authentic Italian Renaissance building outside Italy, and to the west the former **jízdárna** (Riding School; 1695). All three are used as venues for temporary exhibitions of modern art.

A footpath to the west of the Prašný most (on the castle side) leads down into the moat, and doubles back through a modern,

arty (and rather Freudian), red-brick **tunnel** beneath the bridge. If you then follow the path east along the moat you'll eventually end up at Malostranská metro station. A gate on the outer wall of the castle, overlooking the moat, leads to a bomb shelter started by the communists in the 1950s but never completed. Its tunnels run under most of the castle.

THIRD COURTYARD

As you pass through the passage on the eastern side of the Second Courtyard, the huge western façade of **chrám sv Víta** soars directly above you. At first glance it may appear impressively Gothic, but in fact the triple doorway dates only from 1948 to 1953, one of the last parts of the church to be completed.

South of the cathedral is the Third Courtyard, which contains a granite **monolith** (1928) dedicated to the victims of WWI, designed by Jože Plečník, and a copy of a 14th-century bronze **statue of St George** slaying the dragon; the original statue is in the **klášter sv Jiří** (Convent of St George).

The southern doorway of the cathedral is known as the **Zlatá brána** (Golden Gate), an elegant, triple-arched Gothic porch designed by Petr Parler. Above it is a **mosaic of the Last Judgment** (1370–71) – on the left, the godly rise from their tombs and are raised into Heaven by angels; on the right, sinners are cast down into Hell by demons. In the centre, Christ reigns in glory, with six Czech saints – Procopius, Sigismund, Vitus, Wenceslas, Ludmila and Adalbert – below. Beneath them, on either side of the central arch, Charles IV and his wife kneel in prayer.

To the left of the gate is the **Great Tower**, which was left unfinished by Parler's sons in the 15th century; its soaring Gothic lines are capped by a Renaissance gallery added in the late-16th century, and a bulging spire that dates from the 1770s.

CHRÁM SV VÍTA Map p55

St Vitus Cathedral; ☾ **9am-5pm Apr-Oct, to 4pm Nov-Mar; admission free to nave; metro Malostranská**
You enter the cathedral through the western door; everything between here and the crossing was built during the late 19th and early 20th centuries. Inside, the nave is flooded with colour from beautiful **stained-glass windows** created by eminent Czech artists of the early 20th century – note the one by Art Nouveau artist Alfons Mucha (third chapel on the northern side), depicting the lives of SS Cyril & Methodius (1909). Nearby is a wooden sculpture of the **crucifixion** (1899) by František Bílek.

The cathedral's foundation stone was laid in 1344 by Emperor Charles IV, on the site of

Stained-glass windows with Art Nouveau Mucha designs, chrám sv Víta (see above)

a 10th-century Romanesque rotunda built by Duke Wenceslas. Charles' original architect **Matyáš z Arrasu** (Matthias of Arras), began work in 1344 on the choir in the French Gothic style, but died eight years later.

His German successor, **Petr Parler** – a veteran of Cologne's cathedral – completed most of the eastern part of the cathedral in a freer, late-Gothic style before he died in 1399. Renaissance and baroque details were added over the following centuries, but it was only in 1861 during the Czech National Revival that a concerted effort was made to finish the cathedral; it was finally consecrated in 1929.

Walk up to the crossing, where the nave and transept meet, and look at the huge **south window** (1938) by Max Švabinský, depicting the Last Judgement – note the fires of Hell burning brightly in the lower right-hand corner. In the **north transept** are three carved wooden doors.

Just to the right of the southtransept is the entrance to the 96m-tall **Great Tower** (☎ last entry 4.15pm Apr-Oct, closed during bad weather). You can climb the 297 slightly claustrophobic steps to the top for excellent views, and you also get a close look at the clockworks (1597). The tower's Sigismund Bell, made by Tomáš Jaroš in 1549, is Bohemia's largest bell.

You'll need your castle admission ticket (A or B) to enter the eastern end of the cathedral, whose graceful late-Gothic vaulting dates from the 14th century. In the centre lies the ornate **Royal Mausoleum** (1571–89) with its cold marble effigies of Ferdinand I, his wife Anna Jagellonská and son Maximilián II.

On the ambulatory's northern side, just beyond the old sacristy and the confessional booths, a **wooden relief** (1630) by Caspar Bechterle shows Protestant Frederick of the Palatinate (in his horse-drawn coach) legging it out of Prague after the Catholic victory at the battle of Bílá Hora.

As you round the far end of the ambulatory you pass the **tomb of St Vitus** – the brass crosiers set in the floor mark the tombs of bishops – and reach the spectacular, baroque silver **tomb of St John of Nepomuk**, its draped canopy supported by chubby, silver angels (the tomb contains two tonnes of silver in all).

The nearby **Chapel of St Mary Magdalene** contains the grave slabs of Matyáš z Arrasu and Petr Parler. Beyond is the ornate, late-Gothic **Royal Oratory**, a fancy balcony with ribbed vaulting carved to look like tree branches.

Stairs in the corner of the Chapel of the Holy Rood lead down to the crypt, where you can see the remains of earlier churches that stood

Top Five for Kids

- **Bludiště** (Mirror Maze; p66) Fun maze on Petřín hill where kids can distort their facial features with no lasting consequences.
- **Boat trips** (p51)
- **Dětský ostrov** (Children's Island; p65) Leafy riverside retreat with swings and sandpit.
- **Národní technické muzeum** (National Technology Museum; p93) Stuffed with vintage trains, planes and automobiles, many of which kids can clamber aboard.
- **Puppet shows** (p160) Various theatres put on traditional puppet shows aimed at children.

Districts – Prague Castle

on the site of the cathedral, including an 11th-century Romanesque basilica. Beyond, you can crowd around the entrance to the **Royal Crypt** to see the marble sarcophagi (dating only from the 1930s), which contain the remains of Czech rulers, including Charles IV, Wenceslas IV, George of Poděbrady (Jiří z Poděbrad) and Rudolf II.

The biggest and most beautiful of the cathedral's numerous side chapels is Parler's **Chapel of St Wenceslas**. Its walls are adorned with gilded panels containing polished slabs of semiprecious stones. Early-16th-century wall paintings depict scenes from the life of the Czechs' patron saint, while even older frescoes show scenes from the life of Christ.

On the southern side of the Chapel of St Wenceslas, a small door – locked with seven locks – hides a staircase leading to the Coronation Chamber above the Zlatá brána, where the Czech **crown jewels** are kept. Rarely exhibited to the public, the jewels include the gold crown of St Wenceslas, which was made for Charles IV in 1346 from the gold of the original Přemysl crown (for details on the Přemysl dynasty see p41).

STARÝ KRÁLOVSKÝ PALÁC Map p55
Old Royal Palace; admission tickets A or B only; ⏱ 9am-5pm Apr-Oct, to 4pm Nov-Mar; metro Malostranská

The Starý Královský palác (Old Royal Palace), at the courtyard's eastern end, is one of the oldest parts of the castle, dating from 1135. It was originally used only by Czech princesses, but from the 13th to the 16th centuries it was the king's own palace.

At its heart is the **Vladislavský sál** (Vladislav Hall), famous for its beautiful, late-Gothic vaulted

roof (1493–1502) designed by Benedikt Rejt. Though around 500 years old, the flowing, interpenetrating lines of the vaults have an almost Art Nouveau feel, in contrast to the rectilinear form of the Renaissance windows. The vast hall was used for banquets, councils and coronations, and also for indoor jousting tournaments – hence the **Jezdecké schody** (Riders' Staircase) on the northern side, designed to admit a mounted knight. All the presidents of the republic have been sworn in here.

A door in the hall's southwestern corner leads to the former offices of the **České kanceláře** (Bohemian Chancellery). On 23 May 1618, in the second room, Protestant nobles rebelling against the Bohemian estates and the Habsburg emperor threw two of his councillors and their secretary out of the window. They survived, as their fall was broken by the dung-filled moat, but this so-called Second Defenestration of Prague sparked off the Thirty Years' War (for more details about this see p42).

At the eastern end of Vladislavský sál you'll come to a balcony that overlooks **kaple Všech svatých** (All Saints' Chapel); a door to the right leads you to a terrace with great views across the city. To the right of the Jezdecké schody you'll spot an unusual Renaissance doorway framed by twisted columns that leads to the **Sněmovna** (Diet, or Assembly Hall), which displays another beautifully vaulted ceiling. To the left, a spiral staircase leads you up to the **Říšská dvorská kancelář** (New Land Rolls Room), the old repository for land titles, where the walls are covered with the clerks' coats of arms.

NÁMĚSTÍ U SV JIŘÍ

Náměstí U sv Jiří (St George Square), the plaza to the east of the cathedral, lies at the heart of the castle complex.

BAZILIKA SV JIŘÍ Map p55
Basilica of St George; adult/concession/family 50/25/100Kč; ⏱ 9am-5pm Apr-Oct, to 4pm Nov-Mar; metro Malostranská

The striking, brick-red, early-baroque façade that dominates the square conceals the Czech Republic's best-preserved Romanesque church, bazilika sv Jiří (Basilica of St George), established in the 10th century by Vratislav I (the father of St Wenceslas). What you see today is mostly the result of restorations made between 1887 and 1908.

The austerity of the Romanesque nave is relieved by a baroque double staircase leading to the apse, where fragments of 12th-century frescoes survive. In front of the stairs lie the tombs of Prince Boleslav II (d 997; on the left) and Prince Vratislav I (d 921), the church's founder. The arch beneath the stairs allows a glimpse of the 12th-century crypt; Přemysl kings (see p41) are buried here and in the nave.

The tiny baroque chapel beside the entrance is dedicated to St John of Nepomuk (his tomb lies in chrám sv Víta; p57).

KLÁŠTER SV JIŘÍ Map p55
Convent of St George; ☎ 257 320 536; Jiřské náměstí 33; adult/concession 50/20Kč; 10am-6pm Tue-Sun; metro Malostranská

The very ordinary-looking building to the left of the basilica was Bohemia's first convent, klášter sv Jiří (Convent of St George), established in 973 by Boleslav II. Closed and converted to an army barracks in 1782, it now houses a branch of the National Gallery, with an excellent collection of Renaissance and baroque art.

PRAŠNÁ VĚŽ Map p55
Powder Tower; 9am-5pm Apr-Oct, to 4pm Nov-Mar; metro Malostranská

A passage to the north of chrám sv Víta leads to Prašná věž (Powder Tower; also called the Mihulka), built at the end of the 15th century as part of the castle's defences. Later it became the workshop of the cannon- and bell-maker Tomáš Jaroš, who cast the bells for chrám sv Víta. Alchemists employed by Rudolf II also worked here. Today it houses a missable (dull) museum of alchemy, metal-working, and Renaissance life in Prague Castle (labels in Czech only).

JIŘSKÁ
Jiřská (George St) runs from the bazilika sv Jiří (Basilica of St George) to the castle's eastern gate.

LOBKOVICKÝ PALÁC Map p55
Lobkowicz Palace; ☎ 257 535 979; adult/concession 40/20Kč; 9am-5pm Tue-Sun; metro Malostranská

Built in the 1570s this aristocratic palace now houses a branch of the Národní muzeum (National Museum; p84), with a good collection on Czech history from prehistoric times until 1848. Exhibits include the sword of executioner Jan Mydlář (who lopped off the heads of 27 rebellious Protestant nobles in Old Town Square in 1621) and some of the oldest marionettes in

the Czech Republic, but to be honest this is a place for history buffs only.

MUZEUM HRAČEK Map p55
Toy Museum; ☎ 224 372 294; Jiřská 4; adult/concession 50/30Kč; 9.30am-5.30pm; metro Malostranská

In the tower of the Nejvyšší Purkrabství (Burgrave's Palace), across the street from the Lobkovický palác, is the second largest toy museum in the world. It's an amazing collection – with exhibits dating back to ancient Greece – but sure to be frustrating for kids as most displays are hands-off.

ZLATÁ ULIČKA Map p55
Golden Lane; Zlatá ul; 9am-5pm; metro Malostranská

Zlatá ulička (Golden Lane) is a picturesque, cobbled alley running along the northern wall of the castle. Its tiny, colourful cottages were built in the 16th century for the sharpshooters of the castle guard, but were later used by goldsmiths. In the 18th and 19th centuries they were occupied by squatters, and then by artists, including the writer Franz Kafka (who stayed at his sister's house at No 22 from 1916 to 1917; see the boxed text on p26 for more information on Kafka) and the Nobel-laureate poet Jaroslav Seifert. Today, the lane is an overcrowded tourist trap lined with craft and souvenir shops.

At its eastern end is the **Daliborka**, a round tower named after the knight Dalibor of Kozojedy, imprisoned here in 1498 for supporting a peasant rebellion, and later executed. According to an old tale, he played a violin during his imprisonment, which could be heard throughout the castle. Bedřich Smetana (p23) based his 1868 opera *Dalibor* on the tale.

ZAHRADA NA VALECH
At the castle's eastern gate, you can either descend the **Old Castle Steps** (Map p55) to Malostranská metro station, or turn sharp right and wander back to Hradčanské náměstí through the **Zahrada Na Valech** (Garden on the Ramparts; Apr-Oct). The terrace garden enjoys superb views across the roof-tops of Malá Strana and permits a peek into the back garden of the British embassy.

Alternatively, you can descend to Malá Strana through the terraced **Palácové zahrady pod Pražským hradem** (Palace Gardens Beneath Prague Castle; p64).

HRADČANY

Eating p118; Drinking p149; Shopping p167; Sleeping p179

Hradčany is the attractive and peaceful residential area stretching west from Prague Castle to Strahovský klášter (Strahov Monastery). It became a town in its own right in 1320, and twice suffered heavy damage – once in the Hussite wars and again in the Great Fire of 1541 – before becoming a borough of Prague in 1598. After this, the Habsburg nobility built many palaces here in the hope of cementing their influence with the rulers in Prague Castle.

Districts – Hradčany

HRADČANSKÉ NÁMĚSTÍ

Hradčanské náměstí (Hradčany Square), facing the castle entrance, has retained its shape since the Middle Ages, with a central **plague column** by Ferdinand Brokoff (1726) and several former canons' residences (Nos 6 to 12) with richly decorated façades.

ARCIBISKUPSKÝ PALÁC Map pp244-5
Archbishop's Palace; Hradčanské náměstí 16; ☺ only on the day before Good Fri; tram 22, 23

Opposite the Schwarzenberský palác is the rococo Arcibiskupský palác, bought by Archbishop Antonín Brus of Mohelnice in 1562, and the seat of archbishops ever since. The exterior was given a rococo makeover between 1763 and 1765.

SCHWARZENBERSKÝ PALÁC Map pp244-5
Schwarzenberg Palace; Hradčanské náměstí 16; tram 22, 23

The Renaissance Schwarzenberg Palace, acquired by the powerful Schwarzenberg family in 1719, sports a black-and-white *sgraffito* façade as startling as a Hawaiian shirt. It is currently being re-fitted by the National Gallery, and is due to re-open in 2007.

Transport
Tram Both tram Nos 22 and 23 stop at Pohořelec, at the western end of Hradčany.

ŠTERNBERSKÝ PALÁC Map pp244-5
Sternberg Palace; ☎ 220 514 599; adult/child 60/30Kč; ☺ 10am-6pm Tue-Sun; tram 22, 23

Tucked behind the Arcibiskupský palác is the baroque Šternberský palác, home to the National Gallery's valuable collection of 14th- to 18th-century European art, including works by Goya and Rembrandt. Fans of medieval altarpieces will be in heaven; there's also a number of Rubens, some Rembrandt and Breughel, and a large collection of Bohemian miniatures. Pride of the collection is the glowing *Feast of the Rosary* by Albrecht Dürer, an artist better known for his engravings. Painted in Venice in 1505 as an altarpiece for the church of San Bartolomeo, it was brought to Prague by Rudolf II; in the background, beneath the tree on the right, is the figure of the artist himself. It's worth a trip to the back of the 1st floor to see van Heemskerck's

Prague Under the Nazis

'I have fallen totally in love with this city. It exudes the German spirit and must become German again one day.'

Joseph Goebbels, writing about Prague in November 1940

From March 1939 to May 1945 Prague was capital of the Nazi Protectorate of Bohemia and Moravia. Many city landmarks that look innocuous to the visiting tourist still serve as unpleasant reminders of the Nazi occupation; most of them have a memorial of some sort.

- Černínský palác (p61)
- Národní památník obětí heydrichiády (p88)
- Památník protifašistického odboje v Kobylisích (p99)
- Pečkův palác (p85)
- V Holešovičkách (p94)
- Věznice Pankrác (p90)

The Tearful Bride, who seems to have stepped right out of a travesty show.

LORETÁNSKÉ NÁMĚSTÍ

From Hradčanské náměstí it's a short walk west to Loretánské náměstí (Loreta Square), created early in the 18th century when the imposing **černínský palác** (Černín Palace) was built. At the northern end of the square is the **klášter kapucínů** (Capuchin Monastery; 1600–02), whish is Bohemia's oldest working monastery.

ČERNÍNSKÝ PALÁC Map pp244-5
Černin Palace; Loretánské náměstí;
🕙 **closed to the public**
The early baroque 18th-century palace facing the Loreta served as the SS headquarters 1939–45. It now houses the Czech foreign ministry.

LORETA Map pp244-5
☎ **224 510 789; Loretánské náměstí 7; adult/ concession 90/70Kč;** 🕙 **9.15am-12.15pm & 1-4.30pm; photography forbidden; tram 22; 23**
The square's main attraction is the Loreta, a baroque place of pilgrimage founded by Benigna Kateřina Lobkowicz in 1626, designed as a replica of the supposed Santa Casa (Sacred House; the home of the Virgin Mary). Legend says that the original Santa Casa was carried by angels to the Italian town of Loreto as the Turks were advancing on Nazareth. The duplicate **Santa Casa**, with fragments of its original frescoes, is in the centre of the courtyard.

Behind the Santa Casa is the **kostel Narození Páně** (Church of the Nativity of Our Lord), built in 1737 to a design by Kristof Dientzenhofer (for more information on this designer see the boxed text on p34). The claustrophobic interior includes two skeletons – of the Spanish saints Felicissima and Marcia – dressed in nobles' clothing with wax masks over their skulls.

At the corner of the courtyard there is the startling **kaple Panny Marie Bolestné** (Chapel of Our Lady of Sorrows), featuring a crucified bearded lady. She was St Starosta, pious daughter of a Portuguese king who promised her to the king of Sicily against her wishes. After a night of tearful prayers she awoke with a beard, the wedding was called off, and her father had her crucified. She was later made patron saint of the needy and the godforsaken.

The most eye-popping attraction is the **treasury** (1st floor). It's been ransacked several times over the centuries, but some amazing items remain. Most over-the-top is the 90cm-tall **Pražské slunce** (Prague Sun), made of solid silver and gold and studded with 6222 diamonds.

Above the Loreta's entrance 27 bells, made in Amsterdam in the 17th century, play *We Greet Thee a Thousand Times* every hour.

Photography is not allowed, and the rule is enforced with a 1000Kč fine.

STRAHOVSKÝ KLÁŠTER

In 1140 Vladislav II founded **Strahovský klášter** (Strahov Monastery; Map pp244–5; Strahovské nádvoří 1) for the Premonstratensian order. The present monastery buildings, completed in the 17th and 18th centuries, functioned until the communist government closed them down and imprisoned most of the monks, who returned in 1990.

Inside is the 1612 **kostel sv Rocha** (Church of St Roch), which is now an exhibition hall. The **kostel Nanebevzetí Panny Marie** (Church of the Assumption of Our Lady) was built in 1143, and heavily decorated in the 18th century in the baroque style. Mozart is said to have played the organ here.

Façade of kostel Nanebevzetí Panny Marie (see above)

MUZEUM MINIATUR Map pp244-5

Miniature Museum; ☎ 233 352 371;
www.muzeumminiatur.cz; Strahovské II.nádvoří;
adult/child 50/30Kč; ◷ 10am-5pm; tram 22, 23

The 'write your name on a grain of rice' movement may have undermined the respectability
of miniature artists, but Siberian technician
Anatoly Konyenko will restore your faith with
his microscopic creations. Konyenko used to
manufacture tools for eye microsurgery, but
these days he'd rather spend seven-and-a-half
years crafting a pair of gold horseshoes for a
flea. See those, plus the world's smallest book
and strangely beautiful silhouettes of cars on
the leg of a mosquito.

STRAHOVSKÁ KNIHOVNA Map pp244-5

Strahov Library; ☎ 220 516 671; www.strahovmon
astery.cz; Strahovské I.nádvoří; adult/concession
70/50Kč; ◷ 9am-noon & 1-5pm; tram 22, 23

The biggest attraction of Strahovský klášter is
the Strahovská knihovna (Strahov Library), the
largest monastic library in the country, with its
two magnificent baroque halls. You can peek
through the doors but, sadly, you can't go into
the halls themselves – it was found that fluc-
tuations in humidity caused by visitors' breath
was endangering the frescoes.

The stunning interior of the two-storey-high
Filozofický sál (Philosophy Hall; 1780–97) was
built to fit around carved and gilded, floor-to-
ceiling walnut shelving that was rescued from
another monastery in South Bohemia (access
to the upper gallery is via spiral staircases concealed in the corners). The feeling of height is
accentuated by a grandiose ceiling fresco, the
Struggle of Mankind to Gain True Wisdom – the
figure of Divine Providence is enthroned in
the centre amid a burst of golden light, while
around the edges are figures ranging from
Adam and Eve to the Greek philosophers.

The lobby outside the hall contains an
18th-century **Cabinet of Curiosities**, displaying

the grotesquely shrivelled remains of sharks,
skates, turtles and other sea creatures, and the
flayed and splayed corpse of a dodo. Another
case (beside the door to the corridor) contains
historical items, including a miniature coffee
service made for the Habsburg empress Marie
Louise in 1813, which fits into four false books.

The corridor leads to the older but even more
beautiful **Teologiský sál** (Theology Hall; 1679). The
low, curved ceiling is thickly encrusted in ornate baroque stucco-work, and decorated with
painted cartouches depicting the theme of
'True Wisdom', which was acquired, of course,
through piety; one of the mottoes that adorns
the ceiling is 'initio sapientiae timor domini', 'the
beginning of wisdom is the fear of God'.

On a stand outside the hall door is a fac-
simile of the library's most prized possession,
the **Strahov Evangeliary**, a 9th-century codex in a
gem-studded 12th-century binding. A nearby
bookcase houses the **Xyloteka** (1825), a set of
booklike boxes, each one bound in the wood
and bark of the tree it describes, with samples
of leaves, roots, flowers and fruits inside.

In the connecting corridor, look out for the
two long, brown, leathery things beside the
model ship and narwhal tusk – the prudish at-
tendant will tell you they're preserved elephants'
trunks, but they're actually whales' penises.

STRAHOVSKÁ OBRAZÁRNA Map pp244-5

Strahov Picture Gallery; ☎ 220 517 278; www.strahov
monastery.cz; Strahovské II.nádvoří; adult/child
40/20Kč; ◷ 9am-noon & 12.30-5pm Tue-Sun; tram
22, 23

In Strahov Monastery's second courtyard is the
Strahovská obrazárna (Strahov Picture Gallery),
with a valuable collection of Gothic, baroque,
rococo and romantic monastery art on the 1st
floor, and temporary exhibits on the ground
floor. Some of the medieval works are extraordinary – don't miss the very modern-looking
14th-century Jihlava Crucifix.

MALÁ STRANA

Eating p118; Drinking p149; Shopping p167; Sleeping p180

Malá Strana (Little Quarter) clusters around the foot of
Prague Castle. Most tourists climb up to the castle along
part of the Královská cesta (Royal Way; p75), on Mostecká
and Nerudova, but the narrow side streets of this baroque
district also have plenty of interest. Almost too picturesque
for its own good, Malá Strana is now much in demand as a
filming location.

Malá Strana started out initially as a market settlement in the 8th or 9th century. In 1257
Přemysl Otakar II granted the area town status. The district was almost destroyed on two

separate occasions: during battles between the Hussites and the Prague Castle garrison in 1419, and then in the Great Fire of 1541. Following this massive devastation renaissance buildings and palaces replaced the destroyed houses, followed by the baroque churches and palaces in the 17th and 18th centuries that give Malá Strana its present charm.

PRAGUE CASTLE TO CHARLES BRIDGE

Following the tourist crowds downhill from the castle via Ke Hradu, you soon arrive at **Nerudova**, architecturally the most important street in Malá Strana; most of its old Renaissance façades were 'baroquefied' in the 18th century. It's named after the Czech poet Jan Neruda (famous for his short stories, *Tales of Malá Strana*), who lived at the **dům U dvou slunců** (House of the Two Suns; Map pp244-5; Nerudova 47) from 1845 to 1857.

The **dům U zlaté podkovy** U zlaté podkovy (House of the Golden Horseshoe; Map pp244-5; Nerudova 34) is named after the relief of sv Václav (St Wenceslas) above the doorway – his horse was said to be shod with gold.

Hradčany's first pharmacy was opened next door in 1749; the building now houses the **Expozice Historických lékáren** (Historical Pharmacy Exhibition; Map pp244-5; adult/child 20/10Kč; ☼ noon-6pm Tue-Fri, 10am-6pm Sat & Sun Apr-Sep, 11am-5pm Tue-Fri, 10am-5pm Sat & Sun Oct-Mar), with a small collection of pharmaceutical paraphernalia and original furnishings dating from the 19th century.

From 1765 Josef of Bretfeld made his **Bretfeld Palace** (Map pp244-5; Nerudova 33) a centre for social gatherings, with guests such as Mozart and Casanova. The baroque **kostel Panny Marie ustavičné pomoci** (Church of Our Lady of Unceasing Succour; Map pp244-5; Nerudova 24) was a theatre (divadlo U Kajetánů) from 1834 to 1837, and staged Czech plays during the Czech National Revival.

Most of the houses bear emblems of some kind (also see the boxed text on p11). Built in 1566, **St John of Nepomuk** (Map pp244-5; Nerudova 18) is named after one of the Czech's patron saints, whose image was added in around 1730. The **dům U tří houslíček** (House of the Three Fiddles; Map pp244-5; Nerudova 12), a Gothic building rebuilt in Renaissance style during the 17th century, once belonged to a family of violin makers.

Malostranské náměstí (Map pp244–5), Malá Strana's main square, is divided into an upper and lower part by **kostel sv Mikuláše** (St Nicholas Church), the district's most distinctive landmark. The square has been the hub of Malá Strana since the 10th century, though it lost some of its character when Karmelitská was widened early in the 20th century. Today, it's a mixture of official buildings and touristy restaurants, with a tram line through the middle of the lower square.

The nightclub and bar at No 21, **Malostranská beseda** (see p160 for more details), was once the old town hall. Here in 1575 non-Catholic nobles wrote the so-called *České konfese* (Czech Confession), a pioneering demand for religious tolerance addressed to the Habsburg emperor and eventually passed into Czech law by Rudolf II in 1609. On 22 May 1618 Czech nobles gathered at the **Smiřický Palace** (Malostranské náměstí 18) to plot a rebellion against the Habsburg rulers – the next day they flung two Habsburg councillors out of a window in Prague Castle (see p58).

KOSTEL SV MIKULÁŠE Map pp244-5
Church of St Nicholas; Malostranská náměstí 38; adult/child 50/25Kč, belfry 40/30Kč; ☼ 8.30am-4.45pm, belfry 10am-6pm; tram 12, 20, 22, 23

Malá Strana is dominated by the huge green cupola of kostel sv Mikuláše (Church of St Nicholas), one of Central Europe's finest baroque buildings. (Don't confuse it with the other kostel sv Mikuláše on Old Town Square.) It was begun by Kristof Dientzenhofer; his son Kilian continued the work and Anselmo Lurago finished the job in 1755. (See the boxed text on p34 for more details.)

On the ceiling, Johann Kracker's 1770 *Apotheosis of St Nicholas* is Europe's largest fresco

Transport

Metro Malostranská metro station is in northern Malá Strana, about five minutes' walk from Malostranské náměstí.
Tram Note that tram Nos 12, 20, 22 and 23 run along Újezd and through Malostranské náměstí.

Districts – Malá Strana

(clever *trompe l'oeil* technique has made the painting merge almost seamlessly with the architecture). In the first chapel on the left is a mural by Karel Škréta, which includes the church official who kept track of the artist as he worked; he is looking out through a window in the upper corner.

Mozart himself tickled the ivories on the 2500-pipe organ in 1787, and was honoured with a requiem mass here (14 December 1791). Take the stairs up to the gallery to see Škréta's gloomy 17th-century Passion Cycle paintings and the scratchings of bored 1820s tourists and wannabe Franz Kafkas.

MALOSTRANSKÁ MOSTECKÁ VĚŽ
Map pp244-5
Malá Strana Bridge Tower; Charles Bridge; adult/child 40/30Kč; 10am-6pm Apr-Oct; **tram 12, 20, 22, 23**
There are actually two towers at the Malá Strana end of Charles Bridge. The lower one was originally part of the long-gone 12th-century Judith Bridge (see the boxed text on p68), while the taller one was built in the mid-15th century in imitation of the one at the Staré Město end (see p72). The taller tower is open to the public and houses an exhibit on the history of Charles Bridge, though like its Staré Město counterpart the main attraction is the view from the top.

NORTHERN MALÁ STRANA
From the northern side of Malostranské náměstí, Thunovská and the **Zámecké schody** (Castle Steps) lead up to the castle. At the eastern end of Thunovská, on Sněmovní, is the **Sněmovna** (Czech Parliament House; Map pp244-5), seat of the lower house of today's parliament, and formerly of the national assembly that deposed the Habsburgs from the Czech throne on 14 November 1918.

PALÁCOVÉ ZAHRADY POD PRAŽSKÝM HRADEM Map pp244-5
Palace Gardens Beneath Prague Castle; 257 010 401; **Valdštejnské náměstí 3; adult/child 95/40Kč;** 10am-6pm; **tram 12, 20, 22, 23**
These terraced gardens on the steep southern slope of the castle hill date from the 17th and 18th centuries, when they were created for the owners of the adjoining palaces. They were restored in the 1990s and contain a Renaissance loggia with frescoes of Pompeii and a baroque portal with sundial that cleverly catches the sunlight reflected from the water in the triton fountain in front of it.

PRAŽSKÝ KABINET ŠPERKU Map pp244-5
Prague Jewellery Collection; 221 451 333; **www.cihelna.info; Cihelná 2b; adult/child 60/50Kč;** 10am-6pm; **tram 12, 20, 22, 23**
This new museum, part of the Hergetova Cihelna complex (p119), provides a showcase for some of the finest items of jewellery in the collection of the Umělecko-průmyslové muzeum (Museum of Decorative Arts; p74). There are exquisite Art Nouveau and Art Deco designs, as well as several pieces by Tiffany and Fabergé.

VALDŠTEJNSKÁ ZAHRADA Map pp244-5
Wallenstein Garden; Letenská 10; admission free; 10am-6pm Apr-Oct; **metro Malostranská**
This huge walled garden lurks behind the Valdštejnský palác. Its finest feature is the huge **loggia** decorated with scenes from the Trojan Wars, flanked to one side by a fake **stalactite grotto** full of hidden animals and grotesque faces. The **bronze statues** of Greek gods found lining the avenue opposite the loggia are copies – the originals were carted away by marauding Swedes in 1648 and now stand outside the royal palace of Drottningholm near Stockholm.

At the eastern end of the garden is the **Valdštejnská jízdárna** (Wallenstein Riding School), home to changing exhibitions of modern art, and a picturesque pond full of giant carp. There are entrances to the garden on Letenská, beside Malostranská metro station and via the Valdštejnský palác.

VALDŠTEJNSKÝ PALÁC Map pp244-5
Wallenstein Palace; 257 071 111; **www.senat.cz; Valdštejnské náměstí 4; admission free;** 10am-5pm Sat & Sun; **tram 12, 20, 22, 23**
Valdštejnské náměstí, the small square situated to the northeast of Malostranské náměstí, is dominated by a monumental palace built in 1630 by Albrecht of Wallenstein, generalissimo of the Habsburg armies. The palace displaced 23 houses, a brickworks and three gardens, and was financed by the confiscation of properties from the Protestant nobles defeated at the Battle of Bílá Hora (White Mountain) in 1620. The palace now houses the Senate of the Czech Republic, but you can visit some of the rooms on Saturday and Sunday. The fresco on the ceiling of the **Baroque Hall** shows Wallenstein glorified as a warrior at the reins of a chariot, while the unusual oval **Audience Hall** is capped with a fresco of Vulcan at work in his forge.

SOUTHERN MALÁ STRANA

Pretty Maltézské náměstí (Maltese Square; Map pp244–5), to the south of Malostranská náměstí, takes its name from the Knights of Malta, who in 1169 established a monastery beside the austere, early-Gothic towers of the kostel Panny Marie pod řetězem (Church of Our Lady Below the Chain; Map pp244–5).

South of the church is Velkopřevorské náměstí and the French embassy, opposite which is the John Lennon Wall. Before 1989, when most Western pop music was banned by the communists – some Czech musicians were jailed for playing it – the wall was a political focus for Prague youth. After his murder on 8 December 1980 John Lennon became a pacifist hero for many young Czechs. An image of Lennon was painted on the wall, along with political graffiti and Beatles lyrics; the secret police never managed to keep it clean for long. Post-1989 weathering and lightweight graffiti ate away at the political messages and images, until little remained of Lennon but his eyes. Since 1998 the wall has been whitewashed several times, but it soon gets recovered in inconsequential tourist graffiti of the 'we woz ere' variety.

An 'island' separated from the mainland by the Čertovka (Devil's Stream), Kampa (Map pp244–5) is the most peaceful and picturesque part of Malá Strana. In the 13th century the town's first mill, the Sovovský mlýn (Map pp250–1), was built on Čertovka, and other mills followed. Kampa was once used as farmland (the name Kampa comes from campus, Latin for 'field'), but the island was settled in the 16th century after being raised above flood level. In 1939 the river was so low that it was again joined to the mainland and many coins and items of jewellery were found in the dry channel. Keep an eye open for the many little metal plaques marking the water level during the August 2002 floods (see p20 for details) – many are well above your head.

The area where the Čertovka passes under Charles Bridge is sometimes called Prague's Venice – the channel is often crowded with dinky little tour boats (see p51). Cafés beckon from Na Kampě Square, south of the bridge, though the summer sun is ferocious here. The southern part of Kampa, beyond the square, is a pleasant wooded park with views across to Staré Město.

Near the southern end of Kampa lies one of Malá Strana's oldest Gothic buildings, the kostel sv Jana Na prádle (Church of St John at the Laundry; Map pp250-1), built in 1142 as a local parish church. Inside are the remains of 14th-century frescoes.

Střelecký ostrov (Marksmen's Island; Map pp250-1), just to the south of Kampa, is crossed by the Legií most (Legion Bridge). The island's name originates in its use in the 16th century as a cannon and rifle target for the Prague garrison. During summer it has an open-air bar and cinema (see Letní bar in the boxed text on p153), and there's a little beach at the northern end.

DĚTSKÝ OSTROV Map pp250-1

Children's Island; access from Nábřežní; admission free; 24hr; metro Anděl

Prague's smallest island offers a leafy respite from the hustle and bustle of the city, with a selection of swings, slides climbing frames and sandpits to keep the kids busy, as well as a rope swing, skateboard ramp, mini football pitch, netball court, and lots of open space for older siblings to run wild. There are plenty of benches to take the strain off weary parental legs, and a decent restaurant at the southern end.

MUZEUM KAMPA Map pp250-1

☎ 257 286 147; www.museumkampa.cz; U sovových mlýnů 2; adult/child 120/60Kč; 10am-6pm; tram 12, 20, 22, 23

Housed in a renovated mill building, this gallery is devoted to contemporary art from Central Europe. The permanent exhibition is based on a private collection featuring the works of František Kupka, a pioneer of abstract art, and cubist sculptor Otto Gutfreund. A 45-minute, private guided tour costs 1000/2000Kč on weekdays/weekends; call ahead to book.

MUZEUM PRAŽSKÉHO JEZULÁTKA
Map pp244-5

Museum of the Infant Jesus of Prague; ☎ 257 533 646; www.karmel.at/prag-jesu; admission by donation; 10am-5.30pm Mon-Sat & 1-5pm Sun, closed 25 Dec & Easter Mon; tram 12, 20, 22, 23

The kostel Panny Marie Vítězné (Church of Our Lady Victorious; Karmelitská), built in 1613, has on its central altar a waxwork figure of the baby Jesus brought from Spain in 1628. Known as the Pražské jezulátko (Infant Jesus of Prague), it is said to have protected Prague from the plague and from the destruction of the Thirty Years' War, and is visited by a steady stream of pilgrims, especially from Italy, Spain and Latin America. An 18th-century German prior, ES

Stephano, wrote about the miracles, kicking off what eventually became a worldwide cult. The Infant's wardrobe consists of 60 costumes donated from all over the world, changed in accordance with a religious calendar.

At the back of the church is the **museum**, displaying a selection of frocks from the Infant's wardrobe. A visit here makes you ponder the Second Commandment ('Thou shalt not make unto thee any graven image…') and the objectives of the Reformation. Jan Hus must be spinning in his grave.

VRTBOVSKÁ ZAHRADA Map pp244-5
Vrtbov Garden; ☎ 257 531 480; www.vrtbovska.cz; Karmelitská 25; adult/child 35/20Kč; ☯ 10am-6pm Apr-Oct

This 'secret garden', hidden along an alley at the corner of Tržiště and Karmelitská, was built in 1720 for the earl of Vrtba, the senior chancellor of Prague Castle. It's a formal baroque garden, climbing steeply up the hillside to a terrace graced with baroque statues of Greek mythological figures by Matthias Braun – see if you can spot Vulcan, Diana and Mars. Below the terrace (on the right, looking down) is a tiny studio once used by Czech painter Mikuláš Aleš, and above is a little lookout with good views of Prague Castle and Malá Strana.

PETŘÍN
This 318m-high hill, called simply Petřín by Czechs, is one of Prague's largest single green spaces. It's great for cool, quiet walks and fine views over the 'city of 100 spires'. There were once vineyards here, and a quarry that provided the stone for most of Prague's Romanesque and Gothic buildings.

Petřín is easily accessible from Hradčany and Strahov, or you can ride the **lanová dráha** (funicular railway; every 10-20min 9.15am-8.45pm) from Újezd up to the top. The funicular uses ordinary public transport tickets – remember to validate your ticket at the bottom station. You can also get off two-thirds of the way up at Restaurant Nebozízek (p119).

In the peaceful **Kinského zahrada** (Kinský Garden), on the southern side of Petřín, is the 18th-century wooden **kostel sv Michala** (Church of St Michael), transferred here, log by log, from the village of Medveďov in Ukraine. Such structures are rare in Bohemia, though still common in Ukraine and northeastern Slovakia.

The 18th-century wooden kostel sv Michala (see left)

BLUDIŠTĚ Map pp250-1
Mirror Maze; adult/child 40/30Kč; ☯ 10am-10pm Apr-Oct, 10am-5pm Sat & Sun Nov-Mar; tram 12, 20, 22, 23

Below the tower is the Bludiště, also built for the 1891 Prague Exposition. Inside is a **mirror maze** that's good for a laugh, as well as a diorama of the 1648 battle between Praguers and Swedes on Charles Bridge. Opposite is the **kostel sv Vavřince** (Church of St Lawrence; Hellichova 18), which contains a ceiling fresco depicting the founding of the church in 991 at a pagan site with a sacred flame.

PETŘÍNSKÁ ROZHLEDNA Map pp250-1
Petřín Tower; adult/child 50/40Kč; ☯ 10am-10pm Apr-Oct, 10am-5pm Sat & Sun Nov-Mar; tram 12, 20, 22, 23

To the north of the observatory is Petřínská rozhledna, a 62m-tall Eiffel Tower lookalike built in 1891 for the Prague Exposition. You can climb its 299 steps for some of the best views of Prague; on clear days you can see the forests of Central Bohemia. On the way to the tower you cross the **Hladová zeď** (Hunger Wall), running from Újezd to Strahov. These fortifications were built in 1362 under Charles IV, and are so named because they were built by the poor of the city in return for food – an early job-creation scheme.

ŠTEFÁNIKOVA HVĚZDÁRNA Map pp250-1

Štefánik Observatory; ☎ 257 320 540; www.observatory .cz; adult/child 30/20Kč; ☷ 6-8pm Tue-Fri, 10am-noon & 2-8pm Sat & Sun Nov-Feb; 7-9pm Tue-Fri, 10am-noon, 2-6pm & 7-9pm Sat & Sun Mar & Oct; 2-7pm & 9-11pm Tue-Fri, 10am-noon, 2-7pm & 9-11pm Sat & Sun Apr-Aug; 2-6pm & 8-10pm Tue-Fri, 10am-noon, 2-6pm & 8-10pm Sat & Sun Sep; tram 12, 20, 22, 23

Just south of the top station is the Štefánikova hvězdárna, a 'people's observatory' where you can view the stars on clear nights, or look at photos and old instruments.

STARÉ MĚSTO

Eating p121; Drinking p150; Shopping p167; Sleeping p182

By the 10th century a settlement and marketplace existed on the Vltava River's eastern bank. In the 12th century this was linked to the castle district by the forerunner of the Charles Bridge (Judith Bridge; see the boxed text on p68 for details), and in 1231 Wenceslas I honoured it with a town charter and the start of a fortification. This 'Old Town' – Staré Město – has since been Prague's working heart. The town walls are long gone, but their line is still traced by the streets Národní třída, Na příkopě and Revoluční.

Staré Město shared in the boom when Charles IV gave Prague a Gothic face befitting its new status as capital of the Holy Roman Empire. Charles founded the Karolinum (Charles University; p78) in Staré Město in 1348, and commissioned Charles Bridge in 1357. When Emperor Joseph II united Prague's towns into a single city in 1784 Staroměstská radnice (Old Town Hall) became its seat of government.

Many of Staré Město's buildings have Gothic interiors and Romanesque basements. To ease the devastation of frequent flooding by the Vltava River, the level of the town was gradually raised, beginning in the 13th century, with new construction simply rising on top of older foundations. A huge fire in 1689 contributed to an orgy of rebuilding during the Catholic Counter-Reformation of the 17th and 18th centuries, giving the formerly Gothic district a heavily baroque face.

The only intrusions into Staré Město's medieval layout have been the appropriation of a huge block in the west for the Jesuits' massive college, the **Klementinum** (p76), in the 16th and 17th centuries, and the 'slum clearance' of Josefov, the Jewish quarter, at the end of the 19th century.

At the centre of everything is **Old Town Square**. If the maze of alleys around the square can be said to have an 'artery' it's the so-called **Královská cesta** (Royal Way), the ancient coronation route to Prague Castle, running from the Prašná brána (Powder Gate) along Celetná to Old Town Square and Malé náměstí, then along Karlova and over Charles Bridge.

Transport

Metro Staroměstská station is a few minutes' walk northwest of Old Town Square, and Můstek station is five minutes' walk to the south.

Tram No trams run close to Old Town Square. Tram Nos 17 and 18 run along the western edge of Staré Město near the river, while Nos 5, 8 and 14 stop at náměstí Republiky across the street from the Obecní dům. Tram Nos 6, 9, 18, 21, 22 and 23 run along Národní třída on the southern edge of Staré Město.

OLD TOWN SQUARE

Old Town Square (Staroměstské náměstí, often called Staromák) is one of Europe's biggest and most beautiful spaces. It's been Prague's principal public space since the 10th century, and was its main marketplace until the beginning of the 20th century.

Despite the over-the-top commercialism and crowds of tourists that swarm the square, it's impossible not to enjoy – the cafés spilling onto the pavement, the omnipresent buskers and performing dogs, and the horse-drawn beer wagons. There are also alfresco concerts, political meetings, and even fashion shows. Its colourful baroque, neo-Renaissance and rococo façades reveal nothing of the often crumbling interiors, and there's hardly a hint of the harrowing history that the square has witnessed (see the boxed text on p72).

Charles Bridge (Karlův most)

Strolling across Charles Bridge is everybody's favourite Prague activity. However, by 9am it's a 500m-long fairground, with an army of tourists squeezing through a gauntlet of hawkers and buskers, beneath the impassive gaze of the imposing baroque statues that line the parapets. If you want to experience the bridge at its most atmospheric it's best appreciated at dawn.

In 1357 Charles IV commissioned Petr Parler (architect of chrám sv Víta) to replace the 12th-century Judith Bridge, which had been washed away by floods in 1342. (You can see the only surviving arch of the Judith Bridge by taking a boat trip with Prague Venice; see p52 for details).

The new bridge was completed around 1400, and only took Charles' name in the 19th century – before that it was known simply as Kamenný most (Stone Bridge). Despite occasional flood damage, it withstood wheeled traffic for 600 years – thanks, legend says, to eggs mixed into the mortar – until it was made pedestrian-only after WWII.

In the crush, don't forget to look at the bridge itself (climb one of the bridge towers; see p64 and p72 for a great view) and the grand vistas up and down the river. Gangs of pickpockets work the bridge day and night, so keep track of your purse or wallet.

Towers & Statues

The bridge's first monument was the crucifix near the eastern end, erected 1657. The first, and most popular statue – the Jesuits' 1683 monument to St John of Nepomuk – inspired other Catholic orders, and over the next 30 years a score more went up, like ecclesiastical billboards. New ones were added in the mid-19th century, and one (plus replacements for some lost to floods) in the 20th century.

As most of the statues were carved from soft sandstone, several weathered originals have been replaced with copies. Some of the originals are housed in the *kasematy* (casemates) at Vyšehrad (p90), while others are in the Lapidárium in Holešovice (p92).

Starting from the western (Malá Strana) end, the statues that line the bridge:

1 SS Cosmas & Damian (1709) Charitable 3rd-century physician brothers.

2 St Wenceslas (sv Václav; 1858)

3 St Vitus (sv Víta; 1714)

4 SS John of Matha & Félix de Valois (1714) Twelfth-century French founders of the Trinitarian order, for the ransom of enslaved Christians (represented by a Tatar standing guard over a group of them), with St Ivo (see No 30).

5 St Philip Benizi (sv Benicius; 1714)

6 St Adalbert (sv Vojtěch; 1709) Prague's first Czech bishop, canonised in the 10th century. Replica.

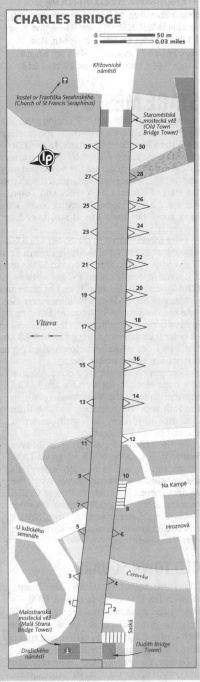

CHARLES BRIDGE

0 —— 50 m
0 —— 0.03 miles

Křižovnické náměstí

kostel sv Františka Serafínského
(Church of St Francis Seraphinus)

Staroměstská mostecká věž
(Old Town Bridge Tower)

Vltava

Na Kampě

Hroznová

U lužického semináře

Čertovka

Saská

Malostranská mostecká věž
(Malá Strana Bridge Tower)

Dražického náměstí

(Judith Bridge Tower)

7 St Cajetan (1709) Italian founder of the Theatine order in the 15th century.

8 The Vision of St Luitgard (1710) Agreed by most to be the finest piece on the bridge, in which Christ appears to the blind saint and allows her to kiss his wounds.

9 St Augustine (1708) Replica.

10 St Nicholas of Tolentino (1706) Replica.

11 St Jude Thaddaeus (1708) Apostle and patron saint of hopeless causes. Further along on the right, beyond the railing, is a column with a statue of the eponymous hero of the 11th-century epic poem, *Song of Roland* (Bruncvík).

12 St Vincent Ferrer (1712) A 14th-century Spanish priest, and St Procopius, Hussite warrior-priest.

13 St Anthony of Padua (1707) The 13th-century Portuguese disciple of St Francis of Assisi.

14 St Francis Seraphicus (1855)

15 St John of Nepomuk (1683) Bronze. Patron saint of Czechs: according to the legend illustrated on the base of the statue, Wenceslas IV had him trussed up in a suit of armour and thrown off the bridge in 1393 for refusing to divulge the queen's confessions (he was her priest), though the real reason had to do with the bitter conflict between church and state; the stars in his halo allegedly followed his corpse down the river. Legend has it that if you rub the bronze plaque, you will one day return to Prague.

16 St Wenceslas as a boy (c 1730) With his grandmother and guardian St Ludmilla, patroness of Bohemia.

17 St Wenceslas with St Sigismund (1853) Son of Charles IV and Holy Roman Emperor and St Norbert, 12th-century German founder of the Premonstratensian order.

18 St Francis Borgia (1710) A 16th-century Spanish priest.

19 St John the Baptist (1857) Further ahead on the right, a bronze cross on the railing marks the place where St John of Nepomuk was thrown off (see No 15).

20 St Christopher (1857) Patron saint of travellers.

21 SS Cyril & Methodius (1938) The newest statue. These two brought Christianity and a written language to the Slavs in the 9th century.

22 St Francis Xavier (1711) A 16th-century Spanish missionary celebrated for his work in the Orient. Replica.

23 St Anne with Madonna & Child (1707)

24 St Joseph (1854)

25 Crucifix (1657) Gilded bronze. With an invocation in Hebrew saying 'holy, holy, holy Lord', funded by the fine of a Jew who had mocked it (in 1696); the stone figures date from 1861.

26 Pietá (1859)

27 Madonna with St Dominic (1709) Spanish founder of the Dominicans in the 12th century, and St Thomas Aquinas. Replica.

28 SS Barbara, Margaret & Elizabeth (1707) St Barbara – 2nd-century patron saint of miners; St Margaret – 3rd- or 4th-century patron saint of expectant mothers; and St Elizabeth – a 13th-century Slovak princess who renounced the good life to serve the poor.

29 Madonna with St Bernard (1709) Founder of the Cistercian order in the 12th century. Replica.

30 St Ivo (1711) An 11th-century bishop of Chartres. Replica.

Ladislav Šaloun's brooding Art Nouveau sculpture of **Jan Hus** dominates the square in the same way that Hus' mythic memory dominates Czech history (see the boxed text on p42). It was unveiled on 6 July 1915, the 500th anniversary of Hus' death at the stake, to patriotic approval but less than unanimous critical acclaim. The steps at its base – once the only place in the square where you could sit down without having to pay for something – have now been protected by a ring of flower beds, but the police seem to have given up on ordering people to keep off, and there's now a beaten path through the flowers.

The brass strip on the ground nearby is the so-called **Prague Meridian**. Until 1915 the square's main ornament was a 17th-century column (see the boxed text on p94), whose shadow used to cross the meridian at high noon.

DŮM U KAMENNÉHO ZVONU

Map pp246-7

House at the Stone Bell; ☎ 224 827 526; Staroměstské náměstí 13; adult/child 90/50Kč; ☯ 10am-6pm Tue-Sun; metro Staroměstská

Next door to the palác Kinských (p72) is the dům U Kamenného Zvonu, its 14th-century Gothic dignity rescued in the 1960s from a second-rate baroque renovation. Inside, two restored Gothic chapels now serve as branches of the Prague City Gallery, with changing exhibits of modern art, and as chamber-concert venues.

DŮM U ZLATÉHO PRSTENU Map pp246-7

House at the Golden Ring; ☎ 224 827 022; Týnská 6; adult/child 60/30Kč; ☯ 10am-6pm Tue-Sun; metro Staroměstská

In the restored Renaissance dům U zlatého prstenu, on the corner of Týnská, just outside the western entrance to Týnský dvůr, is a branch of the Prague City Gallery, with a fine collection of 20th-century Czech art. Note the original painted ceiling beams in some rooms.

KOSTEL PANNY MARIE PŘED TÝNEM

Map pp246-7

Church of Our Lady Before Týn; Staroměstské náměstí; admission free; ☯ services at 4.30pm Mon-Fri, 1pm Sat, 11.30am & 9pm Sun; metro Staroměstská

The distinctive, spiky-topped Týn Church is early Gothic, though it takes some imagination to visualise the original in its entirety because it's partly hidden behind the four-storey Týn School (not a Habsburg plot to obscure this 15th-century Hussite stronghold, but almost contemporaneous with it).

Though Gothic on the outside, the church's interior is smothered in heavy baroque. Two of the most interesting features are the huge rococo **altar** on the northern wall, and the **tomb of Tycho Brahe**, the Danish astronomer who was one of Rudolf II's most illustrious 'consultants' (he died in 1601 of a burst bladder during a royal piss-up – he was too polite to leave the table to relieve himself). On the inside of the southern wall of the church are two small windows – they are now blocked off, but once opened into the church from rooms in the neighbouring house at Celetná 3, where the teenage Franz Kafka once lived (from 1896 to 1907).

As for the exterior of the church, the **north portal** overlooking Týnská ulička is topped by a remarkable 14th-century tympanum showing the Crucifixion, carved by the workshop of Charles IV's favourite architect Petr Parler (this is a copy; the original is in the Lapidárium; see p92).

The Týn Church is an occasional concert venue and has a very grand-sounding pipe organ.

The entrance to the church is along a passage from the square, through the second (from the left) of the Týn School's four arches. It's only open for services and occasional concerts, not ordinary tourist visits, but you can peer at the interior through the glass doors.

The Týn Church's name originates from a courtyard called **Týnský dvůr**, or just Týn, behind the church on Štupartská. Originally a sort of medieval caravanserai for visiting foreign merchants, the attractively renovated courtyard now houses shops, restaurants and hotels.

KOSTEL SV JAKUBA Map pp246-7

St James Church; Malá Štupartská 6; ☯ 9.30am-12.30pm & 2.30-4pm Mon-Sat; metro Staroměstská

The great Gothic mass of kostel sv Jakuba (St James Church), to the east of Týnský dvůr, began in the 14th century as a Minorite monastery church, but was given a baroque face-lift in the early 18th century. Pride of place inside goes to the over-the-top tomb of Count Jan Vratislav of Mitrovice, an 18th-century lord chancellor of Bohemia, in the northern aisle.

In the midst of the gilt and stucco is a grisly memento: on the inside of the western wall (look up to the right as you enter) hangs a shrivelled human arm. The story goes that around 1400 a thief tried to steal the jewels from the statue of the Virgin. Legend claims the Virgin grabbed his wrist in such an iron grip that his arm had to be lopped off. (The truth may not be far behind: the church was a favourite of the guild of butchers, who may have administered their own justice.)

The Astronomical Clock

The Staroměstská radnice (Old Town Hall) tower was given a clock in 1410 by the master clockmaker Mikuláš of Kadaně; this was improved in 1490 by one Master Hanuš, producing the mechanical marvel you see today. Legend has it that Hanuš was afterwards blinded so he could not duplicate the work elsewhere, and in revenge crawled up into the clock and disabled it. (Documents from the time suggest that he carried on as clock master for years, unblinded, although the clock apparently didn't work properly until it was repaired in about 1570.)

Four figures beside the clock represent the deepest civic anxieties of 15th-century Praguers: Vanity (with a mirror), Greed (with his money bag; originally a Jewish moneylender, cosmetically altered after WWII), Death, and Pagan Invasion (represented by a Turk). The four figures below these are the Chronicler, Angel, Astronomer and Philosopher.

On the hour, Death rings a bell and inverts his hourglass, and the 12 Apostles parade past the windows above the clock, nodding to the crowd. On the left side are Paul (with a sword and a book), Thomas (lance), Jude (book), Simon (saw), Bartholomew (book) and Barnabas (parchment); on the right side are Peter (with a key), Matthew (axe), John (snake), Andrew (cross), Philip (cross) and James (mallet). At the end, a cock crows and the hour is rung.

On the upper face, the disk in the middle of the fixed part depicts the world known at the time – with Prague at the centre, of course. The gold sun traces a circle through the blue zone of day, the brown zone of dusk (Crepusculum in Latin) in the west (Occasus), the black disc of night, and dawn (Aurora) the east (Ortus). From this the hours of sunrise and sunset can be read. The curved lines with black Arabic numerals are part of an astrological 'star clock'.

The sun-arm points to the hour (without any daylight-saving time adjustment) on the Roman-numeral ring; the top XII is noon and the bottom XII is midnight. The outer ring, with Gothic numerals, reads traditional 24hr Bohemian time, counted from sunset; the number 24 is always opposite the sunset hour on the fixed (inner) face.

The moon, with its phases shown, also traces a path through the zones of day and night, riding on the offset moving ring. On the ring you can also read which houses of the zodiac the sun and moon are in. The hand with a little star at the end of it indicates sidereal (stellar) time.

The calendar-wheel beneath all this astronomical wizardry, with 12 seasonal scenes celebrating rural Bohemian life, is a duplicate of one painted in 1866 by the Czech Revivalist Josef Mánes. You can have a close look at the beautiful original in the Muzeum hlavního města Prahy (Prague City Museum; p81). Most of the dates around the calendar-wheel are marked with the names of their associated saints; 6 July honours Jan Hus.

It's well worth a visit to enjoy St James' splendid pipe organ and famous acoustics. Recitals – free ones at 10.30am or 11am after Sunday Mass – and occasional concerts are not always advertised by ticket agencies, so check the notice board outside.

KOSTEL SV MIKULÁŠE Map pp246-7
Church of St Nicholas; Staroměstské náměstí; admission free; ☉ noon-4pm Mon, 10am-4pm Tue-Sat, noon-3pm Sun; metro Staroměstská

The baroque wedding cake in the northwestern corner of the square is kostel sv Mikuláše (Church of St Nicholas), built in the 1730s by Kilian Dientzenhofer (not to be confused with at least two other St Nicholas churches in Prague, including the Dientzenhofers' masterwork in Malá Strana). Considerable grandeur has been worked into a very tight space; originally the church was wedged behind Staroměstská radnice's northern wing (destroyed in 1945). Chamber concerts are often held beneath its stucco decorations, a visually splendid (though acoustically mediocre) setting.

Statue of the Angel on the façade of Staroměstská radnice (p72), Stare Město

Historical Milestones in Old Town Square

1338 John of Luxembourg grants Staré Město the right to a town hall, and a private house is purchased for this purpose.

1422 Execution of Jan Želivský, the Hussite preacher who led Prague's first defenestration (see p41 and p89), touching off the Hussite Wars.

1437 Execution of 57 more Hussites.

1458 Election of the Hussite George of Poděbrady as king of Bohemia, in the town hall.

1621 Twenty-seven Protestant nobles beheaded on 21 June after the Battle of Bílá Hora.

1784 The town hall becomes the governmental seat of a newly unified Prague city.

1915 Statue of Jan Hus unveiled on 6 July, the 500th anniversary of his martyrdom.

1918 On 2 November, five days after the declaration of Czechoslovak independence, the 270-year-old Marian Column is toppled.

1945 On 8 May Nazi SS units attempt to demolish the Staroměstská radnice (Old Town Hall) as German troops begin pulling out after three days of fighting against Prague residents; the following day, the Red Army marches in.

1948 On 21 February Klement Gottwald proclaims a communist government from the balcony of palác Kinských (Goltz-Kinský Palace).

1968 On 21 August Warsaw Pact tanks roll across the square as the 'Prague Spring' comes to an end; the Jan Hus statue (Map pp246–7) is draped in black.

PALÁC KINSKÝCH Map pp246-7

Goltz-Kinský Palace; ☎ 224 301 003; Staroměstské náměstí 12; adult/child 100/50Kč; ⏱ 10am-5.30pm; metro Staroměstská

Fronting the late-baroque palác Kinských is probably Prague's finest rococo façade, finished in 1765 by the redoubtable Kilian Dientzenhofer (for more details see the boxed text on p34). Alfred Nobel, the Swedish inventor of dynamite, once stayed here; his crush on pacifist Bertha Kinský may have influenced him to establish the Nobel Peace Prize. Many living Praguers have a darker memory of the place, for it was from its balcony in February 1948 that Klement Gottwald proclaimed communist rule in Czechoslovakia. These days it's a branch of the National Gallery, showing temporary exhibitions.

STAROMĚSTSKÁ MOSTECKÁ VĚŽ

Map pp246-7

Old Town Bridge Tower; Charles Bridge; adult/child 40/30Kč; ⏱ 10am-6pm; metro Staroměstská

Perched at the eastern end of Charles Bridge, the elegant late-14th-century Staroměstská mostecká věž was, like the bridge itself, designed by Petr Parler. Here, at the end of the Thirty Years' War, an invading Swedish army was finally repulsed by a band of students and Jewish ghetto residents. Today, it houses a fairly humdrum collection of vintage musical instruments, but the main attraction is the amazing view from the top.

Looking out from the eastern face of the tower towards Karlova are the figures of SS Adalbert & Procopius, and below them Charles IV, St Vitus and Wenceslas IV. The tower also features a bit of 'Gothic porn': look below these worthies on the left-hand corner of the tower, just above the bridge parapet, and you'll find a stone carving of a man with his hand up the skirt of what appears to be a nun. Naughty.

STAROMĚSTSKÁ RADNICE Map pp246-7

Old Town Hall; ☎ 12 444; Staroměstské náměstí 1; adult/child 40/30Kč, separate tickets for historic halls, Gothic chapel & tower; ⏱ 11am-6pm Mon, 9am-6pm Tue-Sun Apr-Oct, 9am-5pm Tue-Sat, 11am-5pm Sun Nov-Mar; metro Staroměstská

Prague's Old Town Hall, founded in 1338, is a hotch-potch of medieval buildings presided over by a tall Gothic tower, acquired piecemeal over the years by a town council that was short of funds. Most notable is dům U minuty, the arcaded building on the corner covered with Renaissance *sgraffito* – Franz Kafka lived here (1889–96) as a child just before the building was bought for the town hall.

History hangs heavy here. A plaque on the town hall's eastern face lists the 27 Protestant nobles beheaded in 1621 after the Battle of Bílá Hora; white crosses on the ground mark where the deed was done. Another plaque commemorates a critical WWII victory by Red Army and Czechoslovak units at Dukla Pass in Slovakia, and yet another the Czech partisans who died during the Prague Rising on 8 May 1945. If you look at the neogothic eastern gable, you can see that its right-hand edge is broken – the wing that once extended north from here was blown up by the Nazis in 1945, on the day before the Soviet army marched into the city.

This is one of the most crowded corners of Old Town Square, especially during the hourly show put on by the town hall's splendid **Astronomical Clock** (see the boxed text on p71). You can see the interior workings, including parade of Apostles from behind the scenes, by buying a ticket for the Gothic chapel. Apart from the clock, the town hall's best feature is the view from the 60m-tall **tower**, which is certainly worth the climb. There's a lift that allows access for wheelchair users.

JOSEFOV

The slice of Staré Město bounded by Kaprova, Dlouhá and Kozí contains the remains of the once-thriving quarter of Josefov, Prague's former Jewish ghetto, where half-a-dozen old synagogues and the town hall survive along with the powerfully melancholy **Starý židovský hřbitov** (Old Jewish Cemetery). In an act of grotesque irony, the Nazis preserved these places as part of a planned 'museum of an extinct race'. Instead they have survived as a memorial to seven centuries of oppression.

Despite their association with the demise of the Jewish quarter, **Pařížská třída** (Paris Avenue) and the adjacent streets are themselves a kind of museum. When the ghetto was cleared at the turn of the 20th century, this broad Parisian-style boulevard was driven in a straight line through the heart of the old slums. It was a time of general infatuation with the French Art Nouveau–style, and the avenue and its side streets were lined with courtly residential buildings adorned with stained glass and sculptural flourishes. In recent years Pařížská has become a glitzy shopping strand, studded with expensive brand names, such as Dior, Louis Vuitton and Fabergé (see p166).

Náměstí Jana Palacha (Jan Palach Square; Map pp246–7) is named after the young Charles University student who in January 1969 set himself alight in Wenceslas Square in protest against the Soviet invasion (see the boxed text on p86). On the eastern side of the square, beside the entrance to the philosophy faculty building where Palach

was a student, is a bronze memorial plaque with a ghostly death mask.

Presiding over the square is the **Rudolfinum** (Map pp246-7; náměstí Jana Palacha 1, Staré Město; metro Staroměstská), home to the Czech Philharmonic Orchestra. This and the Národní divadlo (p157), both designed by architects Josef Schulz and Josef Zítek, are considered Prague's finest neo-Renaissance buildings. Completed in 1884, the Rudolfinum served between the wars as the seat of the Czechoslovak parliament, and during WWII as the administrative offices of the occupying Nazis (see the boxed text below).

KLÁŠTER SV ANEŽKY Map pp246-7
Convent of St Agnes; ☎ 224 810 628; www.ngprague .cz; U milosrdných 17; adult/child 100/50Kč; ☯ 10am-6pm Tue-Sun; tram 5, 8, 14

In the northeastern corner of Staré Město is the former klášter sv Anežky, Prague's oldest surviving Gothic building, now restored and used by the National Gallery. The 1st-floor rooms hold the National Gallery's permanent collection of medieval art (1200–1550) from Bohemia and Central Europe.

In 1234 the Franciscan Order of the Poor Clares was founded by the Přemysl king

Districts – Staré Město

Mendelssohn is on the Roof

The roof of the Rudolfinum – a complex of concert halls and offices built in the late 19th century – is decorated with statues of famous composers. It housed the German administration during WWII, when the Nazi authorities ordered that the statue of Felix Mendelssohn – who was Jewish – should be removed.

In *Mendelssohn Is on the Roof*, a darkly comic novel about life in wartime Prague, the Jewish writer Jiří Weil weaves a wryly amusing story around this true-life event. The two Czech labourers given the task of removing the statue can't tell which of the two dozen or so figures is Mendelssohn – they all look the same, as far as they can tell. Their Czech boss, remembering his lectures in 'racial science', tells them that Jews have big noses. 'Whichever one has the biggest conk, that's the Jew.'

So the workmen single out the statue with the biggest nose – 'Look! That one over there with the beret. None of the others has a nose like him.' – sling a noose around its neck, and start to haul it away. As their boss walks across to check on their progress, he gapes in horror as they start to topple the figure of the only composer that he does recognise – Richard Wagner.

Wenceslas I, who made his sister Anežka (Agnes) its first abbess. Agnes was beatified in the 19th century, and with timing that could hardly be accidental Pope John Paul II canonised her as St Agnes of Bohemia just weeks before the revolutionary events of November 1989.

In the 16th century the buildings were handed over to the Dominicans, and after Joseph II dissolved the monasteries, they became a squatter's paradise. They've only been restored in the last few decades.

The complex consists mainly of the cloister, a sanctuary and a church in French Gothic style. The graves of St Agnes and of Wenceslas I's Queen Cunegund are in the kaple Panny Marie (Chapel of the Virgin Mary) in the **svatyně sv Salvatora** (Sanctuary of the Holy Saviour). Alongside this is the smaller **kostel sv Františka** (Church of St Francis), where Wenceslas I is buried. Part of its ruined nave and other rooms have been rebuilt as a chilly concert and lecture hall.

The gallery is fully wheelchair accessible, and the ground-floor cloister has a tactile presentation of 12 casts of medieval sculptures with explanatory text in Braille.

UMĚLECKO-PRŮMYSLOVÉ MUZEUM
Map pp246-7
Museum of Decorative Arts; ☎ 251 093 111; www.upm.cz; 17.listopadu 2; permanent collection adult/child 80/40Kč, temporary exhibitions 60/30Kč, combined 120/60Kč; ☼ 10am-6pm Tue-Sun; metro Staroměstská
This neo-Renaissance museum, opened in 1900, arose as part of a European movement to encourage a return to the aesthetic values sacrificed to the Industrial Revolution. Its four halls are a feast for the eyes, full of 16th- to 19th-century artefacts, including furniture, tapestries, porcelain and a fabulous trove of glasswork.

The building itself is a work of art, the façade decorated with reliefs representing the various decorative arts and the Bohemian towns that are famous for them. The **staircase** leading up from the entrance hall to the main exhibition on the 2nd floor is beautifully decorated with colourful ceramics, stained-glass windows and frescoes representing graphic arts, metal-working, ceramics, glass-making and gold-smithing. It leads to the ornate **Votivní sál** (Votive Hall), which houses the **Karlštejn Treasure**, a hoard of 14th-century silver found hidden in the walls of Karlštejn Castle (see p198) in the 19th century.

To the right is a textiles exhibit, but the good stuff is to the left in the **glass and ceramics** hall – exquisite baroque glassware, a fine collection of Meissen porcelain, and a range of Czech glass, ceramics and furniture in Cubist, Art Nouveau and Art Deco styles, the best pieces by Josef Gočár and Pavel Janák. The **graphic arts** section has some fine Art Nouveau posters, and the **gold and jewellery** exhibit contains some real curiosities – amid the Bohemian garnet brooches, 14th-century chalices, diamond-studded monstrances and Art Nouveau silverware you will find a Chinese rhino-horn vase in a silver mount, a delicate nautilus shell engraved with battle scenes, and a silver watch-case in the shape of a skull.

Labels are in Czech but detailed English and French texts are available in each room. What you see is only a fraction of the collection; other bits appear now and then in single-theme exhibitions.

ŽIDOVSKÉ MUZEUM PRAHA
Prague Jewish Museum; ☎ 222 317 191; www.jewishmuseum.cz; full ticket adult/child 500/340Kč; ☼ 9am-6pm Sun-Fri Apr-Oct, 9am-4.30pm Sun-Fri Nov-Mar, closed on Jewish hols
Josefov retains a fascinating variety of Jewish monuments, all of which are now part of the Židovské muzeum Praha (Prague Jewish Museum). The Staronová synagoga (Old-New Synagogue) is still used for religious services; the others have been converted into memorials and exhibition halls holding what is probably the world's biggest collection of sacred Jewish artefacts, many of them saved from demolished Bohemian synagogues.

The various sights are well worth visiting; tickets are sold at the Obřadní Síň (Ceremonial Hall), Pinkasova synagóga (Pinkas Synagogue) and Španělská synagóga (Spanish Synagogue). You also have the option of buying a ticket for the Staronová synagóga only (200/140Kč per adult/child) or for all the sights except the Staronová (300/200Kč).

Completed around 1270, the **Staronová synagóga** (Old-New Synagogue; Map pp246-7; Červená 1) is Europe's oldest working synagogue and one of Prague's earliest Gothic buildings. You step down into it because it predates the raising of Staré Město's street level to guard against floods. Men must cover their heads (a hat or bandanna will do; paper yarmulkes are handed out at the entrance). Around the central chamber are an entry hall, a winter prayer hall and the room from which women watch the men-only services. The interior, with a pulpit surrounded by a 15th-century wrought-iron grill, looks much as it would have 500 years ago. The 17th-century scriptures on the walls were recovered from under a later 'restoration'. On the eastern wall is the Holy Ark that holds the Torah scrolls. In a glass case at the rear, little light bulbs beside the names of the prominent deceased are lit on their death days.

With its steep roof and Gothic gables, this looks like a place with secrets, and at least one version of the golem legend (see the boxed text on p44) ends here. Left alone on the Sabbath, the creature runs amok; Rabbi Löw rushes out in the middle of a service, removes its magic talisman and carries the lifeless body into the synagogue's attic, where some insist it still lies.

Opposite the Staronová synagóga is the elegant 16th-century **Vysoká synagóga** (High Synagogue; Map pp246–7), so called because its prayer hall (closed to the public) is upstairs. On the ground floor is a Jewish Museum shop. Built by Maisel in 1586 and given its rococo façade in the 18th century, the **Židovská radnice** (Jewish Town Hall; Map pp246-7; ☻ closed to the public) has a clock tower with one Hebrew face whose hands, like the Hebrew script, run 'backwards'.

The baroque **Klauzová synagóga** (Klaus Synagogue; Map pp246-7; U Starého hřbitova 1) by the cemetery entrance houses a good exhibit on Jewish ceremonies of birth and death, worship and special holy days. The nearby **Obřadní Síň** (Ceremonial Hall; U Starého hřbitova 3) was built around 1906. Inside is an exhibit on Jewish traditions, similar to that in the Klauzová synagóga.

The handsome **Pinkasova synagóga** (Pinkas Synagogue; Široká 3) was built in 1535 and used for worship until 1941. After WWII it was converted into a powerful memorial, with the names, birth dates, and dates of disappearance of the 77,297 Czech victims of the Nazis inscribed across wall after wall. It also has a collection of paintings and drawings by children held in the Terezín concentration camp during WWII (see p201).

The neogothic **Maiselova synagóga** (Maisel Synagogue; Map pp246-7; Maiselova 10) replaced a Renaissance original built by Maisel and destroyed by fire. It houses another exhibit of synagogue silver, textiles, prints and books.

Named after its striking Moorish interior, the **Španělská synagóga** (Spanish Synagogue; Map pp246-7; Vězeňská 1), dating from 1868, has an exhibit on Jews in the Czech Republic from emancipation to the present day.

Founded in the early 15th century, the **Starý židovský hřbitov** (Old Jewish Cemetery; Map pp246–7) is Europe's oldest surviving Jewish cemetery. It has a palpable atmosphere of mourning even after two centuries of disuse (it was closed in 1787). Some 12,000 crumbling stones (some brought from other, long-gone cemeteries) are heaped together, but beneath them are perhaps 100,000 graves, piled in layers because of the lack of space. Most bear the name of the deceased and his or her father, the date of death (and sometimes of burial), and poetic texts. Elaborate markers from the 17th and 18th centuries have bas-relief and sculpture, some of it indicating the deceased's occupation and lineage. The oldest standing stone (now replaced by a replica), dating from 1439, is that of Avigdor Karo, a chief rabbi and court poet to Wenceslas IV.

The most prominent graves, marked by pairs of marble tablets with a 'roof' between them, are near the main gate. They include those of Mordechai Maisel and Rabbi Löw.

Since the cemetery was closed, burials have taken place at Olšanské hřbitovy (Olšany Cemetery; p96) in Žižkov. There are remnants of another old Jewish burial ground at the foot of the TV tower in Žižkov (see p96).

You enter the cemetery through the Pinkasova synagóga on Široká and exit through a gate between Klauzová synagóga and the Obřadní Síň on U starého hřbitova. Remember that this is one of Prague's most popular sights, so if you're hoping to have a moment of quiet contemplation you'll probably be disappointed (try one of the Žižkov cemeteries for a more solitary experience).

ALONG KRÁLOVSKÁ CESTA

The **Královská cesta** (Royal Way) was the processional route followed by Czech kings on their way to chrám sv Víta for coronation. The route leads from the **Prašná brána** (Powder Gate; Map pp246–7) along Celetná, through Old Town Square and Malé náměstí, along Karlova and across Charles Bridge to Malostranské náměstí, before climbing up Nerudova to the castle.

Pedestrianised **Celetná** between the Powder Gate and Old Town Square is an open-air museum of well groomed, pastel-painted baroque façades over Gothic frames resting on Romanesque foundations, deliberately buried to raise Staré Město above the Vltava River's floods. But the most interesting building dates only from 1912 – Josef

Gočár's delightful Cubist façade (see Muzeum Českého Kubismu; opposite).

Malé náměstí (Little Square; Map pp246–7), the southwestern extension of Old Town Square, has a Renaissance fountain and 16th-century wrought-iron grill. Here several fine baroque and neo-Renaissance exteriors adorn some of Staré Město's oldest structures. The most colourful is the **VJ Rott Building** (1890; Map pp246–7), decorated with wall paintings by Mikuláš Aleš, and now housing four floors of crystal, garnet and jewellery shops (see p171).

A dog-leg from the southwestern corner of the square leads to narrow, cobbled **Karlova** (Charles St; Map pp246–7), which continues as far as Charles Bridge – this section is often choked with tourist crowds. On the corner of Liliová is the house called **U zlatého hada** (At the Golden Snake; Map pp246–7), the site of Prague's first coffee house, opened in 1708 by an Armenian named Deomatus Damajan.

Karlova sidles along the massive southern wall of the Klementinum before opening out at the riverside on Křižovnické náměstí. To the right (north) of the Old Town Bridge Tower is the 17th-century **kostel sv Františka Serafinského** (Church of St Francis Seraphinus; Map pp246–7), its dome decorated with a fresco of the Last Judgment. The church belongs to the Order of Knights of the Cross, the only Bohemian order of Crusaders that is still in existence.

Just south of the bridge, at the site of the former Old Town mill, is **Novotného lávka** (Map pp246–7), a riverside terrace full of sunny, overpriced *vinárny* (wine bars) with great views of the bridge and castle, dominated by a statue of composer Bedřich Smetana.

ČESKÉ MUZEUM VÝTVARNÍCH UMĚNÍ

Map pp246-7

Czech Museum of Fine Arts; ☎ 222 220 218; www.cmvu
.cz; Husova 19-21; adult/child 50/20Kč; ⏱ 10am-6pm
Tue-Sun; metro Staroměstská

Housed in three beautifully restored Romanesque and Gothic buildings, this often-overlooked little gallery stages temporary exhibitions of 20th-century and contemporary art, though it's worth the admission fee just for a look at the architecture.

KLEMENTINUM Map pp246-7

Entrances to courtyards on Křížovnická, Karlova &
Mariánské náměstí; metro Staroměstská

To boost the power of the Roman Catholic Church in Bohemia, the Habsburg emperor Ferdinand I invited the Jesuits to Prague in 1556. They selected one of the city's choicest pieces of real estate and in 1587 set to work on **kostel Nejsvětějšího Spasitele** (Church of the Holy Saviour or St Salvator), Prague's flagship of the Counter-Reformation – the Jesuit's original church. The western façade of the kostel Nejsvětějšího Spasitele faces Charles Bridge, its sooty stone saints glaring down at the traffic jam of trams and tourists on Kižovnické náměstí.

After gradually buying up most of the adjacent neighbourhood, the Jesuits started building their college, the Klementinum, in 1653. By the time of its completion a century later it was the largest building in the city after Prague Castle. When the Jesuits fell out with the pope in 1773, it became part of Charles University.

The Klementinum is a vast complex of beautiful baroque and rococo halls, now occupied by the Czech National Library. Most of it is closed to the public, but you can visit the baroque **Library Hall & Astronomical Tower** (☎ 221 663 111; adult/child 100/30Kč; ⏱ 2-7pm Mon-Fri, 10am-7pm Sat & Sun) on a guided tour. Gates on Křižovnická, Karlova and Seminářská allow free access to the Klementinum's courtyards, which offer a less crowded alternative to Karlova if you're walking to or from Charles Bridge.

Three churches line the southern wall of the Klementinum. The **kostel sv Klimenta** (St Clement Church; ⏱ services 8.30am & 10am Sun), lavishly redecorated in the baroque style from 1711 to 1715 to plans by Kilian Dientzenhofer, is now Greek Catholic. Conservatively dressed visitors are welcome to attend the services.

Karlova takes a bend around the elliptical **Vlašská kaple Nanebevzetí Panny Marie** (Assumption Chapel), built in 1600 for the Italian artisans who worked on the Klementinum (it's still technically the property of the Italian government).

The Klementinum's **Zrcadlová kaple** (Chapel of Mirrors) is a popular concert venue (programme and tickets are available at most ticket agencies (see the boxed text on p149). Dating from the 1720s, the interior is an ornate confection of gilded stucco, marbled columns, fancy frescoes and ceiling mirrors – think of baroque on steroids.

MUZEUM BEDŘICHA SMETANY

Map pp246-7

Smetana Museum; ☎ 222 220 082; adult/child
50/20Kč; ⏱ 10am-noon & 12.30-5pm Wed-Mon;
metro Staroměstská

This small museum is devoted to Bedřich Smetana, Bohemia's favourite composer. It isn't that interesting unless you're a Smetana fan, and only has limited labelling in English. There's a good exhibit on popular culture's feverish response to Smetana's opera *The Bartered Bride* – it seems Smetana was the Britney Spears of his day.

MUZEUM ČESKÉHO KUBISMU

Map pp246-7
Museum of Czech Cubism; ☎ 224 301 003; Ovocný trh 19; adult/child 100/50Kč; ✿ 10am-6pm Tue-Sun; metro Náměstí Republiky

Though dating from 1912, Josef Gočár's **dům U černé Matky Boží** (House of the Black Madonna) – Prague's first and finest example of Cubist architecture – still looks modern and dynamic. It now houses three floors of Czech Cubist paintings and sculpture, as well as furniture, ceramics and glassware in Cubist designs.

MUZEUM LOUTEK Map pp246-7

Museum of Marionettes; ☎ 222 220 928; www .puppetart.com; Karlova 12; adult/child 100/50Kč; ✿ noon-8pm; tram 17, 18

Rooms peopled with a multitude of authentic, colourful marionettes illustrate the evolution of this wonderful Czech tradition from the late-17th to early-19th centuries. The star at-

tractions are the Czech children's favourites, Spejbl and Hurvínek (kids and adults alike can see the Czech equivalent of Punch and Judy at divadlo Spejbla a Hurvínka; p161).

OBECNÍ DŮM Map pp246-7

Municipal House; ☎ 222 002 100; www.obecni-dum .cz; náměstí Republiky 5; guided tours 150Kč; ✿ bldg 7.30am-11pm, information centre 10am-6pm; metro Náměstí Republiky

Prague's most exuberant and sensually beautiful building stands on the site of the Royal Court, seat of Bohemia's kings from 1383 to 1483 (when Vladislav II moved to Prague Castle), and demolished at the end of the 19th century. Between 1906 and 1912 the Obecní dům was built in its place – a lavish joint effort by around 30 of the leading artists of the day, creating a cultural centre that was to be the architectural climax of the Czech National Revival. Restored in the 1990s after decades of neglect during the communist era, the entire building was a labour of love, every detail of the design and decoration carefully considered, every painting and sculpture loaded with symbolism.

The mosaic above the entrance, *Homage to Prague*, is set between sculptures representing the oppression and rebirth of the Czech people; other sculptures ranged along the top of the façade represent history, literature, painting, music and architecture. You pass beneath a

Detail above main entrance of Obecní dům (see above)

wrought-iron and stained-glass canopy into an interior that is Art Nouveau down to the doorknobs (you can look around the lobby and the downstairs bar for free). The restaurant (see Francouzská Restaurace; p121) and the *kavárna* (café) flanking the entrance are like walk-in museums of design.

Upstairs are half a dozen over-the-top halls and assembly rooms which you can visit by guided tour. You can book tours at the building's **information centre**, which is through the main entrance, and around to the left of the stairs.

First stop on the tour is the **Smetana Hall** (p157), Prague's biggest concert hall, with seating for 1200 ranged beneath an Art Nouveau glass dome. The stage is framed by sculptures representing the Vyšehrad legend (to the right) and Slavonic dances (to the left).

Following are several impressive official apartments, but the highlight of the tour is the octagonal **Primatorský sál** (Lord Mayor's Hall), whose windows overlook the main entrance. Every aspect of its decoration was designed by Alfons Mucha (see the boxed text on p22 for more information), who also painted the superbly moody murals that adorn the walls and ceiling. Above you is an allegory of *Slavic Concord*, with intertwined figures representing the various Slavic peoples watched over by the Czech eagle. Figures from Czech history and mythology, representing the civic virtues, occupy the spaces between the eight arches, including Jan Hus as *Spravedlnost* (justice), Jan Žižka as *Bojovnost* (militancy), and the Chodové (medieval Bohemian border guards) as beady-eyed *Ostražitost* (vigilance).

On 28 October 1918 an independent Czechoslovak Republic was declared in the Smetana Hall, and in November 1989 meetings took place in the building between Civic Forum and the Jakeš regime. The Prague Spring (Pražské jaro) music festival always opens on 12 May, the anniversary of Smetana's death, with a procession from Vyšehrad to the Obecní dům, followed by a gala performance of his symphonic cycle *Má Vlast* (My Country) in the Smetana Hall.

PRAŠNÁ BRÁNA Map pp246-7

Powder Gate; Na příkopě; adult/child 40/30Kč;
🕙 **10am-6pm Apr-Oct; metro Náměstí Republiky**

The 65m-tall Prašná brána was begun in 1475 on the site of one of Staré Město's original 13 gates. Built during the reign of King Vladislav II Jagiello as a ceremonial entrance to the city, it was left unfinished after the king moved from the neighbouring Royal Court to Prague

Castle in 1483. The name comes from its use as a gunpowder magazine in the 18th century. Josef Mocker rebuilt, decorated and steepled it between 1875 and 1886, giving it its neo-gothic icing. There are great views from the top, and a tiny exhibit about the tower.

HAVELSKÉ MĚSTO

In about 1230 a market district named Havelské Město (St Gall's Town), named after the 7th-century Irish monk who helped introduce Christianity to Europe, was laid out for the pleasure of the German merchants invited to Prague by Wenceslas I.

Modern-day Rytířská and Havelská were around that time a single plaza, surrounded by arcaded merchants' houses. Specialist markets included those for coal (Uhelný trh; Map pp246-7) at the western end of the plaza and for fruit (Ovocný trh; Map pp246-7) at the eastern end. In the 15th century an island of stalls was built down the middle.

All that remains of St Gall's market today is the touristy **open-air market** (Map pp246-7) on Havelská, and the clothes hawkers in adjacent V kotcích. Though no match for the original, it's still Prague's most central open-air market.

At the eastern end of Havelská is the **kostel sv Havla** (Church of St Gall; Map pp246-7), as old as St Gall's Town itself, where Jan Hus and his predecessors preached religious reform. The Carmelites took possession of it in 1627, and in 1723 added its present shapely baroque façade. The Czech baroque painter Karel Škréta (1610–74) is buried in the church.

At the western end of Havelská is the former Uhelný trh (coal market), and nearby is the plain 12th-century **kostel sv Martina ve zdi** (Church of St Martin in the Wall; Map pp252-3), a parish church enlarged and Gothicised in the 14th century. The name comes from its having had the Old Town wall built right around it. In 1414 the church was the site of the first-ever Hussite communion service *sub utraque specie* (with both bread and wine), from which the name 'Utraquist' derives.

CHARLES UNIVERSITY

Univerzita Karlova; www.cuni.cz
Central Europe's oldest university, founded by Charles IV in 1348 – was originally housed in the so-called **Rotlev House** (Železná 9). With

Protestantism and Czech nationalism on the rise, the reforming preacher Jan Hus became rector in 1402 and soon persuaded Wenceslas IV to slash the voting rights of the university's German students – thousands of them left Bohemia when this was announced.

The facilities of the ever-expanding university were concentrated here in 1611, and by the 18th century the old burgher's house had grown into a sizable complex, known as the **Karolinum**. After the Battle of Bílá Hora it was handed over to the Jesuits, who gave it a baroque makeover. When they were booted out in 1773 the university took it back. Damage in WWII led to remodelling and expansion. Charles University now has faculties all over Prague, and the Karolinum is used only for some medical faculty offices, the University Club and occasional academic ceremonies.

Among pre-university Gothic survivals is the **kaple sv Kosmas a Damian** (Chapel of SS Cosmas & Damian), with its extraordinary oriel protruding from the southern wall. Built around 1370, it was renovated in 1881 by Josef Mocker.

STAVOVSKÉ DIVADLO Map pp246-7

Estates Theatre; ☎ 224 215 001; www.narodni-divadlo .cz; Ovocný trh 1; metro Náměstí Republiky
Beside the Karolinum is Prague's oldest theatre and its finest neoclassical building, the Stavovské divadlo, where the premiere of Mozart's *Don Giovanni* was performed on 29 October 1787, with the maestro himself conducting. Opened in 1783 as the Nostitz Theatre (after its founder, Count Anton von Nostitz-Rieneck), it was patronised by upperclass German citizens. It came to be called the Stavovské divadlo (Estates Theatre) – the Estates being the traditional nobility – and is still commonly known by this name.

After WWII it was renamed the Tylovo divadlo (Tyl Theatre) in honour of the 19th-century Czech playwright Josef Kajetán Tyl. One of his claims to fame is the Czech national anthem, *Kde domov můj?* (Where Is My Home?), which came from one of his plays. In the early 1990s the theatre's name reverted to Stavovské divadlo. Around the corner is the 17th-century **Kolowrat Theatre** (Ovocný trh 6), now also a Národní divadlo venue. Also see p157 for more information on classical-music venues.

SOUTHWESTERN STARÉ MĚSTO

The meandering lanes and passageways between Karlova (Map pp246-7) and Národní třída (Map pp252-3) are Prague's best territory for aimless wandering. When the crowds thin out late in the day, this area can cast such a spell that it's quite a surprise to return to the 21st century outside its borders.

The charm goes a bit cold along **Bartolomějská** (Map pp252-3), however, and not just because it is lined with police offices. Before November 1989, the block was occupied by the StB (Státní bezpečnost, or State Security), the hated secret police. Czechs are still understandably twitchy about police of any shade and it's a common suspicion that a few former StB officers are still around, just wearing new uniforms.

Backing onto Bartolomějská is an old convent and the once-lovely 18th-century **kostel sv Bartoloměje** (St Bartholomew Church; Map pp252-3; ☿ closed to the public), for a time part of the StB complex but now returned to the Franciscans. Although the church is closed to the public, the enterprising Pension Unitas (p185) has rented space from the nuns, and guests can now spend the night in refurbished StB prison cells, including one where former dissident (and now ex-president) Václav Havel spent a night.

BETLÉMSKÁ KAPLE Map pp252-3

Bethlehem Chapel; ☎ 224 2448 595; Betlémské náměstí 3; adult/child 35/20Kč; ☿ 9am-6.30pm Tue-Sun Apr-Oct, to 5.30pm Nov-Mar; tram 6, 9, 18, 21, 22, 23
On Betlémské náměstí is one of Prague's most important churches, the Betlémská kaple, the true birthplace of the Hussite cause. In 1391, Reformist Praguers won permission to build a church where services could be held in Czech instead of Latin, and proceeded to construct the biggest chapel Bohemia had ever seen, able to hold 3000 worshippers. Architecturally it was a radical departure, with a simple square hall focused on the pulpit rather than the altar. Jan Hus preached here from 1402 to 1412, marking the emergence of the Reform movement from the sanctuary of the Karolinum (where he was rector).

In the 18th century the chapel was torn down. Remnants were discovered around 1920, and from 1948 to 1954 – because Hussitism had official blessing as an antecedent of communism – the whole thing was painstakingly reconstructed in its original form, based on old drawings, descriptions, and traces of the original work. It's now a national cultural monument.

Only the southern wall of the chapel is brand new. You can still see some original parts in the eastern wall: the pulpit door, several windows and the door to the preacher's quarters. These quarters, including the rooms used by Hus and others, are apparently original, also; they are now used for exhibits. The wall paintings are modern, and are based on old Hussite tracts. The indoor well predates the chapel.

The chapel has an English text available at the door. Every year on the night of 5 July, the eve of Hus' burning at the stake in 1415, a commemorative celebration is held here, with speeches and bell ringing.

KAPLE SV KŘÍŽE Map pp252-3
Rotunda of the Holy Cross; Konviktská; ☿ services 5pm Sun & Tue, in English 5.30pm on 1st Mon of each month; tram 6, 9, 18, 21, 22, 23
The tiny Romanesque kaple sv Kříže is one of Prague's oldest buildings. It started out as a parish church in about 1100. Saved from demolition and restored in the 1860s by a collective of Czech artists, it still has the remnants of some 600-year-old wall frescoes, though you may have to attend Mass to see them.

KOSTEL SV JILJÍ Map pp246-7
St Giles Church; cnr Zlatá & Husova; tram 6, 9, 18, 21, 22, 23
With stocky Romanesque columns, tall Gothic windows, and an exuberant baroque interior, kostel sv Jiljí is a good place to ponder the architectural development of Prague's religious buildings. The church was founded in 1371. The proto-Hussite reformer Jan Milíč of Kroměříž preached here before the Betlémská kaple was built. The Dominicans gained possession during the Counter-Reformation, built a cloister next door and 'baroquefied' it in the 1730s. Václav Reiner, the Czech painter who created the ceiling frescoes, is buried here.

NÁPRSTKOVO MUZEUM Map pp252-3
Náprstek Museum; ☎ 224 497 500; www.aconet .cz/npm; Betlémské náměstí 1; adult/child 60/30Kč; ☿ 9am-5.30pm Tue-Sun; tram 6, 9, 18, 21, 22, 23
The small Náprstkovo Muzeum houses an ethnographical collection of Asian, African and American cultures, founded by Vojta Náprstek, a 19th-century industrialist with a passion for both anthropology and modern technology (his technology exhibits are now part of the Národní Technické muzeum in Holešovice; p93).

NOVÉ MĚSTO

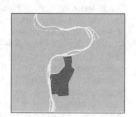

Eating p127; Drinking p152; Shopping p172; Sleeping p185
Nové Město means 'New Town', although this crescent-shaped district east and south of Staré Město was only new when it was founded by Charles IV in 1348.

Most of Nové Město's outer fortifications were demolished and knocked down in 1875 – a section of wall does still survive in the south, facing Vyšehrad – but the original street plan of the area has been essentially preserved, with three large market squares that once provided the district's commercial focus – Senovážné náměstí (Hay Market), Wenceslas Square (Václavské náměstí; originally called Koňský trh, or Horse Market) and Karlovo náměstí (Charles Square; originally called Dobytčí trh, or Cattle Market).

Though originally medieval, most of the surviving buildings in this area are from the 19th and early 20th centuries, many of them among the city's finest. Many blocks are honeycombed with pedestrian-only passages, and are often lined with shops, cafés and theatres.

Nové Město extends eastwards from Revoluční and Na příkopě to Wilsonova and the main railway line, and south from Národní třída to Vyšehrad.

NORTHERN NOVÉ MĚSTO
The northern part of Nové Město stretches from the Vltava River down to Wenceslas Square. The area is mostly rather nondescript, but there are a few gems hidden away among the bland façades.

JINDŘIŠSKÁ VĚŽ Map pp246-7
Jindřišská Tower; ☎ 224 232 429; www.jindrisskavez .cz; Jindřišská 1; adult/child 60/30Kč; ☿ 9am-8pm Mon-Fri, 10am-8pm Sat & Sun; tram 3, 9, 14, 24
This Gothic bell tower, dating from the 15th century but rebuilt in the Gothic style in the 1870s, dominates the northern end of

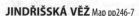

Transport

Metro The city's three metro lines all intersect in Nové Město, at Muzeum and Můstek stations at the eastern and western ends (respectively) of Wenceslas Square. Florenc station on lines B and C is in northern Nové Město, while Karlovo náměstí station on Line B serves southern Nové Město.

Tram Cutting across the middle of Wenceslas Square, tram Nos 3, 9, 14 and 24 run along Vodičkova and Jindřišská. Nos 17 and 21 run along the river embankment in the west.

Jindřišská, a busy street running northeast from Wenceslas Square. Having stood idle for decades, the tower was renovated and re-opened in 2002 as a tourist attraction, complete with shop, café and restaurant. On the 6th floor there is a museum display on the Spires of Prague, and on the 10th you'll find a lookout gallery.

JUBILEJNÍ SYNAGÓGA Map pp246-7
Jubilee Synagogue; Jeruzalémská 7; admission 30Kč; ⏰ 1-5pm Sun-Fri, closed on Jewish hols; metro Hlavní nádraží

The colourful Moorish façade of the Jubilee Synagogue, also called the Velká (Great) synagóga, dates from 1906. Note the names of the donors on the stained-glass windows, and the grand organ above the entrance.

MUCHOVO MUZEUM Map pp252-3
Mucha Museum; ☎ 221 451 333; www.mucha.cz; Panská 7; adult/child 120/60Kč; ⏰ 10am-6pm; metro Můstek

A fascinating (and busy) museum, the Muchovo features the sensuous Art Nouveau posters, paintings and decorative panels of Alfons Mucha (1860–1939), as well as many sketches, photographs and other memorabilia. The exhibits include countless artworks showing Mucha's trademark Slavic maidens with flowing hair and piercing blue eyes, bearing symbolic garlands and linden boughs; photos of the artist's Paris studio, one of which shows a trouserless Gaugin playing the harmonium; a powerful canvas entitled *Old Woman In Winter*; and the original of the 1894 poster of actress Sarah Bernhardt as Giselda which shot him to international fame. The fascinating 30-minute video documentary on his life is well-worth watching, and helps put his achievements in perspective. For more information also see the boxed text on p22.

MUZEUM HLAVNÍHO MĚSTA PRAHY
Map pp258-9

Prague City Museum; ☎ 224 816 772; www.muzeumprahy.cz; Na poříčí 52; adult/child 60/30Kč; 1st Thu of each month 1Kč; ⏰ 9am-6pm Tue-Sun, to 8pm 1st Thu of each month; metro Florenc

This excellent museum, built between 1896 and 1898, is devoted to the history of Prague from prehistoric times to the 20th century. Among the many intriguing exhibits are the brown silk funeral cap and slippers worn by astronomer Tycho Brahe when he was interred in the Týn Church (kostel Panny Marie Před Týnem; p70) in 1601 (they were removed in 1901), and the Astronomical Clock's original 1866 calendar-wheel with Josef Mánes' beautiful painted panels representing the months – that's January at the top, toasting his toes by the fire, and August near the bottom, sickle in hand, harvesting the corn (for more details see the boxed text on p71).

But what everybody comes to see is Antonín Langweil's astonishing 1:480 scale model of Prague as it looked between 1826 and 1834. The display is most rewarding after you get to know Prague a bit, as you can spot the changes – look at chrám sv Víta, for example, still only half-finished.

Most labels are in English as well as Czech, but you'll need the English text (available at the ticket desk) for Room I (prehistory to medieval).

POŠTOVNÍ MUZEUM Map pp246-7
Postal Museum; ☎ 222 312 006; Nové mlýny 2; adult/child 25/10Kč; ⏰ 9am-5pm Tue-Sun; tram 5, 18, 14

Philatelists will love this tiny museum with its letter boxes, mail coach and drawers of old postage stamps, including a rare Penny Black. Look for the beautiful stamps created in the early 20th century by Czech artists Josef Navrátil and Alfons Mucha.

Across the street is the **Petrská vodárenská věž** (Petrská Waterworks Tower), built about 1660 on the site of earlier wooden ones. From here, wooden pipes once carried river water to buildings in Nové Město.

Top Five Nové Město

- **Muchovo muzeum** (Mucha Museum; p81)
- **Muzeum hlavního města Prahy** (Prague City Museum; p81)
- **Národní divadlo** (National Theatre; p85)
- **Palác Lucerna** (p85)
- **Wenceslas Square** (p82)

PRAHA HLAVNÍ NÁDRAŽÍ Map pp252-3

Prague Main Train Station; Wilsonova; ☻ closed 12.40-3.15am; metro Hlavní nádraží

What? The train station is actually a tourist attraction? Perhaps not all of it, but it's worth heading up to Level 4 for a look at the grimy, soot-blackened splendour of the original Art Nouveau building designed by Josef Fanta and built between 1901 and 1909. The domed interior is adorned with two nubile ladies framing a mosaic with the words *Praga: mater urbium* (Prague, Mother of Cities) and the date '28.října r:1918' (28 October 1918 – Czechoslovakia's Independence Day).

A statue at the northern end of the park in front of the station was meant to celebrate the Soviet liberation of Prague at the end of WWII but has always been vaguely insulting, with its submissive Czech soldier embracing his bigger Soviet comrade. Now stripped of its plaque, it looks more like a celebration of gay love in the military.

WENCESLAS SQUARE & AROUND

Originally a medieval horse market, and more of a broad, sloping boulevard than a classical square, Wenceslas Square (Václavské náměstí, also called Václavák) got its present name during the nationalist revival of the mid-19th century; since then it has witnessed a great deal of Czech history. A giant Mass was held in the square during the revolutionary upheavals of 1848, and in 1918 the creation of the new Czechoslovak Republic was celebrated here.

Following the police attack on a student demonstration held on 17 November 1989 (see the boxed text on p86), angry citizens gathered here in their thousands night after night. A week later, in a stunning mirror-image of Klement Gottwald's 1948 proclamation of communist rule in Staroměstské náměstí, Alexander Dubček and Václav Havel stepped onto the balcony of the Melantrich Building to a thunderous and tearful ovation, and proclaimed the end of communism in Czechoslovakia.

At the southern end of the square is Josef Myslbek's muscular equestrian **statue of St Wenceslas** (sv Václav; Map pp252–3), the 10th-century pacifist duke of Bohemia and the 'Good King Wenceslas' of Christmas carol fame – never a king but decidedly good. Flanked by other patron saints of Bohemia – Prokop, Adalbert, Agnes, and Wenceslas' grandmother Ludmila – he has been plastered with posters and bunting at every one of the square's historical moments. Near the statue, a small **memorial to the victims of communism** (Map pp252–3) bears photographs and handwritten epitaphs to

Pedestrian traffic along Wenceslas Square

Tour of Wenceslas Square

Noteworthy buildings surrounding Wenceslas Square (from the northern side of the square, even numbers on the western side):

- **No 25 Grand Hotel Evropa** (1906) The most beautiful building on the square, Art Nouveau inside and out; have a peep at the French restaurant at the rear of the ground floor, and at the 2nd-floor atrium.
- **No 36 Melantrich Building** (1914) Where Havel and Dubček appeared on the balcony in November 1989.
- **No 34 Wiehl House** (1896) With a façade decorated with neo-Renaissance murals by Mikuláš Aleš and others, named after its designer, Antonín Wiehl.
- **No 12 Peterkův dům** (Peterka House; 1901) Art Nouveau building by Jan Kotěra.
- **No 6 Baťa shoe store** (1929) Designed by Ludvík Kysela for Tomáš Baťa, art patron, progressive industrialist and founder of the worldwide shoe empire.
- **No 4 Lindt Building** (1927) Also designed by Ludvík Kysela, and one of the republic's first constructivist buildings.
- **No 1 Koruna Palace** (1914) An Art Nouveau design by Antonín Pfeiffer, with a tower topped with a crown of pearls; note its charming tiny façade around the corner on Na příkopě.

Jan Palach (see the boxed text on p86 for more information) and other anticommunist rebels (see Palác Lucerna on p85 for more details).

In contrast to the solemnity of this shrine, the square beyond it has become a monument to capitalism, a gaudy gallery of cafés, fast-food outlets, expensive shops, greedy cabbies and pricey hotels. See the boxed text above for more information on notable buildings surrounding this square.

KOSTEL PANNY MARIE SNĚŽNÉ

Map pp252-3
Church of Our Lady of the Snows; Jungmannovo náměstí 18; metro Můstek
The most sublime attraction in the neighbourhood is the Gothic kostel Panny Marie Sněžné at the northern end of Wenceslas Square. It was begun in the 14th century by Charles IV but only the chancel was ever completed, which accounts for its proportions – seemingly taller than it is long. Charles had intended it to be the grandest church in Prague; the nave is higher than that of chrám sv Víta, and the altar is the city's tallest. It was a Hussite stronghold, ringing to the sermons of Jan Želivský, who led the 1419 defenestration that touched off the Hussite Wars.

The church is approached through an arch in the Austrian Cultural Institute on Jungmannovo náměstí. Beside the church is the **kaple Panny Marie Pasovské** (Chapel of the Pasov Virgin), now a venue for temporary art exhibitions.

You can rest your feet in the neighbouring **Františkánská zahrada** (Franciscan Garden), a former monastery garden built beside the church and now a peaceful park in the middle of the block (see p103).

MUSEUM OF COMMUNISM Map pp252-3
☎ 224 212 966; www.museumofcommunism.com; Na příkopě 10; adult/child 180/140Kč; ⏰ 9am-9pm; metro Můstek
It would be difficult to think of a more ironic site for a museum of communism – it occupies part of an 18th-century aristocrat's palace, stuck between a casino on one side and a McDonald's burger restaurant on the other. Put together by an American expat and his Czech partner, the museum tells the story of Czechoslovakia's years behind the Iron Curtain in photos, words and a fascinating and varied collection of…well, stuff. The empty shops, corruption, fear and double-speak of life in socialist Czechoslovakia are well conveyed, and there are rare photos of the Stalin monument that once stood on Letná terrace – and its spectacular destruction. Make sure to watch the video about protests leading up to the Velvet Revolution: you'll never think of it as a pushover again.

NA PŘÍKOPĚ
Na příkopě – meaning 'on the moat' – along with Revoluční, 28.října (28 October 1918; named for Czechoslovak Independence Day) and Národní třída, follows the line of the moat that once ran along the foot of Staré Město's city walls (the moat was filled in at the end of the 18th century).

Na příkopě meets Wenceslas Square at **Na můstku** (On the Little Bridge; Map pp252–3). A small stone bridge once crossed the moat here – you can still see a remaining arch in the underground entrance to Můstek metro station, on the left just past the ticket machines.

In the 19th century this fashionable street was the haunt of Prague's German café society.

Designer Buildings

There are several interesting buildings lining Na příkopě (from northeast to southwest):

- **Živnostenská Banka Headquarters** (No 20) With a very grand Art Nouveau interior completed in 1896 by Osvald Polívka, co-architect of the Obecní dům (p77).
- **Myslbek Building** (Nos 19–21) A flashy shopping complex built in 1996, with a bland glass-and-metal front, but a more daring façade overlooking Ovocný trh at the other end.
- **Čedok Main Office** (No 18) Also designed by Polívka (1912) and linked with No 20 by a bridge over Nekázanka ulice.
- **Dům U Černé růže** (House of the Black Rose; No 12) Upstairs, in an ornate and charming neo-Renaissance interior by Josef Fanta (1880), is the Moser crystal shop (see p172).
- **Palác Sylva-Taroucca** (Sylva-Taroucca Palace; No 10) A rococo masterpiece by Kilian Dientzenhofer (1751), and the oldest building on the street.

Today it is (along with Wenceslas Square and Pařížská) the city's main upmarket shopping precinct, lined with banks, shopping malls and tourist cafés.

NÁRODNÍ MUZEUM Map pp252-3

National Museum; ☎ 224 497 111; www.nm.cz; adult/child 100/50Kč, admission free 1st Mon of each month; ☾ 10am-6pm May-Sep, 9am-5pm Oct-Apr, closed 1st Tue of month; metro Muzeum

Looming above Wenceslas Square is the neo-Renaissance bulk of the Národní muzeum designed in the 1880s by Josef Schulz as an architectural symbol of the Czech National Revival.

The museum was founded in 1818 as a natural history collection by a group of Czech aristocrats. However, it was Caspar Sternberg who originally conceived the idea of a national museum and who is credited with most of the work of establishing it. Its first home was at the Šternberský palác in Hradčany, but in 1846 it was moved to a building on Na příkopě where the Živnostenská bank now stands. Today's Národní muzeum building was built from 1885 to 1891 on the site of the former Horse Gate.

The main displays of rocks, fossils and stuffed animals have a rather old-fashioned feel – serried ranks of glass display cabinets arranged on creaking parquet floors – but even if trilobites and taxidermy are not your thing it's still worth a visit just to enjoy the marbled splendour of the interior and the views down Wenceslas Square. The opulent **main staircase** is an extravaganza of polished limestone and serpentine, lined with paintings of Bohemian castles and medallions of kings and emperors. The domed **pantheon**, with four huge lunette paintings of (strangely womanless) Czech legend and history by František Ženíšek and Václav Brožík, houses bronze busts and statues of the great and the good of Czech art and science.

The light-coloured areas on the façade of the museum are patched-up bullet holes. In 1968 Warsaw Pact troops apparently mistook the museum for the former National Assembly or the radio station, and raked it with gunfire. It's also here where you'll find a cross-shaped monument set into the pavement to the left of the fountain in front of the museum that marks the spot where Jan Palach fell (see the boxed text on p86 for details).

Across the road to the northeast is the former Federal Assembly building, built in 1973 on the site of the former Stock Exchange (1936–38; parts of its walls can be seen inside). It's now the headquarters of **Radio Free Europe**; since 11 September 2001 it has been guarded by the military because of the threat of terrorist attack.

NÁRODNÍ TŘÍDA

Národní třída (National Avenue) is central Prague's 'high street', a stately row of mid-range shops and grand public buildings, notably the Národní divadlo at the Vltava River end.

Fronting Jungmannovo náměstí, at the eastern end, is an imitation Venetian palace known as the **Adria Palace**. Its distinctive, chunky architectural style, dating from the 1920s, is known as 'rondocubism'. Note how the alternating angular and rounded window pediments echo similar features in neoclassical baroque buildings, such as Černíský palác (p61).

Beneath it is the **Adria Theatre**, birthplace of Laterna Magika and meeting place of Civic Forum in the heady days of the Velvet Revolution. From here, Dubček and Havel walked to the Lucerna Passage and their 24 November 1989 appearance on the balcony of the Melantrich Building. Wander through the arcade for a look at the lovely marble, glass and brass decoration; the main atrium has a 1920s 24hr clock flanked by sculptures depicting the signs of the zodiac, once the entrance to the offices of the Adriatica insurance company (hence the building's name).

Along the street, inside the arcade near No 16, is a **bronze plaque** on the wall with a cluster of hands making the peace sign and the date '17.11.89', in memory of the students clubbed in the street by police on that date (see the boxed text on p86).

West of Voršilská, the lemon-yellow walls of the **klášter sv Voršila** (Convent of St Ursula) frame a pink church, which has a lush baroque interior that includes a battalion of Apostle statues. Out front is the figure of St John of Nepomuk, and in the façade's lower right niche is a statue of St Agatha holding her severed breasts – one of the more gruesome images in Catholic hagiography.

Across the road at No 7 is the fine Art Nouveau façade (by Osvald Polívka) of the **Viola Building**, former home of the Prague Insurance Co, with the huge letters 'PRAHA' entwined around five circular windows, and mosaics spelling out *život, kapitál, důchod, věno* and *pojišťuje* (life, capital, income, dowry and insurance). The building next door, a former publishing house, is also a Polívka design.

On the southern side at No 4, looking like it has been bubble-wrapped by environmental artist Christo, is the **Nová Scéna** (1983), the 'New National Theatre' building, now home of Laterna Magika (see p161 for details).

Finally, facing the Vltava River near Smetanovo nábřeží, is the **Národní divadlo**, the neo-Renaissance flagship of the Czech National Revival and one of Prague's most impressive buildings. Funded entirely by private donations and decorated inside and out by a roll call of prominent Czech artists, architect Josef Zítek's masterpiece burned down within weeks of its 1881 opening but, incredibly, was funded again and restored under Josef Schulz in less than two years. It's now mainly used for ballet and opera performances (see p157).

Across from the theatre is the **Kavárna Slavia** (see p128), known for its Art Deco interior and river views, once *the* place to be seen or to grab an after-theatre meal. Now renovated, it's once again the place to be seen – though mainly by other tourists.

PALÁC LUCERNA Map pp252-3
Lucerna Palace; Vodičkova 36; tram 3, 9, 14, 24
The most elegant of Nové Město's many passages runs beneath the Art Nouveau Lucerna Palace (1920) between Štěpánská and Vodičkova. This shopping arcade was designed by Václav Havel (grandfather of the ex-president), and is still partially owned by the family. The Lucerna complex includes theatres, a cinema, shops, a rock club-cum-restaurant, and several cafés and restaurants. In the marbled

David Černý's Statue of St Wenceslas (see below)

atrium hangs artist David Černý's wryly amusing counterpart to the equestrian statue of St Wenceslas in Wenceslas Square. Here St Wenceslas sits astride a horse that is decidedly dead; Cerny never comments on the meaning or symbolism of his works, but it's safe to assume that this Wenceslas (Václav in Czech) is a reference to Václav Klaus, former prime minister and now president of the Czech Republic.

The neighbouring **Novák Arcade**, connected to the Lucerna and riddled by a maze of passages, has one of Prague's finest Art Nouveau façades (overlooking Vodičkova), complete with mosaics of country life.

PEČKŮV PALÁC Map pp252-3
Peček Palace; Politických vězňů 20; closed to the public; metro Muzeum
This gloomy neo-Renaissance palace served as the wartime headquarters of the Gestapo. A memorial on the corner of the building honours the many Czechs who were tortured and executed in the basement detention cells. Today, it is home to the Ministry of Trade and Industry.

ALONG THE RIVER
The Nové Město riverfront, stretching south from the Národní divadlo to Vyšehrad, is lined with some of Prague's grandest 19th- and early-20th-century architecture – a great place for an evening stroll (see p112).

Student Sacrifices

Throughout Czech history – from the time of Jan Hus to the Velvet Revolution – Prague's university students have not been afraid to stand up for what they believe; many of them sacrificed their lives for their beliefs. Two student names that have gone down in 20th-century history are Jan Opletal and Jan Palach.

On 28 October 1939 – the 21st anniversary of the declaration of Czechoslovak independence – Jan Opletal, a medical student, was shot and fatally injured by police attempting to break up an anti-Nazi demonstration. After his funeral on 15 November Prague students again took to the streets, defacing German street signs, chanting anti-German slogans and taunting the police. The Nazi retaliation was swift and savage.

In the early hours of 17 November – a day now known in Czech as *den boje studentů za svobodu a demokracii* (the day of the students' fight for freedom and democracy) – the Nazi authorities raided Prague's university dormitories and arrested around 1200 students before carting them off to various concentration camps. Some were executed and many others died in the camps. Prague's universities were closed down for the duration of WWII.

The street in northwestern Staré Město called 17.listopadu (17 November; Map pp246–7) was named in honour of the students who suffered death and deportation on 17 November 1939. Exactly 50 years later students marching along Národní třída in memory of that day were attacked and clubbed by police. The national outrage triggered by this event pushed the communist government towards its final collapse a few days later. There's a memorial plaque inside the arcade at Národní třída 16 (see p84).

Thirty years after Opletal's death, on 16 January 1969, university student Jan Palach set himself on fire on the steps of the Národní muzeum (National Museum; p84) in protest at the Warsaw Pact invasion of Prague. He staggered down the steps in flames and collapsed on the pavement at the foot of the stairs. The following day around 200,000 people gathered in the square in his honour.

It took three agonising days before Jan died, and his body was buried in Olšanské hřbitovy in Žižkov (see p96). But his grave became a focus for demonstrations and in 1974 his remains were moved to his home village. By popular demand he was re-interred in Olšanské hřbitovy in 1990. A cross-shaped monument set into the pavement to the left of the fountain in front of the Národní muzeum marks the spot where he fell.

But Palach was not the only person to make such an extreme gesture. Several other Czechs burnt themselves to death that year, including another student, 18-year-old Jan Zájic. Fearing that things were returning to normal after Palach's death, and choosing the symbolic date of 25 February 1969 – the 21st anniversary of Victorious February, the communist coup – he set himself alight in a passage at No 39 Wenceslas Square, and died on the spot.

Masarykovo nábřeží (Masaryk Embankment) sports a series of stunning Art Nouveau buildings. At No 32 is the duck-egg green **Goethe Institut** (the German Cultural Institute; Map pp252–3), once the East German embassy, while **No 26** is a beautiful apartment building with owls perched in the decorative foliage that twines around the door, dogs peeking from the balconies on the 5th floor, and birds perched atop the balustrade.

No 16 is the **House of the Hlahol Choir**, built in 1906 by Josef Fanta for a patriotic choral society associated with the Czech National Revival. It's decorated with elaborate musical motifs topped by a giant mosaic depicting *Music* – the motto beneath translates as 'let the song reach the heart; let the heart reach the homeland'.

At the next bridge is **Jiráskovo náměstí** (Jirásek Square), dedicated to writer Alois Jirásek (1851–1930), author of *Old Czech Legends* (studied by all Czech schoolchildren) and an influential figure in the drive towards Czechoslovak independence. His statue is overlooked by the famous **Tančící dům** (Dancing Building; Map pp252–3).

A little further along the riverbank is **Rašínovo nábřeží 78**, an apartment building designed by the grandfather of ex-president Václav Havel – this was where Havel first chose to live (in preference to Prague Castle) after being elected as president in December 1989, surely the world's least pompous presidential residence. He later moved to a house on the outskirts of Prague 6.

Two blocks south, sitting on Palackého náměstí, is Stanislav Sucharda's extraordinary Art Nouveau **František Palacký Memorial** (Map pp252–3) – a swarm of haunted bronze figures (allegories of the writer's imagination) swirling around a stodgy statue of the 19th-century historian and giant of the Czech National Revival.

GALERIE MÁNES Map pp252-3

Mánes Gallery; ☎ 224 930 754; Masarykovo nábřeží 1; adult/child 40/20Kč; ☯ 10am-6pm Tue-Sun; tram 17, 21

Beneath the tower is the Mánes Building (1927–30), which houses an art gallery founded in the 1920s by a group of artists headed by painter Josef Mánes, as an alternative to the Czech Academy of Arts. It still has one of Prague's better displays of contemporary art, with changing exhibits. The building itself, designed by Oskar Novotný, is considered a masterpiece of Functionalist architecture.

SLOVANSKÝ OSTROV Map pp252-3
Slav Island; Masarykovo nábřeží; tram 17, 21
This island is a sleepy, dog-eared sandbank with pleasant gardens, river views and several boat-hire places. Its banks were reinforced with stone in 1784, and a spa and a dye works were built in the early part of the following century. Bohemia's first train had a demonstration run here in 1841, roaring down the island at 11km/h. In 1925 the island was named after the Slav conventions that had taken place here since 1848. In the middle is a 19th-century meeting hall and a restaurant. At the southern end is **Šítovská věž**, a 15th-century water tower (once part of a mill) with an 18th-century onion-dome roof, and the **Galerie Mánes** (above).

TANČÍCÍ DŮM Map pp252-3
Dancing Bldg; Rašínovo nábřeží 80; tram 17, 21
The junction where Resslova meets the river at Rašínovo nábřeží is dominated by the famous Dancing Building, built in 1996 by architects Vlado Milunič and the American Frank O Gehry. The curved lines of the narrow-waisted glass tower clutched against its more upright and formal partner led to it being christened the 'Fred & Ginger Building', after the legendary dancing duo of Fred Astaire and Ginger Rogers. It's surprising how well it fits in with its ageing neighbours.

KARLOVO NÁMĚSTÍ & AROUND

At over seven hectares, Karlovo náměstí (Charles Square; Map pp252–3) is the city's biggest square; it's more like a small park, really. Presiding over it is **kostel sv Ignáce** (St Ignatius Church), a 1660s baroque *tour de force* designed by Carlo Lurago for the Jesuits.

The baroque palace at the southern end of the square belongs to Charles University. It's known as **Faustův dům** (Faust House) because, according to a popular story, Mephisto took Dr Faust to hell through a hole in the ceiling here, and because of associations with

Rudolf II's English court alchemist, Edward Kelley, who toiled here in the 16th century trying to convert lead to gold.

Resslova runs west from Karlovo náměstí to the river. Halfway along is the baroque **kostel sv Cyril a Metoděj** (Church of SS Cyril & Methodius), a 1730s work by Kilian Dientzenhofer (for more details on this designer see the boxed text on p34) and Paul Bayer. The crypt now houses the moving **Národní památník obětí heydrichiády** (p88).

On the other side of Resslova there is the 14th-century Gothic **kostel sv Václava na Zderaze** (Church of St Wenceslas in Zderaz), the former parish church of Zderaz, a village that predates Nové Město. On its western side are parts of a wall and windows from its 12th-century Romanesque predecessor.

The area which is to the east of Karlovo náměstí is occupied by Charles University's medical faculty, and is full of hospitals and clinics.

Halfway between Žitná and Ječná is the 14th-century **kostel sv Štěpána** (St Stephen Church), with a 15th-century tower, 17th- and 18th-century chapels, and an 1870s neogothic face-lift by Josef Mocker. Behind it on Na Rybníčku II is one of Prague's three surviving Romanesque rotundas, the **rotunda sv Longina** (Rotunda of St Longinus; closed to the public), built in the early 12th century.

BOTANICKÁ ZAHRADA UNIVERZITY KARLOVY Map pp260-1
Charles University Botanical Garden; ☎ 221 953 142; **Viničná 7; admission free;** 9am-6pm; tram 18, 24
Just south of Karlovo náměstí (entrances on Viničná and Vyšehradská) is Charles University's botanical garden. Founded in 1775 and moved from Smíchov to its present site in 1898, it's the country's oldest botanical garden. The steep, hillside garden concentrates on Central European flora and is especially pretty in spring.

KLÁŠTER EMAUZY Map pp260-1
Emmaus Monastery; Vyšehradská 49; 8am-6pm **Mon-Fri, services noon Mon-Fri, 10am Sun; tram 18, 24**
Founded for a Slavonic Benedictine order at the request of Charles IV, and originally called Na Slovanech, klášter Emauzy dates from 1372. Charles persuaded the pope to allow the Old Church Slavonic liturgy here, possibly in the hope of undermining the Orthodox Church in

Façade of klášter Emauzy (see p87), Nové Město

neighbouring Slavonic states. These un-Roman Catholic beginnings probably saved it from later Hussite plundering. Spanish Benedictines renamed it Emmaus.

During WWII the monastery was seized by the Gestapo and the monks were sent to Dachau concentration camp, and in February 1945 it was almost destroyed by a stray Allied fire-bomb. Some monks returned after the war, but the reprieve was short-lived: in 1950 the communists closed down the monastery, and tortured the prior to death. It was finally restored to the Benedictine order in 1990 and reconstruction has been going on ever since.

The monastery's Gothic **kostel Panny Marie** (St Mary Church), badly damaged by the 1945 bombing, re-opened in 2003, though the swooping, twin spires were added back in the 1960s. The atmospheric Gothic cloisters have some fine, but faded, original frescoes dating from the 14th century, salted with bits of pagan symbolism.

Across Vyšehradská is the baroque **kostel sv Jana Nepomuckého na Skalce** (Church of St John of Nepomuk on the Rock), built in 1739, one of the city's most beautiful Dientzenhofer churches.

KOSTEL NANEBEVZETÍ PANNY MARIE A KARLA VELIKÉHO Map pp260-1
Church of the Assumption of the Virgin Mary & Charlemagne; Ke Karlovu; metro IP Pavlova
At the southern end of Ke Karlovu is a little church with a big name, founded by Charles IV in 1350 and modelled on Charlemagne's burial chapel in Aachen. In the 16th century it acquired its fabulous ribbed vault, whose revolutionary unsupported span was attributed by some to witchcraft.

From the terrace beyond the church you can see some of Nové Město's original fortifications, and look out towards ancient Vyšehrad and the modern **Nuselský most** (Nusle Bridge), which vaults the valley of the Botič creek, with six lanes of traffic on top and the metro inside.

MUZEUM ANTONÍNA DVOŘÁKA
Map pp252-3
Dvořák Museum; ☎ 224 918 013; Ke Karlovu 20; adult/child 40/20Kč; ☽ 10am-1.30pm & 2-5pm Tue-Sun Apr-Sep, from 9.30am Oct-Mar; metro IP Pavlova
The most striking building in the drab neighbourhood south of Ječná is the Vila Amerika, a 1720s, French-style summerhouse designed by (you guessed it) Kilian Dientzenhofer. It's one of the city's finest baroque buildings, and now houses a museum dedicated to the composer Antonín Dvořák. Special concerts of Dvořák's music are staged here (see p159).

NÁRODNÍ PAMÁTNÍK OBĚTÍ HEYDRICHIÁDY Map pp252-3
National Memorial to the Victims of Post-Heydrich Terror; ☎ 224 920 686; Resslova 9; adult/child 50/20Kč; ☽ 10am-5pm Tue-Sun May-Sep, to 4pm Oct-Apr; metro Karlovo Náměstí
In 1942 seven Czech paratroopers that were involved in the assassination of Reichsprotektor Reinhardt Heydrich (see p46 for the details of the assassination) hid in the crypt of the kostel

sv Cyril a Metoděj for three weeks after the killing, until their hiding place was betrayed by the Czech traitor Karel Čurda. The Germans besieged the church, first attempting to smoke the paratroopers out and then flooding the church with fire hoses. Three paratroopers were killed in the ensuing fight; the other four took their own lives rather than surrender to the Germans. The crypt now houses a moving memorial to the men, with an exhibit and video about Nazi persecution of the Czechs. In the crypt itself you can still see the bullet marks and shrapnel scars on the walls, and signs of the paratroopers' last desperate efforts to dig an escape tunnel to the sewer under the street. On the Resslova side of the church the narrow gap in the wall of the crypt is still pitted with bullet marks.

NOVOMĚSTSKÁ RADNICE Map pp252-3
New Town Hall; Karlovo náměstí 23; admission 30Kč;
10am-6pm Tue-Sun Apr-Sep; metro Karlovo Náměstí
The historical focus of Karlovo náměstí is the New Town Hall, which was built when the New Town was still new. From this hall's windows

two of Wenceslas IV's Catholic councillors were flung to their deaths in 1419 by followers of the Hussite preacher Jan Želivský, giving 'defenestration' (throwing out of a window) a lasting political meaning, and sparking off the Hussite Wars. (This tactic was repeated at Prague Castle in 1618.) The 23m-tall **tower** was added to the building 35 years later. You can climb the 221 steps to the top, and visit the Gothic Hall of Justice, which is the site of the defenestration.

U KALICHA Map pp252-3
At the Chalice; ☎ 224 912 557; www.ukalicha.cz;
Na bojišti 12; 11am-11pm; metro IP Pavlova
A few blocks east of Karlovo náměstí is the pub U kalicha. This is where the eponymous antihero was arrested at the beginning of Jaroslav Hašek's comic novel of WWI, *The Good Soldier Švejk* (which Hašek cranked out in instalments from his own local pub). The pub is milking the connection for all it's worth. It's an essential port of call for Švejk fans, but the rest of us can find cheaper beer and dumplings elsewhere.

OUTER SUBURBS
Eating p130; Drinking p153; Shopping p175; Sleeping p188
Clustered around the city's historic core are the ancient citadel of Vyšehrad and the suburbs of Holešovice, Bubeneč, Libeň, Žižkov, Karlín, Vinohrady, Smíchov and Dejvice. Also gathered together here are the various attractions that lie scattered around the more outer fringes of the city; these work clockwise with Troja in the north, followed by Kobylisy, Kbely, Zbraslav, Barrandov, Střešovice and Břevnov.

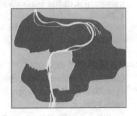

VYŠEHRAD
Vyšehrad (High Castle) is regarded as Prague's mythical birthplace. According to legend the wise chieftain Krok built a castle here in the 7th century. Libuše, the cleverest of his three daughters, prophesised that a great city would rise here. Taking as her king a ploughman named Přemysl, she founded the city of Prague and the Přemysl dynasty.

Archaeologists know that various early Slavonic tribes set up camp at Vyšehrad, a crag above the Vltava River south of the Nusle Valley. Vyšehrad may in fact have been permanently settled as early as the 9th century, and Boleslav II (r 972–99) may have lived here for a time. There was

a fortified town by the mid-11th century. Vratislav II (r 1061–92) moved his court here from Hradčany, beefing up the walls and adding a castle, the bazilika sv Vavřince (St Lawrence Basilica), kostel sv Petra a Pavla (Church of SS Peter & Paul) and the Rotunda sv Martina (Rotunda of St Martin). His successors stayed until 1140, when Vladislav II returned to Hradčany.

Vyšehrad then faded until Charles IV, aware of its symbolic importance, repaired the walls and joined them to those of his new town, Nové Město. He built a small palace, and decreed that the coronations of Bohemian kings should begin with a procession from here to Hradčany.

Nearly everything on the hilltop was wiped out during the Hussite Wars. The hill remained a ruin – except for a township of artisans and traders – until after the Thirty Years' War, when Leopold I refortified it.

The Czech National Revival generated new interest in Vyšehrad as a symbol of Czech history. Painters painted it, poets sang about the old days, Smetana set his opera *Libuše* here. Many fortifications were dismantled in 1866 and the parish graveyard was converted into a national memorial cemetery.

Vyšehrad retains a place in Czech hearts and is a popular destination for weekend family outings. Since the 1920s the old fortress has been a quiet park, with splendid panoramas of the Vltava Valley. Take along a picnic and find a quiet spot among the trees, or on the battlements with a view over the river.

KASEMATY Map pp260-1
Casemates; Vratislavova; adult/child 30/20Kč; 9.30am-6pm Apr-Oct, to 5pm Nov-Mar; metro Vyšehrad

At the 19th-century **Cihelná brána** (Brick Gate) on the northern side of the fortress is the entrance to the vaulted casemates beneath the ramparts. The chambers now house a museum exhibit explaining the history of Prague's fortifications.

Also buried deep in the ramparts, and entered via the Cihelná brána, is the barrel-vaulted **Gorlice Hall** (admission 10Kč), which served as an air-raid shelter and potato store during WWII. It now houses six of the original baroque statues from Charles Bridge, including *St Ludmila with the Young St Wenceslas* by Matthias Braun (the other originals are in the Lapidárium; see p92), as well as temporary art exhibitions in summer.

KOSTEL SV PETRA A PAVLA Map pp260-1
Church of SS Peter & Paul; ☎ 249 113 353; K rotundě 10; admission 20Kč; 9am-noon & 1-5pm Wed-Mon; metro Vyšehrad

Vratislav II's kostel sv Petra a Pavla has been built and rebuilt over the centuries, culminating in a neogothic work-over by Josef Mocker in the 1880s. The twin steeples, a distinctive feature of the Vyšehrad skyline, were added in 1903. The interior is a swirling acid-trip of colourful Art Nouveau frescoes, painted in the 1920s by various Czech artists.

ROTUNDA SV MARTINA Map pp260-1
St Martin's Rotunda; V Pevnosti; closed to the public; metro Vyšehrad

Vratislav II's little chapel, the rotunda sv Martina, built in the 11th century, is Prague's oldest surviving building. In the 18th century it was used as a powder magazine. The door and frescoes date from a renovation made about 1880.

Nearby are a 1714 plague column and the baroque **kaple Panny Marie v hradbách** (St Mary Chapel in the Ramparts), dating from about 1750, and behind them the remains of the 14th-century **kostelík Stětí sv Jana Křtitele** (Church of the Beheading of St John the Baptist).

VĚZNICE PANKRÁC Map pp242-3
Pankrác Prison; Táborská 988; closed to the public; metro Pankrác

During WWII, the Nazis used Prague's notorious Věznice Pankrác as a place of incarceration, interrogation, torture and execution. A guillotine installed in 1943 had claimed the lives of 1075 people by the end of the war. The grim and overcrowded prison, southeast of Vyšehrad, remains in use today as a state prison.

VYŠEHRAD CITADEL Map pp260-1
☎ 241 410 348; www.praha-vysegrad.cz; V Pevnosti 5; admission free; grounds 24hr, information office 9.30am-6.30pm; metro Vyšehrad

The main entrance to the citadel is through the **Táborská brána** (Tábor Gate) at the southeastern end. On the other side of the brick ramparts and ditch are the scant remnants of the Gothic **Špička brána** (Peak Gate) – a fragment of arch that is now part of the information office – all that remains of Charles IV's 14th-century fortifications. Beyond that lies the grand, 17th-century **Leopoldova brána** (Leopold Gate), the most elegant of the fortress' gates. In the course of re-fortification after the Thirty Years' War Táborská brána and Leopoldova brána were erected, and the Špička brána pulled down.

It's possible to walk most of the perimeter battlements, where there are grand views over the river and city. Beside the southwestern

Cubist Architecture

If you've taken the trouble to come out to Vyšehrad, don't miss the chance to see some of Prague's finest Cubist buildings. Cubist architecture, with its eye-catching use of elementary geometric forms, is more or less unique to the Czech Republic, and particularly to Prague.

Neklanova, northeast of the Vyšehrad citadel, is a dingy street of sooty, pastel-hued neoclassical façades lifted out of the ordinary by the striking planes and angles of the apartment block at **Neklanova 30**, designed by the dean of Czech Cubist architects, Josef Chochol. Other buildings by Chochol are the **Villa Libušina** at the corner of Vnislavova and Rašínovo nábřeží, and an elegant terrace of three houses at **Rašínovo nábřeží 6–10**, just before it tunnels beneath Vyšehrad rock. All date from around 1912 to 1913. Other Cubist works by lesser lights are scattered around the neighbourhood.

For more information on this architectural style see p36.

bastion are the foundations of a small **royal palace** built by Charles IV, but dismantled in 1655. Perched on the bastion itself is the **galérie Vyšehrad** (Vyšehrad Gallery; admission 10Kč; 9.30am-5.30pm Tue-Sun), which holds temporary exhibitions. Below the bastion are some ruined guard towers poetically named **Libuše's Bath**.

South of the kostel sv Petra a Pavla lie the **Vyšehradské sady** (Vyšehrad Gardens), with four imposing statues by Josef Myslbek based on Czech legends. Prague's progenitors Libuše and Přemysl are in the northwestern corner; in the southeast are Šárka and Ctirad (see the boxed text below right). On Sundays in May, June and August, open-air concerts are held here at 2.30pm, with anything from jazz to oompah to chamber music.

You can also examine the foundations of the 11th-century Romanesque **bazilika sv Vavřince** (St Lawrence Basilica; admission 10Kč; 11am-6pm). Ask for the key at the snack bar next door.

In the northwestern corner is the former **Nové proboštství** (New Provost's House), built in 1874. In the adjacent park, Štulkovy sady, there is an open-air **Letní scéna** (Summer Theatre) where you can catch a concert or cultural show from 6pm on most Thursdays or the odd children's performance on Tuesday afternoon (usually around 2pm).

The information centre has an informative booklet about Vyšehrad's buildings.

VYŠEHRADSKÝ HŘBITOV Map pp260-1

Vyšehrad Cemetery; ☎ 249 198 815; K rotundé 10; admission free; 8am-4pm; metro Vyšehrad

For Czechs, the Vyšehradský hřbitov is the hill's main attraction. In the late-19th century, the parish graveyard was made into a memorial cemetery for famous figures of Czech culture, with a graceful, neo-Renaissance arcade running along the northern and western sides. For the real heroes, an elaborate pantheon called the **Slavín** (loosely, Hall of Fame), designed by Antonín Wiehl, was added at the eastern end in 1894; its 50-odd occupants include painter Alfons Mucha, sculptor Josef Mýslbek and architect Josef Gočár. The motto reads 'AČ ZEMEŘELI JEŠTĚ MLUVÍ' ('Though dead, they still speak').

The 600 or so graves in the rest of the cemetery include those of composers Smetana and Dvořák, and writers Karel Čapek, Jan Neruda and Božena Němcová; there's a directory of famous names at the entrance. One word that you will see all over the place is 'rodina' – it means 'family'.

Many of the tombs and headstones are themselves works of art – Dvořák's is a sculpture by Vladislav Šaloun, the Art Nouveau sculptor who created the Jan Hus monument in Staroměstské náměstí (p67). To find it from the gate beside the church, head straight across to the colonnade on the far side, and turn left; it's the fifth tomb on your right. To find Smetana's grave, go to the Slavín and stand facing the monument; it's the pale grey obelisk to your right.

The Prague Spring (Pražské jaro) music festival (see p157) kicks off every 12 May, the anniversary of Smetana's death, with a procession from his grave at Vyšehrad to the Obecní dům (see p77).

Love Hurts

According to Czech legend Šárka was one of a renegade army of women who fled across the Vltava River after the death of Libuše, mother of the Přemysl line. She was chosen as a decoy to trap Ctirad, captain of the men's army. Unfortunately she fell in love with him, and when her fellow amazons killed him she threw herself into the Šárka Valley in remorse. The women were slaughtered by the men of Hradčany in a final battle.

You can see a monumental statue of Šárka and Ctirad in the Vyšehradské sady (Vyšehrad Gardens; see p90).

HOLEŠOVICE & BUBENEČ

This patch of Prague inside the Vltava River's big bend grew from two old settlements: Holešovice and the fishing village of Bubny. Both remained small until industry arrived in the mid-19th century and the Hlávkův most (1868) linked it to Nové Město. Close behind came a horse-drawn tram line, a river port and the exhibition grounds. The area became part of Prague in 1884.

The vast exhibition area of Výstaviště in the northern part of the district emerged around the buildings erected for the 1891 Jubilee Exhibition. These include the **Pavilón hlavního města Prahy** (Prague Pavilion), which houses the Lapidárium, and the grand, Art Nouveau **Průmyslový palác** (Palace of Industry; Map pp256–7).

Výstaviště was once the venue for the big spring and autumn trade fairs, but these are moving to a **new exhibition centre** (Prazvský Veletržní areál Prague Exhibition Centre; Map pp242-3; ☎ 225 291 611; www.pva.cz; Beranových 667, Letňany; bus 758 from metro Českomoravská) at Letňany in the northeastern suburbs, now partially open and due for final completion in 2006. Výstaviště still hosts the popular annual funfair **Matějská pouť** (St Matthew's Fair) in March, when it's full of roller-coasters, candyfloss, and half of Prague having fun.

EKOTECHNICKÉ MUZEUM Map p255

Ecotechnical Museum; ☎ 233 325 500; www.ekotech nickemuzeum.cz; Papírenská 6, Bubeneč; adult/child 80/50Kč; ☯ 10am-4.30pm Sat & Sun May-Oct; bus 131 from metro Hradčanská

Near the banks of the Vltava is this museum, Prague's former Waste Water Treatment Plant, built between 1895 and 1906 following a design by the English architect WH Lindley. Surprisingly, as the plant was designed to service a city of 500,000 people, it remained in service until 1967 by which time Prague had a population of over a million. Several steam-powered engines are on display and more are being repaired; there are guided tours of the labyrinth of sewers beneath the building. During one weekend in September all the steam-driven machinery is demonstrated in full working order.

KŘIŽÍKOVA FONTÁNA Map pp256-7

Křižík Fountain; ☎ 220 103 280; www.krizikova fontana.cz; U Výstaviště 1, Holešovice; shows around 200Kč; ☯ performances hourly 8-11pm Mar-Oct; tram 5, 12, 14, 15, 17

Transport

Metro Vltavská and Nádraží Holešovice metro stations on line C serve the southern and northern parts of Holešovice respectively.

Tram You'll find tram Nos 5, 12, 14, 15 and 17 run along Dukelských hrdinů, the main north-south street in Holešovice, while Nos 1, 8, 15, 25 and 26 run east-west on Milady Hořákové, serving both Holešovice and Bubeneč.

Each evening from spring to autumn the musical Křižíkova Fontána performs its computer-controlled light-and-water dance. Performances range from classical music such as Dvořák's *New World* symphony to modern works by Jean Michel Jarre and Vangelis, rock music by Queen, and theme music from popular films. Call or check out the website for details of what's on. The light show is best after sunset – from May to July go for the later shows.

Behind the fountain pavilion there is the **divadlo Spirála** (Spiral Theatre), a venue for Czech-language musicals. **Dětský svět** (Children's World) is a children's theatre with regular weekend performances.

LAPIDÁRIUM Map pp256-7

☎ 233 375 636; U Výstaviště 1, Holešovice; adult/child 40/20Kč; ☯ noon-5pm Tue-Fri, 10am-5pm Sat & Sun; tram 5, 12, 14, 15, 17

An outlying branch of the National Gallery, and an often overlooked gem of a museum, the Lapidárium is a repository for some 400 sculptures from the 11th to the 19th centuries. The exhibits include the Lions of Kouřim – Bohemia's oldest surviving stone sculpture – parts of the Renaissance Krocín Fountain that once stood in Old Town Square, 10 of Charles Bridge's original statues, and many other superb sculptures. See also the boxed text on p94.

LETNÁ Map pp256-7

Letná is a vast area between Milady Horáková and the river, with a parade ground to the north and a peaceful park, the **Letenské sady** (Letná Gardens), in the south, descending towards the Vltava with postcard views of the city and its bridges. In the summer you'll find here an open-air beer garden (see p153 for details). In 1261 Přemysl Otakar II held his coronation celebrations here, and during communist times Letná was the site of Moscow-style May Day military parades. In 1989 around 750,000 people gathered here in support of the Velvet Revolution, and in 1990 Pope John Paul II gave an open-air Mass here to more than a million people. See also the boxed texts on p94 and p98.

In the southwestern corner is the charming neobaroque **Hanavský Pavilón**, built by Otto Prieser for the 1891 Jubilee Exposition (see p143).

LETNÁ TERÁSA Map pp246-7
Letná Terrace

The monumental, stepped terrace overlooking the river on the southern edge of Letenské sady dates from the early 1950s, when a huge statue of Stalin, the world's biggest, was erected here by the Communist Party of Czechoslovakia, only to be blown up in 1962 by the same sycophants when Stalin was no longer flavour of the decade (see the boxed text on p94). A peculiar giant metronome – a symbolic reminder of the passing of time – has stood in its place since 1991.

MAROLDOVO PANORAMA Map pp256-7
☎ 220 103 210; U Výstaviště 1, Holešovice; adult/child 20/10Kč; 2-5pm Tue-Fri, 10am-5pm Sat & Sun; tram 5, 12, 14, 15, 17

The Maroldovo Panorama is an impressive 360-degree diorama (11m high and 95m long) of the 1434 battle of Lipany (in which the Hussite Taborites lost to the Hussite Utraquists and Emperor Zikmund's forces). It was painted by Luděk Marold in 1898.

NÁRODNÍ TECHNICKÉ MUZEUM
Map pp256-7

National Technology Museum; ☎ 220 399 111; www .ntm.cz; Kostelní 42, Holešovice; adult/child 70/30Kč, with audioguide 120/80Kč; 9am-5pm Tue-Fri, 10am-5pm Sat & Sun; tram 1, 8, 15, 25

This fun museum has a huge main hall full of vintage trains, planes and automobiles, including 1920s and '30s Škoda and Tatra cars and a fine collection of Bugattis. The motorcycle exhibit has a 1926 BSA 350-L in perfect nick, and among the vintage bicycles you'll find a 1921 predecessor of the 1970s Raleigh Chopper. Upstairs you can fool around with the cameras in a working TV studio, or head to the basement for a tour down a simulated mineshaft.

PLANETÁRIUM PRAHA Map pp256-7
☎ 233 376 452; www.planetarium.cz; Královská obora 233, Holešovice; exhibition adult/child 10/5Kč, shows 40-120Kč; 8.30am-noon & 1-8pm Mon-Thu, from 9.30am Sat & Sun; tram 5, 12, 14, 15, 17

The Planetarium, in Stromovka park just west of Výstaviště, presents various slide and video shows in addition to the astronomical shows, as well as an exhibition in the main hall. Most shows are in Czech only, but one or two of the more popular ones provide a text summary in English.

STROMOVKA Map pp256-7
tram 5, 12, 14, 15, 17

Stromovka, west of Výstaviště, is Prague's largest park. In the Middle Ages it was a royal hunting preserve, which is why it's sometimes called the Královská obora (Royal Deer Park). Rudolf II had rare trees planted here and several lakes created (fed from the Vltava River via a still-functioning canal). It's now the preserve of strollers, joggers, cyclists and inline skaters (see p109).

VELETRŽNÍ PALÁC Map pp256-7
Trade Fair Palace; ☎ 224 301 111; Dukelských hrdinů 47, Holešovice; adult/child from 100/50Kč for any 1 floor to 250/120Kč for all 4 floors; 10am-6pm Tue-Sun; tram 5, 12, 14, 15, 17

In 1996 the huge, grimly Functionalist Veletržní palác (1928) became the new home of the National Gallery's **Centre for Modern & Contemporary Art**. Its superb collection of 19th- and 20th-century Czech and European art is spread over four floors of the vast, ocean-linerlike building.

You could easily spend a whole day here, but if you only have an hour to spare, head for the 3rd floor (Czech Art 1900–30, and 19th- and 20th-century French Art) to see the *Sunbeam Motorcyclist* sculpture by Otokar Sveč; the paintings of František Kupka, pioneer of abstract art; and the art, furniture and ceramics of the Czech Cubists. The French section includes some sculpture by Rodin, a few unexceptional Impressionist works, Gaugin's *Flight* and Van Gogh's *Green Wheat*.

Highlights of the 4th floor (19th-century Czech Art) include the Art Nouveau sculpture of Josef Myslbek, Stanislav Sucharda and Bohumil Kafka; the glowing portraits by Josef Mánes; and the forest landscapes by Július Mařák.

The 1st floor (20th-century Foreign Art) includes works by Picasso, Warhol and Lichtenstein, while the 2nd floor (Czech Art 1930 to present day) has early examples of kinetic art, some Socialist Realist stuff from the communist era and various amusing works by contemporary artists – check out the grotesque *Dog Family* by Karel Pauzer.

LIBEŇ

V HOLEŠOVIČKÁCH Map pp242-3

tram 10, 24

The spot in the suburb of Libeň where Reich-sprotektor SS Obergruppenführer Reinhard Heydrich was assassinated (for details see the boxed text on p46) has changed considerably since 1942 – the tram tracks have gone and a modern road intersection has been built. It's where the slip road exits north from V Holešovičkách to Zenklova. The neighbouring streets, Gabčíkova and Kubišova, are named after the parachutists who carried out the attack. Take tram No 10 or 24 to the Zenklova stop and walk south for a few minutes.

ŽIŽKOV & KARLÍN

Named after the one-eyed Hussite hero, Jan Žižka, who defeated Holy Roman Emperor Sigismund here in 1420, Žižkov has always been a rough-and-ready, working-class neighbourhood, full of revolutionary fizz

well before 1948. Streets near the centre are slowly getting a face-lift but much of the district is still grimy and run down. It's famous for its numerous bars and night-clubs, and the views from Vítkov and the futuristic TV Tower.

The famous battle of Vítkov – it was not renamed Žižkov Hill until much later – took place in July 1420 on the long, narrow ridge that separates the Žižkov and Karlín districts. A colossal **statue of Jan Žižka** (Map pp258-9), the Hussite general, was erected here in 1950, commanding superb views across Staré Město to Prague Castle. It's said to be the biggest equestrian statue in the world. Behind it is the **Národní památník** (National Monument; for more information see opposite).

The mostly residential suburb of Karlín lies north of Žižkov, squeezed between Žižkov Hill and the Vltava River. There's nothing to see here, but the district is home to several hotels – see p190.

The Missing Monuments

Prague witnessed several profound changes of political regime during the 20th century: from Habsburg Empire to independent Czechoslovak Republic in 1918; to Nazi Protectorate from 1938 to 1945; to communist state in 1948; and back to democratic republic in 1989.

Each change was accompanied by widespread renaming of city streets and squares to reflect the heroes of the new regime. The square in front of the Rudolfinum in Staré Město, for example, was known variously as Smetanovo náměstí (Smetana Square; 1918–39); Mozartplatz (Mozart Square; 1939–45); náměstí Krasnoarmějců (Red Army Square; 1948–89); and náměstí Jana Palacha (Jan Palach Square; 1989–present).

This renaming was often followed by the removal of monuments erected by the previous regime. Here are five of Prague's most prominent 'missing monuments'.

The Missing Virgin

If you look at the ground in Old Town Square (Staroměstské náměstí; Map pp246–7) about 50m south of the Jan Hus monument, you'll see a circular stone slab set among the cobblestones. This was the site of a Marian Column (a pillar bearing a statue of the Virgin Mary), erected in 1650 in celebration of the Habsburg victory over the Swedes in 1648. It was surrounded by figures of angels crushing and beating down demons – symbolic of a resurgent Catholic Church defeating the Protestant Reformation.

The column was toppled by a mob – who saw it as a symbol of Habsburg repression – on 3 November 1918, five days after the declaration of Czechoslovak independence. Its remains can be seen in the Lapidárium at Výstaviště (see p92).

The No-Longer Missing Emperor

Before 1918, Smetanovo nábřeží (Smetana Embankment; Map pp246–7), between Charles Bridge and the Národní divadlo (National Theatre), was known as Emperor Francis I Embankment, after the Habsburg ruler. A block north of the theatre is a little garden with an elaborately pinnacled neogothic monument. The equestrian statue of Francis I that once again occupies the pedestal was removed in 1918 and languished in the Lapidárium until 2003. Plans to replace it with a statue of Smetana never materialised, and the plinth remained empty for 85 years.

The Missing General

Another victim of the change of regime in 1918 was the statue of Field Marshal Václav Radecký (1766–1858) – or Count Josef Radetzky, to give him his Austrian name – that once stood in the lower part of Malostranské náměstí (Map pp252–3);

ARMÁDNÍ MUZEUM Map pp258-9

Army Museum; ☎ 220 204 924; www.militarymuseum
.cz; U Památníku 2; Žižkov; admission free;
🕒 10am-6pm Tue-Sun; metro Florenc

On the way up Žižkov Hill battle freaks can stop at this grim-looking barracks of a museum, which displays a courtyard full of rusting tanks, and exhibits on the history of the Czechoslovak army and resistance movement from 1918 to 1945. There are occasionally more interesting temporary exhibitions covering the anniversaries of important battles and military events.

NÁRODNÍ PAMÁTNÍK Map pp258-9

National Monument; ☎ 222 781 676; U Památníku
1900, Žižkov; guided tour 30/20Kč; 🕒 2pm on 1st Sat
of each month Sep-Jun; metro Florenc

Although not, strictly speaking, a legacy of the communist era – it was completed in the 1930s – the huge monument atop Žižkov Hill is, in the minds of most Praguers over a certain age, inextricably linked with the Communist Party of Czechoslovakia, and in particular with Klement Gottwald, the country's first 'worker-president'.

Designed in the 1920s as a memorial to the 15th-century Hussite commander Jan Žižka, and to the soldiers who had fought for Czechoslovak independence, it was still under construction in the late 1930s. The occupation of Czechoslovakia by Nazi Germany in 1939 made the 'Monument to National Liberation', as it was called, seem like a sick joke.

After 1948 the Communist Party appropriated Jan Žižka and the Hussites for the purposes of propaganda, extolling them as shining examples of Czech peasant power. The communists completed the Národní památník with the installation of the Tomb of the Unknown Soldier, and Bohumil Kafka's gargantuan bronze statue of Žižka. But they didn't stop there.

In 1953 the monument's mausoleum – originally intended for the remains of Tomáš Masaryk, Czechoslovakia's founding father –

it is now in the Lapidárium. Although Radecký was a Czech, his fame derived from leading the Habsburg armies to victory against Napoleon and crushing the Italians at the battles of Custoza and Novara. (Composer Johann Strauss the Elder wrote the *Radetzky March* in his honour.) A baroque religious sculpture now occupies the site of Radecký's former pedestal.

The Missing Dictator

If you stand on Old Town Square (Map pp246–7) and look north along the arrow-straight avenue of Pařížská you will see, on a huge terrace at the far side of Čechův most (Bohemia Bridge), a giant metronome. If the monumental setting seems out of scale that's because the terrace was designed to accommodate the world's biggest statue of Stalin. Unveiled in 1955 – two years after Stalin's death – the 30m-high, 14,000-tonne colossus showed Uncle Joe at the head of two lines of communist heroes, Czech on one side, Soviet on the other. Cynical Praguers used to constant food shortages quickly nicknamed it *'fronta na maso'* ('the meat queue').

The monument was dynamited in 1962, in deference to Krushcev's attempt to airbrush Stalin out of history. The demolition crew were instructed: 'It must go quickly, there mustn't be much of a bang, and it should be seen by as few people as possible'. The Museum of Communism (p83) has a superb photo of the monument – and of its destruction.

The Missing Tank

Náměstí Kinských (Map pp250–1), at the southern edge of Malá Strana, was until 1989 known as náměstí Sovětských tankistů (Soviet Tank Crews Square), named in memory of the Soviet soldiers who 'liberated' Prague on 9 May 1945. For many years a Soviet T-34 tank – allegedly the first to enter the city – squatted menacingly atop a pedestal here (in fact it was a later Soviet 'gift').

In 1991 artist David Černý decided that the tank was an inappropriate monument to the Soviet soldiers and painted it bright pink. The authorities had it painted green again, and charged Černý with a crime against the state. This infuriated many parliamentarians, 12 of whom re-painted the tank pink. Their parliamentary immunity saved them from arrest and secured Černý's release. For more on Černý see the boxed text on p23.

After complaints from the Soviet Union the tank was removed. Its former setting is now occupied by a circular fountain surrounded by park benches; the vast granite slab in the centre is split by a jagged fracture, perhaps symbolic of a break with the past. The tank still exists, and is still pink – it's at the Military Museum in Lešany, near Týnec nad Sázavou, 30km south of Prague.

received the embalmed body of Klement Gott-wald, displayed to the public in a refrigerated glass chamber, just like his more illustrious comrade Lenin in Moscow's Red Square. It soon became a compulsory outing for school groups and bus-loads of visiting Soviet-bloc tourists.

Gottwald's morticians, however, were apparently not as adept as the Russians – by 1962 the body had decayed so badly that it had to be cremated. Since 1989 the monument has been closed to the public except on a few special occasions, although you can wander freely around the exterior. This is a pity; although the massive memorial building has all the elegance of the reactor house at a nuclear power station, the interior is a spectacular extravaganza of polished marble and gilt, and its memorials – Soviet as well as Czech – allow a glimpse of a period of Czech history that many would prefer to forget. At the time of writing, it was possible to visit the interior only on a pre-booked tour; you can book through any PIS office (see p222 for contact details).

OLŠANSKÉ HŘBITOVY Map pp258-9

Olšany Cemetery; Vinohradská 153, Žižkov; admission free; ☙ **8am-7pm May-Sep; 8am-6pm Mar, Apr & Oct; 9am-4pm Nov-Feb; metro Flora**

Huge and atmospheric, Prague's main burial place was founded in 1680 during a plague epidemic; the oldest stones are in the north-western corner, near the 17th-century **kaple sv Rocha** (St Roch Chapel). There are several entrances to the cemetery along Vinohradská, east of Flora metro station, and beside the chapel on Olšanská. **Jan Palach**, the student who set himself on fire in January 1969 in protest at the Soviet invasion (see the boxed text on p86), is buried here. To find his grave, enter the main gate (flanked by flower shops) on Vinohradská and turn right – it's about 50m along on the left of the path.

TELEVIZNÍ VYSÍLAČ Map pp258-9

TV Tower; ☎ **267 005 778; www.tower.cz; Mahlerovy sady 1, Žižkov; adult/child 150/30Kč;** ☙ **10am-11pm; metro Jiřího z Poděbrad**

Prague's tallest landmark and – depending on your tastes, either its ugliest or its most futuristic – is the 216m-tall Televizní vysílač, erected between 1985 and 1992. The viewing platforms, reached by high-speed lifts, have comprehensive information boards in English and French explaining what you can see. There is also a restaurant (at 63m; see p143 for

details). But the most bizarre thing about it is the 10 giant crawling babies with coin-slots for faces that appear to be exploring the outside of the tower – an installation called *Miminka* (Mummy) by artist David Černý.

The tower is built on the site of a **Jewish cemetery** (admission 20Kč; ☙ 9am-1pm Tue & Thu). The cemetery was opened after the Old Jewish Cemetery in Josefov (see p73) was closed. This cemetery remained in use until the year 1890, when the Židovské Hřbitovy (below) opened. What's left of the cemetery is just north of the tower.

ŽIDOVSKÉ HŘBITOVY Map pp258-9

Jewish Cemetery; Izraelská, Žižkov; admission free; ☙ **9am-5pm Sun-Thu & 9am-2pm Fri Apr-Oct, 9am-4pm Sun-Thu & 9am-2pm Fri Nov-Mar, closed on Jewish hols; metro Želivského**

Franz Kafka is buried in this cemetery, which opened around 1890 when the previous Jewish cemetery – now at the foot of the Televizní vysílač – was closed. To find Kafka's grave, follow the main avenue east (signposted), turn right at row 21, then left at the wall; it's at the end of the 'block'. Fans make a pilgrimage on 3 June, the anniversary of his death.

The entrance is beside Želivského metro station; men should cover their heads (yarmulkes are available at the gate). Last admission is 30 minutes before closing.

Tombstones, Zídovské Hřbitovy

VINOHRADY

Vinohrady occupies a rounded hill above the valley of the Botič creek, east of Nové Město and south of Žižkov. The name means 'vineyards' and refers to the vines that were cultivated here in centuries past; as recently as 200 years ago there was little urbanisation. Today, it is an upmarket residential district of elegant, early-20th-century apartment blocks and wooded parks.

Vinohrady's physical and commercial heart is **náměstí Míru** (Peace Square), dominated by the neogothic **kostel sv Ludmily** (St Ludmila Church). Right behind it is the neo-Renaissance **Národní dům** (National House), housing exhibition and concert halls. On the north side of the square is the **divadlo na Vinohradech** (Vinohrady Theatre; p161), built in 1909, it's a popular drama venue.

KOSTEL NEJSVĚTĚJŠÍHO SRDCE PÁNĚ
Map pp258-9

Church of the Most Sacred Heart of Our Lord; náměstí Jiřího z Poděbrad 19; ☯ services 8am & 6pm Mon-Sat, 7am, 9am, 11am & 6pm Sun; metro Jiřího z Poděbrad This church was built in 1932 and is one of Prague's most original and unusual pieces of 20th-century architecture. It's the work of Jože Plečník, the Slovenian architect who also raised a few eyebrows with his additions to Prague Castle. Inspired by Egyptian temples and early Christian basilicas, the glazed-brick building sports a massive, tombstone-like bell tower pierced by a circular glass clock-window. Another architectural surprise from the same period is Josef Gočár's constructivist **kostel sv Václava** (St Wenceslas Church; Map pp242-3; náměstí Svatopluka Čecha). Built in 1930 it has a fragile-looking tower and climbs the hillside.

SMÍCHOV

The suburb of Smíchov became part of Prague in 1838 and grew into an industrial quarter full of chimney stacks, railway yards and the sprawling Staropramen brewery. It is currently undergoing a wave of renovation and renewal, and is now home to the vast Nový Smíchov shopping centre (p175) and the trendy Anděl's Hotel (p192).

BERTRAMKA Map pp242-3

Mozart Museum; ☎ 257 317 465; www.bertramka.cz; Mozartova 169; adult/child 110/50Kč, concerts 390/250Kč; ☯ 9.30am-6pm Apr-Oct, to 5pm Nov-Mar; tram 4, 7, 9, 10

Transport

Metro Note that metro line B has stations at Anděl, in the heart of Smíchov, and Smíchovské Nádraží in the south of the suburb.
Tram The tram Nos 4, 7, 10 and 14 rumble across Palackého most from Karlovo náměstí to Smíchov; from Malá Strana take tram Nos 12 or 20 south from Malostranské náměstí or Újezd.

Mozart stayed at the elegant 17th-century Vila Bertramka during his visits to Prague in 1787 and 1791, as guest of composer František Dušek. Here he finished his opera *Don Giovanni*. Today, the house is a modest Mozart museum. Regular concerts are held in the salon (see p159 for more details), and in the garden (April to October only).

FUTURA GALLERY Map pp250-1

☎ 251 511 804; www.futuraprojekt.com; Holečkova 49; admission free; ☯ noon-7pm Wed-Sun; tram 4, 7, 9, 10

Opened in June 2003, Futura is a new gallery focussing on all aspects of contemporary art, ranging from painting, photography and sculpture to video, installations and performance art. The gallery spaces, which include two floors of 'white cube' halls, a more intimate brick-vaulted cellar, and an attractive garden with children's play area, host changing exhibitions by both Czech and international artists. The most notorious exhibit is the permanent installation in the garden by David Černý (see the boxed text on p23).

DEJVICE

Sprawling Dejvice, to the north of Hradčany, is a mix of university campuses and residential areas in the west, merging into the leafy backstreets of Prague's embassy district in the east. There's not too much to see out here, but there are some good restaurants (see p145) and accommodation options (see p193).

Transport

Metro The metro station Dejvická is the northwestern terminus of line A; Hradčanská, the last stop but one, serves the southern part of the district.
Tram Conveniently, tram Nos 2, 8, 20 and 26 all pass through Vítězné náměstí in the centre of Dejvice.

Districts – Outer Suburbs

Communist Prague

Here are a few prominent reminders of Prague's 41 years as a communist capital.

Hotel Crowne Plaza The silhouette of this huge Stalinist 1950s building will be familiar to those who have been to Moscow (see p98).

Letná Terása It is here at this monumental terrace overlooking the river that the world's largest statue of Stalin once stood (see p93).

Museum of Communism This museum tells the story of Czechoslovakia's years behind the Iron Curtain (see p83).

Národní Památník Although not, strictly speaking, a legacy of the communist era, this huge monument is, in the minds of most Praguers over a certain age, inextricably linked with the Communist Party of Czechoslovakia (see p95).

Just north of Dejvice is the unusual 1930s villa suburb of **Baba**, a Functionalist project by a team of artists and designers to build cheap, attractive, single-family houses. The **Hanspaulka** suburb to its southwest was a similar project, built between 1925 and 1930.

BÍLKOVA VILA Map pp246-7
Bílek Villa; ☎ 224 322 021; Mickiewiczova 1; adult/child 50/20Kč; ☷ 10am-6pm Tue-Sun mid-May–mid-Oct, 10am-5pm Sat & Sun mid-Oct–mid-May; tram 18, 22, 23

In the deep south of Dejvice, near the northeastern edge of Hradčany, is the striking, redbrick villa designed by the sculptor František Bílek in 1911 as his own home. It now houses a museum of his unconventional stone and wood reliefs, furniture and graphics. See p109 for a description of a walking tour of this area.

HOTEL CROWNE PLAZA Map p255
☎ 224 393 111; www.crowneplaza.cz; Koulova 15; tram 8

The silhouette of this huge Stalinist building in northern Dejvice will be familiar to anyone who has visited the Russian capital. Originally called the Hotel International, it was built in the 1950s to a design inspired by the tower of Moscow University, right down to the Soviet-style star on top of the spire (though this one is green, not red).

Nip into the gleamingly restored, marble-clad lobby bar (to the right), and take a look at the large tapestry hanging on the wall in the far left-hand corner. Entitled *Praga Regina Musicae* (Prague, Queen of Music), and created by Cyril Bouda around 1956, it shows an exaggerated aerial view of central Prague. Bang in the centre is the former Stalin Monument on Letná terása, and at the bottom edge you can spot the now-departed Soviet Tank memorial (see the boxed text on p94). See also this hotel's review on p193.

TROJA

Troja is a mostly residential suburb on the south-facing hillside overlooking the Vltava River north of Holešovice.

TROJSKÝ ZÁMEK Map pp242-3
Troja Chateau; ☎ 283 851 614; U Trojského zámku 1; adult/child 140/70Kč; ☷ 10am-6pm Tue-Sun Apr-Oct, 10am-5pm Sat & Sun Nov-Mar; bus 112 from metro Nádraží Holešovice

Trojský zámek is a 17th-century baroque palace that now houses the Prague City Gallery's collection of 19th-century Czech art, and modern Czech sculpture (1900–70). On the walls and ceiling of the main hall is a vast, obsequious mural depicting the Habsburgs in full transcendental glory. There's free admission to the palace grounds, where you can wander in the beautiful French gardens, watched by a gang of baroque stone giants on the balustrade outside the southern door.

ZOO PRAHA Map pp244-5
☎ 296 112 111; U Trojského zámku 120; adult/child 80/50Kč Apr-Sep, 50/30Kč Oct-Mar; ☷ 9am-7pm Jun-Aug, to 6pm Apr, May, Sep & Oct, to 5pm Mar, to 4pm Nov-Feb; bus 112 from metro Nádraží Holešovice

Prague's attractive zoo is set in 60 hectares of wooded grounds on the banks of the river. Pride of place, at the top of the hill, goes to a herd of Przewalski's horses, little steppe-dwellers that still survive in the wilds of Mongolia and are successfully bred in captivity here.

Transport
Boat Take a boat trip (see p51) from the city centre to the Troja landing.
Bus Take bus No 112 from Nádraží Holešovice metro station to the end of the line.
On Foot Walk from Výstaviště to Troja through Stromovka (see p109).

KOBYLISY

PAMÁTNÍK PROTIFAŠISTICKÉHO ODBOJE V KOBYLISÍCH Map pp242-3
Kobylisy Anti-Fascist Resistance Memorial; Žernosecká; admission free; ⓨ 24hr; tram 10, 17, 24

This grassy quadrangle of earthen embankments, ringed by trees and overlooked by apartment blocks, was once the Kobylisy Rifle Range. More than a hundred Czechs were executed here by firing squads during WWII. Today it's the site of a national memorial; a huge bronze plaque lists all the names of the dead, and – such was Nazi bureaucracy – the dates and times of their executions. Take tram No 10, 17 or 24 to the terminal at Ďáblická, then walk west for 10 minutes along Žernosecká.

KBELY

Far-flung Kbely lies on the northeastern outskirts of the city.

LETECKÉ MUZEUM Map pp242-3
Aircraft Museum; ☎ 220 207 504; Mladoboleslavská; admission free; ⓨ 10am-6pm Tue-Sun May-Oct; bus 185 or 259 from metro Českomoravská

The Kbely airfield in northeastern Prague is home to this aircraft museum where you can have a close look at Russian MiG fighter planes and a host of exhibits on aeronautics and space flight. The impressive collection amounts to no less than 275 aircraft.

ZBRASLAV

This small town on the western bank of the Vltava, 10km south of the centre, was only recently incorporated into Greater Prague.

ZÁMEK ZBRASLAV
☎ 257 921 638; Bartoňova 2; adult/child 80/40Kč; ⓨ 10am-6pm Tue-Sun; bus 129, 241 or 243 from metro Smíchovské Nádraží

As early as 1268 Přemysl Otakar II built a hunting lodge and a chapel here, later rebuilt as a Cistercian monastery. In 1784 it was converted into a baroque chateau which now houses the National Gallery's permanent collection of Asian art, with copies of well-known Czech sculptures in the gardens.

BARRANDOV

The southern suburb of Barrandov, on the western bank of the Vltava River, was devel-oped in the 1930s by Václav Havel, the father of ex-president Havel. It is famous for the Barrandov Studios, the film studios founded by Miloš Havel (the ex-president's uncle) in 1931, and increasingly popular today with Hollywood producers – *Amadeus* (1984), *Mission Impossible* (1996), *Blade II* (2002), *The League of Extraordinary Gentlemen* (2003) and *Shanghai Knights* (2003) were shot here.

The suburb was named after the 19th-century French geologist, Joachim Barrande, who studied the fossils in the contorted limestone of the Barrandovské skály (Barrandov Cliffs; Map pp242–3) – hundreds of them are on display in the Národní muzeum (p84).

STŘEŠOVICE

Střešovice is a largely residential suburb stretching to the west of Hradčany.

MÜLLEROVA VILA Map pp242-3
Müller Villa; ☎ 224 312 012; www.mullerovavila.cz; Nad hradním vodojemem 14; guided tours in Czech 300/200Kč, in English or German 400/300Kč; ⓨ 9am-6pm Tue, Thu, Sat & Sun Apr-Oct, 10am-5pm Tue, Thu, Sat & Sun Nov-Mar; tram 1, 2, 18

Fans of Functionalist architecture will enjoy this masterpiece of domestic design. It was built in 1930 for construction entrepreneur František Müller, and designed by the Viennese architect Adolf Loos, whose clean-cut, ultramodernist exterior contrasts with the polished wood, leather and oriental rugs of the classically decorated interior. The villa can be visited only by guided tour, which must be booked in advance.

MUZEUM MHD Map pp244-5
Public Transport Museum; ☎ 296 124 900; Patočkova 4; adult/child 40/20Kč; ⓨ 9am-5pm Sat, Sun & hols Apr-Oct; tram 1, 2, 18

The museum at the Střešovice tram depot has a large collection of trams and buses, from an 1886 horse-drawn tram to present-day vehicles. It's great for kids as they can climb into some of the vehicles.

Transport
Tram The tram Nos 1, 2 and 18 run along Střešovická, the main drag.

BŘEVNOV

Břevnov, a sprawling, low-density residential suburb that consists mostly of open green space, takes its name from the 1000-year-old monastery of Břevnovský klášter.

BÍLÁ HORA Map pp242-3

White Mountain; access from Karlovarská; tram 22, 25

The 381m-high Bílá Hora – more of a hillock really – on the western outskirts of Prague was the site of the 1620 Protestant military collapse that ended Czech independence for almost 300 years. The only reminder of the battle is a small memorial cairn located on a mound in the middle of a field, with the roof of the Letohrádek Hvězda (below right) poking above the forest to the northeast.

Take the tram to the end of the line, then continue west past the **kostel Panny Maria Vítězná** (Church of Our Lady of Victory), an early-18th-century celebration of the Habsburg victory at Bílá Hora, and turn right; the field is visible up ahead.

BŘEVNOVSKÝ KLÁŠTER Map pp242-3

Břevnov Monastery; ☎ 220 406 111; Patočkova 72; gardens admission free, guided tour of church, crypt & monastery 50Kč; ☼ gardens 10am-6pm Sun, tours 10am, 2pm & 4pm Sat & Sun; tram 15, 22, 25

Břevnovský klášter is the Czech Republic's oldest Benedictine monastery, founded in 993 by Boleslav II and Bishop Vojtěch Slavníkovec (later to be canonised as St Adalbert). The two men, from powerful and opposing families intent on dominating Bohemia, met at Vojtěška spring, each having had a dream that this was the place where they should found a monastery. Its name comes from *břevno* (beam), after the beam laid across the spring where they met.

The present baroque monastery building and the nearby **bazilika sv Markéty** (Church of St Margaret) were completed in 1720 by Kristof Dientzenhofer. During the communist era the monastery housed a secret-police archive;

Districts – Outer Suburbs

Transport

Tram The tram Nos 15, 22 and 25 run along Patočkova/Bělohorská, the main drag. No 15 terminates at the Vypich stop, 22 and 25 continue to Bílá Hora.

Divoká Šárka

The valley of the Šárecký potok (Šárka Creek; Map pp242-3) is one of Prague's best-known and most popular nature parks. It's named after the legendary warrior Šárka, who is said to have thrown herself off a cliff here (see the boxed text on p91).

From metro Dejvická, take tram No 20 or 26 west to the terminus at Divoká Šárka. The most attractive area is nearby, among the rugged cliffs near the Džbán Reservoir. People sunbathe on the rocks, and you can swim in the Džbán Reservoir.

From there it's a 7km walk northeast down the valley on a red-marked trail to the suburb of Podbaba, where the creek empties into the Vltava River. There's a bus stop by the Vltava at Podbaba, for the trip back to the centre, or you can walk south about 1.5km on Podbabská to the northern terminus of tram No 8, opposite the Hotel Crowne Plaza in Dejvice (p193). Bus No 116 to Dejvice runs along the lower half of the Šárka Valley, should you want to cut your walk short.

Jan Patočka (1907–77), a leading figure of the Charta 77 movement, who died after interrogation by the secret police, is buried in the cemetery behind the monastery. In 1993 (the 1000th anniversary of the monastery's founding) the restored 1st floor, with its fine ceiling frescoes, and the Romanesque crypt, with the original foundations and a few skeletons, were opened to the public for the first time.

The church, crypt and monastery can be only be visited by guided tour, but you can wander the gardens at your leisure.

LETOHRÁDEK HVĚZDA Map pp242-3

Star Summer Palace; ☎ 235 357 938; Obora Hvězda, entrances on Libocká & Bělohorská; adult/child 30/15Kč; ☼ 10am-5pm Tue-Sun Apr-Oct; tram 15, 22, 25

The Letohrádek Hvězda is a Renaissance summer palace in the shape of a six-pointed star built in 1556 for Archduke Ferdinand of Tyrol. It sits at the end of a long avenue through the lovely wooded park of Obora Hvězda, a hunting reserve established by Ferdinand I in 1530. The palace houses a small museum about its history, and an exhibit on the battle of Bílá Hora.

From the Vypich tram stop, bear right across open parkland to the white archway in the wall; the avenue on the far side leads to the palace (a 15-minute walk from the tram).

Walking Tours

Walking Tours

MALÁ STRANA GARDENS

This walk will lead you through some of the hidden green corners of Malá Strana, visiting the various gardens that once belonged to the quarter's 18th-century aristocratic residents. Begin at the **lookout 1** just outside the eastern entrance to Prague Castle, which offers a fine view over Malá Strana.

Go through the gate into the Zahrada na valech (Garden on the Ramparts; p59) and find the top entrance of the **Palácové zahrady pod Pražským hradem 2** (Palace Gardens Beneath Prague Castle; p64; this entrance is only accessible from April to October; in winter, begin the walk from Malostranská metro station, and walk west to the lower entrance of the Palácové zahrady).

Having explored these lovely terraced gardens, exit via the main gate on Valdštejnská and turn right. On your left is the **Valdštejnský palác 3** (Wallenstein Palace; p64); upon reaching Valdštejnské náměstí, turn left into the main entrance, and go through the courtyard in to the peace of **Valdštejnská zahrada 4** (Wallenstein Garden; p64). Head for the northeastern corner, to the right of the big fishpond, and leave through the gate beside Malostranská metro station.

Walk Facts

Start Prague Castle, tram 22, 23 or metro Malostranská
End Petřín Hill, tram 12, 20, 22, 23 or funicular
Distance 4km
Duration Two hours
Fuel Stops Restaurant Nebozízek (p119); El Centro (p119)

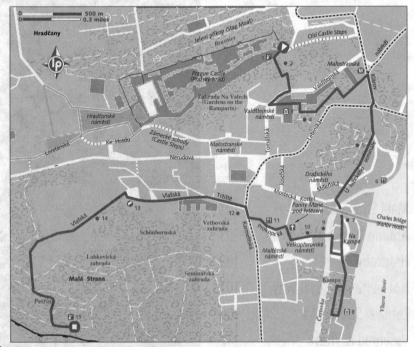

Turn right on Klárov, and go straight across the junction with the tram line, continuing along U lužického semináře. Just past the Černý Orel restaurant, a gate on the right gives access to the **Vojanovy sady** 5, the poor relation of Malá Strana's many gardens. Less manicured but more peaceful than the others, it's a public park where local folk take a breather with the kids, or sit in the sun on the park benches. The nearby riverside terrace of **Hergetova Cihelna** 6 (p119) will beckon hungry walkers.

Keep on walking past the park gate, and bear left across the little bridge over the Čertovka (Devil's Stream) onto Kampa island (p65) and pass under Charles Bridge. To your left, about waist height on the wall to the left of the little gallery under the stairs, is a small **metal plaque** 7 that reads 'Výska vody 4.žáří 1890' (height of waters, 4 September 1890), marking the level reached by the floodwaters of 1890. There are also several similar plaques around Kampa marking the height of the 2002 floods (for more information on these floods see p19), however most of them are above head height! By the way, fans of the film *Mission Impossible*, starring Tom Cruise, might recognise this little square – many of the night scenes in the movie were shot here.

Head on through the square and into the leafy riverside park known simply as Kampa (from the Latin campus, meaning 'field'), one of the city's favourite chill-out zones, usually littered with lounging bodies in summer. If the mood strikes, go for a wander among the recently restored mill buildings that house the **Muzeum Kampa** 8 (p65), specialising in modern art.

Return north but, as soon as you reach the cobblestones before Kampa Square, bear left along Hroznová, a back street that leads to a little bridge over the Čertovka beside Prague's most photographed **water wheel** 9. The bridge leads on to a tiny cobbled square with **John Lennon Wall** 10 (p65) on one side, and the baroque palace that is the French embassy on the other. The far end of the square curves right, past the severe Gothic towers of kostel Panny Marie pod řetězem (Church of Our Lady Below the Chain). Just beyond the church, on the right, is the embassy of the Knights of Malta, which featured in the movie *Amadeus* as the house of Salieri.

Turn left opposite the church and bear right along Prokopská; if you fancy a drink, and you may well do by now, **El Centro** 11 (p119) is on your right. At the end of Prokopská, cross busy Karmelitská and turn right. Just past U malého Glena pub is the alley that leads to **Vrtbovská zahrada** 12 (Vrtbov Garden; p66), one of Malá Strana's least visited, but most beautiful gardens. After visiting the gardens, turn left along Tržiště and its continuation Vlašská, passing in turn the Irish, US and **German embassy** 13. A few hundred metres beyond the German embassy there's a little **park** 14 and playground on the left; wander over to the rear wall, and you'll be able to peek into the back garden of the German embassy to see David Černý's famous sculpture of a Trabant car perched on four human legs. It was installed in this spot where a group of East German asylum seekers sought refuge during the communist era.

Follow Vlašská to its end and climb the steps that lead up to the top of Petřín Hill and finish your walk at the lookout tower **Petřínská rozhledna** 15 (Petřín Tower; p66). From here you can take the funicular railway (12Kč; every 10 to 20 minutes from 9.15am to 8.45pm) back down to Újezd or slowly wander down one of the many footpaths. Halfway down the funicular is Restaurant Nebozízek (p119), which is a great spot for a snack with a view after your stroll through the gardens.

AROUND WENCESLAS SQUARE

Start at the steps in front of the neo-Renaissance **Národní muzeum** 1 (National Museum), which dominates the upper end of Wenceslas Square (Václavské náměstí). From the steps you have a grand view down the square, a focal point of Czech history since the 19th century. At the foot of the steps is a pavement memorial to student Jan Palach (see the boxed text on p86).

Cross the busy traffic artery of Mezibranská to Prague's famous landmark, the equestrian **statue of sv Václav** 2 (St Wenceslas), the Christmas carol's 10th-century 'Good King Wenceslas'. Below the stature is a modest **memorial** 3 to those who died for their resistance to communism.

Wander down the middle of the square, admiring the grand buildings on either side. The finest is the 1906 Art Nouveau **Grand Hotel Evropa** 4 (p186) at No 25, about halfway down on the right. Across the street at No 36 is the **Melantrich Building** 5, from whose balcony the death of Czech communism was pronounced by Alexander Dubček and Václav Havel on 24 November 1989.

Turn left into Hvězda Pasáz, a shopping arcade directly across the street from the Grand Hotel Evropa. It leads to the central atrium of the **Palác Lucerna 6**, graced by David Černý's ironic twist on the St Wenceslas statue (p85) in the square outside (it helps to know that the first prime minister of the Czech Republic was also a Václav).

Walk Facts

Start Národní muzeum (National Museum), metro Muzeum
End Na můstku, metro Můstek
Distance 1.5km
Duration 30 minutes
Fuel stop Downtown Café Praha (p127)

Turn right beneath the dead horse (you'll see when you get here), and follow the passage to Vodičkova. Bear right across the street and enter the Světozor arcade. Up ahead you'll see a stained-glass window dating from the late 1940s – it's actually an advertisement for Tesla Radio, an old Czech electronics company.

At the far end of the Hvězda Pasáz, turn left into the **Františkánská zahrada 7** (Franciscan Garden), which is a hidden oasis of peace and greenery. Make your way diagonally to the far northern corner of the garden, where you'll find an exit to Jungmannovo náměstí. Go past the arch leading to the **kostel Panny Marie Sněžné 8** (Church of Our Lady of the Snows; p83) and turn right.

Keep to the right of the Lancôme shop, and you will come to what must be the only **Cubist lamppost 9** in the entire world, dating from 1915. Turn left here and then duck right through the short Lindt arcade so that you return to Wenceslas Square. Look up and to the left and you will see the corner tower of the Art Nouveau **Koruna Palace 10**, complete with its crown of pearls.

You can now head right along Na příkopě to the Obecní dům (Municipal House; p77) and the beginning of the walking tour of Malá Strana, or retire to one of the many nearby bars and cafés. **Downtown Café Praha 11** is only a few paces away.

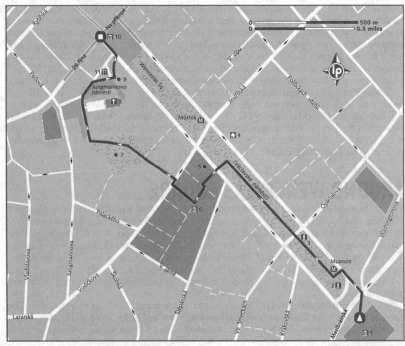

HRADČANY

Although Prague Castle is usually crammed with crowds of tourists, there are many peaceful corners in the surrounding Hradčany district. This walk will lead you to them.

As you leave the top of the escalators in Hradčanská metro station, turn right and head for the stairway in the right-hand corner marked 'Pražský hrad'. At street level turn right, and then go right again through the gap in the building opposite the railway level crossing on the other side of the street. This leads to the street called K Brusce – head for the stone gateway of the **Písecká brána** 1 (Sand Gate) that you'll see straight ahead. The baroque gateway, decorated with carved military emblems, was built by Giovanni Battisti for Charles VI in 1721 as part of Prague's new fortifications; the streets on either side still follow the outlines of the bastions of sv Jiří (St George) to the right, and sv Ludmila to the left. A century later, in 1821, the gate became the terminus of Prague's first horse-drawn railway.

Walk Facts

Start Hradčanská metro station
End Petřín Hill, tram 12, 20, 22, 23 or funicular
Distance 2.5km
Duration One hour
Fuel stop U zlaté hrušky (p118)

Bear right past the gate, then turn right on U Písecké brány, and then left at the end onto Tychonova. Here you will pass two attractive **Cubist houses** 2 designed by Josef Gočár. When you reach Mariánské hradby (the street with the tram lines), cross it and enter the Královská zahrada (Royal Garden; p56) beside the beautiful, Renaissance **Letohrádek** 3 (Summer Palace; p56). The gardens are open from April to October only; at other times of the year you'll have to go right along Mariánské hradby and enter the castle via U Prašného mostu.

Turn right beyond the Letohrádek, continuing past the equally stunning **Míčovna** 4 (Ball-Game House; p56), and follow the upper rim of the Stag Moat to the western end of the gardens. Go through the gate and turn left to enter the Second Courtyard of Prague Castle via the **Prašná most** 5 (Powder Bridge); that's powder as in gunpowder, not a reference to the poor quality construction. Visit the castle if you wish, but for the moment we'll leave the courtyard via the first gate on the right, which leads past a window giving a glimpse into the ruins of a Romanesque chapel, and into Hradčanské náměstí.

Královská zahrada (p56), Hradčany

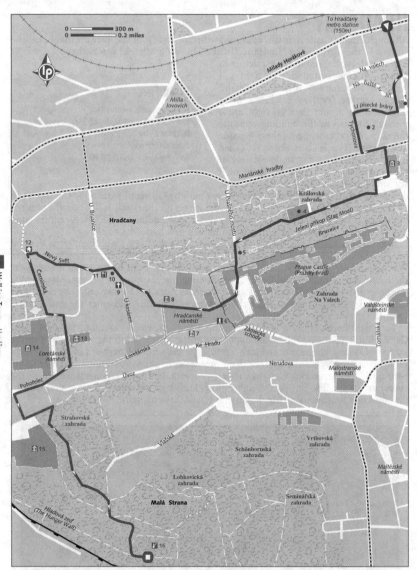

This square, now dominated on the left by a **statue of TG Masaryk** 6, the first president of Czechoslovakia, was once the social heart of the aristocratic quarter of Hradčany; in the wake of the Thirty Years War, many Catholic nobles built their palaces here to be close to the power centre of the castle. On the southern side of the square is the extravagant Renaissance status symbol of the **Schwarzenberský palác** 7 (Schwarzenberg Palace; p60), while on the northern side you can see the rococo Arcibiskupský palác (Archbishop's Palace) and the *sgrafitto*-covered **Martinický palác** 8 (Martinic Palace), which served as Hradčany's town hall. More recently the palace was used as Mozart's house in the film *Amadeus*.

At the far end of the square, bear right down the narrow cobbled street of Kanovnická, and pass the pretty little **kostel sv Jan Nepomucký** 9 (Church of St John Nepomuk), built in 1729 by the king of Prague baroque, Kilian Dientzenhofer (see the boxed text p34). Take the first lane on the left downhill from the church. This is called Nový Svět (New World) and is a picturesque cluster of little cottages once inhabited by court artisans and tradesmen, a far cry from the fancy palaces at the top of the hill. **No 1 Nový Svět 10** was the humble home of court astronomer Tycho Brahe and, after 1600, his successor Johannes Kepler. The atmospheric restaurant **U zlaté hrušky** 11 (p118), serving a selection of traditional Czech dishes, is just next door.

Continue downhill to where Nový Svět ends in a leafy hollow occupied by the **Romantik Hotel U Raka 12** (p180). Turn left and climb slowly up Černínská to the pretty square in front of the extravagantly baroque **Loreta 13** (p61), a shrine to the Virgin Mary and a hugely popular place of pilgrimage for Roman Catholics. Facing it is the imposing 150m-long façade of the **Černínský palác 14** (Černín Palace; p61), which dates from 1692.

At the southern end of the square turn right into Pohořelec and continue to the far western side. A little alley at No 9 leads into the courtyard of **Strahovský klášter 15** (Strahov Monastery; p61), where you can visit the library before exiting the eastern end of the courtyard into the gardens above Malá Strana. Turn right on the footpath here (signposted) and finish the walk with a stroll along to the lookout tower **Petřínská rozhledna 16** (p66).

NOT QUITE THE ROYAL WAY

The Královská cesta (Royal Way; p67) is an ancient processional route from the Prašná brána (Powder Gate) to the castle via Charles Bridge. In Staré Město it leads along Celetná to Old Town Square, and then on by Karlova to the bridge, but the only procession that makes its way along these streets today is the daily crush of tourists shouldering their way through a gauntlet of gaudy souvenir shops and bored-looking leaflet touts. This walk follows the general direction of the Royal Way, but dodges the main route – and the crowds – at every opportunity.

At the starting point, náměstí Republiky (Republic Square), three ages of Prague architecture face each other across the intersection of Na příkopě and Celetná – the sooty Gothic tracery of the **Prašná brána 1**, the elegant Art Nouveau convolutions of the Obecní dům (Municipal House; p77), and the stern Functionalist façades of the Česká národní banka (Czech National Bank) and the Komerční banka (Commercial Bank). As you look west

Horse-drawn carriages on Old Town Square (p67), Staré Město

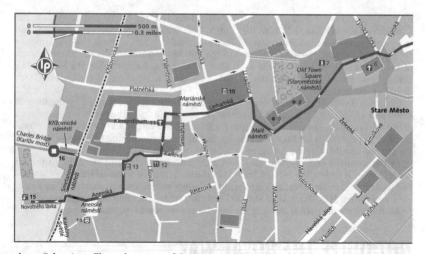

along Celetná you'll see the tower of the Staroměstská Radnice (Old Town Hall) framed in the end of the street like a target in a gunsight; set off towards it.

As well as the many souvenir shops, Celetná is lined with many interesting buildings, but as you reach the open space of Ovocný trh you'll see an unusual, origami-like façade on the left. It belongs to the **dům U černé Matky Boží 2** (House of the Black Madonna; p77), one of Prague's finest examples of Cubist architecture.

A little further along Celetná, turn right into the passage at No 17, which leads to a peaceful little courtyard beside the **divadlo v Celetné 3** (Celetná Theatre; p161). Head up the stairs to Café Gaspar Kasper (p126) if you fancy a coffee or a cold beer. The passage on the far side of the courtyard leads out onto Štupartská; go straight ahead along Malá Štupartská for a look at the baroque sculptures adorning the façade of **kostel sv Jakuba 4** (p70), and if it's open, go inside for a peek at its gloomy, gilded splendour and the grisly exhibit hanging next to the door.

Retrace your steps for a few metres and turn right through the cobbled passage just beyond Big Ben Bookshop, to enter the **Týnský dvůr 5** (p70). This lovely little courtyard is lined with posh shops, good restaurants and a Renaissance loggia, and has a fine view of the twin steeples of Týn Church. Exit at the western end, and go around to the right of **kostel Panny Marie před Týnem 6** (Church of Our Lady Before Týn; p70), stopping to look up at the semicircular tympanum above the northern door, decorated with a superb Gothic relief of the Last Judgment (this is actually a copy – the original is in the Lapidárium; p92).

A narrow alley continues along the northern side of the church and spits you out into the melee of Old Town Square (p67), dominated by the brooding **statue of Jan Hus 7** and the Gothic tower of the **Staroměstská Radnice 8** (Old Town Hall; p72). If you've timed it right, you'll be able to join the crowd at the foot of the tower to watch a performance by the Astronomical Clock (p71). Beyond the clock, keep right and enter the Gothic arcade at the foot of the *sgraffito*-clad **dům U minuty 9** (p72), and follow it around to the right into the neighbouring square of Malé náměstí (Little Square). You'll see the main tourist throng bearing left into Karlova, but head for the opposite end of the square and then turn left into Linhartská.

This leads to the quieter space of Mariánské náměstí, dominated by **City Hall 10**, whose façade is framed by brooding Art Nouveau statues by Ladislav Šaloun, the same chap who created the Jan Hus Monument in Old Town Square. Facing City Hall across the square is the main gate of the Klementinum (p76); go through the gate into the

Walk Facts

Start Náměstí Republiky, metro Náměstí Republiky
End Charles Bridge, tram 17, 18
Distance 1.5km
Duration 45 minutes
Fuel stops Café Gaspar Kasper (p126); Reykjavík (p124)

Walking Tours – Not Quite the Royal Way

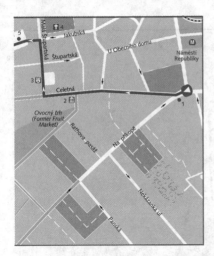

courtyard and turn left; on your right is the entrance to the **Zrcadlová kaple** 11 (Chapel of Mirrors); if you've booked to see a concert here, well, now you know where it is! Continue past the chapel through the next arch, and head for the doorway straight ahead. This leads out into the heaving crowds of Karlova and the old-fashioned, bar-like dining room of **Reykjavík** 12 (p126), which lies just across the street.

Allow the flow of the crowd to pull you west along narrow Karlova as far as the muzeum Loutek 13 (Museum of Marionettes; p77), then duck left into the museum entrance passage which leads to a courtyard. Another passage at the far side of the courtyard (bear right) leads out onto Anenská; turn right and you'll find yourself in the near-deserted Anenské náměstí, a hundred metres and a million miles away from crowded Karlova. At the far side of the square is **divadlo Na Zábradlí** 14 (Theatre on the Balustrade; p160), where ex-president Havel spent many of his formative years as a playwright.

Continue along Anenská and cross the busy traffic artery of Smetanovo nábřeží, and walk out to the end of the café-fringed terrace called Novotného lávka, where you'll find a **viewpoint** 15 with a picture-postcard view of Charles Bridge and the castle. Retrace your steps and turn left into the gaudy arcade that leads north to Křížovnické náměstí, at the eastern end of Charles Bridge. End your walk by climbing up **Staroměstská mostecká věž** 16 (Old Town Bridge Tower; p72).

LETNÁ & STROMOVKA

This is a long walk through some of the leafiest parts of Prague; make a half-day, or even a full-day expedition out of it. Instead of taking the bus and metro from Troja back to the city centre, you could time it so as to catch a boat trip back (see p52).

Begin at the Letohrádek (Summer Palace; p56) at the eastern end of the Královská zahrada (Royal Garden), north of Prague Castle. A path at the southern end of the Letohrádek leads east into the neighbouring park of Chotkovy sady; in the centre you'll find a little **stone grotto** 1 dedicated to the historical novelist Josef Zeyer and, nearby, a park bench with a superb view over the river and Staré Město. This part of the route is only possible from April to October, as the Royal Garden is closed in winter. An alternative start involves taking tram 18 to the Chotkova stop, and following Gogolova east into Letenské sady (Letná Park). You can visit Chotkovy sady by doubling back across the bridge at the eastern end of the gardens.

A footbridge at the eastern end of the gardens leads across Chotkova and into the huge Letenské sady, crossing a broad grassy ditch lined with red-brick walls that once formed part of Prague's fortifications (see also Písecká brána; p105). Follow the main path which bears right from the park entrance, but detour further right to visit the **Hanavský pavilón** 2 (p143), where you can enjoy a superb panorama and, perhaps a little lunch.

The path continues along the top of a bluff directly above the Vltava, with great views over the river and the eastern and southern parts of the city, before arriving at the monumental stepped terrace topped by a giant, creaking **metronome** 3. Designed

Walk Facts

Start Letohrádek, tram 22, 23
End Troja, bus 112 to metro Nádraží Holešovice
Distance 6km
Duration Two to three hours
Fuel stops Hanavský pavilón (p143); La Crêperie (p143)

Walking Tours – Letná & Stromovka

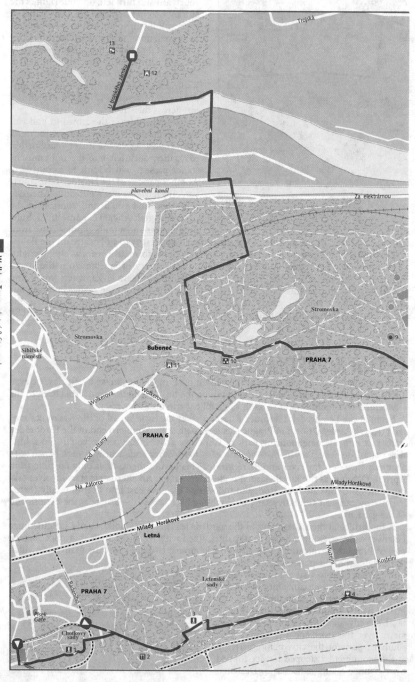

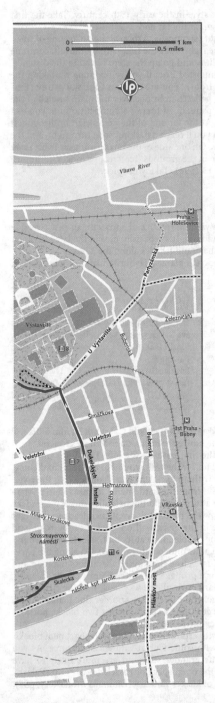

by artist David Černý, who also created the babies on the Televizní vysílač (TV Tower; p96) and the Trabant on legs in the garden of the German embassy (p103), the metronome sits on a spot once occupied by a giant statue of Stalin (see the boxed text on p95).

Continue east along the path at metronome level and you will eventually arrive at Letenské sady's popular **beer garden 4** (p153), where it is almost certainly compulsory to stop for a cold one. Beyond the beer garden, the path slopes down through pretty flower gardens and along an avenue of plane trees, past the futuristic **Expo 58 Restaurant 5**. Built for the Brussels World Exposition of 1958, and later re-erected here, it is no longer a restaurant but has been beautifully renovated and now houses some fortunate office workers. If the Hanavský Pavilón didn't tempt you into a lunch stop, perhaps cosy **La Crêperie 6** (p143) on nearby Janovského will.

Leave the park and continue downhill on Skalecka, then turn left along busy Dukelských hrdinů. Follow this street north for 400m – stopping to visit the **Výstaviště palác 7** (Trade Fair Palace; p93), Prague's premier collection of modern art, if you wish – to the entrance of **Výstaviště exhibition grounds** (p92); if you don't fancy walking this section, hop on a tram for a couple of stops (No 5, 12 or 17 will do).

If the Veletržní palác has whet your appetite for cultural attractions (or maybe it's just started raining), you might like to detour into the **Lapidárium 8** (p92) for a wander among some of the city's finest sculptures. Otherwise, bear left at the entrance to Výstaviště and follow the path just to the left of the No 5 tram line's terminal loop, passing the dome of the **Planetárium Praha 9** (p93) on your right as you enter the former royal hunting ground, Stromovka (p93).

Follow your nose as the path curves to the left, past people playing *boules* on the gravel verge, and a run-down 1960s 'space-age' children's playground, then bear right towards the pond. Turn left when you reach a broad main path (signposted Dejvice & Bubeneč), which leads between a series of artificial lakes on the right, and a once-grand but now ruined **old restaurant 10** and bandstand on the left. Beyond this you'll see the Renaissance **Místodržitelský letohrádek 11** (Summer Palace) perched on a hill to the left, the place where Bohemian royals used to hang out on their hunting trips to

Stromovka. It was re-modelled in neogothic style in the early 19th century. Take the first path on the left as it curves around to the right at the far end.

At the T-junction below the palace, go right (signposted Troja) along an avenue of trees, and follow the path as it curves around to the right. Take the first path on the left, continue through the short tunnel under the railway line, and go up the steps ahead in the distance. Cross the bridge and go left, then right (signposted Zoo; if you're planning on taking the boat back into town, this is where it leaves from). You are now on Císařský ostrov (Emperor's Island); the road leads to a sweeping pedestrian bridge over the main branch of the Vltava, with a canoe slalom course visible upstream (if there's a competition on, you can guarantee there'll be a beer tent there also). At the far end of the pedestrian bridge go left along the riverbank path, and in about 300m you'll reach a parking area; turn right, and the road will lead you to the No 112 bus terminus. On one side of the bus terminus is **Trojský zámek 12** (Troja Chateau; p98), with a welcome café in the grounds (ice-cream sundaes, mmmm); and on the other is the entrance to **Zoo Praha 13** (p98). Take your pick.

VYŠEHRAD & VLTAVA

This walk begins with the ancient citadel of Vyšehrad (p89), and ends with an easy riverside stroll past some of Nové Město's grandest buildings. It's especially nice in the late afternoon or early evening, when the setting sun gilds the grand façades along the Vltava.

You exit from the metro station into a concrete plaza, a favourite haunt of local skaters, beneath the concrete façade of the **Kongresové centrum 1** (Congress Centre). Set off with the centre on your left and a view towards the twin spires of kostel sv Petra a Pavla off to your right. At the far end of the plaza go down the steps and follow Na Bučance towards the Vyšehrad battlements. Go past the first bastion you come to and turn right to enter the fortress through the **Táborská brána 2** (Tábor Gate). It's soon followed by the scant remains of the **Špička brána 3** (Peak Gate), with the brick-and-stone lined ditches of the 17th-century fortifications in between. You then pass through the much more impressive **Leopoldova brána 4** (Leopold Gate), which film buffs will recognise from its appearance at the end of the movie *Amadeus*, after Mozart's funeral.

Walk Facts

Start Vyšehrad metro station
End Nádodní divadlo (National Theatre), metro Národní Třída
Distance 3km
Duration One hour
Fuel stops Le Bistrot de Marlène (p128); Kavárna Slavia (p128)

Just beyond the Leopoldova brána, take the first path on the left. This leads up to the citadel's southern battlement. Turn right and follow the wall around to the point of the next bastion, where there are three park benches with an excellent **view 5** south along the river; this is a good spot for a picnic lunch. Descend from the battlements towards **kostel sv Petra a Pavla 6** (Church of SS Peter & Paul), and take a turn around the neighbouring Vyšehradský hřbitov (Vyšehrad cemetery; p91), then follow the road, Štulcová, which leads to the right as you exit the church. Go through the gate in the brick wall on the left of the road, and descend the long staircase. Turn left along the cobbled lane at its foot, which leads around to the main road next to the **Cubist villa 7** (p91) at Rašínovo nábřeží 6–10. Go along the pavement past the villa to a pedestrian crossing just before the tunnel, then cross the road and double back along the far side of the river for a proper view of the Cubist façade.

The rest of the walk follows the river embankment all the way back into the city centre. Just before you pass under the railway bridge, you can admire another fine Cubist house, the **Villa Libušina 8** (p91), on the right. **Le Bistrot de Marlène 9** (p128) is just two blocks north of the villa and is a good spot to sample some exquisite French cuisine.

The embankment near the bistro is lined with crumbling Art Nouveau apartment blocks, and a huge Functionalist apartment block with some Cubist-influenced features. As you continue further north the buildings become grander still, and are more likely to have been renovated. Opposite the next bridge is the open space of Palackého náměstí (Palacký Square), backed by the swooping twin spires of klášter Emauzy (Emmaus Monastery; p87),

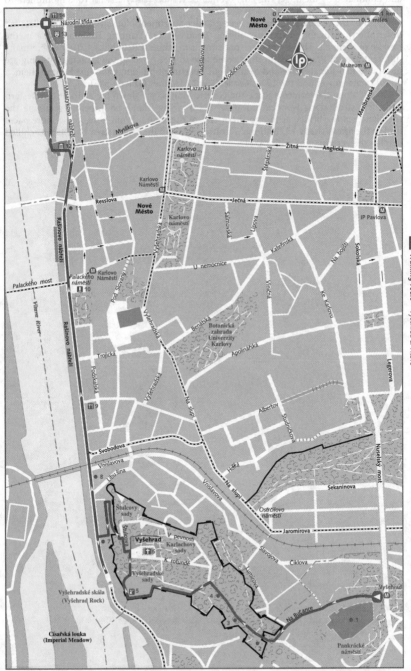

and dominated by the huge, swirlingly romantic **František Palacký Memorial** 10, a monument to the country's best-known historical writer.

North of the square you pass by ever-grander apartment blocks (see p85 for a detailed description), with the attention-grabbing **Tančící dům** 11 (Dancing Building; p87) in the middle of them all. This is another spot similar to náměstí Republiky (p107) where many different ages of Prague architecture come face to face – facing the Dancing Building are grandiose neo-Renaissance and neobaroque apartment buildings and just beyond them, a Gothic water tower and the 1920s **Galerie Mánes** 12 (Mánes Gallery; p86).

Go left along the terrace outside the Galerie Mánes, and down the stairs at the western end for a stroll along wooded Slovanský ostrov (Slav Island; p87), before rejoining the mainland via the bridge at the northern end of the island. From here, a few more paces lead to the **Národní divadlo** 13 (National Theatre; p85) and the **Kavárna Slavia** 14 (p85), its chilled display shelves groaning with cakes.

Eating

Eating

In recent years Prague has enjoyed a welcome upsurge in the number, quality and variety of its restaurants. You can now sample all manner of foreign fare, from Afghan to Argentinean, Korean to Cantonese, and even – miracle of miracles – expect service with a smile in a majority of eating places.

However, don't let this kaleidoscope of cuisines blind you to the pleasures of good old-fashioned Czech grub. The city's many pubs dish up tasty pork and dumplings, often at very low prices, and a lot of the more-upmarket restaurants offer gourmet versions of classic Bohemian dishes such as pork knuckle or roast duck.

Opening Hours

In general, lunch is served from noon to 3pm, and dinner from 6pm to 9pm. Most Prague restaurants, however, are open all day, from 10am or noon to 10pm or 11pm, allowing a laid-back approach to meal times (ie diners are not confined to rigid meal times). Cafés are usually open from 8am; see the boxed text on p130 for breakfast recommendations.

How Much?

On average, you can expect to pay around 250Kč to 500Kč per person for a meal in a mid-range restaurant, not including drinks. In the more upmarket places you can double that, and in the very best restaurants the bill will be in the area of 1500Kč per person before drinks.

On the other hand, it's possible to eat well for very little. You can fill up in a pub or café for less than 200Kč per person – and that includes a glass of beer. The Cheap Eats options listed in this chapter have an average main course price of around the 100Kč mark.

Unless otherwise indicated, price ranges quoted in restaurant reviews are for main courses at dinner; prices for main courses at lunch are sometimes cheaper.

Booking Tables

It's always a good idea to reserve a table at upmarket restaurants, especially during the high season; almost without fail the phone will be answered by someone who speaks English. That said, we spent months researching in Prague and we mostly did just fine without making any reservations at all.

Tipping

It's pretty much unheard of for Prague restaurants to include a service charge on your bill (check). In most places the helpful message 'Tips Not Included', in English (hint, hint) is printed on the bill.

Vegetarian selection, Country Life (p126), Staré Město

Spanish Birds & Moravian Sparrow

Many Czech dishes have names that don't offer a clue as to what's in them, but certain words will give you a hint: *šavle* (sabre; something on a skewer); *tajemství* (secret; cheese inside rolled meat or chicken); *překvapení* (surprise; meat, capsicum and tomato paste rolled into a potato pancake); *kapsa* (pocket; a filling inside rolled meat); and *bašta* (bastion; meat in spicy sauce with a potato pancake).

Two strangely named dishes that all Czechs know are *Španělský ptáčky* (Spanish birds; veal rolled up with sausage and gherkin, served with rice and sauce) and *Moravský vrabec* (Moravian sparrow; a fist-sized piece of roast pork). But even Czechs may have to ask about *Meč krále Jiřího* (the sword of King George; beef and pork roasted on a skewer), *Tajemství Petra Voka* (Peter Voka's mystery; carp with sauce), *Šíp Malínských lovců* (the Malín hunter's arrow; beef, sausage, fish and vegetables on a skewer) and *Dech kopáče Ondřeje* (Digger Ondřej's breath; fillet of pork filled with extremely smelly Olomouc cheese slices).

Normal practice in pubs, cafés and mid-range restaurants is to round up the bill to the next 10Kč (or the next 20Kč if it's over 150Kč). The usual protocol is for the staff to hand you the bill and for you, as you hand over the money, to tell them the total amount you want to pay with the tip included.

Change is usually counted out starting with the big notes, on down to the littlest coins. If you say *děkuji* (thank you) during this process the staff will stop and assume the rest is a tip.

Self-Catering

There is a wide variety of self-catering options available from *potraviny* (grocery or food shops) and supermarkets everywhere, the best stocked and priciest being in flash department stores near the centre. Note that some perishable supermarket food items bear a date of manufacture *(datum výroby)* plus a 'consume-within...' *(spotřebujte do...)* period, whereas others (such as long-life milk) have a stated minimum shelf-life *(minimální trvanlivost)* date, after which the freshness of the product is not guaranteed.

For supermarket supplies, head to the basement of **Kotva** (Map pp246-7; ☎ 224 801 111; náměstí Republiky; ☽ 9am-8pm Mon-Fri, 9am-6pm Sat, 10am-6pm Sun; metro Náměstí Republiky) or **Tesco** (Map pp252-3; ☎ 222 003 111; Národní třída 26; ☽ 8am-9pm Mon-Fri, 9am-8pm Sat, 10am-8pm Sun; metro Národní Třída). In Malá Strana you'll find the handy **Vacek Bio-Market** (Map pp244-5; ☎ 257 330 488; Mostecká 3; ☽ 7am-10pm Mon-Sat, 10am-10pm Sun), a well stocked minisupermarket.

The city has several open-air produce markets (Map pp246-7). The biggest one in the city centre is the tourist-oriented **open-air market** (Havelská; ☽ 8am-6pm), south of the Old Town Square. More authentic neighbourhood markets – mainly open in the mornings only and closed on Sundays – include the open-air market on Dejvická, near Hradčanská metro station in Dejvice.

In Staré Město, **Bakeshop Praha** (Map pp246-7; Kozí 1; ☽ 7am-7pm) is quite a fantastic bakery that sells some of the best bread in the city, along with pastries, cakes and takeaway sandwiches, salads and quiche. Another good bakery near Old Town Square is **Michelské pekářství** (Map pp246-7; Dlouhá 1; ☽ 6.30am-6pm Mon-Fri, 11am-6pm Sun), which sells a wide range of freshly baked breads and freshly prepared sandwiches.

Delicatessens that are good for stocking up on picnic supplies include **Fruits de France** (Map pp252-3; ☎ 224 220 304; Jindřišská 9, Nové Město; ☽ 9.30am-6.30pm Mon-Fri, 9.30am-1pm Sat; metro Můstek) sells French wine, cheese, pastries and more. Next door is the similar **Paris-Praha** (Map pp252-3; ☎ 224 222 855; Jindřišská 7, Nové Město; ☽ 7am-6.30pm Mon-Fri; metro Můstek).

Cellarius (Map pp252-3; ☎ 224 210 979; Hvězda pasáž, Václavské náměstí 36, Nové Město; ☽ 9.30am-9pm Mon-Sat, 3-9pm Sun; metro Můstek), which is located at the intersection of the Lucerna and Hvězda passages, is the place to head to if you are looking for Czech and imported wines. There is also a branch situated in the **Vinohradský Pavilón shopping centre** (Map pp260-1; Vinohradská 50, Vinohrady; ☽ 9am-9pm Mon-Sat, 3-8pm Sun).

Top Five Romantic Restaurants

- Kampa Park (p119)
- La Provence (p123)
- U Maltézských rytířů (p120)
- U modré kachničky (p120)
- U zlaté hrušky (right)

HRADČANY

There aren't too many eateries in the castle district, and the whole area is pretty quiet in the evenings. The following places, which are a cut above the usual tourist restaurants regarding character and cuisine, are worth seeking out – Peklo and U zlaté hrušky for Czech food with some atmosphere, Saté and Malý Buddha for authentic Asian cooking.

MALÝ BUDDHA   Map pp252-3   *Vietnamese*

☎ 220 513 894; Úvoz 46; mains 60-200Kč;
⊗ 1-10.30pm Tue-Sun; tram 22, 23

This hippy-influenced eatery is easy to find – just follow the incense fumes. It's an oriental tearoom, complete with Buddhist shrine, offering carefully prepared vegetarian and seafood dishes, plus 'healing wines' ranging from ginseng wine to Chinese rose liqueur. Crab, shark and crocodile are on the menu, but credit cards are not.

RESTAURANT PEKLO

Map pp252-3   *Modern Czech*

☎ 220 516 652; Strahovské nádvoří 1/132;
mains 250-600Kč; ⊗ 6pm-midnight Mon,
11am-midnight Tue-Sun; tram 22, 23

Set in a vaulted subterranean wine-cellar in the courtyard of the Strahovský klášter (p61) grounds, this eerily atmospheric restaurant serves Czech and Italian cuisine. The name means 'Hell' – because the gardens above are called 'Paradise' – but the only suffering that happens is when you have to pay the bill. The house speciality is *pstruh* (trout) fresh from the cellar's own pond.

SATÉ   Map pp252-3   *Indonesian/Malaysian*

☎ 220 514 552; Pohořelec 3; mains 80-110Kč;
⊗ 11am-10pm; tram 22, 23

Saté is a down-to-earth, no-frills restaurant, just five minutes' walk west of the castle, serving tasty and inexpensive Indonesian and Malaysian dishes, such as *nasi goreng* (fried rice with veggies, prawns and egg), beef rendang (coconut-based curry), Javanese beefsteak and a string of tasty vegetarian dishes.

U ZLATÉ HRUŠKY   Map pp244-5   *Czech*

☎ 220 514 778; Nový svět 3; mains 400-600Kč;
⊗ 11.30am-3pm & 6.30pm-midnight; tram 22, 23

'At The Golden Pear' is a cosy, wood-panelled gourmet's corner, serving beautifully prepared Czech fish, fowl and game dishes. It's frequented as much by locals as by tourists and visiting dignitaries (the Czech foreign ministry is just up the road). In summer you can opt for a table in its leafy *zahradní restaurace* (garden restaurant) across the street.

MALÁ STRANA

You'll be spoilt for choice when it comes to looking for somewhere to eat in Malá Strana. The tourist crowds are swelled by hungry office workers from the district's many embassies and government offices, and this well-heeled clientele means that there are lots of quality restaurants offering a wide range of cuisines. Many of the best restaurants take advantage of a riverside location, or are perched on a hillside with a view over the city.

ART DIOGENES

Map pp244-5   *Mediterranean*

☎ 224 931 220; Nerudova 43; mains 135-325Kč;
⊗ 8am-midnight; tram 12, 20, 22, 23

A friendly, family-run restaurant and piano bar with a sunny Mediterranean mood, Diogenes dishes up Greek classics, such as tangy feta cheese salad, smoky *melitzanosalata* (aubergine and garlic puree), taramasalata and calamari, as well as a range of pasta dishes, steaks, chops and seafood – the sea bass baked in a salt crust is excellent.

CIRCLE LINE BRASSERIE

Map pp244-5   *French*

☎ 257 530 023; Malostranské náměstí 12;
mains 395-645Kč; ⊗ noon-11pm Mon-Fri,
11am-11pm Sat & Sun; tram 12, 20, 22, 23

The Circle Line is one of the city's top French restaurants, with dining on separate levels in a

Top Five Malá Strana

- Circle Line Brasserie (above)
- Hergetova Cihelna (p119)
- Kampa Park (p119)
- U Maltézských rytířů (p120)
- U Zlaté studně (p120)

Eating – Hradčany

plush Gothic and baroque palace. Frequented by local bon viveurs and business people on expenses, it offers a five-course *menu dégustation* for 1590Kč, plus 890Kč for wines to accompany each course.

EL CENTRO Map pp244-5 *Spanish*
☎ 257 533 343; Maltézské náměstí 9; mains 150-320Kč, tapas 70-200Kč; ☼ noon-midnight; tram 12, 20, 22, 23
Bright colours, chunky wooden furniture and Spanish-speaking staff lend an authentic atmosphere to this classic tapas bar. Here you can nibble on snackettes of chorizo, calamari and *gambas pil-pil* (prawns in garlic) over a bottle of Rioja, or splash out on a full meal of steak, grilled chicken or paella washed down with a jug of sangria. The cocktail bar offers a range of port, sherry and Spanish brandies, and there's a neat little garden courtyard out back.

HERGETOVA CIHELNA
Map pp244-5 *Modern Czech*
☎ 257 535 534; Cihelná 2b; mains 200-550Kč; ☼ 9am-2am; metro Malostranská
A converted *cihelná* (brickworks) may not sound like a promising spot for a restaurant, but this beautifully restored 18th-century building enjoys one of Prague's hottest locations, with a riverside terrace offering sweeping views of Charles Bridge and Staré Město. The food is of equally high quality, from pizzas and burgers to steaks and seafood. Be aware that there are two wine lists.

KAMPA PARK
Map pp244-5 *Seafood/Modern Czech*
☎ 257 532 685; Na Kampě 8b; mains 500-800Kč; ☼ 11.30am-1.30am; tram 12, 20, 22, 23
Kampa Park is a celebrity magnet at the northern tip of Kampa island – Princess Caroline of Monaco, Johnny Depp, Lou Reed, Michael Douglas and Hilary Clinton have all over-tipped the staff here, and even Salman Rushdie has been seen skulking in a corner. The interior is a designer's wet dream, while the rustic riverside terrace offers a panorama of Charles Bridge and the Staré Město skyline. The cuisine is as famous as the clientele, from the seared scallops with salmon roe and lobster foam ('foam' is a big feature of the menu here) to the seared yellowfin tuna with porcini risotto, black truffle and gari ginger foam (told you!). For a romantic dinner, reserve a candlelit table on the narrow, cobble-stoned terrace right beside the river, with the lights of Charles Bridge glittering on the water.

MEDUZZY Map pp246-7 *Greek/Italian*
☎ 251 510 557; Mělnická 13; mains 90-270Kč; ☼ 11.30am-11pm; tram 6, 9, 12, 20
Meduzzy strikes a Mediterranean note with its blond pine and terracotta décor, and windmill and Medusa motifs. Service is friendly, and the food is fairly authentic, too – *choriatiki* salad (feta cheese, olives, tomato and cucumber), freshly made pitta bread, and *tsatziki* (yogurt, cucumber and garlic dip) with enough raw garlic to stun a horse.

PÁLFFY PALÁC CLUB
Map pp244-5 *French/International*
☎ 257 320 570; Valdštejnská 14; mains 475-585Kč; ☼ 11am-midnight; metro Malostranská
In the same neobaroque palace as the Prague Conservatoire (music school), the Pálffy is a local institution patronised at lunch time by workers from the nearby government ministries. The cuisine is high-quality, but the main attraction is the terrace views of the palace gardens. There are good-value set-lunch menus offering dishes like salad of smoked trout and tomato vinaigrette, and grilled saddle of rabbit with Dijon mustard cream sauce, available on weekdays, ranging in price from 240Kč to 520Kč.

PASHA Map pp244-5 *Lebanese*
☎ 257 532 434; U lužického semináře 23; mains 350-500Kč; ☼ 11.30am-11.30pm; metro Malostranská
Decked out in deep blues, plush reds and sensuous silks, decadent Pasha offers a lush menu of Lebanese *mezzes* (appetisers) with which to carpet your table. Service is polite and attentive, though the staff keep topping up your wine glass just a little too often…

RESTAURANT NEBOZÍZEK
Map pp250-1 *Czech*
☎ 257 315 329; Petřínské sady 411; mains 200-450Kč; ☼ 11am-11pm; tram 12, 20, 22 or 23, then Petřín funicular
Set halfway up Petřín hill (p66), Nebozízek serves Czech standards – including a succulent roast pork with potato pancakes, fish dishes and good salads. The food is served in a terrace-conservatory with panoramic views across the Vltava River to Staré Město.

RYBÁŘSKÝ KLUB Map pp250-1 *Czech*
☎ 257 533 170; U sovových mlýnů 1; mains 180-270Kč; ☼ 11am-11pm; tram 6, 9, 22, 23
Český rybářský svaz, the old Fishermen's Guild, offers diners great value in a riverside location,

provided you enjoy fish – there's precious little else on the menu. It has a peaceful setting at the southern end of Kampa island, with wooden benches indoors and a handful of outdoor tables beside the river. The menu specialises in freshwater fish, including carp, trout and catfish; try the delicious *candát* (pikeperch) with mushroom sauce, or pike with herb butter.

SQUARE Map pp244-5   *Mediterranean*
☎ 257 532 109; Malostranské náměstí 5; mains 200-500Kč; ☽ 9am-12.30am; tram 12, 20, 22, 23

Chic, sleek and unashamedly modern, this stylish restaurant and bar occupies the premises of the old Café Radetzky (later renamed Malostranská kavárna), established in 1874 and frequented by Czech literary lions, such as Jan Neruda and Franz Kafka. Its latest incarnation specialises in tapas, pasta and seafood, serving dishes such as *porcini pappardelle*, risotto with seared pheasant and black truffle, and lobster with linguini in tomato and basil sauce. The cocktail bar mixes a mean *mojito*, too.

SUSHI BAR Map pp252-3   *Japanese*
☎ 603 244 882; Zborovská 49; mains 180-480Kč, sushi boxes 440-680Kč; ☽ 11am-10pm; tram 6, 9, 22, 23

This dinky little sushi bar is as compact and neatly ordered as, well…a plate of sushi. The menu includes sashimi (raw fish thinly sliced and elegantly arranged), *maki sushi* (raw fish and rice rolled in a thin sheet of crisp seaweed) and *nigiri sushi* (a piece of fish or other seafood pressed onto a pad of vinegared rice, with soy sauce for dipping), with sake (rice wine), *mogi-shochu* (Japanese spirit) and Kirin beer to wash it down. It's run by a seafood importer – there's a fresh fish shop next door – so your sushi is always superbly fresh.

U MALÍŘŮ Map pp244-5   *French*
☎ 257 530 000; Maltézské náměstí 11; mains 630-1080Kč; ☽ 11.30am-10pm; tram 12, 20, 22, 23

'The Painter's House' is an opulent enclave of colourful frescoes, starched linen and *haute cuisine*; the vaulted 15th-century dining room received its painted decoration in the 1930s. Opinions vary as to whether the standard of the food is as consistently high as the prices – the lobster in chardonnay sauce (2890Kč per person) is going to be a big letdown if it's the head chef's night off – but when it's good it's very, very good. The *prix fixe* three-course *menu St Hubert* costs 1190Kč.

U MALTÉZSKÝCH RYTÍŘŮ
Map pp244-5   *Czech/International*
☎ 257 533 666; Prokopská 10; mains 210-350Kč; ☽ 11am-11pm; tram 12, 20 22, 23

'At the Maltese Knights' is a cosy and romantic olde-worlde restaurant, with tables tucked in niches in the downstairs Gothic vaults. Typical dishes include roast saddle of boar with bramble sauce and grilled fillet of pikeperch with olives and paprika. It's a popular spot, so book well ahead.

U MODRÉ KACHNIČKY
Map pp252-3   *Czech*
☎ 257 320 308; Nebovidská 6; mains 280-480Kč; ☽ noon-4pm & 6.30-11.30pm; tram 12, 20, 22, 23

A chintzy, baroque hunting lodge hidden away on a quiet side street, 'At the Blue Duckling' is a plush, old-fashioned place with quiet, candlelit nooks perfect for a romantic dinner. The menu is heavy on duck, game and fish dishes, with selections such as roast duck with walnut stuffing and potato dumplings, or rump of venison with rosehip sauce and potato pancakes.

U ZLATÉ STUDNĚ
Map pp244-5   *French/International*
☎ 257 533 322; U Zlaté studně 4; mains 525-950Kč; ☽ 7am-11pm; metro Malostranská

'At the Golden Well' enjoys one of the best locations in Prague, perched beneath the castle gardens and commanding a view across the rooftops of Malá Strana to the river. The food and wine are superb too. The menu, which has a Mediterranean motif, includes dishes such as terrine of foie gras with apricot coulis, roast duck on red cabbage with forest honey sauce, and baked monkfish with saffron risotto, and the wine list offers a good selection of French and Italian wines.

Cheap Eats
BOHEMIA BAGEL Map pp250-1   *Café*
☎ 257 310 694; Újezd 18; snacks 60-120Kč; ☽ 7am-midnight Mon-Fri, 8am-midnight Sat & Sun; tram 6, 9, 12, 20, 22, 23

Endlessly popular with travellers, Bohemia Bagel is like a little outpost of America. It offers bagels, quiches, soups, salads and all-you-can-drink soft drinks and coffee, as well as an Internet café, which all keep people coming back over and over. It's also a great place to meet people. There's another branch in **Staré Město** (p126).

RESTAURACE BAR BAR

Map pp250-1   *International*
☎ 257 312 246; Všehrdova 17; mains 80-200Kč;
🕑 noon-midnight Sun-Thu, noon-2am Fri & Sat;
tram 12, 20, 22, 23

Bar Bar is a cellar bar serving giant salads and a zillion kinds of tasty crepes, ranging from savoury pancakes stuffed with smoked bacon, sauerkraut and cheese to sweet offerings, such as crepe with fruit salad and maple syrup. Other main courses include mushroom risotto with parmesan, poached fillet of pikeperch with pesto and sun-dried tomatoes, and steak teriyaki with grilled veggies. The food stops at midnight, but drinks go on till 2am.

ST NICHOLAS CAFÉ Map pp244-5   *Café*
☎ 257 530 205; Tržiště 7; mains 80-160Kč; 🕑 noon-2am Sun-Thu, noon-3am Fri & Sat; tram 12, 20, 22, 23

St Nicholas offers a quiet Gothic cellar, a favourite midday refuge in the heart of the tourist zone. Slump into an armchair with your coffee and cake, fuel up on tasty pizza, or enjoy a cocktail before dinner.

U ZELENÉHO ČAJE

Map pp244-5   *Tearoom*
☎ 257 530 027; Nerudova 19; tea 40-65Kč;
🕑 11am-10pm; tram 12, 20, 22, 23

'At the Green Tea' is a charming little olde-worlde tea house on the way up to the castle. The menu offers around a hundred different kinds of tea from all over the world, ranging from classic green and black teas from China and India to fruit-flavoured teas and herbal infusions, as well as tempting cakes and tasty sandwiches.

STARÉ MĚSTO

The Old Town is littered with tourist traps, especially around Old Town Square, but there are also lots of excellent restaurants. The maze of streets leading away from Old Town Square contains many hidden gems, while the swanky strip of Pařížská boasts

a more obvious string of stylish, upmarket eateries. The classic Staré Město dining room is in a brick-lined cellar – you'll soon become a connoisseur of subterranean décor.

AMBIENTE PASTA FRESCA

Map pp246-7   *Italian*
☎ 224 230 244; Celetná 11; mains 110-200Kč;
🕑 11am-midnight; metro Náměstí Republiky

Slick styling, service with a smile and a wide selection of Italian wines complement excellent dishes, such as succulent, melt-in-the-mouth *carpaccio* of beef, piquant spaghetti *aglio-olio* with chilli and crisp pancetta, and rich risotto with *porcini*, at this busy Italian restaurant. There is also a long, narrow, coffee-coloured café at street level, and you'll fina a more formal, more intimate cellar restaurant located down below.

ARIANA Map pp246-7   *Afghan*
☎ 222 323 438; Rámová 6; mains 170-230Kč;
🕑 11am-11pm; tram 5, 8, 14

Ariana is a welcoming little place decked out with Persian rugs and photos of Kabul, with Asian music wailing in the background. It serves a range of unusual Afghani dishes, including *ashak* (a sort of ravioli containing chopped leeks, with a rich sauce of minced lamb and yogurt), various lamb and chicken kebabs and tasty vegetarian specialities, served with light, fluffy *nan-i-dashi* (hot bread) on the side.

BELLEVUE Map pp252-3   *French*
☎ 224 221 387; Smetanovo nábřeží 18;
mains 590-890Kč; 🕑 noon-3pm & 5.30-11pm Mon-Sat, 11am-3pm & 7-11pm Sun; tram 17, 18

Snappy service, crisp linen and the clink of crystal accompany top-notch *nouvelle cuisine* at this long-standing French favourite, famed for its outdoor terrace tables with a majestic view of the river, Charles Bridge and the castle. Sunday features a champagne brunch (795Kč) with live jazz from 11am to 3.30pm.

Eating – Staré Město

121

BODEGUITA DEL MEDIO

Map pp246-7   *Cuban*

☎ 224 813 922; Kaprova 5; mains 300-500Kč;
☼ 10am-2am; metro Staroměstská

The Prague incarnation of the famous Havana cocktail-bar and restaurant chain brings a whiff of Hemingway to the Old Town streets, with its chunky wooden tables, ceiling fans and cigars. And, of course, its classic *mojito* cocktails (well, it did invent them, after all). The seafood is excellent, especially the zingy *gambas Punta Arenas* (prawns with chilli, lime and ginger), the cappuccinos are froth-topped caffeine bombs, and the pavement tables catch the sun at lunch time…perfecto.

CAFÉ-RESTAURANT METAMORPHIS

Map pp246-7   *Italian/Czech*

☎ 221 771 068; Týnský dvůr, Malá Štupartská 5;
mains 85-250Kč; ☼ 9am-1am; metro Náměstí Republiky

Metamorphis is the place to go if you want romantic outdoor dining (April to October) with a view of the Týn Church spires, but without the crowds and inflated prices of places on Old Town Square. The menu is mainly Italian, including good pizzas and pasta dishes, such as fusilli with salmon and caper sauce. It also offers excellent service and a good range of wines. There's a more formal restaurant (mains 150Kč to 400Kč) in the atmospheric Romanesque cellar downstairs.

CHEZ MARCEL Map pp246-7   *French*

☎ 222 315 676; Haštalská 12; mains 130-250Kč;
☼ 8am-1am Mon-Fri, 9am-1am Sat & Sun; tram 5, 8, 14

Chez Marcel is a French café-bar done up in yellow ochre and dark wood, and it's a popular hang-out for French expats – here you can you can smoke your Gitanes, sip *café au lait*, and order a *croque monsieur*. The menu also has good bistro dishes, such as rabbit with mustard sauce, and tagliatelle with salmon and basil.

CLEMENTINUM Map pp246-7   *French/Czech*

☎ 224 813 892; Platnéřská 9; mains 100-300Kč;
☼ 11am-11pm; metro Staroměstská

A minimalist look combining cream walls, burgundy floor and stainless-steel bar with colourful art and a few strategic pot plants complements the beautifully prepared dishes in this modern restaurant. Choose between the likes of *poulet Lyonnais* (chicken in a tart tomato and tarragon sauce) and *staročeská kachna* (crispy roast duck with red and white cabbage and herby dumplings).

DAHAB

Map pp246-7   *North African/Middle Eastern*

☎ 224 827 375; cnr Rybná & Haštalská; mains 125-245Kč;
☼ noon-1am; tram 5, 8, 14

Dahab is a shadowy *souq* scattered with rugs and cushions, where you can sit at a low table and sip Moroccan mint tea to an oriental-jazz-ragga soundtrack. The menu ranges from baklava and other sweet snacks to more substantial couscous, *tajine* (meat and vegetable stew), lamb and chicken dishes, and there are teas from India, China and Turkey. Or you can just kick back with a hookah (hubble-bubble pipe); 155Kč gets you a chunk of perfumed baccy that'll last around 45 minutes.

FRANCOUZSKÁ RESTAURACE

Map pp246-7   *French*

☎ 222 002 770; Obecní dům, náměstí Republiky 5;
mains 625-845Kč; ☼ noon-4pm & 6-11pm;
metro Náměstí Republiky

The 'French Restaurant' in the Obecní dům (p77) is a stunning Art Nouveau dining room offering gourmet dishes, like carpaccio of tuna with quail egg and caper-and-pistachio oil, *coq au vin bordelaise*, and pork tenderloin marinated in Provençal herbs. It's hugely popular with visitors, so book to avoid disappointment. The à la carte menu is complemented by a two-/three-course set lunch menu for 850/950Kč. It also has a café, **Kavárna Obecní** (below).

JALAPEÑOS Map pp246-7   *Mexican*

☎ 222 312 925; Valentínská 8; mains 145-245Kč;
☼ 11am-midnight Mon-Sat, 11.30am-midnight Sun;
metro Staroměstská

This is a cheerful, mock-adobe Tex-Mex place, tricked out in orange and ochre with basket-work chairs, sombreros and ceiling fans. It dishes up decent fajitas, burritos, tacos and nachos, which are accompanied by nicely chilled Sol and Corona beers.

KAVÁRNA OBECNÍ DŮM

Map pp246-7   *Café*

☎ 222 002 763; Obecní dům, náměstí Republiky 5;
mains 70-360Kč, breakfast 170Kč; ☼ 7.30am-11pm;
metro Náměstí Republiky

The spectacular café in the Obecní dům (p77) offers the opportunity to crunch your cornflakes or slurp you morning coffee amid an orgy of Art Nouveau splendour. The menu also extends to more filling fare, such as sandwiches, salads and cold meat and fish platters. Also see its restaurant counterpart **Francouzská restaurace** (above).

Patrons sitting outdoors at Kavárna Obecní dům (see opposite), Staré Město

KLUB ARCHITEKTŮ
Map pp252-3   *International*
☎ 224 401 214; Betlémské náměstí 5; mains 150-220Kč;
☯ 11.30am-11.30pm; metro Národní Třída
Part of a slightly smug complex dedicated to modern architecture, this place pulls in the crowds with its atmospheric stone-cellar dining room and inventive, reasonably priced dishes. As well as plenty of vegetarian options, it also offers a couple of (apparently) vegan dishes. Upstairs, the outdoor café by Betlémská kaple (p79) serves salads and light meals.

KOLKOVNA
Map pp246-7   *Czech*
☎ 224 819 701; V Kolkovně 8 ; mains 160-250Kč;
☯ 11am-midnight; metro Staroměstská
Owned and operated by the Pilsner Urquell brewery, Kolkovna is a stylish, modern take on the traditional Prague beer hall, with décor by top Czech designers and posh (but hearty) versions of classic Czech dishes, such as goulash, roast duck and roast pork, including the Czech favourite pork and dumplings. All washed down with exquisite Urquell beer, of course.

LA PROVENCE
Map pp246-7   *French*
☎ 257 535 050; Štupartská 9; mains 400-750Kč;
☯ noon-midnight; metro Náměstí Republiky
With its dark-wood beams, cushion-strewn benches, dim yellow lighting and shelves crammed with cooking implements, La Provence makes a good fist of passing itself off as a French country kitchen. The menu matches the décor, ranging from *bouillabaisse Marseillaise* to *cassoulet du Midi;* the wine list is respectable, and the service professional. In the evening, when candlelight and soft piano music add to the atmosphere, it's an ideal spot for a romantic *tête-à-tête.*

LE SAINT-JACQUES
Map pp246-7   *French*
☎ 222 322 685; Jakubská 4; mains 350-750Kč,
3-course menu 650Kč; ☯ noon-3pm & 6pm-midnight
Mon-Fri, 6pm-midnight Sat; metro Náměstí Republiky
This is an elegant and intimate, family-run restaurant with abundant white linen, lacy curtains and candlelit tables merging to create *une ambiance féerique* (a fairytale atmosphere), ideal for a special dinner. The menu includes all the French classics: oysters (in season), frogs' legs and snails to *coquilles* St Jacques, *tournedos* Rossini and Châteaubriand.

LES MOULES
Map pp246-7   *Belgian*
☎ 222 315 022; Pařížská 19; mains 275-395Kč;
☯ 8am-midnight; tram 17
This impressive, wood-panelled, Belgian-style brasserie serves up steaming pans of mussels in a range of sauces, from traditional *marinière* (white wine, cream and garlic) to Thai-style curry, steaks, pork ribs, *boeuf bourgignon* and lobster fresh from the *vivier* (live tank). The bar offers a selection of Belgian beers, including Leffe and Hoegaarden on tap.

ORANGE MOON
Map pp246-7   *Asian*
☎ 222 325 119; Rámová 5; mains 165-220Kč;
☯ 11.30am-11.30pm; tram 5, 8, 14
An oriental restaurant combining sunny colours upstairs and red-brick cellar downstairs (with Thai woodcarvings and sleekly modern fittings), Orange Moon offers friendly service and a menu of mouth-wateringly authentic Thai, Burmese and Indian dishes.

PRAVDA
Map pp246-7   *International*
☎ 222 326 203; Pařížská 17; mains 325-600Kč;
☯ 11am-midnight; metro Staroměstská
Cosmopolitan Pravda (Truth) occupies a prime corner location opposite the Staronová synagóga (p74) – to the right is the restaurant, all crisp linen and sparkling chandeliers, to the left the bar, in minimalist black and red leather, steel and glass. There are plenty of mirrors for the mobile phone–flaunting clientele to check themselves out in. The menu meanders

from Italy (*risotto nero*) to Thailand (an almost authentic *tom yam goong*) by way of Mexico (tacos). The menu also includes caviar, oysters and champagne, of course.

RASOI Map pp246-7 *Indian*
☎ 222 328 400; Dlouhá 13; mains 275-500Kč;
🕒 11.30am-3pm & 5-11.30pm Mon-Fri, 11.30am-11pm Sat & Sun; tram 5, 8, 14

Rasoi is in a cellar below the busy Bombay cocktail bar, with a refined, semiformal atmosphere, and friendly and attentive service. The excellent subcontinental cuisine draws an appreciative crowd of expat Brits, hankering after authentic tandoori chicken and *rogan josh*.

RED, HOT & BLUES
Map pp246-7 *American*
☎ 222 314 639; Jakubská 12; mains 140-390Kč;
🕒 9am-11pm, breakfast to 11.30am Mon-Fri, brunch to 4pm Sat & Sun; metro Náměstí Republiky

This is a New Orleans–style place with ceiling fans, a little courtyard, traditional jazz on the sound system, and live jazz or blues nightly. Pulling in the crowds with great nachos, burgers, burritos and shrimp creole, plus some wicked desserts, it also serves a range of Western breakfasts, including pancakes and maple syrup, and a full British fry-up. Its 'Home Run Special' (bacon, eggs, hash browns, pancakes and toast) will soak up the heaviest hangover, and lay a firm foundation for further debauchery.

RESTAURACE U MEDVÍDKŮ
Map pp252-3 *Czech*
☎ 224 211 916; Na Perštýně 5-7; mains 100-250Kč;
🕒 11.30am-11pm, bar to 3am Mon-Sat, to 1am Sun; metro Národní Třída

'At The Little Bear' is a touristy but authentic Czech beer hall and wine bar with a nonsmoking restaurant and a pleasant beer garden out back. The meaty Bohemian menu includes classics, such as pork knuckle, dumplings, roast wild boar and venison, but there are also half-a-dozen *bezmasa* (meat-free) dishes to cater for contemporary tastes.

REYKJAVÍK
Map pp246-7 *Seafood/International*
☎ 222 221 218; Karlova 20; mains 250-500Kč;
🕒 11am-midnight; metro Staroměstská

Reykjavík has an appealingly old-fashioned, bar-like dining room, all dark wood, gleaming brass, dim globes and candlelight, with musical instruments all over the place. Though billed

as an Icelandic restaurant – not too many of them around here – the menu is not noticeably Scandinavian, though the seafood is superb. As well as vaguely northern dishes, such as cod fillet with caramelised root vegetables and beetroot sauce, and salmon marinated in vodka, lime and rose pepper, there's succulent seared tuna, baked salmon in mushroom and tarragon sauce, and a selection of steaks and burgers.

SIAM-I-SAN Map pp246-7 *Thai*
☎ 224 814 099; Valentínská 11; mains 150-300Kč;
🕒 10am-midnight; metro Staroměstská

This unusual little restaurant is tucked away at the back of the designer boutique **Arzenal** (p168), in a colourful room designed by a local architect – dramatically lit-up bar, grey, orange and yellow décor, colourful print tablecloths, and arty glass *objets* from the neighbouring shop. Even the coffee-cups have a designer touch, with an asymmetric sway reminiscent of the Tančící dům or Dancing Building (p87). The cuisine is authentic Thai – probably the best Thai food in Prague – with a wide range of dishes, including many vegetarian ones.

STAROMĚSTSKÁ RESTAURACE
Map pp246-7 *Czech/International*
☎ 224 213 015; Staroměstské náměstí 19;
mains 100-300Kč; 🕒 9am-midnight Apr-Oct, 11am-midnight Nov-Mar; metro Staroměstská

This is easily the best-value place on Old Town Square. The meaty Czech and international menu is big, the food good and the service pleasant. If you're watching the pennies, it's cheaper to eat indoors than at the outside tables – food and beer prices on the terrace outside are up to 50% higher than those charged inside.

U BENEDIKTA Map pp246-7 *Czech*
☎ 222 311 527; Benediktská 11; mains 60-200Kč;
🕒 11am-11pm; tram 5, 8, 14

'At Benedict's' is a homely little place with rustic décor, done up to look like a traditional Czech country tavern. The menu of traditional Czech poultry, fish, steak and game dishes includes old Bohemian classics, such as *pečené vepřové koleno s horčicí a křenem* (roast pork knuckle with mustard and horseradish) and *pečená kachna s červeným a bílým zelím* (roast duck with red and white cabbage).

U MODRÉ KACHNIČKY II
Map pp246-7 *Czech*
☎ 224 213 418; Michalská 16; mains 280-450Kč;
🕒 11.30am-11.30pm; metro Můstek

The Staré Město branch of 'At the Blue Duckling' in **Malá Strana** (p118) is altogether grander in scale, more country house than hunting lodge, but with the same comfortably olde-worlde atmosphere and hearty Bohemian menu based around all things duck and game. We can recommend the medallions of venison with juniper berries flambéed in Borovička (juniper-flavoured spirit). Celebrity guests include ex-president Václav Havel and ex-German chancellor Helmut Kohl.

V ZÁTIŠÍ
Map pp252-3   *International/Modern Czech*
☎ 222 221 155, Liliová 1; mains 395-795Kč;
🕒 noon-3pm & 5.30-11pm; tram 17

'Still Life' is regularly voted one of Prague's most excellent restaurants, though local opinion holds that, service-wise, the restaurant has been resting on its laurels lately. Still, the food remains near-flawless, and it's one of the few top places that offers gourmet versions of traditional Czech dishes – for example the crispy roast duckling with red cabbage and herb dumplings is superb. The main dining room mimics a bright summer garden, with white wrought-iron chairs, sprigs of greenery and floral murals, but there are also more intimate nooks with warm ochre walls and candlelight. There's a two-course lunch menu, including one drink (495Kč), or you can lash out on the dinner menu (1075Kč; 600Kč extra for local wines to match the dishes). The vegetarian menu (all mains 395Kč) is original and interesting, offering dishes such as crispy goat's cheese with smoked tomatoes, pickled girolle mushrooms and pomegranate-juice dressing, including a 'cappuccino' of roasted butternut squash with radicchio ravioli and cinnamon cream.

Cheap Eats
AU GOURMAND Map pp246-7   *Café*
☎ 222 329 060; Dlouhá 10; snacks 60-100Kč;
🕒 9am-7pm; metro Staroměstská

Au Gourmand is a French-style patisserie and café gaily decked out in colourful 19th-century tiles and wrought-iron furniture. It offers baguettes, pastries and a joyously bewildering array of cakes and its caffè latte is among the best in town.

BEAS VEGETARIAN DHABA
Map pp246-7   *Vegetarian/Indian*
☎ 777 165 478; Týnská 19; meals 78-93Kč;
🕒 8.30am-8pm Mon-Fri, 10am-6pm Sat & Sun;
metro Náměstí Republiky

Tucked in a courtyard off Týnská, this stylish and friendly little place offers a vegetarian curry (changes daily) served with rice, salad, chutneys and raita; an extra 15Kč gets you a drink and dessert. It's good value, and a great place to meet Czechs of an alternative bent.

French pastries at au Gourmand (see above), Staré Město

BOHEMIA BAGEL Map pp246-7   *Café*

☎ 224 81 25 60; Masná 2; snacks 60-120Kč;
🕑 7am-midnight Mon-Fri, 8am-midnight Sat & Sun;
metro Náměstí Republiky

Another branch of the popular café in **Malá Strana** (See p120 for more information).

CAFÉ GASPAR KASPER

Map pp246-7   *Café*

☎ 222 326 843; Celetná 17; snacks 10-35Kč;
🕑 9am-midnight; metro Náměstí Republiky

Gaspar Kasper is a convivial, nonsmoking café-bar in an L-shaped nook overlooking the courtyard at the divadlo v Celetné (Celetná Theatre; p161), hidden away from the tourist crowds on nearby Celetná. Its arty credentials include lots of theatrical literature lying around for your perusal, and a naked scarlet lady with green nipples perched above the bar. The inexpensive snack menu includes sandwiches, potato pancakes and cheeseburgers.

COUNTRY LIFE Map pp246-7   *Vegetarian*

☎ 224 213 366; Melantrichova 15; mains 75-150Kč;
🕑 8.30am-7pm Mon-Thu, 8.30am-4pm Fri, 11am-6pm
Sun; metro Můstek

This place is an all-vegan cafeteria and sandwich bar offering inexpensive salads, sandwiches, pizzas, goulash, sunflower-seed burgers, soy drinks etc. This is Prague's best health-food shop and vegetarian eatery. This branch has plenty of seat-

Top Five Tables with A View

- **Hanavský pavilón** (p143)
- **La Perle de Prague** (p128)
- **Restaurace Televizní Věž** (p143)
- **Restaurant Nebozízek** (p119)
- **U Zlaté studně** (p120)

ing in the courtyard out back; the branch in **Jungmannova** (p129) is more a takeaway place, with only four small tables upstairs. Both get crowded at lunchtime, so go early or get some takeaway.

EBEL COFFEE HOUSE Map pp246-7   *Café*

☎ 222 222 018; Týn 2; snacks 60-80Kč;
🕑 9am-10pm; metro Náměstí Republiky

Superb coffee only a few minutes' walk from Old Town Square – if you can't face the watery instant served up with your hotel breakfast, head to Ebel for a jolt of full-fat, 98-octane arabica, accompanied by a yummy toasted bagel with herby cream cheese. This branch is in a top people-watching spot in a corner of the Týnský dvůr (p70); there's another **branch** (Map pp246-7; Řetězová 9), a block south of Karlova.

KÁVA.KÁVA.KÁVA Map pp252-3   *Café*

☎ 224 228 862; Platýz pasáž, Národní třída 37;
snacks 20-80Kč; 🕑 7am-10pm; metro Národní Třída

Shopping at Country Life (see above), Staré Město

Top Five Vegetarian Restaurants

- **Albio** (p127)
- **Beas Vegetarian Dhaba** (p125)
- **Café FX** (p144)
- **Country Life** (p126)
- **U Góvindy** (p130)

Tucked away in the peaceful Platýz courtyard, this American-owned café has some of the best coffee in town – the *grande cappuccino* is big enough to bathe in – and a selection of bagels, croissants, chocolate brownies, carrot cake and other goodies. There's also Internet access via desktop computers and a wireless hotspot. A second branch opened recently at Lidická 42 in **Smíchov** (p145).

PIVNICE RADEGAST Map pp246-7 Czech

☎ 222 328 237; Templová 2; mains 60-120Kč;
🕑 11am-12.30am; metro Náměstí Republiky

Don't expect smiles and flirtatious behaviour from the staff at this good old-fashioned Prague pub; do expect your food and beer to turn up quick smart, however, and do expect to pay a cover if you don't wave away the bread and sauces left on your table. This has to be the cheapest place in the neighbourhood, and offers all the Czech classics. It's always packed with locals, so it's doing something right.

NOVÉ MĚSTO

The New Town hosts an eclectic collection of eating places, with lots of cafés and traditional Czech pubs as well as a range of international restaurants. The main eating streets are Wenceslas Square and Na příkopě, lined with restaurants offering cuisines that crisscross the world from Italy to India and from Argentina to Japan, but there are also lots of less obvious eateries hidden in the back streets between Wenceslas Square and the river.

ALBIO Map pp246-7 Vegetarian

☎ 222 317 902; Truhlářská 18; mains 100-180Kč;
🕑 11.30am-10pm Mon-Fri; metro Náměstí Republiky

This friendly wholefood place is as bright and fresh as an Alpine morning, decked out in white pine, ropework and rustic timber. It sources all its food from local organic farmers and operates its own onsite bakery, shop and advice counter

offering tips on organic food and healthy eating. The menu includes vegetable sauté with ginger and black mushrooms, pasta with goat's-cheese sauce, spinach and walnuts, and a couple of fish dishes, such as baked trout fillet stuffed with hazel and cashew nuts.

BUFFALO BILL'S Map pp252-3 Tex-Mex

☎ 224 948 624; Vodičkova 9; mains 180-380Kč;
🕑 noon-midnight; tram 3, 9, 14, 24

Mosey on down to Bill's saloon for a touch of the Old West – dark wood panelling and brass rails, tall bar stools and bentwood chairs, wagon wheels, John Wayne posters and photos of Native Americans. The menu bulges with Tex-Mex classics, from nachos and enchiladas to fajitas and BBQ ribs, with jugs of frozen margaritas to slake that midsummer thirst.

DOWNTOWN CAFÉ PRAHA
Map pp252-3 Café

☎ 724 111 276; Jungmannovo náměstí 21; snacks 60-150Kč; 🕑 9am-11pm Mon-Thu, 9am-midnight Fri, 10am-midnight Sat, 10am-11pm Sun; metro Můstek

Gay-owned and -operated Downtown – does any other café have a 'wait-staff hair styled by…' credit in its menu? – is a cool little place with cakes and cocktails that are almost as gorgeous as the staff. It has a range of breakfast offerings, from a minimalist fruit salad and champagne, to jumbo baguette with ham and cheese, yogurt, muesli and fruit juice. Grab a seat on the shady terrace and lap up the eye candy.

EL GAUCHO Map pp252-3 Argentinean

☎ 221 629 410; Václavské náměstí 11; mains 350-950Kč;
🕑 11.30am-midnight; metro Můstek

El Gaucho is carnivore heaven – a big, rustic, rug-draped basement serving a range of charcoal-grilled steaks with *chimichuri* sauce (oil, garlic and herbs), and also – for the offally adventurous only – beef heart, liver, pickled tongue and all the other bits of a cow you just never knew what to do with. Watch out when the staff asks if you'd like a large beer – large here means a whole litre.

Top Five Nové Město

- **El Gaucho** (above)
- **Kogo** (p128)
- **La Perle de Prague** (p128)
- **Le Bistrot de Marlène** (p128)
- **Restaurant Pod Křídlem** (p128)

GRAND HOTEL EVROPA

Map pp252-3   *Café*

☎ 224 228 117; Václavské náměstí 25; mains 100-300Kč;
◷ 9.30am-11pm; metro Můstek

The Grand Hotel Evropa sports the most stylish café on Wenceslas Square, a fading museum of over-the-top Art Nouveau – despite second-rate cakes and coffee, and high tourist prices (including a music cover charge after 3pm on public holidays), it's almost always packed out.

KAVÁRNA IMPERIAL

Map pp246-7   *Café*

☎ 222 316 012; Na poříčí 15; mains 100-200Kč;
◷ 9am-11pm; metro Náměstí Republiky

The Habsburg-era Imperial has beautiful, turn-of-the-20th-century décor – oak parquet, ornate cream-and-mustard ceramic tiles, and a colourful mosaic ceiling. It's popular with locals and tourists alike, who gather for the live jazz on Friday and Saturday evenings. The food is a bit of an anticlimax, though, with a menu of unremarkable omelettes, curries and salads. Stick to the coffee and cakes, and watch out for the flying doughnuts.

KAVÁRNA SLAVIA

Map pp252-3   *Café*

☎ 224 220 957; Národní třída 1; mains 100-250Kč;
◷ 8am-midnight Mon-Fri, 9am-midnight Sat & Sun;
metro Národní Třída

The Slavia is the most famous of Prague's old cafés, a cherrywood and onyx shrine to Art Deco elegance, with polished limestone-topped tables and big windows overlooking the river. With the Národní divadlo (National Theatre; p157) across the street, it has been a celebrated literary meeting place since the 1920s, though these days there are more tourists than theatre people. The menu ranges from wicked cream cakes to fresh salads, pastas and vegetarian dishes; specialities of the house include spicy grilled pork knuckle with cabbage, and steak and chips.

KOGO Map pp246-7   *Italian*

☎ 221 451 259; Slovanský dům, Na příkopě 10;
pizzas 150-250Kč, mains 200-450Kč;
◷ 9am-midnight; metro Náměstí Republiky

Chic but child-friendly (high-chairs provided), Kogo is a stylish but laid-back place serving top-notch pizza, pasta, steak and seafood – the rich, tomatoey *zuppa di pesce* (fish soup) is delicious – and a good range of wines is available

by the glass. On summer evenings, tables filled with conversation and candlelight spill over into the leafy courtyard.

LA PERLE DE PRAGUE

Map pp252-3   *French*

☎ 221 984 160; Rašínovo nábřeží 80; mains 470-690Kč,
4-course menu 900Kč; ◷ noon-2pm & 7-10.30pm
Tue-Sat, 7-10.30pm Mon; metro Karlovo Náměstí

Located on the 7th floor of the spectacular Tančiči dům (p87), La Perle de Prague's dining room and outdoor terrace offer stunning views across the river to Malá Strana and Prague Castle. The cuisine is French, with the accent on seafood and meat dishes – nothing for veggies here – and the atmosphere is crisply formal. A six-course *menu dégustation* (for the whole table only) costs 2500Kč per head.

LE BISTROT DE MARLÈNE

Map pp260-1   *French*

☎ 224 921 853; Plavecká 4; mains 400-600Kč;
◷ noon-10.30pm; tram 3, 7, 16, 17, 21

One of Prague's top French restaurants, Marlène is elegant and formal, a favourite haunt of diplomats and business people. From *escargots* to crêpes suzettes by way of beef tenderloin, scallops or duck, the menu is classically French, and there's a respectable range of fine French wines to choose from.

MIYABI Map pp252-3   *Japanese*

☎ 296 233 102; Navrátilova 10; mains 100-300Kč;
◷ 11am-11pm Mon-Fri, noon-11pm Sat & Sun;
tram 3, 9, 14

Miyabi is a relaxed, café-style Japanese restaurant with minimalist décor and modern art on the walls – a refreshing change from more formal Japanese places. There's a small sushi menu, and main courses that include tempura (prawns and pieces of vegetables dipped in batter and deep-fried), *sakana no amiyaki* (grilled salmon marinated in saki) and *karaage* (grilled chicken marinated with ginger). The good-value set Japanese lunch is served from 11am to 2pm Monday to Friday.

RESTAURANT POD KŘÍDLEM

Map pp252-3   *Modern Czech*

☎ 224 951 741; cnr Voršilska & Národní třída;
mains 300-600Kč; ◷ 10am-midnight Mon-Fri,
11.30am-midnight Sat & Sun; tram 6, 9, 18, 21 22, 23

'Under the Wing' is a stylish restaurant and bar with Art Deco décor, bottle-juggling cocktail staff and live jazz at weekends. The menu gives a modern spin to traditional Czech dishes, and also includes succulent Aberdeen Angus steaks, roast rack of lamb, and various fish dishes. The staff will recommend some good Czech wine to match your meal.

TAJ MAHAL Map pp252-3 *Indian*
☎ 224 225 566; Škrétova 10; mains 195-295Kč; ⊗ 11.30am-11.30pm; metro Muzeum

Hldden away behind the Národní muzeum (see p84), the Taj Mahal is one of the city's better Indian restaurants, complete with live sitar-twanging in the evenings. There are separate smoking and nonsmoking dining rooms, and though the food is delicious the atmosphere can be a little formal and restrained. Indian Cobra and Kingfisher beers are available, and on weekdays there's a set lunch menu (11.30am to 3pm) for only 178Kč.

TITANIC STEAK HOUSE
Map pp252-3 *International*
☎ 296 226 282; Štěpánská 22; mains 90-190Kč; ⊗ 11am-11pm Mon-Sat, 3-11pm Sun; metro Karlovo Náměstí

Not the most propitious name for a business, you might think – perhaps the food goes down nicely. Whatever. The Titanic is a cool and quiet place with terracotta tiles, ochre walls and cane chairs, only a few minutes' walk from Wenceslas Square. It offers a range of salads and steaks with various sauces. And there's no sinking feeling when you get the bill…

Cheap Eats
BRANICKÝ SKLÍPEK Map pp252-3 *Czech*
U Purkmistra; ☎ 224 237 103; Vodičkova 2 ains 70-260Kč; ⊗ 9am-11pm Mon-Fri, 11am-11pm Sat & Sun; metro Můstek

This is a rough-and-ready, old-fashioned beer hall and restaurant, serving meaty, good-value Czech dishes and cheap beer. Menus and staff are Czech only, which puts off most tourists, but persevere – this is the real deal, and serves up the finest pork, dumplings and sauerkraut in town (look for *purkmistrová mísa* on the menu). Nonsmokers, beware – the atmosphere is smoky enough to kipper a truckload of herring.

BREAK CAFE Map pp252-3 *Café*
☎ 222 231 065; Štěpánská 32; mains 65-250Kč; ⊗ 8am-10pm Mon-Fri, 9.30am-7pm Sat, breakfast until 11am; metro Můstek

The Break Cafe is a buzzing American-style diner that serves big Western breakfasts – coffee and croissants, bacon and eggs, fresh fruit and yogurt. It also has hot chocolate to die for.

CAFÉ LOUVRE Map pp252-3 *Café*
☎ 224 930 949; 1st fl, Národní třída 2; mains 120-240Kč; ⊗ 8am-11pm Mon-Fri, 9am-11pm Sat & Sun; metro Národní Třída

Established in 1902, the Louvre is an elegant, French-style dining room with smart apron-and-waistcoated staff serving reasonably priced Czech lunch and supper dishes. It's famed for its big breakfast menu (5Kč to 120Kč), which offers Czech, British, French and American options. There's a billiard room next door and an art gallery on the first landing.

ČESKÁ HOSPODA V KRAKOVSKÉ
Map pp252-3 *Czech*
☎ 222 210 204; Krakovská 20; mains 65-155Kč; ⊗ 11am-11pm; metro Muzeum

Fuel up on pork, dumplings and *pivo* at this welcoming and convivial Bohemian pub, whose slightly smoky atmosphere is brightened by polished wood, chequered tablecloths and fresh flowers. Specialities of the house include *Staročeská pánev* (Old Bohemian platter – smoked pork, red cabbage, potato pancake and bread dumplings with ham) and *svíčková* (slices of beef in a cream sauce with bread dumpling and cranberries).

COUNTRY LIFE Map pp252-3 *Vegetarian*
☎ 257 044 419; Jungmannova 1; mains 75-150Kč; ⊗ 9.30am-6.30pm Mon-Sat, 10am-4pm Sun; tram 3, 9, 14, 24

Country Life is a cafeteria-style health-food restaurant with all-vegan food and buffet service – load up your plate, and pay by weight (that's right! you weigh in at the till). There are only four tables at this branch, which caters mainly to the takeaway trade – if you want a better chance of a seat, head for the branch in **Staré Město** (p126).

DOBRÁ ČAJOVNA Map pp252-3 *Tearoom*
☎ 224 231 480; Václavské náměstí 14; snacks 50-150Kč; ⊗ 10am-9.30pm Mon-Fri, 3-9.30pm Sat & Sun; metro Můstek

This tearoom, tucked up a passage off Wenceslas Square, is a little haven of oriental rugs and cushions away from the heaving crowds on the street. It takes its tea seriously here, and you can choose from a wide range of Chinese,

Indian, Sri Lankan, Japanese and Turkish teas. It also serves cakes and vegetarian snacks, such as hummus and pitta bread.

GLOBE BOOKSHOP & CAFÉ
Map pp252-3   *Café*
☎ 224 916 264; Pštrossova 6; mains 90-150Kč;
☽ 10am-midnight; metro Karlovo Náměstí
The Globe is a relaxed and popular expat hangout, sharing space with an excellent English-language **bookshop** (p173). There's a good range of filling veggie sandwiches and healthy snacks, including hummus and pitta bread and black-bean burritos, plus burgers, spag bog, nachos etc. It also has Internet access; see p217.

INSTITUT FRANÇAIS Map pp252-3   *Café*
☎ 224 216 630; Štěpánská 35; snacks 20-80Kč;
☽ 9am-6pm Mon-Fri; metro Karlovo Náměstí
Prague's French cultural institute has a nice little café at the back (go in the main entrance and bear right), frequented by French expats but open to all, where you can read the latest issues of *Le Monde* and *Le Figaro* over *café au lait* and a croissant or *pain au chocolat*.

JIHOČESKÁ RESTAURACE U ŠUMAVY
Map pp252-3   *Czech*
☎ 224 921 145; Štěpánská 3; mains 90-160Kč;
☽ 10am-11pm Mon-Fri, 11am-11pm Sat & Sun;
metro Karlovo Náměstí
'At the Šumava' is a smoky, wood-panelled Prague institution, serving tasty, traditional *jihočeská* (South Bohemian) dishes, such as roast duck and baked carp, and of course, pork and dumplings.

PIZZERIA KMOTRA Map pp252-3   *Pizza*
☎ 224 934 100; V jirchářích 12; pizza 70-160Kč;
☽ 11am-midnight; metro Národní Třída
One of Prague's oldest and best pizzerias, 'The Godmother' can rustle up more than two dozen varieties, from Margherita to Marinara, cooked in a genuine, wood-fired pizza oven. It gets busy after 8pm, so try to snag a table before then.

Top Five Breakfasts
- Bohemia Bagel (p120)
- Break Café (p129)
- Café Louvre (p129)
- Káva.Káva.Káva (p126)
- Red Hot & Blues (p124)

Top Five Pork & Dumplings
- Branický sklípek (p129)
- Česká hospoda V Krakovské (p129)
- Jihočeská restaurace u Šumavy (left below)
- Kolkovna (p123)
- Restaurace U medvídků (p124)

U GÓVINDY Map pp246-7   *Vegetarian*
☎ 224 816 631; Soukenická 27; mains 50-75Kč;
☽ 11am-5.30pm Mon-Sat; metro Náměstí Republiky
U Góvindy takes a 'donation' of around 50Kč, which gets you a generous, imaginatively seasoned set meal of vegetable soup, salad, rice, cake and herbal tea. It's run by Hare Krishnas, but nobody's proselytising.

OUTER SUBURBS
Eateries in the outer suburbs are for the most part less touristy and less expensive than their city-centre counterparts, catering to a clientele of local residents and expats. You'll find some great-value dining here, and have more chance of mixing with real Praguers.

Vyšehrad
JAMES COOK Map pp260-1   *International*
☎ 224 936 652; Oldřichova 14; mains 80-250Kč;
☽ 11am-11pm Mon-Fri, noon-11pm Sat & Sun;
tram 7, 18, 24
Terracotta tiles, earth-toned walls and timber beams draped with fishing nets and nautical knick-knacks lend a vaguely exotic air to this unassuming place in the shadow of Vyšehrad's citadel. The menu ranges across the globe, promising kangaroo steaks and roast shark as well as more familiar Asian, American and European dishes. There are no less than eight vegetarian options.

U VYŠEHRADSKÉ ROTUNDY
Map pp260-1   *Italian/Czech*
☎ 224 919 970; K rotundě 3; mains 80-200Kč;
☽ 11am-11pm; metro Vyšehrad
Situated just inside the Leopold Gate in the Vyšehrad citadel (p90), this quiet restaurant has a pleasant garden where you can enjoy beer and sausages while you gaze at Prague's oldest Romanesque rotunda. The menu offers a big list of pizzas, pastas and steak dishes.

(Continued on page 143)

1 Cobblestoned Thunovská at night (p64), Malá Strana
2 Festival in Old Town Square (p67), Staré Město **3** Charles Bridge Swing Band, Charles Bridge (p68) **4** Statues on Charles Bridge (p68)

1 Stained-glass windows, chrám sv Víta (p57), Prague Castle
2 Façade of Loreta (p61), Hradčany 3 Views to Prague Castle (p53) 4 Statue of praying saint and tower, kostel Nanebevzetí Panny Marie (p61), Hradčany

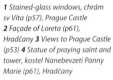

*1 People strolling, Petřín (p66), Malá Strana **2** Blue House on Zlatá Ulička (p59), Prague Castle **3** Baroque ceiling fresco, Teologiský sál, Strahovský klášter (p62), Hradčany **4** Changing of the guard (p55), Prague Castle*

1 *Detail of Astronomical Clock (p71), Staré Město* 2 *Marionettes on display* 3 *Front roofline of Staronová synagóga (p74), Josefov* 4 *Detail of front façade of Umělecko-průmyslové muzeum (p74), Josefov* 5 *Tombstones, Židovské hřbitovy (p96), Žižkov*

1 *Detail of Tančící dům (p87), Nové Město* 2 *Façade of Národní muzeum (p84), Nové Město* 3 *Bronzed statues in Pantheon (p84), Nové Město* 4 *Poster art work, Muchovo muzeum (p81), Nové Město*

1 French pastries on display
2 Interior reflection, au Gourmand
(p125), Staré Město 3 Stone cellar
interior, Klub architektů (p123),
Staré Město 4 Fresh fish on ice

1 Copper beer vats, Pivovarský dům (p152), Nové Město 2 Bar tender pouring wine 3 Bottles of Absinthe 4 Radost FX (p156), Vinohrady

1 People arriving at the Národní divadlo (p157), Nové Město
2 Cinema poster 3 Marionettes on display 4 Poster at Palace Cinemas (p162), Nové Město

1 Art stands on Charles Bridge (p68) 2 Soap display, Botanicus (p168), Staré Město 3 Wooden toys for sale, Sparkys (p171), Staré Město 4 Mannequin on Saská, Malá Stana

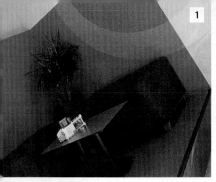

1 Café at Hotel Imperial (p188), Nové Město 2 Façade of Hotel Paříž (p184), Staré Město 3 Lobby of Hotel Josef (p183), Staré Město 4 Medieval suit of armour, Best Western Hotel Kampa (p180), Malá Strana

1 View of turrets, Konopiště Chateau (p199), Konopiště
2 Historic building, Kutná Hora (p204) 3 Theresienstadt Concentration Camp (p201), Terezín
4 Statue of Masaryk, Vlašský dvůr (p205), Kutná Hora

(Continued from page 130)

Holešovice & Bubeneč
HANAVSKÝ PAVILÓN
Map pp246-7   *Czech/International*

☎ 233 323 641; Letenské sady, Bubeneč;
mains 490-890Kč; ⏱ 11am-1am, terrace till 11pm;
tram 18, 22, 23

Perched on a terrace high above the river, this ornate, neobaroque pavilion dating from 1891 houses a smart restaurant with a postcard-perfect view of the Vltava bridges – from April to September you can dine on the outdoor terrace. There's a three-course set menu (from 490Kč) of Czech classics.

HONG KONG Map pp256-7   *Chinese*

☎ 233 376 209; Letenské náměstí 5, Holešovice;
mains 140-380Kč; ⏱ 11am-3pm & 6-11pm; tram 1,
8, 15, 25, 26

When you see members of the local Chinese community eating in a Chinese restaurant, you know it must be the real thing, and you'll see them eating in the Hong Kong. There's a wide-ranging menu (mostly Cantonese dishes) and a separate nonsmoking area, and the staff even have the compassion to turn the Canto-pop on the speakers down to a bearable level.

LA BODEGA FLAMENCA
Map pp256-7   *Spanish*

☎ 233 374 075; Šmeralová 5, Holešovice; tapas
35-70Kč, mains 90-120Kč; ⏱ noon-1am Sun-Thu,
noon-3am Fri & Sat; tram 1, 8, 15, 25, 26

La Bodega is an atmospheric, red-brick cellar painted and plastered to look like an adobe shack. It has the low buzz of conversation, Latin music turned down low, flickering candlelight and an authentically Spanish menu – its list of delicious tapas includes *tortilla español, chorizo al vino tinto* (chorizo sausage stewed in red wine) and *gambas pil-pil* (prawns in garlic and chilli). You can order a paella for four (790Kč), and the drinks list includes a selection of good Spanish wines and Mexican beers.

LA CRÊPERIE Map pp250-1   *French*

☎ 220 878 040; Janovského 6, Holešovice;
mains 50-100Kč; ⏱ 9am-11pm Mon-Sat, 9am-10pm
Sun; metro Vltavska

A cosy little basement with old pine tables and creaky wooden chairs, this place sports the Breton flag on the walls and authentic *galettes* (savoury pancakes) and nicely chilled Breton cider

on the menu. It's quiet in the afternoons – curl up with a good book and excellent coffee on the old sofa hidden under the stair – but it livens up later with a young and mostly local crowd.

RESTAURANT CORSO
Map pp256-7   *International*

☎ 220 806 541; Dukelských hrdinů 7, Holešovice;
mains 100-300Kč; ⏱ 9am-11pm; tram 5, 12, 17

The Corso has 'interesting' décor – something like a cross between Aztec and Art Nouveau on acid, with more painted glass and ceiling decoration than most of the city's churches. The food is good though – top-notch traditional Czech cuisine, steaks, pasta dishes and half a dozen decent veggie options, and the wine list offers more than 20 different Czech wines.

Žižkov
HANIL Map pp258-9   *Japanese/Korean*

☎ 222 715 867; Slavíkova 24; mains 200-400Kč;
⏱ 11am-2.30pm & 5.30-11pm Mon-Sat, 5.30-11pm
Sun; metro Jiří z Poděbrad

White walls, blond-wood lattice screens, paper lanterns and polished granite tables create a relaxed and informal setting. Here a mixed crowd of business people, locals and expats enjoy authentic Japanese and Korean cuisine without the fuss and formality of more expensive Japanese restaurants.

MAILSI Map pp258-9   *Pakistani*

☎ 290 059 706; Lipanská 1; mains 160-275Kč;
⏱ noon-3pm & 6-11pm; tram 5, 9, 26

Mailsi was Prague's first Pakistani restaurant, and is still one of the city's best for curry cuisine. The outside is inconspicuous, and it's only the qawwali music that gives it away. Service is courteous, the food authentic and prices modest for a speciality restaurant – though helpings are often small. Dishes with prawns are more expensive (up to 450Kč).

RESTAURACE TELEVIZNÍ VĚŽ
Map pp258-9   *Czech/International*

☎ 267 005 778; Mahlerovy sady 1; mains 200-450Kč;
⏱ 10am-11pm; metro Jiřího z Poděbrad

This restaurant sits 63m above ground level, halfway up the TV Tower in Žižkov (p96). It serves so-so Czech and international dishes at modest prices, but the main attraction is the view. You have to pay the normal admission fee (150/75Kč per adult/child) for the tower's sightseeing deck, but this gets you 10% off the menu prices.

Eating – Outer Suburbs

U RADNICE Map pp258-9 *Czech*
☎ 222 782 713; Havlíčkovo náměstí 7; mains 50-110Kč;
🕑 11am-11pm Mon-Fri, 11am-10pm Sat & Sun;
tram 5, 9, 26

'At the Town Hall' is a cheerful neighbourhood *pivnice* (with its own six- to 10-person sauna, no less!) where you can wash down generous helpings of Czech standards, such as pork and dumplings or roast duck with red cabbage, with excellent Budvar beer. The sauna needs to be booked in advance.

Vinohrady

AMBIENTE Map pp260-1 *International*
☎ 222 727 851; Mánesova 59; mains 140-240Kč;
🕑 11am-midnight Mon-Fri, 1pm-midnight Sat & Sun;
metro Jiřího z Poděbrad

The sunny yellow décor in this bright and cheerful restaurant is so bright you'll have to wear shades. The menu also dazzles, offering a huge range of salads (including Caesar, goat's cheese, roast veggies, avocado), tasty pasta dishes, barbecue ribs, and Tex-Mex fajitas, burritos and quesadillas.

CAFÉ FX Map pp252-3 *Vegetarian*
☎ 224 254 776; Bělehradská 120; mains 110-230Kč;
🕑 11.30am-2am; metro IP Pavlova

FX offers some of the best food in Prague in its price range – and it's all veggie. This hippy-chic restaurant at the entrance to the nightclub **Radost FX** (p156) – looking like a faded bordello with its draped chiffon, tasselled lampshades and distressed walls – comes up with imaginative dishes ranging from Indian-spiced aubergine with mint yogurt to Thai veggies in coconut sauce.

CAFFÉ KAABA Map pp258-9 *Café*
☎ 222 254 021; Mánesova 20; snacks 40-100Kč;
🕑 8am-10pm Mon-Sat; tram 11

Kaaba is a colourful little architect-designed café-bar with furniture and décor straight out of the 1959 Ideal Homes Exhibition – you half expect to see a Kenwood Chef sitting on the counter. It serves excellent coffee (made with freshly ground imported beans) and home-baked cakes, and has an extensive list of Czech and imported wines.

LA LAVANDE Map pp260-1 *French*
☎ 222 517 406; Zahřebská 24; mains 260-390Kč;
🕑 noon-3pm & 7-11pm Mon-Fri; metro Náměstí Míru

La Lavande is another classy French dining room that goes for the farmhouse kitchen feel, with lots of wooden beams, pot plants, and walls and shelves cluttered with homely bric-a-brac, but we prefer a table in the little garden terrace out back. Chef's specials include a warm salad of chicken livers cooked in Madeira, and roast veal in olive, black truffle

Dining alfresco

and mushroom sauce. There's a two-course business lunch available for just 99Kč.

MODRÁ ŘEKA Map pp252-3 *Yugoslavian*
☎ 222 251 601; Mánesova 13; mains 100-200Kč; 3-11pm Mon-Fri, 5-11pm Sat & Sun; tram 11
The 'Blue River' is a homely Yugoslav restaurant run by a couple who fled to Prague from Serbia in 1992. The deliciously spicy menu includes Yugoslav classics, such as *čevapčiči* (minced meat kebabs) with *adžvar* (roasted red-pepper puree), and *gibanica* (a rich cake filled with fruit, nuts and poppy seeds).

OSMIČKA Map pp252-3 *International*
☎ 222 826 211; Balbínova 8; mains 80-180Kč; 11am-11pm; metro Náměstí Míru
This is an underground eatery packed with lots of old paintings, mirrors and chandeliers, with a battered piano in the corner. It serves traditional Czech specialities with a modern 'fusion' twist, such as roast duck in Calvados (apple-brandy sauce), as well as pasta dishes, steak and fish.

TAI WAN Map pp260-1 *Chinese*
☎ 224 247 549; Vinohradská 48; mains 100-150Kč; 11am-11pm; metro Náměstí Míru
Tai Wan is a great little no-frills Chinese restaurant, with authentic Taiwanese cuisine and good-value set lunch menus (49Kč to 79Kč) from 11am to 3pm on weekdays.

TIGER TIGER Map pp260-1 *Thai*
☎ 222 512 048; Anny Letenské 5; mains 175-275Kč; 11.30am-11pm Mon-Fri, 5-11pm Sat & Sun; metro Náměstí Míru
Tiger Tiger has an dapper little dining room in cheerful yellow with smart navy upholstery, a restrained and elegant setting for some of the city's best Thai cuisine. Authentic specialities include *tom yam kung* (hot and sour prawn soup), *som tam* (spicy carrot salad) and *kaeng ped gai* (chicken in red curry sauce); symbols on the menu rate the chilli levels.

Smíchov

IL GIARDINO Map pp242-3 *Mediterranean*
☎ 257 154 262; Mozartová 1; mains 400-900Kč; noon-11pm; tram 4, 7, 9, 10
Il Giardino is a smart, modern restaurant – think tortellini and seared tuna – in the smart, modern Mövenpick Hotel. Perched on top of a high-rise, its rooftop terrace commands a great view across the city towards Vyšehrad, while

the rustic interior with its wooden beams, marble columns and murals of Italian landscapes makes a cosy retreat for a romantic dinner.

KÁVA.KÁVA.KÁVA Map pp260-1 *Café*
☎ 257 314 277; Lidická 42; snacks 20-80Kč; 7am-10pm; metro Anděl
This is the new branch of the popular café in **Staré Město** (p126).

NA VERANDÁCH Map pp242-3 *Czech*
☎ 257 191 200; Nádražní 84; mains 75-150Kč; 11am-midnight; metro Anděl
This big, brassy, modern bar and restaurant is part of Smíchov's Staropramen brewery, so there's no shortage of quality beer (there are five varieties of Staropramen on tap) to wash down their traditional Czech pub grub such as *utopenec* (pickled sausage), *guláš* and *vepřové koleno* (pork knuckle). It also offers overseas classics, such as fish and chips, and buffalo wings.

PIZZERIA CORLEONE
Map pp242-3 *Italian*
☎ 251 511 244; Na Bělidle 42; mains 70-130Kč; 11am-11pm; metro Anděl
This is a popular and lively neighbourhood restaurant, with a wood-fired pizza oven and a taste for the art of Jack Vettriano, whose paintings are reproduced in several large murals.

Dejvice

HAVELI Map p255 *Indian*
☎ 233 344 800; Dejvická 6; mains 200-300Kč; 11am-11pm; metro Hradčanská
Indian music and a waft of incense will guide you towards this popular and authentic curry restaurant with tables split between an informal street-level bar and a cosy red-brick and whitewash cellar. The onion *bhaji* is light and crisp, the naan bread soft and buttery, and the curry dishes nicely spiced.

PIZZERIA GROSSETO Map p255 *Italian*
☎ 233 342 694; Jugoslávských partyzánů 8; mains 70-125Kč; 11.30am-11pm; metro Dejvická
This is a lively and friendly pizzeria that pulls in crowds of students from the nearby university campus with its genuine, wood-fired pizza oven and Moravian Radegast beer. As well as a huge choice of tasty pizza varieties, the menu also offers salads, pastas, risotto, roast chicken, steak, and grilled salmon. The main dining room, where you can watch the pizza chefs twirling

their dough, is complemented by an attractive timber-decked conservatory out back.

RESTAURACE SOKOLOVNA

Map p255 *Czech*

☎ 224 317 834; Dejvická 2; mains 50-70Kč;
🕙 10.30am-10.30pm Mon-Fri, 11.30am-10.30pm Sat & Sun; metro Hradčanská

Sokolovna is a warren of small, smoky, wood-panelled rooms frequented by a regular crowd of local workers tucking into hearty helpings of pork and dumplings – you won't find cheaper nosh than this in the city.

RESTAURANT U CEDRU

Map pp246-7 *Lebanese*

☎ 233 342 974; Národní obrany 27; mains 200-300Kč;
🕙 11am-11pm; metro Dejvická

'At the Cedar' is a welcoming Lebanese restaurant offering tasty *mezzes* (appetisers) such as *baba ganoush* (smoky aubergine and garlic puree), tabouleh salad and stuffed vine leaves. Rather than agonise over the selection on the menu, you can order a spread of 10 *mezzes* (775Kč), which the chef will select for you – a great start to dinner, or a lunch in itself.

Entertainment

Entertainment

Across the spectrum, from ballet to blues, jazz to rock, theatre to tennis, there's a bewildering range of entertainment on offer in this eclectic city. Prague is now as much a European centre for jazz, rock and hip-hop as it is for classical music. The big draw, however, is still the Prague Spring (Pražské jaro; p157) festival of classical music and opera.

For reviews, day-by-day listings and an up-to-the-minute directory of venues, consult the 'Night & Day' section of the weekly *Prague Post* (www.praguepost.cz). Monthly listings booklets include *Culture in Prague* and the Czech-language *Přehled*, available from PIS offices (see p222 for contact details). The fortnightly pamphlet *Do města – Downtown*, available for free at bars and restaurants, lists clubs, galleries, cinemas and theatre events. For online listings and reviews, check out www.prague.tv. It's also worth keeping an eye on the posters and bulletin boards around town. *Houser* is a free weekly mag with film, theatre and club listings, available in cinemas, pubs and clubs. It's in Czech only, but the listings are easily understood.

Tickets & Reservations

For classical music, opera, ballet, theatre and some rock concerts – even with the most thoroughly 'sold-out' events – you can often find a ticket or two on sale at the theatre's box office a half-hour or so before show time.

If you want to be sure of a seat, Prague is awash with ticket agencies (see the boxed text on p149). Their advantage is convenience: most are computerised, quick, and accept credit cards. Their drawback is a probable 10% to 15% mark-up. Touts will sell tickets at the door, but avoid them unless all other avenues have been exhausted.

Many venues have discounts for students and sometimes for the disabled. Most performances have a certain number of tickets set aside for foreigners. For rock and jazz clubs you can turn up at the door, but advance bookings are recommended for big names.

Live music at one of Prague's jazz venues

Buying Tickets

The 'wholesalers' with the largest agency networks are Bohemia Ticket International (BTI), FOK and Ticketpro; the others probably get their tickets from them.

Bohemia Ticket International (BIT; Map pp246-7; ☎ 224 227 832; www.ticketsbti.cz; Malé náměstí 13, Staré Město; ☼ 9am-5pm Mon-Fri, 9am-2pm Sat) BIT provides tickets for all kinds of events. Tickets are also available at another **branch** (Map pp246-7; ☎ 224 227 832; Na příkopě 16, Nové Město; ☼ 10am-7pm Mon-Fri, to 5pm Sat, to 3pm Sun).

FOK Box Office (Map pp246-7; ☎ 222 002 336; U obecního domu 2, Staré Město; ☼ 10am-6pm Mon-Fri) For classical concert tickets.

Ticketcentrum (Map pp246-7; Rytířská 31, Staré Město; ☼ 8.30am-8.30pm) Walk-in centre for all kinds of tickets; branch of Ticketpro.

Ticketpro (Map pp246-7; ☎ 296 329 999; www.ticketpro.cz; Salvátorská 10, Staré Město; ☼ 9am-12.30pm & 1-5.15pm Mon-Fri) Tickets are available here for all kinds of events. It also has branches in PIS offices (see p222 for contact details) and in many other places.

Ticketpro Melantrich (Map pp252-3; ☎ 224 228 455; Pasáž Rokoko, Václavské náměstí 36, Nové Město; ☼ 9.30am-1pm & 2-6pm Mon-Fri) This is a good agency for rock-concert tickets.

DRINKING

Bars come and go with alarming speed in Prague, and trendspotters are forever flocking to the latest 'in' place only to desert it as soon as it becomes mainstream. There's only space here to list the best of the long-term survivors, along with a few of the newer places; pick up a listings magazine to check what the latest 'in' places are (see p148).

Most pubs serve beer snacks; some of the most popular are *utopenci* (sliced sausage pickled in vinegar with onion), *topinky* (fried toast) and, of course, the famous *Pražská šunka* (Prague ham) with gherkin. Many of the following places also serve more substantial meals.

HRADČANY

PIVNICE U ČERNÉHO VOLA Map pp244-5
☎ 220 513 481; Loretánské náměstí 1; ☼ 10am-10pm; tram 22, 23

The 'Black Ox' is an authentic and surprisingly cheap beer hall barely a bottle's throw from the tourist-thronged Loreta. Its lip-smackingly delicious draught beer, Velkopopovický Kozel, comes from a small town southeast of Prague, and is one of the country's favourite brews.

MALÁ STRANA

BAZAAR Map pp244-5
☎ 257 535 050; Nerudova 40; ☼ noon-11pm, music bar 10pm-2am Wed-Sat; tram 12, 20, 22, 23

It's possible we dreamed this place. Nestled under the castle wall, Bazaar is a multifloored warren of dim candlelit nooks and crannies, Arabian nights'–style canopied beds complete with hookahs, barstools in the form of swings and a sweeping roof-top garden with a view over the rooftops of Malá Strana. The drinks aren't cheap – a small *pivo* will set you back 40Kč – but the atmosphere more than makes up for it.

BLUE LIGHT Map pp244-5
☎ 257 533 126; Josefská 1; ☼ 6pm-3am; tram 12, 20, 22, 23

The Blue Light is an appropriately dingy and atmospheric jazz cavern where you can enjoy a relaxed drink and cast an eye over the vintage posters and records that deck the walls. Sadly the background jazz music comes recorded rather than live.

HOSTINEC U KOCOURA Map pp244-5
☎ 257 530 107; Nerudova 2; ☼ 11am-11pm; tram 12, 20, 22, 23

'The Tomcat' is a long-established pub, still enjoying its reputation as a former favourite of ex-president Havel, and still managing to pull in a mostly Czech crowd despite being in the heart of tourist-ville. It has good cheap beer for this part of town – 24.50Kč for 0.5L of draught Budvar.

JO'S BAR Map pp244-5
☎ 257 533 342; Malostranské náměstí 7; mains 100-150Kč; ☼ 11am-2am; tram 12, 20, 22, 23

Top Five Traditional Pubs
- Hostinec U kocoura (above)
- Pivnice U Černého vola (left)
- Pivovarský dům (p152)
- U Vystřeleného oka (p153)
- U Zlatého Tygra (p152)

Jo's is a cheerful bar serving foaming beers (plus sandwiches, salads, burgers and Tex-Mex dishes) to crowds of young expats and backpackers. In the heaving club downstairs (no cover charge), the drinks keep flowing till 5am (see p155 for details).

KLUB ÚJEZD Map pp250-1
☎ 257 316 537; Újezd 18;
⏱ 11am-4am; tram 12, 20, 22, 23
A former live-rock venue tamed by noise complaints, Klub Újezd remains an agreeably grungy bar, with a wide range of mood music (harder sounds downstairs, mellower upstairs), a retro underground setting and a youngish crowd.

TLUSTÁ MYŠ Map pp250-1
☎ 605 282 506; Všehrdova 19;
⏱ 11am-midnight Mon-Thu, 2pm-1am Fri & Sat, 3-11pm Sun; tram 12, 20, 22, 23
The subterranean 'Fat Mouse' is very much a local pub, with a couple of small rooms filled with long tables for those convivial evening drinking sessions. The extensive list of inventive cocktails may keep you longer than anticipated, and there are small displays of local art to admire over a quiet afternoon drink.

U KRÁLE BRABANTSKÉHO Map pp244-5
☎ 257 310 929; Thunovská 15;
⏱ noon-11pm; tram 12, 20, 22, 23
'The King of Brabant', around the corner from Hostinec U kocoura, is another long-established, cramped and crowded Gothic beer hall filled with tables awash in suds and laughter, and Pilsner Urquell on draught for only 26Kč per 0.5L.

U MALÉHO GLENA Map pp244-5
☎ 290 003 967; www.malyglen.cz; Karmelitská 23;
⏱ 10am-2am; tram 12, 20, 22, 23
Little Glen's is a popular expat bar and hangout for local musicians (with Guinness on tap), as well as a café, restaurant and jazz club (see p159). You can chill out over a late breakfast of bagels and coffee, or relax with a beer in the afternoon, but in the evenings the place really starts to rock.

ZANZI BAR Map pp244-5
☎ 602 780 076; cnr Lázeňská & Saská; ⏱ 5pm-3am; tram 12, 20, 22, 23
Zanzi Bar is a little haven of cool jazz and superb cocktails tucked away in the medieval lanes beside Charles Bridge. The drinks list is the size of a

Jeffrey Archer novel, but far more interesting – the house cocktail is a refreshing mix of light rum, apricot brandy, orange curacao, lime juice, almond syrup and orange juice.

STARÉ MĚSTO

BAMBUS Map pp246-7
☎ 224 828 110; Benediktská 12; ⏱ 9am-1am Mon-Fri, 11am-2am Sat, 11am-11pm Sun; metro Náměstí Republiky
Bambus is a laid-back café-bar whose bamboo chairs are filled by a mixed crowd of young locals, including backpackers who have found their way from nearby hostels.

BARFLY Map pp252-3
☎ 222 222 141; U Dobřenských 3; ⏱ noon-2am Mon-Sat, till midnight Sun; tram 17
Barfly is a snug cellar bar with a laid-back ambience, obviously established by a fan of the famously hard-drinking American novelist Charles Bukowski (Barfly is the title of his autobiography, and there are pics of him behind the bar). Perfect for an evening drink with someone special, it has a particularly good selection of Czech wines, and serves a menu of pasta and steak dishes.

BAROCK Map pp246-7
☎ 222 329 221; Pařížská 24; ⏱ 8.30am-1am; metro Staroměstská
This is a place to see and be seen – there are photos on the walls of famous Czech fashion models, while the models themselves can often be seen air-kissing their way through the crowd at the bar. Big mirrors let you check out your new hairstyle while keeping one eye on the beautiful people coming and going in the background.

BLATOUCH Map pp246-7
☎ 222 328 643; Vězeňská 4; ⏱ 11am-midnight Mon-Thu, to 2am Fri, 1pm-2am Sat, 1pm-midnight Sun; tram 17
Blatouch is a pleasantly relaxed literary hangout, with a long, narrow bar lined with antique bookcases and Edward Hopper prints, and a tiny garden courtyard at the back. The perfect place to read the papers over an afternoon glass of wine.

BLOODY FREDDY'S BAR Map pp252-3
☎ 224 223 312; Vejvodova 6; ⏱ 4pm-2am; metro Národní Třída

This is a trendy little bar hidden away on a side street off Michalská, popular with both backpackers and local youth alike. There's a long menu of powerful cocktails on offer, including some curious absinthe concoctions, and a selection of salads and sandwiches to munch while watching whatever happens to be on Eurosport.

CHATEAU Map pp246-7
**☎ 222 326 242; cnr Malá Štupartská & Jakubská;
⏰ noon-5am; metro Náměstí Tříída**
Chateau is a very red, British-style pub where the cheap beer never fails to pull in a big crowd of expat regulars, Czechs and tourists; by mid-evening it's often standing-room only. Everything in this pointedly cool bar is back-lit, including the smiles of the clientele; black T-shirt compulsory.

FRIENDS Map pp252-3
**☎ 224 236 772; Bartolomějská 11; ⏰ 4pm-5am;
metro Národní Tříída**
Recently re-opened in a new venue, Friends is a welcoming gay music-and-video bar serving excellent coffee and wine. It's a good spot to sit back with a drink and check out the crowd, or join in the party spirit on assorted theme nights, which range from Czech music and movies to hits of the 60s. DJs add their own spin from 10pm onwards.

JAMES JOYCE Map pp246-7
**☎ 224 248 793; Liliová 10; ⏰ 11am-12.30am;
metro Staroměstská**
The James Joyce is a small but often raucous Irish pub in the dům U krále Jiřího (p182), full of good-timers knocking back expensive Guinness (95Kč for 0.4L). The pub serves a tasty and filling Irish stew and beef-and-Guinness hotpot.

KONVIKT PUB Map pp252-3
**☎ 224 232 427; Bartolomějská 11; mains 50-100Kč;
⏰ 9am-1am Mon-Fri, noon-1am Sat & Sun;
metro Národní Tříída**
The Konvikt – set on a street filled with police offices – is a down-to-earth Czech bar and café serving good beer and solid Bohemian fare, such as smoked pork, sauerkraut and dumplings – excellent value.

KOZIČKA Map pp246-7
**☎ 224 818 308; Kozí 1; ⏰ noon-4am Mon-Fri,
6pm-4am Sat & Sun; metro Staroměstská**

The 'Little Goat' is a permanently buzzing, red-brick basement bar with taped mainstream music, a young clientele and standing-room only after midnight. There's Krušovice on tap at 30Kč per 0.5L, and a food menu that includes good steaks and mixed grills.

MOLLY MALONE'S Map pp246-7
**☎ 224 818 851; U obecního dvora 4;
⏰ 4pm-1am Mon-Thu, 4pm-2am Fri, 11am-2am Sat,
11am-1am Sun; metro Náměstí Republiky**
Molly's is a convivial Irish bar serving not only draught Guinness (80Kč for 0.4L) but also an excellent menu of high-cholesterol comfort food – this is the place to come for a great bacon sandwich, *boxty* (Irish potato pancake), bangers and mash, or a bacon-and-egg fry-up, even at midnight.

O'CHE'S CUBAN-IRISH BAR Map pp246-7
**☎ 222 221 178; Liliová 14; ⏰ 10am-1am;
metro Staroměstská**
Yes, you read that correctly – O'Che's is an expat bar that juxtaposes Cuban flags and images of Che Guevara with Guinness taps and dartboards. The only revolutionary spirit you're likely to find, however, is on the shelves behind the bar – there are more than 75 varieties to choose from. The bar also caters to sports fans with a large-screen TV.

O'Che's Cuban-Irish Bar (see above)

U ZLATÉHO TYGRA Map pp246-7

☎ 222 221 111; Husova 17; ⏰ 3-11pm; metro Staroměstská

The 'Golden Tiger' is one of the few old-town drinking holes that has hung on to its soul – and its low prices (26Kč per 0.5L of Pilsner Urquell). It was novelist Bohumil Hrabal's favourite hostelry – there are photos of him on the walls – and the place that Václav Havel took fellow president Bill Clinton in 1994 to show him a real Czech pub.

NOVÉ MĚSTO

BOULDER BAR Map pp252-3

☎ 222 231 244; V Jámě 6; ⏰ 10am-midnight Mon-Fri, noon-midnight Sat & Sun; metro Muzeum

This unlikely enclave of mountain machismo is hidden away in a Nové Město side street, with skis, skates, snowboards and alpine photography on the walls, and lots of little metal figures clambering all over the bar. If it all makes you feel like climbing the walls, then you can – the two circular windows allow a peek into the climbing wall at the back (60Kč for two hours), where you can work on the overhangs before working on your hangover.

JÁGR'S SPORT BAR Map pp252-3

☎ 224 032 481; Palác Blaník, Václavské náměstí 56; ⏰ 11am-midnight; metro Muzeum

Owned by NHL ice-hockey superstar Jaromír Jágr – mainstay of the Pittsburgh Penguins in the '90s, and winner of Olympic gold with the Czech national team in '98 – this cavernous sports bar offers fans four large projection screens and no fewer than 40 TVs, so you needn't miss a moment of that important match. Get in early – it fills up quickly before big events.

JÁMA Map pp252-3

☎ 224 222 383; V jámě 7; ⏰ 11am-1am; metro Muzeum

The Hollow, southeast off Vodičkova, is a popular American expat bar and restaurant, with a leafy little beer garden out back shaded by lime and walnut trees. The clientele includes a mix of expats, tourists and young Praguers, and the beer is medium priced at 42Kč for 0.5L of Pilsner Urquell.

NOVOMĚSTSKÝ PIVOVAR Map pp252-3

☎ 224 233 533; Vodičkova 20; 8am-11.30pm Mon-Fri, 11.30am-11.30pm Sat, noon-10pm Sun; tram 3, 9, 14, 24

Like U Fleků (right), the Novoměstský pivovar (New Town Brewery) brews its own beer on the premises. It also suffers from coach-party invasions, but it's considerably cheaper (30Kč for 0.5L), and the food is not only edible but actually rather good, including a delicious *svíčková* (beef and dumplings with cream sauce).

PIVOVARSKÝ DŮM Map pp252-3

☎ 296 216 666; cnr Ječná & Lipová; ⏰ 11am-11pm; metro Karlovo Náměstí

This is the best of Prague's microbreweries – while the tourists flock to U Fleků (below), locals gather here to sample the classic Czech lager (in light, dark and mixed varieties; 28.50Kč per 0.5L) that is produced on the premises, as well as wheat beer and a range of flavoured beers (including coffee, banana and cherry). You can even buy a 5L keg to take away. The pub itself is a pleasant place to linger, decked out with polished copper vats and brewing implements and smelling faintly of malt and hops.

ROCKY O'REILLYS Map pp252-3

☎ 222 231 060; Štěpánská 32; ⏰ 10am-1am; metro Muzeum

No prizes for guessing this is an Irish bar – Guinness on tap, and pictures of James Joyce and George Bernard Shaw on the walls. It pulls in a boisterous crowd of British, Irish and American expats and tourists, with live sports on TV and a separate restaurant serving good-value pub grub.

U FLEKŮ Map pp252-3

☎ 224 934 019; Křemencová 11; ⏰ 9am-11pm; metro Karlovo Náměstí

A festive warren of drinking and dining rooms, U Fleků is a Prague institution, though increasingly clogged with tour groups high on oompah music and the tavern's home-brewed, 13° black beer (49Kč for 0.4L) – see the boxed text on p154 for more information on Czech beer. Purists grumble but go along anyway because everybody has a good time, though tourist prices have nudged out many locals. You might still find an empty seat at 7pm on a weekday, but probably not.

VELRYBA Map pp252-3

☎ 224 912 484; Opatovická 24; ⏰ 11am-midnight Sat-Thu, 11am-2am Fri; metro Národní Třída

The 'Whale' is an arty café-bar – quiet enough to have a real conversation – with vegetarian-friendly snacks, a smoky back room and a basement art gallery. A clientele of young Czechs and plenty of backpackers keep the place jumping.

Beer Gardens

On a hot summer day, what could be finer than sitting outdoors with a chilled glass of Bohemia's finest beer, admiring a view over river or city. Many of Prague's pubs have small beer gardens or courtyards, but the following summer-only spots are truly out in the open air. Opening times are weather-dependent, but typically noon to midnight June to September.

Letenské sady (Map pp256-7; Letná Gardens, Bubeneč) This slew of rickety benches and tables spread along a dusty scarp beneath the trees at the eastern end of Letná Gardens enjoys one of the city's most stunning views, looking across the river to the spires of Staré Město, and southwest to Malá Strana. Also see p92 for more information.

Letní bar (Map pp250-1; Střelecký ostrov, Malá Strana) Basically a shack serving Budvar in plastic cups, this is the place to pick up a beer before hitting the little beach at the northern end of the island. See p65 for other details.

Park Café (Map pp258-9; Riegrovy sady, Vinohrady) Perched on top of precipitous Riegrovy Park, this bustling beer garden has awesome night-time views of the castle, a big screen showing sport and plenty of chances to play table football and table hockey with half of Prague.

ZLATÁ HVĚZDA Map pp252-3
☎ 296 222 292; Ve smečkách 12; ☽ noon-2am Tue-Thu, to 4.30am Fri & Sat, till midnight Mon; metro Muzeum

Pilsner Urquell at 35Kč per 0.5L, big pizzas and a couple of large-screen TVs make the 'Golden Star' a popular port of call for sports fans. It has a bit more character than most sports bars, and there's a more intimate brick-lined cellar bar down below.

OUTER SUBURBS
Žižkov
HAPU Map pp258-9
☎ 222 720 158; Orlická 8; ☽ 6pm-2am; metro Jiřího z Poděbrad

Low-ceilinged, plush-chaired, dimly lit and immensely cool, Hapu is almost in Vinohrady – geographically and socially on the opposite side of Žižkov from U Vystřeleného oka (right). It's a tiny, smoky bar with a comprehensive cocktail list and friendly staff who wield a mean shaker – and all the fruit juice in those mixed drinks is freshly squeezed.

PIANO BAR Map pp258-9
☎ 222 727 496; Milešovská 10; ☽ 5pm-midnight or later; metro Jiřího z Poděbrad

The Piano Bar is a homely little cellar bar cluttered with junk and bric-a-brac, and yes, there is a piano where you can play chopsticks until someone raps a pool cue across your knuckles. It's a stalwart of the Prague gay scene, frequented mainly by locals, a good spot for a quiet drink and a chat.

U VYSTŘELENÉHO OKA Map pp258-9
☎ 226 278 714; U Božích bojovníků 3; ☽ 4.30pm-1am Mon-Sat; bus 133, 207

You've got to love a pub that has vinyl forehead rests on the wall above the gents' urinals. 'The Shot-Out Eye' – the name pays homage to the one-eyed Hussite hero atop the hill behind the pub (see p94) – is a bohemian (with a small 'b') hostelry with a raucous beer garden whose cheap food and beer pulls in a typically heterogeneous Žižkov crowd, ranging from art students and writers to lost backpackers and tattooed bikers.

Vinohrady
BOND'S COCKTAIL BAR Map pp258-9
☎ 222 733 871; Polská 7; ☽ 5pm-2am Mon-Sat, 5pm-midnight Sun; metro Jiřího z Poděbrad

Operating under the motto 'Mixing Enjoy and Girls', Bond's must be Prague's most self-consciously hip cocktail bar. With stylishly uncomfortable leather seating, Walther PPK motifs, and plenty of backlit Bond-girl silhouettes, it serves cocktails to American expats taking a meeting and local hipsters SMSing like their lives depend on it.

CLUB STELLA Map pp260-1
☎ 224 257 869; Lužická 10; ☽ 8pm-5am; tram 4, 22, 23

Club Stella is an intimate, candlelit café-bar that seems to be the first place everyone recommends when you ask about gay bars in Prague. There's a long narrow bar where you can just squeeze onto a bar stool, and an armchair-filled lounge that looks like somebody's living room. Ring the doorbell to get in.

Pivo

Pivo is Czech for beer, and the Czech Lands, including Prague, have been famous for centuries as one of the finest producers of the amber liquid. The first-ever historical documentation of beer-making and hop-growing goes back to 1088 and the founding charter of Opatovice monastery in East Bohemia. Apparently the taste of beer was quite different in those days and by today's standards it would be considered undrinkable. It was not until 1842 that a smart group of Plzeň brewers pooled their experience, installed 'modern' technology and founded a single municipal brewery, with spectacular results. Their golden lager beer, labelled Plzeňský Prazdroj (*prazdroj* is old Czech for 'the original source') – Pilsner Urquell in German – is now one of the world's best, and most imitated, beers.

The Czech Republic has the largest per capita beer consumption (158L per head of population) of any country in the world, easily beating both Germany and Australia. This means, of course, that the 'average' adult drinks about 330L per year.

The world famous Pilsner Urquell and Budvar (Budweiser) beers are brewed in the smaller, provincial towns of the Czech Republic, but Prague has its own brews. The largest concern is Prague Breweries, which operates the Staropramen and Braník breweries in Prague, and the Ostravar brewery in Ostrava (in Northern Moravia). Its brands include the traditional Staropramen lager, and the newer Kelt stout and Velvet bitter, and account for around 13% of the domestic beer market. Prague Breweries is owned by the Belgian company Interbrew, the second-largest brewery in the world after Anheuser Busch.

There are several microbreweries in Prague – beer halls that brew their own beer on the premises. The most famous, and probably the oldest, is **U Fleků** (p152), a Prague institution. Though very touristy its 13° black beer is still excellent. The newer **Novoměstský pivovar** (p152) is another place that brews its own beer but is cheaper all-round. The **Pivovarský dům** (p152) produces some very unusual flavoured beers, as well as classic Czech lager.

Czech beers are predominantly bottom-fermented lagers. As in neighbouring Germany, there are no chemicals in the beer. The whole fermentation process uses only natural ingredients – water, hops and barley.

The strong beer culture here is centuries old and is one of the few traditions to survive the communist era relatively intact. Today, the art of beer drinking is celebrated at numerous Czech festivals (note, too, there are some great open-air beer gardens strewn about town; see the boxed text on p153 for a list of some popular spots). Beer-inspired competitions include speed drinking (the record for 1L of beer is 3.44 seconds) and the largest beer gut, to name but a few.

Czechs have many sayings that celebrate beer drinking, but their claims are often dubious. One of the favourites is *'Pivo dělá pěkná těla'* (Beer makes beautiful bodies). And home-brew fans might adopt *'Kde se pivo vaí tam se dobe daí'* (Life flourishes where beer is brewed).

KAVÁRNA MEDÚZA Map pp260-1
☎ 222 515 107; Belgická 17; ◷ 11am-1am; metro Náměstí Míru

The perfect Prague coffee house, Medúza is an oasis of old, worn furniture, dark wood, armchairs and an antique sugar bowl on every table, with an atmosphere that invites you to sink into a Kafka novel or indulge in a conversation on the nature of self. Coffees and teas of all types, plenty of alcohol (including Velvet on tap for 26Kč per 0.5L), pancakes and massive banana splits will sustain you through the most bohemian moments.

POTREFENÁ HUSA Map pp258-9
☎ 267 310 360; Kolínská 19; ◷ 11.30am-1am; metro Jiřího z Poděbrad

The 'Wounded Goose' is one of a chain of modern pubs owned by Prague's Staropramen brewery. Bright, bustling and always busy, this place serves good beer at local neighbourhood prices, and has excellent food as well – from grilled salmon steaks to *halušky s brynzou*

(which are little potato dumplings grilled with sheep's-milk cheese).

ZVONAŘKÁ Map pp260-1
☎ 224 251 990; Šafaříkova 1; ◷ 11am-11pm Mon-Thu, noon-midnight Fri & Sat, noon-11pm Sun; metro IP Pavlova

Recently renovated with a chic new interior, Zvonařká sits at the far end of a quiet residential street where Vinohrady spills over into the Nusle Valley. Enjoy a glass of Budvar (28Kč for 0.5L) at an outdoor table on the tree-shaded terrace, which commands a wide view across the valley towards Vyšehrad.

CLUBBING

With few exceptions, Prague's dance clubs cater to teenagers weaned on MTV Europe and techno/tribal beats – if you want to dance to anything other than hip-hop, R&B or house, you'll have to look long and hard.

Top Five Clubs

- Gejzee..r (below)
- Palác Akropolis (below right)
- Mecca (below right)
- Radost FX (p156)
- Sedm Vlků (p156)

Most venues open late (after 10pm) and keep the music going until 4am or 5am. Clubs have notoriously short life spans; check *Houser* weekly magazine or www.prague.tv for up-to-date listings.

ANGEL CLUB Map pp250-1

☎ 257 316 127; www.clubangel.cz; Kmochova 8, Smíchov; ⏰ 8pm-4am Mon-Thu, 7pm-7am Fri & Sat; tram 4, 7, 9, 10

The Angel is a gay club, with a tiny, mirrored dance floor, karaoke sessions, a Green Room full of chill-out sofas, a black-light Dark Room out back, and a romantic, candlelit Red Room.

FUTURUM Map pp250-1

☎ 257 328 571; www.musicbar.cz; Zborovská 7, Smíchov; cover 80-130Kč; ⏰ 9pm-3am; metro Anděl

Futurum is a former heavy-metal venue where DJs now play techno, garage and tribal. There are record launches and live alternative bands a couple of times a week, but mostly it's a case of back to the future – lots of exposed metal, brick walls and weird lighting forming the backdrop for regular '80s and '90s parties.

GARÁŽ Map pp244-5

☎ 257 533 342; Malostranské náměstí 7; ⏰ 6pm-5am; tram 12, 20, 22, 23

Garáž is a dark and decadent dance venue in the basement of Jo's Bar (p149), popular with backpackers who flock here for the four-hour happy hour (6pm to 10pm). There's no cover charge.

GEJZEE..R Map pp258-9

☎ 222 516 036; Vinohradská 40, Vinohrady; cover 50-70Kč, admission free Thu & before 10.30pm Fri & Sat; ⏰ 8pm-4am Thu, 9pm-6am Fri & Sat; metro Náměstí Míru

Prague's biggest G&L club, with two bars, a huge dance floor, video-projection system, dark room and erotic cinema, Gejzee..r pulls in large crowds at weekends and for special 'meet a partner' evenings.

KARLOVY LÁZNĚ Map pp246-7

☎ 222 220 502; www.karlovylazne.cz; Novotného lávka 1, Staré Město; admission 50-120Kč; ⏰ 9pm-5am; tram 17, 18

Down by the river near Charles Bridge, Karlovy Lázně is Central Europe's biggest music club. A single cover charge admits you to four venues – MCM Café (various live bands); Discotheque (classic disco music); Kaleidoskop ('60s, '70s and '80s revival); and Paradogs (house, techno, drum'n'bass etc).

KLUB 007 STRAHOV Map pp250-1

☎ 257 211 439; www.klub007strahov.cz; Block 7, Chaloupeckého, Strahov; cover 50-200Kč; ⏰ 7.30pm-1am Tue-Sat; bus 143, 149, 217

Klub 007 is one of several grungy student clubs in the basements of the big dormitory blocks in Strahov, offering a menu of hip-hop, ragga, punk, ska and reggae served very, very loud.

MALER Map pp260-1

☎ 222 013 116; www.maler-club.cz; Blanická 28, Vinohrady; ⏰ 9am-11pm Mon-Thu, 9am-4am Fri & Sat, 1-10pm Sun; metro Náměstí Míru

Maler is a small and intimate café-club with a thriving lesbian scene and it pulls in a mixed crowd through the week. There are lesbian discos on Friday and Saturday (cover 50Kč) and the so-called 'Ladies Secret Club' night once a month.

MECCA Map pp256-7

☎ 283 870 522; www.mecca.cz; U Průhonu 3, Holešovice; admission 150-250Kč; ⏰ 10pm-6am Fri & Sat; metro Nádraží Holešovice

This ultrafashionable dance venue is all stark colours, space-age vinyl couches and the sort of chairs that challenge you to sit on them. Prague's fashionistas, models, film stars, DJs and a legion of clubbers flock to Mecca's industrial-chic club to dance the night away to house, drum'n'bass and techno.

PALÁC AKROPOLIS Map pp258-9

☎ 296 330 911; www.palacakropolis.cz; Kubelíkova 27, Žižkov; tram 5, 9, 26

The Akropolis is a Prague institution, a labyrinthine, sticky-floored shrine to alternative music and drama. Its various performance spaces host a smorgasbord of musical and cultural events, from club nights to string quartets to Macedonian Roma bands to local rock gods to visiting talent – Marianne Faithfull, the Dead Kennedys and the Strokes have all played here.

Entertainment – Clubbing

RADOST FX Map pp252-3

☎ 224 254 776; www.radostfx.cz; Bělehradská 120, Vinohrady; cover 100-250Kč; ⏰ 10pm-5am; metro IP Pavlova

Prague's slickest, shiniest and most self-assured club is the best place in town to catch top local DJs spinning hip-hop, house and funk. It has a bohemian lounge area with stainless-steel walls, leopard-skin sofas, mosaic-topped tables and lava lamps – yeah, baby! – while the club downstairs is where the city's beautiful people go to strut their stuff.

ROXY Map pp246-7

☎ 224 826 296; www.roxy.cz; Dlouhá 33, Staré Město; cover 50-250Kč; ⏰ 1pm-1am; metro Náměstí Republiky

The expansive floor of this iconic, ramshackle old theatre complex has seen many a DJ and band over the years. Roxy's displayed a surprising longevity as an 'experimental space', staging drama and dance, experimental cinema, live music and some of Prague's most popular club nights. All those shadowy nooks and crannies fill up quickly once the doors open.

SEDM VLKŮ Map pp258-9

☎ 222 711 725; www.sedmvlku.cz; Vlkova 7, Žižkov; ⏰ 5pm-3am Mon-Sat; tram 5, 9, 26

The 'Seven Wolves' is a cool, two-level, art-studenty kind of café-bar and club. Upstairs,

Gay & Lesbian Prague

- Angel Club (p155)
- Club Stella (p153)
- Downtown Café Praha (p127)
- Friends (p151)
- Gejzee..r (p155)
- Maler (p155)
- Piano Bar (p153)
- Pension Arco (p192)
- Prague Room (p181)
- Termix (below)

there's candlelight, booths and dimmed lamps, and the music's low enough to have a conversation without shouting; down in the darkened cellar, the DJs pump out drum'n'bass and ragga.

TERMIX Map pp260-1

☎ 222 710 462; www.club-termix.cz; Třebízckého 4a, Vinohrady; admission free; ⏰ 8pm-5am; metro Jiřího z Poděbrad

Termix is Prague's newest gay bar and club, with an industrial/high-tech vibe (lots of steel, glass and a car sticking out of one wall), cute bar staff, a regular house/techno night (Thursday) and a dark room (if you feel like being naughty).

The bar at Radost FX (see above), Vinohrady

MUSIC
CLASSICAL MUSIC, OPERA & BALLET

Don't believe anyone who says it's impossible to get concert tickets. There are half-a-dozen concerts of one kind or another almost every day during the summer, making a fine soundtrack to accompany the city's visual delights. Many of these are chamber concerts performed by aspiring musicians in the city's churches – gorgeous but chilly (take an extra layer, even on a summer day) and not always with the finest of acoustics. An increasing number of church concerts have been second-rate, despite the premium prices that foreigners pay.

In addition to the hours indicated here in the individual reviews, box offices are also open from 30 minutes to one hour before the start of a performance.

DVOŘÁK HALL Map pp246-7
☎ 227 059 352; www.rudolfinum.cz; náměstí Jana Palacha 1, Staré Město; tickets 150-900Kč; ⏲ box office 10am-12.30pm & 1.30-6pm Mon-Fri; metro Staroměstská

The Dvořák Hall in the neo-Renaissance Rudolfinum is home to the world-renowned Česká filharmonie (Czech Philharmonic Orchestra). Sit back and be impressed by some of the best classical musicians in Prague.

NÁRODNÍ DIVADLO Map pp252-3
National Theatre; ☎ 224 901 448; www.narodni-divadlo.cz; Národní třída 2, Nové Město; tickets 310-930Kč; ⏲ box office 10am-6pm; metro Národní Třída

The glorious, golden-roofed centrepiece of the Czech National Revival, the National Theatre provided a stage for the re-emergence of

Czech culture in the late-19th and early-20th century. Today, traditional opera, drama and ballet by the likes of Smetana, Shakespeare and Tchaikovsky share the programme with more modern works by composers and playwrights, such as Philip Glass and John Osborne.

SMETANA HALL Map pp246-7
☎ 220 021 01; www.fok.cz; náměstí Republiky 5, Staré Město; tickets 200-1200Kč; ⏲ box office 10am-6pm; metro Náměstí Republiky

The Smetana Hall, centrepiece of the stunning Obecní dům (Municipal House; p77), is the city's largest concert hall with seating for 1200. This is the home venue of the Symfonický orchestr hlavního města Prahy (Prague Symphony Orchestra), and also stages performances of folk dance and music, and musical shows such as *Rockquiem* (a 'rock' version of Mozart's *Requiem*, if you can imagine it).

STÁTNÍ OPERA PRAHA Map pp252-3
Prague State Opera; ☎ 224 227 832; www.opera.cz; Wilsonova 4, Nové Město; opera tickets 400-1200Kč, ballet tickets 200-550Kč; ⏲ box office 10am-5pm Mon-Fri, 10am-noon & 1-5pm Sat & Sun; metro Muzeum

The impressive neorococo home of the Prague State Opera provides a glorious setting for performances of opera and ballet. The annual Verdi festival takes place here in August and September, and less conventional shows, such as Leoncavallo's rarely staged version of *La Bohème*, have also been performed here.

STAVOVSKÉ DIVADLO Map pp246-7
Estates Theatre; ☎ 224 901 638; www.narodni-divadlo.cz; Ovocný trh 1, Staré Město; tickets 190-1950Kč; ⏲ box office 10am-6pm Mon-Fri, to 12.30pm Sat & Sun; metro Můstek

The Stavovské divadlo (also see p79) is the oldest theatre in Prague, famed as the place

---

Prague Spring

Prague Spring (Pražské jaro) is the Czech Republic's best-known annual cultural event, and is now a major tourist attraction too. It begins on 12 May, the anniversary of Smetana's death, with a procession from his grave at Vyšehrad (p91) to the Obecní dům (p77), and a performance there of his song cycle *Má vlast* (My Homeland). The festival runs until 3 June. The beautiful venues are as big a drawcard as the music.

The cheapest tickets are to be had through the official **Prague Spring Box Office** (Map pp246-7; ☎ 296 329 999; www.festival.cz). Bookings can also be made through **Ticketpro** (see the boxed text on p149) outlets.

If you want a guaranteed seat at a Prague Spring concert book it by mid-March. A few seats may still be available as late as the end of May: watch the papers.

Other Concert Venues

Prague's numerous churches and baroque palaces also serve as concert venues, staging anything from choral perform-ances and organ recitals to string quartets, brass ensembles and occasionally full orchestras. You can get comprehensive details of these concerts from PIS offices (see p222). We've listed here a selection of the more popular venues around town.

Hradčany & Malá Strana

Bazilika sv Jiří (Basilica of St George; Map p55; Prague Castle) The Czech Republic's best-preserved Romanesque church (see p58 for more information).

Chrám sv Víta (St Vitus Cathedral; Map p55; 3rd Courtyard, Prague Castle, Hradčany; metro Malostranská) Inside this cathedral the nave is flooded with colour from beautiful stained-glass windows (see p57).

Kostel sv Mikuláše (Church of St Nicholas; Map pp244-5; Malostranská náměstí 38, Malá Strana; metro Malostranská) Mozart himself tickled the ivories on the 2500-pipe organ here in 1787.

Kostel sv Vavřince (Church of St Lawrence; Map pp250−1; Hellichova 18, Malá Strana) Located opposite the Bludiště (p66).

Lichtenštejnský palác (Liechtenstein Palace; Map pp246-7; Malostranské náměstí, Malá Strana; tram 12, 20, 22, 23) Home to the Music Faculty of the Akademie múzických umění v Praze (Prague Academy of Performing Arts).

Lobkovický palác (Lobkowicz Palace; Map p55; Jiřská 3, Prague Castle, Hradčany; metro Malostranská) Built in the 1570s (see p59 for details).

Strahovský klášter (Strahov Monastery; Map pp244-5; Strahovské nádvoří 1, Hradčany; tram 22, 23) Mozart is said to have played the organ here.

Valdštejnský palác (Wallenstein Palace; Map pp244-5; ☎ 257 071 111; www.senat.cz; Valdštejnské náměstí 4, Malá Strana; metro Malostranská) The palace now houses the Senate of the Czech Republic.

Vrtbovská zahrada (Vrtbov Garden; Map pp244-5; ☎ 257 531 480; www.vrtbovska.cz; Karmelitská 25, Malá Strana; tram 12, 20, 22, 23) A formal baroque garden (see p66 for details).

Staré Město

Betlémská kaple (Bethlehem Chapel; Map pp252-3; ☎ 224 2448 595; Betlémské náměstí 1; tram 6, 9, 18, 21, 22, 23) This 14th-century chapel was torn down during the 18th century and painstakingly reconstructed between 1948 and 1954 (see p79 for more details).

Klášter sv Anežky (Convent of St Agnes; Map pp246-7; ☎ 224 810 628; www.ngprague.cz; U milosrdných 17; tram 5, 8, 14) Prague's oldest surviving Gothic building (see p73 for details).

Kostel sv Františka (Church of St Francis; Map pp246-7; Křížovnické náměstí; tram 5, 8, 14) Alongside the complex of Klášter sv Anežky (see p76).

Kostel sv Mikuláše (Church of St Nicholas; Map pp246-7; Staroměstské náměstí; metro Staroměstská) Built in the 1730s by Kilian Dientzenhofer (see p71 for more details).

Zrcadlová kaple (Chapel of Mirrors; Map pp246-7; Klementinum, Mariánské náměstí; tram 17, 18, 53) Dating from the 1720s this chapel's interior is ornate (see p76).

Take care when buying tickets through people who hand out flyers in the street – some of these concerts are OK, but some may turn out to be a disappointment. Make sure you know exactly where the concert will be held – if you are told just 'the Municipal House', don't expect the magnificent Smetana Hall, as it may well be in one of the smaller concert halls.

where Mozart conducted the premiere of *Don Giovanni* (29 October 1787), a touristy version is staged here by the Opera Mozart company each summer; the rest of the year sees various opera and ballet productions. The theatre is equipped for the hearing-impaired and has wheelchair access (wheelchair bookings can be made up to five days in advance); the box office is around the corner in the Kolowrat Palace.

MUZEUM ANTONÍNA DVOŘÁKA

Map pp252-3

Dvořák Museum; ☎ 224 918 013; Ke Karlovu 20, Nové Město; tickets 545Kč; ⊙ concerts 8pm Tue & Fri Apr-Oct; metro IP Pavlova

The pretty little Vila Amerika was built in 1717 as a count's immodest summer retreat. These days it's home to the Muzeum Antonína Dvořáka (p88), and its salon stages performances of Dvořák's vocal and instrumental works by the Original Music Theatre of Prague, complete with period costume. Tickets are available through BTI (see the boxed text on p149).

VILA BERTRAMKA Map pp242-3

☎ 257 317 465; www.bertramka.cz; Mozartova 169, Smíchov; tickets 350-565Kč; ⊙ salon 5pm, garden 7pm Tue-Sat Apr-Oct; tram 4, 7, 9, 10

Mozart stayed in the Vila Bertramka during his visits to Prague. It now houses a museum (p97) and serves as a charming venue for classical concerts held in the salon and garden.

FOLK & TRADITIONAL MUSIC

DLABAČOV HALL Map pp242-3

☎ 233 373 475; Bělohorská 24, Střešovice; tickets 450Kč; ⊙ shows 8.30pm Mon-Sat Apr-Nov; tram 15, 22, 23, 25

Dlabačov Hall, in the Hotel Pyramida, is the home venue of the Český soubor písní a tanců (Czech Song & Dance Ensemble), the only professional troupe of its kind in the Czech Republic. Performances, a stylised amalgam of traditions from around Bohemia, are undeniable crowd-pleasers.

JAZZ & BLUES

Prague has lots of good jazz clubs, and many have been around for decades. Unless otherwise indicated, most charge a cover of 50Kč to 150Kč.

AGHARTA JAZZ CENTRUM Map pp252-3

☎ 222 211 275; www.agharta.cz; Krakovská 5, Nové Město; ⊙ 7pm-1am, music from 9pm; metro Muzeum

A venerable basement venue with '70s décor, a café (open 7pm to midnight) and a music shop (open 5pm to midnight Monday to Friday and 7pm to midnight Saturday and Sunday), AghaRTA has been staging top-notch modern Czech jazz, blues, funk and fusion since 1991. Don't worry if you turn up and no one else is

there – the audience tends to drift in about half an hour before showtime.

METROPOLITAN JAZZ CLUB Map pp252-3

☎ 224 947 777; Jungmannova 14, Nové Město; ⊙ 6pm-1am Mon-Fri, 7pm-1am Sat, music from 9pm; metro Národní Třída

A basement jazz'n'blues haunt with an easily digestible menu of ragtime and swing, the Met shows a similar preference for substance over style in its choice of décor, with a plain tiled floor and general lack of adornment.

RED, HOT & BLUES Map pp246-7

☎ 222 323 364; Jakubská 12, Staré Město; ⊙ 9am-11pm, music 7-10pm; metro Náměstí Republiky

Red, Hot & Blues is a New Orleans–style restaurant (also see p124) with live blues or jazz most nights (check the board outside), playing to a mostly tourist and expat crowd.

REDUTA JAZZ CLUB Map pp252-3

☎ 224 912 246; Národní třída 20, Nové Město; cover 280-300Kč; ⊙ 9pm-3am; metro Národní Třída

The Reduta is Prague's oldest jazz club, founded in the communist era. It has an intimate setting, with smartly dressed patrons squeezing into tiered seats and lounges to soak up the big-band, swing and dixieland atmosphere. Book a few hours ahead at the box office (open from 3pm Monday to Friday and from 7pm Saturday and Sunday).

U MALÉHO GLENA Map pp244-5

☎ 290 003 967; www. malyglen.cz; Karmelitská 23, Malá Strana; ⊙ 10am-2am, music from 9pm; tram 12, 20, 22, 23

'Little Glen's' is a good bar (also see p150) where hard-swinging local jazz or blues bands play in the stone cellar most nights. There are regular jam sessions where amateurs are welcome (as long as you're good!). It's a small venue, so get here early.

U STARÉ PANÍ JAZZ CLUB Map pp246-7

☎ 603 551 680; www.jazzinprague.com; Michalská 9, Staré Město; ⊙ 7pm-2am from 9pm Tue-Sat; metro Můstek

Located in the basement of the hotel of the same name (see p184), the long-established U Staré paní Jazz Club caters to all levels of musical appreciation. There's a varied programme of modern jazz, soul, blues and latin rhythms, and a nightly DJ spot from midnight onwards.

ROCK

Prague has a high-energy live-music scene, with rock, metal, punk, rap and newer sounds at a score of legitimate DJ and live-music venues.

During the last five years or so, noise regulations and increasing rents have forced the closure of several big venues in historical city-owned properties, but new ones have since opened in the suburbs (see Sazka Arena on p163). For current listings and reviews check out the media noted on p148 – and watch the posters around town.

BATALION Map pp252-3
☎ 220 108 148; www.batalion.cz; 28.října 3, Staré Město; cover 50-100Kč; ☉ bar 24hr, music from 9pm; metro Můstek

Batalion is a delightfully grungy bar offering anything from rock'n'roll and jazz to punk and death metal performed by up-and-coming Czech bands (plus DJs on most Saturdays). Despite a location in the midst of the tourist hordes, it pulls in a young, mainly local crowd.

KLUB DELTA Map pp242-3
☎ 233 311 398; www.noise.cz/delta; Vlastina 887, Na Dědině; ☉ from 7pm, music from 8pm; bus 218

Klub Delta is a big theatre and exhibition venue that hosts mainly alternative and underground Czech bands. It's almost at the airport – take bus No 218 from Dejvická metro station to the Sídliště Na Dědiňe stop.

LUCERNA MUSIC BAR Map pp252-3
☎ 224 217 108; www.musicbar.cz; Vodičkova 36, Nové Město; cover 50-150Kč; ☉ 8pm-4am; metro Můstek

Nostalgia reigns supreme at this atmospheric old theatre, now looking a little dog-eared, with anything from Beatles tribute bands to mainly Czech artists playing jazz, blues, pop, rock and more. Theme nights include 1980s and '90s video parties, 1960s Czech pop (interesting) and 1950s Americana.

MALOSTRANSKÁ BESEDA Map pp244-5
☎ 257 532 092; Malostranské náměstí 21, Malá Strana; cover 80-100Kč; ☉ bar 5pm-1am, music from 8pm; tram 12, 20, 22, 23

Malá Strana's former town hall now houses a large café-bar that hosts anything from hard rock to bluegrass via jazz and folk, playing to a young and mostly Czech crowd. It packs out early, particularly on weekends.

ROCK CAFÉ Map pp252-3
☎ 224 914 416; www.rockcafé.cz; Národní třída 20, Nové Město; cover 50-100Kč; ☉ 10am-3am Mon-Fri, 5pm-3am Sat, 5pm-1am Sun, music from 8.30pm; metro Národní Třída

Over-commercialised to the hilt, and loving it, the Rock Café is a stripped-down auditorium for DJs and live rock, with a café downstairs, a cinema and an art gallery.

THEATRE

Most Czech drama is, not surprisingly, performed in Czech, which rather diminishes its appeal to non Czech-speakers.

Black-light theatre – occasionally called just 'black theatre' – is a hybrid of mime, drama and puppetry. Live or animated actors wearing fluorescent costumes do their thing on a stage or in front of a black backdrop lit only by ultraviolet light, thus eliminating the usual distractions of stage management and scenery (it's a growth industry in Prague, with at least half a dozen venues).

ČINOHERNÍ KLUB Map pp252-3
Dramatic Club; ☎ 296 222 123; www.cinoherniklub.cz; Ve Smečkách 26, Nové Město; tickets 170-190Kč; ☉ box office 3-7.30pm Mon-Fri, 6-7.30pm Sat & Sun; metro Muzeum

On the go since 1965, the Činoherní klub stages Czech-language modern drama, but is more famous abroad as the venue where the dissident group Civic Forum (see the boxed text on p47), led by Václav Havel, was founded.

DIVADLO MINOR Map pp252-3
☎ 222 231 351; www.minor.cz; Vodičkova 6, Nové Město; ☉ box office 9am-1.30pm & 2.30-8pm Mon-Fri, 11am-8pm Sat & Sun; metro Karlovo Náměstí

Divadlo Minor is a wheelchair-accessible children's theatre that offers a fun mix of puppets, clown shows and pantomime. There are performances at 9.30am Monday to Friday and at 7.30pm Tuesday and Wednesday, and you can usually get a ticket at the door before the show.

DIVADLO NA ZÁBRADLÍ Map pp246-7
Theatre on the Balustrade; ☎ 222 868 868; www.nazabradli.cz; Anenské náměstí 5, Staré Město; tickets 90-250Kč; ☉ box office 2-7pm Mon-Fri, 2hr before show start Sat & Sun; metro Staroměstská

The city's main venue for serious Czech-language drama, this is the theatre where Václav Havel honed his skills as a playwright four decades ago. The theatre dabbled in absurdism early on in its career, and now plays host to a range of more contemporary material.

DIVADLO NA VINOHRADECH

Map pp260-1

Vinohrady Theatre; ☎ 224 25 76 01; náměstí Míru 7, Vinohrady; ✆ box office 11am-7pm Mon-Fri, 1-4pm & 4.30-7pm Sat

On the northern side of náměstí Míru (Peace Square) is the divadlo na Vinohradech, which was built in 1909 and is a popular venue for Czech-language drama and ballet.

DIVADLO SPEJBLA A HURVÍNKA

Map p255

☎ 224 316 784; www.volny.cz/spejblhurvinek; Dejvická 38, Dejvice; ✆ box office 10am-2pm & 3-6pm Tue-Fri, 1-5pm Sat & Sun

Created in 1930 by puppeteer Josef Skupa, the main characters Spejbl and Hurvinek are the Czech equivalents of Punch and Judy, although they are father and son rather than husband and wife.

DIVADLO V CELETNÉ Map pp246-7

Celetná Theatre; ☎ 222 326 843; www.divadlovceletne .cz; Celetná 17, Staré Město; tickets 30-250Kč; ✆ box office 1-7.30pm; metro Náměstí Republiky

The Divadlo v Celetné, in a courtyard between Celetná and Štupartská, stages mainly Czech drama, both old and new, and some foreign plays (including Shakespeare) translated into Czech.

IMAGE THEATRE Map pp246-7

☎ 222 314 448; www.imagetheatre.cz; Pařížská 4, Staré Město; tickets 400Kč; ✆ box office 9am-8pm; metro Staroměstská

This company uses creative black-light theatre along with pantomime, modern dance and video – not to mention liberal doses of slapstick – to tell its stories. The staging can be very effective, but the atmosphere is often dictated by audience reaction.

LATERNA MAGIKA Map pp252-3

Magic Lantern; ☎ 224 931 482; www.laterna.cz; Nova Scéna, Národní třída 4, Nové Město; tickets 690Kč; ✆ box office 10am-8pm Mon-Sat; metro Národní Třída

Since its first cutting-edge multimedia show, interweaving dance, opera, music and film,

caused a stir at the 1958 Brussels World Fair, Laterna Magika has been wowing audiences both at home and abroad. Its imaginative blend of live dance and projected images continues to pull in the crowds.

Nová Scena, the futuristic glass-block building next to the Národní divadlo, has been home to the Laterna Magika show since it moved here from its birthplace in the basement of the Adria Palace in the mid-1970s. Some agencies may tell you it's booked out, but you can often bag a leftover seat at the box office (Nova Scéna) on the day before a performance, or a no-show seat half-hour beforehand.

NÁRODNÍ DIVADLO MARIONET

Map pp246-7

National Marionette Theatre; ☎ 224 819 323; www.mozart.cz; Žatecká 1, Staré Město; tickets 490Kč; ✆ box office 10am-8pm; metro Staroměstská

Loudly touted as the longest-running classical marionette show in the city – the Národní divadlo marionet has been staging performances almost continuously since 1991 – *Don Giovanni* is an operatic, life-sized puppet extravaganza that has spawned several imitations around town. Younger kids' attention might begin to wander fairly early on during this two-hour show.

REDUTA THEATRE Map pp252-3

Jiří Srnec; ☎ 257 921 835; www.blacktheatresrnec.cz; Národní třída 20, Nové Město; tickets 370-490Kč; metro Národní Třída

The Reduta Theatre is home to the Black Theatre of Jiří Srnec, who was a founding member of Prague's original black-light theatre back in the early 1960s. Today, the company's productions include versions of *Alice in Wonderland* and *Peter Pan*, and a compilation of the best of black theatre from the early days. You can buy tickets from Ticketpro or BTI (see the boxed text on p149).

TA FANTASTIKA Map pp246-7

☎ 222 221 366; www.tafanstastika.cz; Karlova 8, Staré Město; tickets 350-549Kč; ✆ box office 11am-9.30pm; metro Staroměstská

Established in New York in 1981 by Czech émigré Petr Kratochvil, Ta Fantastika moved to Prague in 1989. The theatre produces black-light theatre based on classic literature and legends such, as *Gulliver's Travels*, *Alice in Wonderland*, *Excalibur* and *Joan of Arc*.

CINEMA

Prague has over 30 cinemas, some showing first-run Western films, some showing Czech films. For listings check the 'Night & Day' section of the *Prague Post*, or the free bi-monthly pamphlet *Do města – Downtown*.

Most films are screened in their original language with Czech subtitles (*České titulky*), but Hollywood blockbusters are often dubbed into Czech (*dabing*); look for the labels 'tit.' or 'dab.' on cinema listings. Tickets generally cost from 90Kč to 170Kč.

KINO AERO Map pp242-3

☎ 271 771 349; www.kinoaero.cz; Biskupcova 31, Žižkov; tickets 80-90Kč; tram 5, 9, 10, 16, 19

The Aero is Prague's best-loved arthouse cinema, with themed programmes, retrospectives and unusual films, often with English subtitles. This is the place to catch re-runs of classics from *Smrt v Benátkách* (Death in Venice) to *Dobrodružství Priscilly, Královny Pouště* (The Adventures of Priscilla, Queen of the Desert). The same managers run a similar venue in the city centre, see Kino Světozor (below).

KINO MAT Map pp252-3

☎ 224 915 765; www.mat.cz; Karlovo náměstí 19, Nové Město; tickets 95Kč; metro Karlovo Náměstí

Kino Mat is a former film and TV studio's private screening room (there are only 40 seats) turned hip, arthouse cinema, where film buffs sip espressos in the celluloid-decorated downstairs bar while discussing the use of visual metaphor in *Citizen Kane*. The programme includes the latest Czech films (with English subtitles), and the latest European films (with Czech ones).

KINO PERŠTÝN Map pp252-3

☎ 221 668 432; Na Perštýně 6, Staré Město; tickets 80-130Kč; metro Národní Třída

This film-clubbish cinema forgoes those boring old rows of seats for a sociable scattering of tables and chairs, and screens mostly English-and foreign-language films with Czech subtitles. You can bring drinks into the cinema, but smoking is confined to the next-door bar.

KINO SVĚTOZOR Map pp252-3

☎ 224 947 566; www.kinosvetozor.cz; Vodičkova 41, Nové Město; tickets 80-90Kč; metro Můstek

The recently made-over Světozor is now under the same management as Kino Aero (above) but is more central, and has the same emphasis on arthouse and classic cinema – this place

is your best bet for seeing Czech films with English subtitles.

PALACE CINEMAS Map pp246-7

☎ 257 181 212; www.palacecinemas.cz; Slovanský dům, Na příkopě 22, Nové Město; tickets 179Kč; metro Náměstí Republiky

Housed in the posh Slovanský dům shopping centre, this is central Prague's main popcorn palace – a modern 10-screen multiplex showing first-run Hollywood films. There's also a **branch** (Map pp250-1; ☎ 257 181 212; www .palacecinemas.cz; Nový Smíchov, Plzeňská 8, Smíchov; tickets 149Kč; metro Anděl) at the huge new Nový Smíchov shopping centre, which is home to a 12-screen multiplex.

SPORT, HEALTH & FITNESS

FITNESS CENTRES

You can use the *posilovna* (weight room) at the **Sportcentrum YMCA** (p164) for 66Kč per hour. **Esquo Squashcentrum** (p164) has a fitness centre, which costs 40Kč per hour. The weights room at the **Sportcentrum Hotel Čechie** (p164) charges 100Kč to 120Kč for up to three hours. Guests of the hotel can use the pool for free.

The luxurious **Cybex Health Club & Spa** (Map pp258-9; ☎ 224 842 375; www.cybexprg .cz; Pobřežní 1, Nové Město; ⏰ 6am-10pm Mon-Fri, 7am-10pm Sat & Sun; metro Florenc) in the Hotel Hilton Prague (p186) charges 900Kč for a day pass, which gives access to the gym, pool, sauna, Jacuzzi and steam room.

FOOTBALL (SOCCER)

Slavia Praha and Sparta Praha are both leading teams in the national *fotbal* (football) league; two other Prague teams are the **Bohemians** (FC Bohemians Stadium; Map pp242-3; ☎ 271 721 459; www.fc-bohe mians.cz; Vršovická 31, Vinohrady; tickets 50-70Kč; tram 4, 22) and **Viktoria Žižkov** (FK Viktoria Žižkov stadium; Map pp258-9; ☎ 222 722 504; www.fkviktoriazizkov.cz; Seifertova, Žižkov; tickets 40-60Kč; tram 5, 9, 26). Each has its own stadium where you can watch matches, mostly on Sunday afternoons. The season runs from August to December and February to June.

SK SLAVIA PRAHA STADIUM

Map pp242-3

Stadión Evšena Rošického; ☎ 257 213 290; www.slavia .cz; Diskařská 100, Strahov; tickets 40-120Kč; bus 176

Founded in 1892, SK Slavia Praha is one of the oldest sporting clubs in continental Europe and is an honorary member of England's Football Association. Czech National Cup winners in 1997, 1999 and 2002, it holds an unusual record – the design of its distinctive red-and-white strip has remained almost unchanged since 1896. Slavia's 19,000-capacity Stadión Evšena Rošického is in Strahov.

TOYOTA ARENA Map pp256-7

☎ 296 111 400; www.sparta.cz; Milady Horákové 98, Bubeneč; tickets 50-230Kč; tram 1, 8, 15, 25, 26

The all-seater Toyota Arena, with a capacity of 18,761, is the home ground of Sparta Praha – winners of the Czech football league in 2000, 2001 and 2003 – and is also used by the Czech national football team for big international matches.

GOLF

GOLF CLUB PRAHA Map pp242-3

☎ 257 216 584; Plzeňská 401/2, Motol; green fees 500Kč Mon-Fri, 600Kč Sat, Sun & hols; tram 7, 9 or 10

Prague has one nine-hole golf course, the Golf Club Praha behind the Hotel Golf in the western suburbs. Here you can hire a set of clubs for 800Kč. Take tram No 7, 9 or 10 west to the Hotel Golf stop.

GOLF & COUNTRY CLUB Map pp242-3

☎ 244 460 435; Vltavanů 982, Hodkovičky; admission 50Kč, plus 50Kč per 50 balls; ☉ 8am-9pm May-Oct, 10am-4pm Nov-Apr; tram 3, 17 or 21

The Golf & Country Club, on the southern edge of the city, has a driving range, and chipping and putting greens. Take tram No 3, 17 or 21 south to the Černý kůň stop, and walk west towards the river on V náklích (follow the signs for Hostel Boathouse) for 100m, then turn first right immediately after passing under the railway bridge.

KARLŠTEJN GOLF COURSE

☎ 311 684 716; Běleč 280, Liteň; green fees 1200Kč Mon-Fri, 2400Kč Sat, Sun & hols

The closest 18-hole course to Prague is the prestigious Karlštejn Golf Course overlooking Karlštejn Castle, southwest of the city (see p198). It's several kilometres from Karlštejn village, on the southern bank of the Berounka River.

HORSE RACING

There are horse races every Sunday from April to October. Contact PIS (see p222) about venues and events around Prague as these constantly change.

VELKÁ CHUCHLE ZÁVODIŠTĚ PRAHA

Map pp242-3

Prague Racecourse; ☎ 257 941 431; www.velka-chuchle .cz; Radotínská 69, Velká Chuchle; admission 70Kč, child under 15 free; metro Smíchovské Nádraží

Check out the *dostihy* (racing) scene at Velká Chuchle závodiště Praha. Its website has details of the racing calendar. You can reach the racecourse by taking bus No 129, 172, 243, 244 or 255 from Smíchovské Nádraží metro station.

ICE HOCKEY

The Czech national *lední hokej* (ice-hockey) team has won the European championship 17 times, the world title 10 times and took Olympic gold at the winter Olympics in Nagano in 1998. HC Sparta Praha and HC Slavia Praha are Prague's two big teams. The season runs from September to early April.

SAZKA ARENA Map pp242-3

☎ 266 212 111; www.sazkaarena.cz; Ocelařská 2, Vysočany; metro Českomoravská

Completed in time to host the 2004 Ice Hockey World Championship, the Sazka Arena is Prague's biggest multipurpose venue. It can accommodate up to 18,000 spectators, and is used to host sporting events, rock concerts, exhibitions and other major events.

T-MOBILE ARÉNA Map pp256-7

☎ 266 727 443; Za elektrámou 419, Výstaviště, Holešovice; tickets 40-100Kč; metro Nádraží Holešovice

You can see HC Sparta Praha play at the big T-Mobile Arena beside the Exhibition Grounds in Holešovice (take tram No 12 one stop west from the Nádraží Holešovice metro station).

ICE-SKATING

There are many places to skate in winter. When it's below zero, sections of parks are sprayed with water and turned into ice rinks. Indoor rinks at *zimní stadiony* (winter sports complexes) are open to the public during certain hours from September to March or April.

ZIMNÍ STADIÓN ŠTVANICE Map pp246-7

☎ 233 378 327; Ostrov Štvanice 1125, Holešovice; adult/child under seven 70/20Kč; 🕑 10.30am-noon & 3.30-5.30pm Mon & Tue, 10.30am-noon & 3.30-6pm Wed, 10.30am-noon Thu 10.30am-noon, 3.30-6pm & 7.30-9.30pm Fri, 9-11.30am, 2.30-5pm & 8-11pm Sat, 9-11.30am & 2.30-6.30pm Sun; tram 3, 26

This is the oldest ice-hockey stadium in Central Europe – Czechoslovakia's first ice-hockey match on artificial ice was played here in 1931. You can hire skates for 80Kč per session.

RUNNING
PRAGUE INTERNATIONAL MARATHON

☎ 224 919 209; www.pim.cz; Záhořanského 3, 120 00 Praha 2

The Prague International Marathon (Pražský Mezinárodní maraton), established 1989, is now an annual event (normally held mid- to late May), attracting more foreign runners than Czechs. There's also a half-marathon, held in late March. If you'd like to compete, you can register online or obtain entry forms from the website. Registration fee is €65, and entries must be received at least 10 days before the race.

SWIMMING

Here are some popular swimming venues. You can go swimming for free at the Džbán Reservoir at Divoká Šárka (see the boxed text on p100 for details).

PLAVECKÝ STADIÓN Map pp242-3

Swimming Stadium; ☎ 261 214 343; Podolská 74, Podolí; admission 80/125Kč per 1½/3hr, child under 13 half-price; 🕑 6am-9.45pm; tram 3, 16, 17, 21

There are Olympic-sized indoor and outdoor pools at the Plavecký stadión. To get there, take tram No 3 or 16 to the Dvorce tram stop, from where it's a five-minute walk. Bring footwear for the grotty showers.

SPORTCENTRUM HOTEL ČECHIE

Map pp246-7

☎ 266 194 100; U Sluncové 618, Karlín; 🕑 4-11pm Mon, 1-11pm Tue-Fri, 10am-11pm Sat & Sun; metro Invalidovna

The pool and sauna at the Sportcentrum Hotel Čechie costs 200/100Kč for adult/child under 15 for up to three hours.

SPORTCENTRUM YMCA Map pp246-7

☎ 224 875 811; www.scymca.cz; Na poříčí 12; admission 67.50Kč per hr; 🕑 6.30am-1pm & 4-10pm Mon-Fri, 10am-8.30pm Sat & Sun; metro Náměstí Republiky

There is a 25m-deep pool at the Sportcentrum YMCA. The pool is not available to the public at all times; you should check the website (follow the link Služby/Bázen for the relevant information) – the sessions that are blocked out in green and marked 'veřejnost' are open to the public.

TENNIS & SQUASH
ČESKÝ LAWN TENNIS KLUB Map pp256-7

☎ 224 810 272; Ostrov Štvanice 38, Holešovice; admission 400Kč per hr after 3pm Mon-Fri, 200Kč before 3pm & all day Sat & Sun; 🕑 6am-11pm Apr-Oct; tram 3, 26

Among the many places across the city to play tennis is the prestigious Český Lawn Tennis Klub, which is the oldest tennis club in the country.

ESQUO SQUASHCENTRUM Map pp250-1

☎ 233 109 301; www.squashstrahov.cz; Vaníčkova 2b, Strahov; 🕑 7am-11pm Mon-Fri, 8am-11pm Sat & Sun

The Esquo Squashcentrum offers squash courts for 120Kč to 280Kč per hour, depending on the time of day.

SPORTCENTRUM HOTEL ČECHIE

Map pp246-7

☎ 266 194 100; U Sluncové 618, Karlín; 🕑 7am-11pm Mon-Fri, 8am-11pm Sat & Sun; metro Invalidovna

You can rent outdoor clay courts for 100Kč to 200Kč per hour, and you can book indoor courts for 300Kč to 650Kč per hour at the Sportcentrum Hotel Čechie. It also offers squash courts for 200Kč to 350Kč per hour. There is also a pool here (see left for more information).

Shopping

Shopping

In recent years Prague has succumbed to a wave of rampant consumerism, with glitzy new shopping malls crammed with designer outlets, smart cafés and big Western brand names springing up all over the place. The swanky Slovanský dům (p174) mall, opened in 2001, was followed by the huge Nový Smíchov (p175) in 2002 and Palác Flóra (p175) in 2003.

Imported goods often carry Western European prices, but Czech products remain affordable for Czechs and cheap for Westerners. While tourist gift shops outside Prague (eg in Karlštejn or Mělník, see p198) have smaller selections, prices are significantly lower. If you're hunting for bargains, the word 'sleva' means 'discount'.

Shopping Areas

The city centre's single biggest – and most exhausting – retail zone is around **Wenceslas Square** (Václavské náměstí; Map pp252–3), its pavements jammed with browsing visitors and locals making beelines for their favourite stores. You can find pretty much everything here, from high fashion and music megastores to run-of-the-mill department stores and gigantic book emporia. Many of the more interesting shops are hidden away in arcades and passages, such as the **Palác Lucerna** (Map pp252–3).

The other main shopping drag intersects with the lower end of Wenceslas Square, comprising **Na příkopě** (Map pp256–7), **28.října** (Map pp252–3) and **Národní třída** (Map pp252–3). Most of the big stores and malls are concentrated on Na příkopě.

In Staré Město, the elegant avenue of **Pařížská** (Map pp246–7) is lined with international designer boutiques, including Dior, Boss, Louis Vuitton and Fabergé, while the winding lanes between the Old Town Square and Charles Bridge are thronged with tacky souvenir shops flaunting puppets, Russian dolls and 'Czech This Out' T-shirts.

Opening Hours

Prague shops usually open anywhere between 8am and 10am, and close between 5pm and 7pm on Monday to Friday; major shops, departments stores and tourist businesses open on weekends, too, but more local shops may be closed on Saturday afternoon and Sunday.

Consumer Taxes

Value-added tax (VAT, or DPH in Czech) is applied at 5% on food, hotel rooms and restaurant meals, but 22% on luxury items (including alcohol). This tax is included in the marked price and not added at the cash register.

It is possible to claim VAT refunds for purchases worth more than 1000Kč made in shops displaying the 'Tax Free Shopping' sticker. They will give you a VAT Refund Form, which you then present to customs for validation when you leave the country (which must be within 30 days from the date of purchase). You can then claim your refund from a collecting agency (listed in the ubiquitous *Where to Shop Tax Free – Prague* brochure) within six weeks of the purchase date.

HRADČANY

ANTIQUE MUSIC INSTRUMENTS
Map pp244-5   *Antiques*
☎ 233 353 779; Pohořelec 9; ◷ 9am-6pm;
metro Malostranská

It may not get the prize for Prague's most inventive shop name, but this place is a real

---

Top Five Jewellery Shops

- Belda Jewellery (p172)
- Galerie Vlasta (p169)
- Granát Turnov (p169)
- Fabergé (p169)
- U České orlice (p171)

treasure-trove of vintage stringed instruments. You'll find an interesting stock of antique violins, violas and cellos dating from the 18th century up to the mid-20th century, as well as bows, cases and other musical accessories.

ICONS GALLERY Map pp244-5 *Antiques*
☎ 233 353 777; Pohořelec 9; ⏱ 9am-6pm; metro Malostranská

In the same building as Antique Music Instruments (above), this cluttered little shop has a luminous collection of Russian and Eastern European religious icons, as well as lots of other decorative *objets d'art*, watches, porcelain and Art Nouveau glassware.

MALÁ STRANA

CAPRICCIO Map pp250-1 *Music*
☎ 257 320 165; Újezd 15; ⏱ 9am-5pm Mon-Fri; tram 6, 9, 12, 20

Pick up the score for Mozart's *Don Giovanni* or Dvořák's *From the New World* at this eclectic sheet-music shop. Those who don't play might enjoy the books of country music favourites – who wouldn't want to learn how to sing *Rhinestone Cowboy* in Czech?

MÝRNYX TÝRNYX ECLECTIKS
Map pp244-5 *Fashion*
☎ 224 923 270; Saská; ⏱ 11am-7pm; tram 12, 20, 22, 23

Carefully selected second-hand designer clothes and retro rags share rack space with original designs for brave fashionistas (of both sexes) in this intriguing and exciting fashion store. Mýrnyx represents cutting-edge designers from both the Czech Republic and Germany.

SPORT SLIVKA
Map pp250-1 *Outdoor Sportswear*
☎ 257 007 231; Újezd 42; ⏱ 10am-6pm Mon-Fri, 10am-1pm Sat; tram 12, 20, 22, 23

This shop has vast racks of skis and snowboards, shelves jammed with climbing and camping gear and other outdoor equipment, and inexpensive T-shirts, hoodies and baggy pants. Local brands of camping and climbing gear are often of good quality, and much cheaper than their Western counterparts.

VETEŠNICTVI Map pp250-1 *Antiques*
☎ 257 530 624; Vítezná 16; ⏱ 10am-5pm Mon-Fri, 10am-noon Sat; tram 6, 9, 12, 20, 22, 23

This is an Aladdin's cave of second-hand goods, bric-a-brac and junk with, in all likelihood, some genuine antiques for those who know what they're doing. There's affordable stuff for everyone, from communist-era lapel pins, medals, postcards, old beer mugs and toys to crystal, shot glasses, porcelain, china, pipes and spa cups, all presided over by a bust of Lenin.

STARÉ MĚSTO

ANAGRAM Map pp246-7 *Books*
☎ 224 895 737; Týn 4; ⏱ 10am-8pm Mon-Sat, 10am-6pm Sun; metro Náměstí Republiky

An excellent English-language bookshop, Anagram has a vast range of fiction and nonfiction, with an especially good selection on European history, philosophy, religion, art and travel, as well as Czech works in translation and children's books. Seek out the remainders section for some bargain new books and second-hand offerings on various topics.

ANTIKVARIÁT KAREL KŘENEK
Map pp246-7 *Antiques*
☎ 222 314 734; U Obecního domů 2; ⏱ 10am-6pm Mon-Fri, 11am-6pm Sat; metro Náměstí Republiky

Clothing Sizes
Measurements approximate only, try before you buy

Women's Clothing

Aus/UK	8	10	12	14	16	18
Europe	36	38	40	42	44	46
Japan	5	7	9	11	13	15
USA	6	8	10	12	14	16

Women's Shoes

Aus/USA	5	6	7	8	9	10
Europe	35	36	37	38	39	40
France only	35	36	38	39	40	42
Japan	22	23	24	25	26	27
UK	3½	4½	5½	6½	7½	8½

Men's Clothing

Aus	92	96	100	104	108	112
Europe	46	48	50	52	54	56
Japan	S		M	M		L
UK/USA	35	36	37	38	39	40

Men's Shirts (Collar Sizes)

Aus/Japan	38	39	40	41	42	43
Europe	38	39	40	41	42	43
UK/USA	15	15½	16	16½	17	17½

Men's Shoes

Aus/UK	7	8	9	10	11	12
Europe	41	42	43	44½	46	47
Japan	26	27	27½	28	29	30
USA	7½	8½	9½	10½	11½	12½

This fascinating shop has a huge range of old maps, photographs and watercolours, and books in Czech, German and French dating from the 16th to 19th centuries. There are also antique engravings and decorative graphics, including some views of old Prague.

ART DECO GALERIE

Map pp246-7 *Antiques*

☎ 224 223 076; Michalská 21; ⏰ 2-7pm Mon-Fri; metro Můstek

Specialising in early-20th-century items, this shop has a wide range of 1920s and '30s stuff, including clothes, handbags, jewellery, glassware and ceramics, along with knick-knacks, such as cigarette cases of the sort you might imagine Dorothy Parker pulling from her purse.

ART DÉCORATIF Map pp246-7 *Arts & Crafts*

☎ 224 222 283; Melantrichova 5; ⏰ 10am-8pm; metro Můstek

This is a beautiful shop dealing in Czech-made reproductions of fine Art Nouveau and Art Deco glassware, jewellery and fabrics, including some stunning vases and bowls. It's also an outlet for the gorgeously delicate creations of Jarmila Plockova, granddaughter of Alfons Mucha, who uses elements of his paintings in her work.

ARZENAL Map pp246-7 *Glassware*

☎ 224 814 099; Valentinská 11; ⏰ 10am-midnight; metro Staroměstská

Arzenal is a design salon and showroom for the striking and colourful glassware of Bořek Šípek, one of the Czech Republic's leading architects and designers. Unusually, it is also home to one of the city's best Thai restaurants Siam-I-San (p124).

BIG BEN Map pp246-7 *Books*

☎ 224 826 565; Malá Štupartská 5; ⏰ 9am-6.30pm Mon-Fri, 10am-5pm Sat & Sun; metro Náměstí Republiky

Big Ben is a small but well-stocked English-language bookshop, with shelves devoted to Czech and European history, books on Prague, travel (including Lonely Planet guides), science fiction, children's books, poetry, and all the latest fiction bestsellers. There are also English-language newspapers and magazines at the counter.

BLUE KING GALLERY

Map pp246-7 *Arts & Crafts*

☎ 603 536 488; Týn 1; ⏰ 10.30am-7pm; metro Náměstí Republiky

This gallery tucked in a corner of the Týnský dvůr is a showcase for fine-quality puppets created by Czech craftsmen and women, as well as man-made dolls and glassware. They don't come cheap, though – one of the larger marionettes will cost around €500 to €700.

BOHÉME Map pp246-7 *Fashion*

☎ 224 813 840; Dušní 8; ⏰ 11am-8pm Mon-Fri, 11am-5pm Sat; metro Staroměstská

Opened in 2002, this trendy fashion store showcases the designs of Hana Stocklassa and her associates, with collections of knitwear, leather and suede clothes for women. Sweaters, turtlenecks, suede skirts, linen blouses, knit dresses and stretch denim suits seem to be the stock in trade, and there's a range of jewellery to choose from as well.

BOTANICUS Map pp246-7 *Cosmetics*

☎ 224 895 445; Týn 3; ⏰ 10am-8pm; metro Náměstí Republiky

Prepare for olfactory overload in this always-busy outlet for natural health and beauty products. The scented soaps, herbal bath oils and shampoos, fruit cordials and handmade paper products are made using herbs and plants grown on an organic farm at Ostrá, east of Prague.

BRÍC Á BRAC Map pp246-7 *Antiques*

☎ 224 815 763; Týnská 7; ⏰ 10am-6pm; metro Náměstí Republiky

Hidden up a narrow lane behind the Týn church, this is a wonderfully cluttered Aladdin's cave of old household items and glassware and toys and apothecary jars and 1940s leather jackets and cigar boxes and typewriters and stringed instruments and… Despite the junky look of the place, the knick-knacks are surprisingly expensive; there are two 'showrooms', a small one on Týnská, and a larger one in a nearby courtyard (follow the signs), and the affable Serbian owner can give you a guided tour around every piece in his extensive collection.

EDUARD ČAPEK Map p255   *Bric-a-Brac*
Dlouhá 32; ⏱ **10am-6pm Mon-Fri;**
metro Náměstí Republiky
The Čapek clan has lovingly operated its bric-à-brac shop since 1911 – it was supposedly the only shop to continue in private ownership throughout the communist era – and nothing has ever been thrown away, including the dust. Rolls of recycled electrical wire, rusty tools, dog-eared magazines and battered handbags are among the many, er…treasures awaiting your perusal.

FABERGÉ Map pp246-7   *Jewellery*
☎ **222 323 639; Pařížská 15;** ⏱ **10am-8pm;**
metro Staroměstská
Jewellers to the Russian royal family, Fabergé certainly knows how to put on a dazzling display. This gorgeously stocked store contains its trademark Easter egg pendants, as well as a sparkly array of rings, cufflinks, brooches, bracelets and necklaces.

GALERIE VLASTA Map pp246-7   *Jewellery*
☎ **222 318 119; Staroměstské náměsti 5;** ⏱ **10am-6pm Mon-Fri, 10am-1pm Sat; metro Staroměstská**
This small boutique showcases the delicate creations in gold and silver wire of award-winning contemporary Czech designer Vlasta Wasserbauerová, including a range of highly distinctive net-like brooches, necklaces and earrings.

GRANÁT TURNOV Map pp246-7   *Jewellery*
☎ **222 315 612; Dlouhá 28-30;** ⏱ **10am-6pm Mon-Sat, 10am-1pm Sun; metro Náměstí Republiky**
Part of the country's biggest jewellery chain, and specialising in Bohemian garnet, Granát Turnov stocks a huge range of gold and silver rings, brooches, cufflinks and necklaces showing off these small, dark blood-red stones. It also has pearl and diamond jewellery, as well as less expensive pieces set with the dark green semi-precious stone known in Czech as *vltavín* (moldavite).

IVANA FOLLOVÁ ART & FASHION
GALLERY Map pp246-7   *Fashion*
☎ **224 895 460; Týn 1;** ⏱ **10am-6pm; metro Náměstí Republiky**
Prague designer Ivana Follová specialises in hand-painted silk dresses, many of which can be seen at this chic boutique. Only natural materials are used in her colourful creations. The shop also has accessories, including handmade glass beads, and some excellent, if pricey, locally produced paintings, jewellery and sculpture.

KERAMIKA V UNGELTU
Map pp246-7   *Arts & Crafts*
Týn 7; ⏱ **10am-6pm; metro Náměstí Republiky**
This little shop in a corner of the Týnský dvůr is a good place to look for both traditional Bohemian pottery and modern blue-and-white wares, with prices up to 25% lower than at many other outlets in Staré Město.

KLARA NADEMLÝNSKÁ Map p255 *Fashion*
☎ **224 818 769; Dlouhá 3;** ⏱ **10am-6pm Mon-Fri, 11am-6pm Sat; metro Staroměstská**
Klara Nademlýnská is one of the Czech Republic's top fashion designers, having trained in Prague and worked for almost a decade in Paris. Her clothes are characterised by clean lines, simple styling and quality materials, making for a very wearable range that covers the spectrum from swimwear to evening wear via jeans, halter tops, colourful blouses and sharply styled suits.

KOTVA Map pp246-7   *Department Store*
☎ **224 801 111; náměstí Republiky 8;** ⏱ **9am-8pm Mon-Fri, 10am-7pm Sat, 10am-6pm Sun; metro Náměstí Republiky**
This huge, ugly brown mall has five floors of varied goods, from stationery and cosmetics on the ground floor, through furniture, china, glass kitchenware toys and sports equipment, to electronics and electrical goods on the top floor. There's also a pharmacy and tax-free shopping service on the ground floor, including a supermarket in the basement (see p117 for more details).

KUBISTA Map pp246-7   *Arts & Crafts*
☎ **224 236 378; Ovocný trh 19;** ⏱ **10am-6pm; metro Náměstí Republiky**
Appropriately located in the **Muzeum Českého Kubismu** (p77), Prague's finest Cubist building, this shop specialises in limited-edition reproductions of distinctive Cubist furniture and ceramics, and designs by masters of the form, such as Josef Gočár and Pavel Janák. It also has a few original pieces for serious collectors with serious cash to spend.

LE PATIO LIFESTYLE Map p255 *Homewares*
☎ **222 320 260; Pařížská 20;** ⏱ **10am-7pm Mon-Sat, 11am-7pm Sun; metro Staroměstská**

There are lots of high-quality household accessories here, from wrought-iron chairs and lamps forged by Bohemian blacksmiths to scented wooden chests made by Indian carpenters. Plus you'll find funky earthenware plant pots, chunky crystal wine glasses in contemporary designs, and many more tempting items that you just *know* will fit into your already crammed suitcase…

MANUFAKTURA Map pp246-7   *Arts & Crafts*
☎ 221 632 48; Melantrichova 17; ☽ 10am-7pm
Mon-Thu, to 7.30pm Fri-Sun; metro Můstek

This is the biggest of six shops of the same name scattered between Prague Castle and the Old Town Square, all stocked with quality wooden toys, scented soaps, beeswax candles, ceramics, linen and ironwork – handmade in traditional styles and/or using traditional materials. Things to look out for include painted Easter eggs, wooden kitchen utensils, colourful ceramics with traditional designs and Bohemian lacework.

MAXIMUM UNDERGROUND
Map pp246-7   *Music*
☎ 222 541 333; Jílská 22; ☽ 11am-7pm; metro Můstek

In an arcade just off Jílská, this place is stocked with CDs and LPs of indie, punk, hip-hop, techno and other contemporary genres. It also has a selection of new and second-hand street- and club-wear for those after that Central European grunge look.

MODERNISTA Map pp252-3   *Furniture*
☎ 222 220 113; Konviktská 5; ☽ 2-6pm Mon-Fri,
11am-4pm Sat; metro Národní Třída

Modernista is an elegant gallery specialising in reproduction 20th-century furniture in classic styles ranging from Art Deco and Cubist to functionalist and Bauhaus. Its collection includes those sensuously curved chairs by Jindřich Halabala and an unusual chaise lounge by Adolf Loos, a copy of the one you can see in the drawing room of the **Müllerova Vila** (p99).

PHILHARMONIA Map pp246-7   *Music*
☎ 224 811 258; Pařížská 13; ☽ 10am-6pm; metro
Staroměstská

You can sample entire collections of classics at this superbly stocked store where you'll find the works of top Czech composers, including Dvořák, Smetana and Janáček. You will also find jazz, Czech folk music and Jewish music and an eclectic selection of 'marginal genres', including rockabilly, blues and other random offerings.

Easter eggs for sale, Manufaktura (see above), Staré Město

Browsing through CD selection at Philharmonia (see opposite) , Staré Město

ROTT CRYSTAL Map pp246-7   *Glassware*
☎ 224 229 529; Malé náměstí 3; ⏲ 10am-10pm;
metro Staroměstská

This place is housed in a beautifully restored neo-Renaissance building – originally an iron-mongers' – with 1890s wall paintings on the façade, Rott now has four floors of glassware, jewellery and ceramics, but it's best known for its stock of fine-quality Bohemian and imported crystal.

SANU-BABU Map pp246-7   *Speciality*
☎ 221 632 401; Michalská 20; ⏲ 10.30am-10.30pm;
metro Můstek

This Old Town hideaway is a sandalwood-scented hippie heaven filled with all manner of New Age essentials, including incense sticks and holders, bongs, handmade Nepalese paper, wooden carvings and a colourful range of Nepalese clothes.

SIRIUS DESIGN
Map pp246-7   *Interior Design*
☎ 222 319 536; Dlouhá 32; ⏲ 9am-7pm Mon-Fri,
10am-4pm Sat; metro Náměstí Republiky

The long-established Sirius is one of Prague's top design agencies – its CV ranges from contributions to Expo 1958 to designing the lighting for the exclusive **Kampa Park restaurant** (p119). Its showroom highlights the best in European interior design, including fabrics, lighting, carpets and modular furniture.

SPARKYS Map pp246-7   *Toys*
☎ 224 239 309; Havířská 2; ⏲ 10am-7pm Mon-Sat,
10am-6pm Sun; metro Můstek

Sparkys is an inviting toy store with lots of stuffed animals ranging from small to ultrahuge, as well as model cars, computer games, board games and cartoon videos and DVDs. A second branch located in the **Slovanský dům** (p174) sells baby clothes, prams and toys for tots.

STAROŽITNOSTI ALMA
Map pp246-7   *Antiques*
☎ 222 325 865; Valentinská 7; ⏲ 10am-6pm;
metro Staroměstská

Alma specialises in Art Nouveau and Art Deco antiques, and also has a wide selection of rather twee porcelain and lacy items, rather stuffy furniture and glassware, and a veritable army of scary looking dolls.

STAROŽITNOSTI V. ANDRLE
Map pp246-7   *Antiques*
☎ 222 311 625; Křížovnická 1; ⏲ 10am-7pm Mon-Sat,
10am-6pm Sun; metro Staroměstská

Mr Andrle's shop is a little treasure house of antique gold, jewellery, clocks, watches, glassware and ceramics from all over Central Europe, and is a regular port of call for serious collectors from around the world.

TUPESY LIDOVÁ KERAMIKA
Map pp246-7   *Ceramics*
☎ 224 210 728; Havelská 21; ⏲ 10am-6pm;
metro Můstek

Tupesy Lidová Keramika stocks a good selection of folk ceramícs in traditional blue, green and yellow patterns that come from the Slovácko region of Moravia and the Chodsko region of Bohemia.

U ČESKÉ ORLICE Map pp246-7   *Jewellery*
☎ 224 228 544; Celetná 30; ⏲ 10am-8pm;
metro Náměstí Republiky

'At the Bohemian Eagle' – the symbol of the Czech nation – houses a range of elegant traditional Czech jewellery, including lots of elaborate garnet and chunky amber, as well as more restrained pieces in gold and silver. Exquisite hand-painted porcelain and other *objets d'art* fill out the shop.

NOVÉ MĚSTO

BAŤA Map pp252-3 *Shoes*

☎ 224 218 133; Václavské náměstí 6; ⏰ 9am-9pm Mon-Fri, 9am-7pm Sat, 10am-6pm Sun; metro Můstek

Established by Tomáš Baťa in 1894, the Baťa footwear empire is still in family hands and is one of the Czech Republic's most successful companies. The flagship store on Wenceslas Square, built in the 1920s, is considered a masterpiece of modern architecture, and houses six floors of shoes (including international brands, such as Nike, Salomon and Cat, as well as Baťa's own), handbags, luggage and leather goods.

BAZAR Map pp252-3 *Music*

☎ 602 313 730; Krakovská 4; ⏰ 9am-7pm Mon-Fri, 10am-2pm Sat; metro Muzeum

There's a vast selection of second-hand CDs, LPs and videos to browse through here at Bazar, representing a wide range of genres. Czech and Western pop jostle with jazz, blues, heavy metal, country and world music, though with CDs costing around 300Kč to 400Kč this place is not exactly what you'd call a bargain basement.

BELDA JEWELLERY Map pp252-3 *Jewellery*

☎ 224 910 476; Mikulandská 10; ⏰ 9am-6pm Mon-Fri; metro Národní Třída

Belda & Co is a long-established Czech firm, dating from 1922. Nationalised in 1948 it was revived by the founder's son and grandson, and continues to create gold and silver jewellery of a very high standard. Its range includes its own angular, contemporary designs, as well as reproductions based on Art Nouveau designs by Alfons Mucha.

BONTONLAND Map pp252-3 *Music*

☎ 224 473 080; Václavské náměstí 1-3; ⏰ 9am-8pm Mon-Sat, 10am-7pm Sun; metro Můstek

Supposedly the biggest music megastore in the Czech Republic, this place covers pretty much everything, including Western chart music, classical, jazz, dance, and heavy metal, as well as an extensive collection of Czech pop. Bontonland also sells videos and DVDs, and has a large Playstation arena and Internet café.

DĚTSKÝ DŮM Map pp246-7 *Toys*

☎ 272 142 401; Na příkopě 15; ⏰ 9.30am-8pm Mon-Sat, 10am-6pm Sun; metro Můstek

Top Five English-Language Bookshops

- Anagram (p167)
- Big Ben (p168)
- Globe Bookshop & Café (p173)
- Palác Knih Neo Luxor (p174)
- Shakespeare & Sons (p175)

'House of Children' is a modern mall devoted to kid's stuff, with a number of specialist outlets selling such things as model cars, video games and stuffed toys. Other shops here sell children's shoes and trendy clothes for those diminutive divas who just have to have Kenzo.

DEVÁTÁ VLNA Map pp252-3 *Fashion*

☎ 224 917 773; Pasáž Metro, Národní třída 25; ⏰ 11am-7pm Mon-Sat, 10am-7pm Sun; metro Národní Třída

Young and local Prague designers Dita Ladovská and Kateřina Kašparová whip up extremely wearable, affordable street wear for gals, including skirts, hoodies, trousers and some very cute dresses and even swimsuits. 'Ninth Wave' also stocks covetable T-shirts from other local designers.

FOTO ŠKODA Map pp252-3 *Photography*

☎ 222 929 029; Vodičkova 37; ⏰ 8.30am-8pm Mon-Fri, 9am-6pm Sat; metro Můstek

One of Prague's biggest camera shops, Foto Škoda stocks a wide range of digital and film cameras, video cameras, film (professional as well as amateur) and photographic accessories. It also sells used cameras, and offers a camera repair service.

FRUITS DE FRANCE

Map pp252-3 *Delicatessen*

☎ 224 220 304; Jindřišská 9; ⏰ 9.30am-6.30pm Mon-Fri, 9.30am-1pm Sat; metro Můstek

Francophile foodies will make a beeline for this delectable deli and its range of fine French wines, cheeses, pastries and all manner of fresh, canned and bottled French fare.

GIGASPORT Map pp246-7 *Sportswear*

☎ 224 233 552; Myslbek Bldg, Na příkopě 19-21; ⏰ 9.30am-7pm; metro Můstek

This sporting superstore in the Myslbek Shopping Centre has three floors of sportswear

Shopping – Nové Město

and equipment, covering just about all the activities and big-name brands that you might want. You're not allowed to take large bags into the store – use the lockers just inside the door.

GLOBE BOOKSHOP & CAFÉ

Map pp252-3 *Books*

☎ 224 934 203; Pštrossova 6; ☺ 10am-midnight; metro Karlovo Náměstí

A popular hang-out for book-hunting backpackers, the Globe is a cosy English-language bookshop with a quiet café (p130) in which to peruse your purchases. There's a good range of new fiction and nonfiction, as well as a big selection of second-hand novels.

HELENA FEJKOVÁ GALLERY

Map pp252-3 *Fashion*

☎ 224 211 514; Lucerna Pasáž, Štěpánská 61; ☺ 10am-7pm Mon-Fri, to 3pm Sat; metro Muzeum

Kit yourself out in the latest Czech fashions at this chic boutique and showroom. Contemporary men's and women's fashion and accessories by Prague designer Helena Fejková and others are on display, and private fashion shows can be arranged. There's another branch in the **Kotva department store** (p169).

HUDY SPORT Map pp246-7 *Outdoor Sports*

☎ 224 813 010; Havlíčkova 11; ☺ 9am-6.30pm Mon-Fri, to 1pm Sat; metro Náměstí Republiky

One of the half-dozen branches of this nationwide chain of stores, Hudy Sport provides reasonably priced equipment for hiking, climbing, camping and other outdoor activities and pursuits. There is a good selection of boots, backpacks, sleeping bags, tents, waterproofs and the like, as well as more specialist gear such as crampons, ice axes and climbing ropes. There are seven branches in the city, including another central one at **Na Perštýné 14** (Map pp252-3; ☺ 9am-7pm Mon-Fri, 10am-2pm Sat).

JAN PAZDERA Map pp252-3 *Photography*

☎ 224 216 197; Vodičkova 28; ☺ 10am-6pm Mon-Sat; tram 3, 9, 14, 24

The friendly and knowledgeable staff at this long-standing shop are happy to show you around their impressive stock of second-hand cameras, darkroom gear, lenses, binoculars and telescopes. Models range from the basic but unbreakable Russian-made Zenit to expensive Leicas.

KANZELSBERGER

Map pp252-3 *Books & Maps*

☎ 224 219 214; Václavské náměstí 4; ☺ 9am-7pm; metro Můstek

Housed in the tall, glass-fronted Lindt building at the foot of Wenceslas Square, Kanzelsberger has five floors of bookshelves, with a café on the 1st floor overlooking the square. You'll probably want the top floor, where there's an extensive selection of books in English, German and French, plus hiking and city maps covering the whole of the Czech Republic.

KIWI Map pp252-3 *Books & Maps*

☎ 224 948 455; Jungmannova 23; ☺ 9am-6.30pm Mon-Fri, to 2pm Sat; metro Národní Třída

This small specialist travel bookshop stocks a huge range of maps covering not only the Czech Republic but many other countries. It also has an extensive selection of Lonely Planet guidebooks.

Kanzelsberger bookshop (see above), Wenceslas Square

MARKS & SPENCER

Map pp246-7 *Department Store*

☎ 224 235 735; Myslbek Bldg, Na příkopě 19-21; 🕑 9.30am-8pm Mon-Fri, 10am-7pm Sat, 10.30am-7pm Sun; metro Náměstí Republiky

British high-street fashion comes to Prague, with two floors of men's and women's clothing in M&S's traditional smart-casual style. There's also a small range of kid's clothes and a toiletry section.

MOSER Map pp246-7 *Glassware*

☎ 224 211 293; Na příkopě 12; 🕑 10am-8pm Mon-Fri, 10am-7pm Sat & Sun; metro Můstek

One of the most exclusive and highly respected of Bohemian glass makers, Moser was founded in Karlovy Vary in 1857 and is famous for its rich and flamboyant designs. The shop on Na příkopě is worth a browse as much for the décor as the goods – it's in a magnificently decorated, originally Gothic building called the dům U černé růže (House of the Black Rose).

MOTHERCARE Map pp246-7 *Babycare*

☎ 222 240 008; Myslbek Bldg, Na příkopě 19-21; 🕑 9am-7pm; metro Náměstí Republiky or Můstek

If you're travelling with a baby or toddler, you'll find pretty much everything you need to meet their nonedible demands in this bright and modern babycare shop – toys, clothes, accessories and all manner of other goods for mother and child.

PALÁC KNIH NEO LUXOR

Map pp252-3 *Books*

☎ 221 111 336; Václavské náměstí 41; 🕑 8am-8pm; metro Muzeum

Palác Knih Neo Luxor is Prague's biggest bookshop – head for the basement to find a wide selection of fiction and nonfiction in English, German and French, including Czech authors in translation. You will also find Internet access (1Kč per minute), a café and a good selection of international newspapers and magazines available.

SLOVANSKÝ DŮM

Map pp246-7 *Shopping Centre*

☎ 221 451 400; Na příkopě 22; 🕑 10am-8pm; metro Náměstí Republiky

This is Prague's glitziest shopping mall, at least in terms of its shops if not its appearance, housing numerous upmarket fashion boutiques, a 10-screen multiplex cinema, a

nightclub, and a handful of chic restaurants. There's a pleasant tree-lined courtyard at the back with a beer garden for tired and thirsty shoppers.

STAROŽITNOSTI Z. KRIŽEK

Map pp252-3 *Antiques*

Žitna 3; 🕑 10am-noon & 1-5pm Mon-Fri; metro Karlovo Náměstí

This is a dusty treasure-trove of antique furniture, porcelain toilet bowls, old postcards and photographs, vintage newspapers and magazines, and art books.

SUPRAPHON Map pp252-3 *Music*

☎ 224 948 718; Jungmannova 20; 🕑 9am-7pm Mon-Fri, to 1pm Sat; metro Národní Třída

Music publisher Supraphon is a good option for the serious classical-music buff – not only does it stock recent recordings by top Czech musicians and up-and-coming young performers, Supraphon also has re-releases of archive recordings of great performances of the past. this place also has CDs of traditional Bohemian and Moravian folk music, including spoken-word recordings of Czech legends and fairytales.

SYDNEY STORE Map pp246-7 *Fashion*

☎ 224 398 288; Senovazné náměstí 26; 🕑 9am-7pm Mon-Fri, to 2pm Sat; metro Náměstí Republiky

If you should find yourself in need of an Australian bush hat or Driza-Bone waxed riding coat whilst in Prague, then look no further than this little corner of Aussie style. There is also a range of more conventional clothes from Down Under, of the chequered shirt and chinos variety, as well as the odd pair of hiking boots and a small selection of Australian wine available.

TESCO Map pp252-3 *Department Store*

☎ 222 003 111; Národní třída 26; 🕑 8am-9pm Mon-Fri, 9am-8pm Sat, 10am-8pm Sun; metro Národní Třída

This bustling multistorey maze of consumerism will leave even the hardiest shopaholic feeling dazed and confused. The ground floor minimarket here seems constantly occupied by a shuffling queue of shoppers, but beyond spreads a smorgasbord of quality coffee, chocolates, wine and spirits, stationery and cosmetics. The floors above are crammed with everything from low-priced electrical goods to baby wear, while Tesco's basement houses a rather huge and well-stocked supermarket.

OUTER SUBURBS

Holešovice

PIVNÍ GALERIE Map pp250-1 *Beer*
☎ 220 870 613; U Průhonu 9; ⏱ 10am-8pm Mon-Fri, to 3pm Sat; tram 1, 3, 5, 25

If you think that Czech beer begins and ends with Pilsner Urquell, a visit to the tasting room at Pivní Galerie will soon lift the scales from your eyes. Here you can sample and purchase a huge range of Bohemian and Moravian beers – more than 180 varieties from 34 different breweries – with expert advice from the owner, who speaks both English and Swedish.

Vinohrady

KAREL VÁVRA
Map pp252-3 *Musical Instruments*
☎ 222 518 114; Lublaňská 65; ⏱ 9am-5pm Mon-Fri; metro IP Pavlova

Handmade fiddles decorate the interior of this old-fashioned violin workshop where Karel and his assistants beaver away making and repairing these instruments in time-honoured fashion. Even if you are not in search of a custom-made violin, it's worth a look just for the time-warp atmosphere.

ORIENTÁLNÍ KOBERCE PALÁCKA
Map pp258-9 *Carpets*
☎ 541 214 620; Vinohradská 42; ⏱ 10am-7pm Mon-Fri, to 2pm Sat; metro Náměstí Míru

The 'Oriental Carpet Palace' is a sumptuous showroom stocked with handmade carpets, rugs and wall-hangings from Iran and other Central Asian states. The colourful pieces come in all sizes and prices, in intricate traditional designs, and the knowledgeable staff here will be happy to help you make an informed purchase.

PALÁC FLÓRA
Map pp258-9 *Shopping Centre*
☎ 255 741 712; Vinohradská 151; ⏱ 8am-midnight; metro Flóra

You could be anywhere in the capitalist world in this shiny, glittering shrine to consumerism. Slick cafés share floor space with girly emporia of tiny T-shirts, sparkly makeup and globalised brand names – Hilfiger, Benetton, Puma, Lacoste, Guess, Diesel; a multiplex and IMAX cinema keep the crowds coming in the evenings.

SHAKESPEARE & SONS
Map pp260-1 *Books*
☎ 271 741 839; Krymská 12; ⏱ noon-midnight; tram 4, 22, 23

Though its shelves groan with a formidable range of literature in English, both new and second-hand, Shakes is more than a bookshop – it's a congenial literary hangout, with a café that regularly hosts poetry readings, author events and live jazz, and where you can buy magazines, such as the *New York Review of Books*, *Harpers* and *Atlantic Monthly*, and settle down for a read over coffee and cakes.

VINOHRADSKÝ PAVILÓN
Map pp260-1 *Shopping Centre*
☎ 222 097 111; Vinohradská 50; ⏱ 9.30am-9pm Mon-Sat, noon-8pm Sun; metro Jiřího z Poděbrad

Housed in a lovingly restored 19th-century market pavilion (hence the name), this small but searingly trendy mall has four floors of brand-name boutiques (for example, Tommy Hilfiger, Sergio Tacchini, La Perla), Sony electronics, jewellery, shoes and household goods. Oh, and that obligatory adjunct to all Prague shopping malls – it includes a supermarket in the basement.

Smíchov

MAPIS Map pp250-1 *Maps*
☎ 257 315 459; Štefánikova 63; ⏱ 9am-6.30pm Mon-Fri; tram 6, 9, 12, 20

Mapis is a specialist map shop with a wide selection of local, national and international maps, including hiking maps and city plans covering not jus the city but the whole of the Czech Republic.

NOVÝ SMÍCHOV
Map pp250-1 *Shopping Centre*
☎ 251 511 151; Plzeňská 8; ⏱ 9am-10pm; metro Anděl

Opened in 2002, Nový Smíchov is a vast shopping mall that occupies an area the size of several city blocks. It is an airy, well-designed space with lots of fashion boutiques and niche stores – for example you could check out Pece o Zuby, which has all the dental care products you never knew you needed – a big computer store, a food court, a virtual games hall, a 12-screen multiplex cinema, and it also includes a huge and well-stocked **Carrefour hypermarket** (⏱ 7am-midnight).

Dejvice

ANTIKVITA Map p255   *Antiques*

☎ 233 336 601; Na hutích 9; ☻ 10am-5pm Mon-Fri; **metro Dejvická**

This antique shop is definitely a collector's delight, where·you'll find it is crammed with cases and cabinets overflowing with vintage toys, model trains, dolls, coins, medals, jewellery, clocks, watches, militaria, postcards, porcelain figures, glassware and much, much more. If you have something to sell, Antikvita offers buying sessions on Wednesday and Thursday.

Sleeping

Sleeping

Accommodation Styles

Prague offers a wide range of accommodation options, from cosy, romantic hotels set in historic town houses to luxurious international chain hotels, and from budget hostels and pensions to a new generation of sharply styled boutique hotels. Most mid-range and top-end hotels have rooms with private bathrooms, but some older mid-range places and many budget hotels (especially those outside the centre) still offer cheaper rooms with shared facilities. Note that a 'hotel garni' denotes a hotel that does not have a restaurant.

An increasing number of Prague hotels provide specially adapted rooms and facilities for wheelchair users; we have noted these facilities in the individual listings.

Check-in & Check-out Times

Hotels usually require you to check out on the day of departure between 10am and noon. Later than this and you run the risk of being charged for a further night; check with individual hotels for specific regulations. As to check-in times, there are no hard and fast rules, but if you're going to arrive late in the day, it's probably best to mention this when you book your room. Many hostels will not accept prior reservations for dorm beds, so arrive after 10am and it's first come, first served. Check-out times are often earlier in hostels, typically around 9am.

Price Ranges

A double room in a mid-range hotel in central Prague will cost around 4000Kč to 5000Kč; outside the centre, this might fall to around 3500Kč. Top-range hotels cost from 6000Kč. The 'cheap sleeps' options listed in this chapter charge 2500Kč or less for a double room. Note that some mid-range and top-end hotels quote rates in euros, and a few quote in US dollars. At these hotels you can pay cash in Czech crowns if you like, but the price will depend on the exchange rate on the day you settle the bill.

The rates quoted in this chapter are for high season, which generally covers April to June, September and October, and the Christmas/New Year holidays. July and August are mid-season, and the rest of the year is low season.

Accommodation Agencies

Alfa Tourist Service (Map pp246-7; ☎ 224 230 037; www.alfatourist.cz; Opletalova 38, Nové Město; ✆ 9am-5pm Mon-Fri) Can provide accommodation in student hostels, pensions, hotels and private rooms.

Apartments.CZ (Map pp252-3; ☎ 224 990 900; www.apartments.cz; Ostrovní 7, Nové Město; ✆ 9am-5pm Mon-Fri) Long-established specialist in holiday apartments near the city centre.

AVE (Map pp252-3; ☎ 251 551 011; www.avetravel.cz; Praha-hlavní nádraží, Nové Město; ✆ 6am-11pm) Convenient offices at the main train station, Praha-Holešovice train station, Ruzyně airport and PIS offices (see p222).

Happy House Rentals (Map pp246-7; ☎ 222 312 488; www.happyhouserentals.com; Vodičkova 37; ✆ 9am-5pm Mon-Fri) Specialises in short-term rental apartments.

Hostels in Prague (www.hostel.cz) Website database of around 60 hostels, with a secure online booking system.

Mary's Travel & Tourist Service (Map pp252-3; ☎ 222 253 510; www.marys.cz; Italská 31, Vinohrady; ✆ 9am-9pm) Private rooms, hostels, pensions, apartments and hotels in all price ranges in Prague and surrounding areas.

Stop City (Map pp252-3; ☎ 222 521 233; www.stopcity.com; Vinohradská 24, Vinohrady; ✆ 10am-9pm Apr-Oct, 11am-8pm Nov-Mar) Specialises in apartments, private rooms and pensions in the Vinohrady and Žižkov areas.

Even high-season rates can be inflated by up to 15% on certain dates, notably at New Year, Easter and at weekends (Thursday to Sunday) in May, June and September.

Most hostel, pension and budget hotel rates do not include breakfast; most mid-range and top-end hotel rates do. If only a double-room rate is quoted, then that's what you'll pay for single use, too.

Reservations

Booking your accommodation in advance is strongly recommended (especially if you want to stay in or near the centre), and there are dozens of agencies that will help you find a place to stay – some better than others. The places listed in the boxed text on p178 are reliable, and even if you turn up in peak period without a booking, these agencies should be able to find you a bed.

Longer-Term Rentals

More and more travellers are discovering the pleasures of renting an apartment in Prague. Before you scoff at the idea, consider that the extra cost of a very basic self-catering flat near the centre means minimal transportation costs, access to cheap local food, and the freedom to come and go as you like.

There are many Prague agencies that will find a flat for you (see Reservations; above). Typical rates for a modern two-person apartment with living room/bedroom, bathroom, TV and kitchenette range from around 1000/5000/13,000Kč per night/week/month for a place in the outer suburbs, to around 2200/11,000/28,000Kč for a flat near Old Town Square. All short-term rental apartments are fully furnished and serviced, meaning that utilities (gas, water, electricity) and bed linen are included in the price, and staff will clean up and change the beds at least weekly.

The real estate section of the weekly *Prague Post* (www.praguepost.cz) newspaper also lists dozens of agencies and private individuals with apartments to rent by the month.

HRADČANY

Stay in Hradčany and you're only a few minutes from the castle. It's a mostly peaceful district, as the crowds drain away at the day's end leaving the streets almost deserted.

DOMUS HENRICI Map pp246-7   *Hotel*
☎ 220 511 369; www.domus-henrici.cz;
Loretánská 11; s/d from €140/155; tram 22, 23; 🖳
This historic building in a quiet corner of Hradčany is intentionally nondescript out front, hinting that peace and privacy are top priorities here. There are eight spacious and stylish rooms, half with private fax, scanner/copier and Internet access, and a sunny terrace with sigh-inducing views over the city.

HOTEL HOFFMEISTER Map pp244-5   *Hotel*
☎ 251 017 111; www.hoffmeister.cz; Pod Bruskou 7;
s/d €250/290; metro Malostranská
Named after caricaturist Adolf Hoffmeister, whose works adorn a gallery here, this hotel is

the chosen meeting place for Prague's Rotary Club, which should tell you something about the atmosphere – plush, pink, chintzy and a tad overdressed. It is, however, very comfortable, has excellent service, and is right at the foot of the Old Castle Steps.

HOTEL SAVOY Map pp244-5   *Hotel*
☎ 224 302 430; www.hotel-savoy.cz; Keplerova 6;
d €320; tram 22, 23
The 55-room Savoy boasts spacious rooms (all have a sitting area) and big marble bathrooms, plus a leather-bound library, sky-lit restaurant

and roof terrace. It pampers guests with in-house fitness trainers, hairdressers, sauna and gym, and previous celebrity guests have included Bruce Willis, David Bowie, Tina Turner and Princess Caroline of Monaco.

ROMANTIK HOTEL U RAKA

Map pp244-5   *Hotel*

☎ 220 511 100; www.romantikhotels.com; Černínská 10; s/d 6200/7900Kč; tram 22, 23

Concealed in a manicured rock garden in a quiet corner of Hradčany, the historic Hotel U Raka is an atmospheric, late-18th-century timber cottage with just six elegant doubles ideal for romantic getaways – kids aged under 10 are not allowed. Book a few months ahead in summer.

MALÁ STRANA

Lots of Malá Strana's lovely old Renaissance and baroque buildings have been converted into hotels and apartments, making this a good district to stay in if you're looking for a place with a romantic atmosphere. You'll also be within walking distance of Charles Bridge, ideal for those atmospheric evening strolls.

BEST WESTERN HOTEL KAMPA

Map pp250-1   *Hotel*

☎ 257 320 508; www.euroagentur.cz; Všehrdova 16; s/d €160/190; tram 6, 9, 12, 20, 22, 23; Ⓟ ▣

This comfortable Best Western hotel is set in a quiet and convenient location near the southern end of Kampa island. Subtle décor is not a strong point in the hotel's public areas – the pseudo-Gothic 'Knight's Hall' restaurant is an extravaganza of candelabras and suits of armour – but fortunately the rooms are rather more restrained.

HOTEL ARIA Map pp244-5   *Boutique Hotel*

☎ 225 334 111; www.ariahotel.net; Tržiště 9; d from €195; tram 12, 20, 22, 23; Ⓟ ▣

The Aria offers five-star luxury with a musical theme – each of the four floors is dedicated to a musical genre (jazz, opera, classical and contemporary), and each room celebrates a particular artist or musician and contains a selection of their music that you can enjoy on the in-room hifi system. Other facilities include a music and movie library, screening room, fitness centre and steam room.

HOTEL NERUDA

Map pp244-5   *Boutique Hotel*

☎ 257 535 557; www.hotelneruda-praha.cz; Nerudova 44; s/d €200/220; tram 12, 20, 22, 23; ▣

Set in a tastefully renovated Gothic house dating from 1348, the Neruda offers a refreshingly modern and stylish alternative to the often tacky, so-called 'historic' hotels, which are all too common in Malá Strana. The décor is chic and minimalist in shades of chocolate and cream, with Internet connections in each room and an appealing café in the atrium.

HOTEL SAX Map pp244-5   *Hotel*

☎ 257 531 268; www.sax.cz; Jánský vršek 3; s/d 4100/4400Kč; tram 12, 20, 22, 23

Set in a quiet corner of Malá Strana, the Sax is refreshingly low-key and unpretentious, with tidy, uncluttered rooms and sleek, modern décor. The rates are very reasonable considering its location – less than 10 minutes' walk from the castle's main gate.

HOTEL U PÁVA Map pp244-5   *Hotel*

☎ 257 320 743; www.romantichotels.cz; U lužického semináře 32; s/d from 5400/5900Kč; metro Malostranská; Ⓟ ▣

As its name (At the Peacock) might suggest, this hotel proudly displays its colourfully renovated Gothic and Renaissance interior. The rooms are richly decorated with painted wooden ceilings, rich textiles, antique furniture and stained glass, and some have magical views of Prague Castle.

HOTEL U PŠTROSŮ Map pp244-5   *Hotel*

☎ 257 532 410; www.upstrosu.cz; Dražického náměstí 12; s/d 5900/7900Kč; tram 12, 20, 22, 23; Ⓟ ▣

'At the Ostriches' is a grand old merchant's house at the foot of the Malá Strana bridge tower on Charles Bridge (see the boxed text on p68). Dating from the 15th century, it's filled with interesting historic details, including Renaissance frescoes and painted wooden ceilings. The hotel enjoys an unbeatable location, and many rooms have splendid views across Charles Bridge.

Sleeping – Malá Strana

HOTEL U ZLATÉ STUDNĚ

Map pp244-5   *Hotel*

☎ 257 011 213; www.zlatastudna.cz; U Zlaté studně 4
s/d 6000/6300Kč, ste 7900-9900Kč;
metro Malostranská;

'At the Golden Well' is one of Malá Strana's more tasteful renovations – a Renaissance house that once belonged to Emperor Rudolf II (and once inhabited by astronomer Tycho Brahe) perched on the southern slope of the castle hill, and furnished with reproduction antiques. The hotel has an excellent restaurant (see p120 for details) and a terrace with superb views over the city.

HOTEL WILLIAM

Map pp250-1   *Hotel*

☎ 257 320 242; www.euroagentur.cz; Hellichova 5;
s/d 3840/4160Kč; tram 12, 20 22, 23; Ⓟ ☒ ▢

A relatively new addition to the Malá Strana hotel scene, the William has a great location only five minutes' walk from Charles Bridge. Try to get a room overlooking the garden rather than the street. Depending on your tastes, the décor is either wonderfully 'fairytale' or just plain twee – lots of swagged curtains, frills and flounces – but the staff is delightful.

ROMANTIK HOTEL U KRÁLE KARLA

Map pp244-5   *Hotel*

☎ 257 532 869; www.romantichotels.cz; Úvoz 4;
s/d from 5000/5500Kč; tram 12, 20 22, 23; Ⓟ

The 'King Charles' is a cosy, romantic hotel set in a lovely, 'baroquefied' Gothic building with antique furniture, painted wooden ceilings and stained-glass windows. It's a bit heavy-handed with the pastel pink, but vies with Hotel Neruda (p180) for the title of closest hotel to the castle, it's just a few minutes from the main gate.

Cheap Sleeps

HOTEL COUBERTIN Map pp250-1   *Hotel*

☎ 233 353 109; coubertin@volny.cz; Atletická 4;
s/d 1000/1800Kč; bus 143, 149 or 217 from metro
Dejvická

The Coubertin is a modest three-star place in a quiet but rather remote area beside Strahov Stadium, originally intended for visiting sports teams. However, the rooms are perfectly comfortable, and the views from the roof terrace are five-star.

PRAGUE ROOM Map pp244-5   *Apartments*

☎ 257 532 921; www.pragueroom.com; Nerudova 10;
r €25-39, apt €58; tram 12, 20, 22, 23

This 16th-century building has been converted into five rooms and three apartments, each sleeping at least two people, and offers remarkable value. Some rooms are a little cramped, and in some you may have to share a bathroom, but all are comfortable and nicely decorated, and the management is laid-back, helpful and gay-friendly.

Romantik Hotel U Raka (see opposite), Hradčany

TRAVELLERS HOSTEL ISLAND

Map pp250-1 *Hostel*

☎ 224 932 991; www.travellers.cz; Strelecký ostrov 36; dm 300Kč; open mid-Jun–mid-Sep; tram 6, 9, 22, 23

Set on the island beneath Legii most (Legions Bridge), this is the most attractive of the five Travellers' Hostels in Prague, with huge dorms, a garden bar with barbecue, and an open-air cinema and skate park within spitting distance.

STARÉ MĚSTO

Staré Město offers a wide range of accommodation, from backpacker hostels to some of the city's most luxurious hotels, with everything in between. Be aware that a lot of pensions and mid-range hotels have been squeezed into historic old buildings with no room for a lift – be prepared for a spot of stair climbing.

APOSTOLIC RESIDENCE

Map pp246-7 *Apartments*

☎ 221 632 222; www.prague-residence.cz; Staroměstské náměstí 26; s/d 3990/5700Kč, apt 7600-9890Kč; metro Staroměstská; 🖳

This is a lovely old building on Old Town Square that has been converted into a double room and two luxury apartments (the attic apartment, with its spiral staircase and massive timber beams, is our favourite) with parquet floors, oriental rugs and reproduction antique furniture. The big selling point, though, is its location – you can hang out your window and watch the Astronomical Clock (p71) do its thing.

CLOISTER INN Map pp252-3 *Hotel*

☎ 224 211 020; www.cloister-inn.cz; Konviktská 14; s/d 4000/4200Kč; metro Národní Třída; 🄿 🖳

The Cloister Inn's refurbished convent rooms were once part of the still-operational kostel sv Bartoloměje (St Bartholomew Church; p79). While some architectural touches remain from the convent, they're a little overwhelmed by the hotel's overly cheery colour scheme. It's a comfortable place, and if you can snag one of the top-floor executive rooms you'll also get in-room fax, Internet access and minibar.

DŮM U KRÁLE JIŘÍHO

Map pp246-7 *Pension*

☎ 221 466 100; www.kinggeorge.cz; Liliová 10; s/d 1800/3100Kč; metro Staroměstská

King George's House is an appealing pension with smallish rooms that have been given a

crisp, modern makeover; the attic rooms, with exposed, head-bumping wooden beams, are the most attractive. It's within lurching distance of Old Town Square, although the bar is so comfortable you may not bother venturing outside. Unfortunately there's no lift, only steep stairs.

FOUR SEASONS HOTEL PRAGUE

Map pp246-7 *Hotel*

☎ 221 427 000; www.fourseasons.com/prague; Veleslavínova 2a; r from €295; metro Staroměstská; 🄿 ☒ 🖳

An executive riverside villa for all seasons, this sumptuous hotel boasts some of the largest suites in Prague, many with stunning views across the river to the castle. For grown-ups there's massage on-call, a health club and spa, and for the kids there are video games, mini-bathrobes and milk and cookies at bedtime. Under-18s can stay for free in their parents' room.

GRAND HOTEL BOHEMIA Map p255 *Hotel*

☎ 234 608 111; www.grandhotelbohemia.cz; Královdvorská 4; s/d from €230/335; metro Náměstí Republiky; 🄿 ☒ 🖳

It may have an antique exterior and neobaroque ballroom dating from 1925 but this is a thoroughly modern member of an Austrian hotel chain with efficient service and spacious, businesslike rooms. Kids aged seven to 12 are charged 50%, and children under six stay free of charge.

HOTEL ANTIK Map pp246-7 *Hotel*

☎ 222 322 288; www.hotelantik.cz; Dlouhá 22; s/d 3590/3990Kč; metro Náměstí Republiky

As the name suggests, this place has a passion for bric-a-brac, with an antique shop on the ground floor and various pieces scattered elsewhere throughout the building. The 12 cosy rooms have been thoroughly modernised, however, and there's a lovely garden courtyard out back where you can have breakfast.

HOTEL CASA MARCELLO

Map pp246-7 *Hotel*

☎ 222 310 260; www.casa-marcello.cz; Řásnovka 783; d from €170; ste from €188; apt from €207; tram 5, 8, 14; 🖳

The Casa Marcello is a former aristocratic residence with 20 stylishly furnished rooms, six suites and six apartments. Its small size, antique atmosphere and attentive service make it an ideal romantic hideaway in the heart of Staré Město; room 104, with king-size bed and preserved medieval archway, is our favourite. Added attractions include a sunny garden courtyard where you can enjoy a drink or a snack, and a sauna.

HOTEL CENTRAL Map pp246-7 *Hotel*
☎ 224 812 041; www.orfea.cz; Rybná 8; s/d 3800/4400Kč; metro Náměstí Republiky; Ⓟ

Tucked behind the Kotva department store, the renovated 1930s-era Central retains a slightly dated feel – the public areas have a vaguely Art Deco feel, with stained glass and chandeliers, but the rooms are bright and nicely furnished in 'bland-international' style. Good location though, only a few minutes from both Old Town Square and the metro station.

HOTEL CLEMENTIN Map pp246-7 *Hotel*
☎ 222 221 798; www.clementin.cz; Seminárská 4; s/d 4250/5250Kč; metro Staroměstská

The Clementin is a pretty little place with nine cosy rooms squeezed into a 14th-century town house that is probably the narrowest building in Prague, with a façade just two windows wide. It's on a narrow alley just off the tourist thoroughfare of Karlova, halfway between Charles Bridge and Old Town Square.

HOTEL ČERNÝ SLON Map pp246-7 *Hotel*
☎ 222 321 521; www.hotelcernyslon.cz; Týnská ulička 1; s/d 2900/3600Kč; metro Náměstí Republiky

A lovely historic building barely 30 paces from Old Town Square, the 'Black Elephant' has 13 smallish but comfortable four-star rooms, a Gothic-vaulted dining room and a tiny courtyard garden.

HOTEL JOSEF Map pp246-7 *Boutique Hotel*
☎ 221 700 111; www.hoteljosef.cz; Rybná 20; s/d from €147/167; metro Náměstí Republiky; Ⓟ ⊠ 🖥

The Josef is a stunning boutique hotel designed by London-based Czech architect Eva Jiřičná. Design highlights include the glass-walled en suite bathrooms and the suspended spiral staircase in the stark, white, minimalist lobby. There are two wheelchair-accessible rooms, and a stylish bar and business lounge.

HOTEL LEONARDO Map pp252-3 *Hotel*
☎ 239 009 239; www.hotelleonardo.cz; Karoliny světlé 27; s/d 4500/5000Kč; tram 17; ⊠

One of Staré Město's newest hotels (opened in 2004), the Leonardo building is a harmonious blend of historic and part-Romanesque styles. It has modern comforts, with period features, wooden floors and marble bathrooms, set around a central courtyard on a quiet back street just two blocks away from the river.

HOTEL MEJSTŘÍK
Map pp246-7 *Boutique Hotel*
☎ 224 800 055; www.hotelmejstrik.cz; Jakubská 5; d from 5500Kč; metro Náměstí Republiky; Ⓟ 🖥

Lobby of Hotel Josef (see above), Staré Město

Established back in 1924 (by the father of the present owner), this place got an impressive Art Deco face-lift in 2000 and is now one of Staré Město's more impressive small hotels. It's set on a reasonably quiet back street just around the corner from the Obecní dům (Municipal House; p77), and has an attractive in-house restaurant and bar.

HOTEL METAMORPHIS
Map pp246-7   *Hotel*
☎ 221 771 011; www.metamorphis.cz; Malá Štupartská 5; s/d 4800/5850Kč, ste 6500Kč; metro Náměstí Republiky
Set on historic Týnský dvůr (p70), the Metamorphis has luxuriously renovated rooms and suites dating from the 15th and 16th centuries, some with original timber beams and one with an original Dutch ceramic stove. One of the suites was once used as a family chapel, and retains its Gothic-vaulted ceiling.

HOTEL PAŘÍŽ Map pp246-7   *Hotel*
☎ 222 195 195; www.hotel-pariz.cz; U Obecního domu 1; d from €170; metro Náměstí Republiky; P ⊠ ▣
The Paříž is a monument to Art Nouveau grandeur, with a magnificently marbled and mirrored interior dating from 1904. Its rooms have all the mod cons, including heated bathroom floors, Internet connections and on-call massage, but still manage to retain that early-20th-century feel.

HOTEL ROTT Map pp246-7   *Hotel*
☎ 224 190 901; www.hotelrott.cz; Malé náměstí 4; s/d/apt €200/230/290; metro Staroměstská; P ⊠ ▣
Well located just a few steps west of Old Town Square, this hotel occupies the fine old premises next to the famous VJ Rott Building (p76). It has a fresh, clean atmosphere and offers all the mod cons you could wish for, including interactive TVs in each room for Internet access. Its two-storey studio apartment offers more-spacious accommodation.

HOTEL U KLENOTNÍKA
Map pp252-3   *Hotel*
☎ 224 211 699; www.uklenotnika.cz; Rytířská 3; s/d 2500/3800Kč; metro Můstek
This friendly, central hotel has 11 plain but comfy rooms decorated with unique art and a stylish little restaurant – check out the bizarre painted-glass windows. A nice touch for

Birkenstock-wearing British guests – you get the *Guardian* newspaper free with your breakfast.

HOTEL U PRINCE Map pp246-7   *Hotel*
☎ 224 213 807; www.hoteluprince.cz; Staroměstské náměstí 29; s/d 5890/6090Kč; metro Staroměstská
It would be hard to find a bed closer to Old Town Square unless you camp at the feet of Jan Hus. This recently renovated Gothic and Renaissance building lacks the vast spaces common in other top-end hotels and has only six rooms per floor, lending it a private, personalised feel. It also has a superb roof terrace.

HOTEL U STARÉ PANÍ
Map pp246-7   *Hotel*
☎ 224 228 090; www.ustarepani.cz; Michalská 9; s/d 3250/3950Kč; metro Můstek
'At the Old Lady' offers 18 pleasant, modern, en suite rooms above the jazz club of the same name (see p159), just a few minutes' stroll from Old Town Square. Accommodation is spread over four floors, but there's no lift.

HOTEL U ZLATÉHO STROMU
Map pp246-7   *Hotel*
☎ 222 220 441; www.zlatystrom.cz; Karlova 6; s/d 3790/3990Kč; tram 17
The 22-room 'At the Golden Tree' has a pleasingly historical atmosphere with period features and many timber-ceilinged rooms, and is only a few short steps from Charles Bridge. But unless you're in a party mood try to get a room on the upper floors – the hotel also has a basement disco that rages till 6am.

HOTEL UNGELT
Map pp246-7   *Boutique Hotel*
☎ 224 828 686; hotel@ungelt.cz; Malá Štupartská 1; s/d from 4850/5900Kč; metro Náměstí Republiky; P ▣
The Ungelt, overlooking the pretty Týnský dvůr (p67), has 10 elegant apartments, each with one or two bedrooms, lounge, kitchen and bathroom. The oldest part of the building dates back to the 12th century, and the interior is an interesting mix of Gothic and Renaissance décor with lots of chandeliers and swagged drapery. Rates include breakfast served in your room, washing and ironing, and free Internet access and fax service.

PENSION U LILIE Map pp246-7   *Pension*
☎ 222 220 432; www.pensionulilie.cz; Liliová 15; s/d 1850/2800Kč; metro Staroměstská

Rooms at 'The Lily' are plain but pleasant with en suite bathroom and TV – our favourite is the timber-lined attic room (No 14). Rates are very reasonable considering the central location, just a few minutes' walk from Old Town Square.

PENSION U MEDVÍDKŮ
Map pp252-3 *Pension*
☎ 224 211 916; www.umedvidku.cz; Na Perštýně 7; s/d 2300/3500Kč; metro Národní Třída

Cosy and centrally located, 'At the Little Bear' is a traditional pub and restaurant (see p124) with several attractive rooms upstairs. For a romantic splurge, choose one of the historic attic rooms with exposed wooden beams – No 33 is the best in the house (ie most spacious, most atmospheric)

PENSION U ZLATÉ STUDNY
Map pp246-7 *Pension*
☎ 222 220 262; www.uzlatestudny.cz; Karlova 3; d/ste from 4500/5100Kč; metro Staroměstská

Set in a lovely, elaborately decorated 16th-century house, 'At the Golden Well' has four double rooms and four (two-person) suites, some with original painted wooden ceilings and all with antique furniture and Persian

Pension U Zlaté Studny (see above), Nové Město

rugs. Adding a third bed in a suite adds 1000Kč to the rate.

Cheap Sleeps

HOSTEL TÝN
Map pp246-7 *Hostel*
☎ 224 808 333; www.hostel-tyn.web2001.cz; Týnská 19; dm/d/tr 400/1100/1350Kč; metro Náměstí Republiky; ☒

Spotless two- to six-bed rooms, a superb location only a 200m from Staroměstské náměstí, and a sauna, Jacuzzi and vegetarian restaurant (see Beas Vegetarian Dhaba on p125) in the same courtyard – what more could you ask for?

PENSION UNITAS
Map pp252-3 *Pension*
☎ 224 211 020; www.unitas.cz; Bartolomějská 9; dm per person 270-500Kč, s/d 1100/1400Kč; metro Národní Třída; ☐ ☒

This former convent is an interesting place to stay – many of its cramped rooms were once prison cells (ex-president Havel once did time here – ask for room No P6), with shared bathrooms and a generous breakfast included. You have a choice between cramped dorms or rather more spacious pension rooms, and despite the history it's a very friendly and welcoming place.

NOVÉ MĚSTO

Although there are one or two grand old luxury hotels here, Nové Město's accommodation is mostly in modern chain hotels and upgraded 1930s establishments. What they might lack in historical atmosphere and romantic appeal, they make up for in spaciousness and facilities. Those on Wenceslas Square (Václavské náměstí) are right in the thick of things, but there are quiet corners to be found as well, especially in southern Nové Město (ie Karlovo náměstí and its surrounds).

Northern Nové Město

ATLANTIC HOTEL
Map pp246-7 *Hotel*
☎ 224 811 084; www.hotel-atlantic.cz; Na poříčí 9; s/d 3500/4400Kč; metro Náměstí Republiky; ☐

The Atlantic is a cut above your average mid-range Prague hotel, with imaginative décor and spacious rooms, including three rooms that are designed for wheelchair users.

BOTEL ALBATROS
Map pp246-7 *Hotel*
☎ 224 810 541; www.botelalbatros.cz; nábřeží Ludvíka Svobody 1; s/d €62/76; tram 5, 8, 14; ☐

The Albatros is a converted cruise boat that can be a good bargain in the off-season, when rates fall by 30%. Cabins are small and spartan, and include a tiny private shower and toilet.

HOTEL AXA Map pp246-7 _Hotel_
☎ 224 812 580; www.hotelaxa.com; Na poříčí 40; s/d 3100/3800Kč; metro Florenc; P ⊠

Another of the big 1930s hotels that line Na poříčí, the Axa has rooms that are clean, simple and comfortable and staff who is businesslike and friendly. Facilities include a fitness centre, sauna and a 25m-long indoor pool.

HOTEL CARLO IV Map pp246-7 _Hotel_
☎ 224 593 111; www.boscolohotels.com; Senovážné náměstí 13; d/ste from €260/900; metro Hlavní Nádraží; P ⊠ ⊡ ⊠

Housed in a neo-Renaissance palace that was once a banking headquarters, the five-star Carlo IV is a monument to designer decadence. Acres of marble, glass, leather, wood, silk and linen will have you trailing your fingers across every surface, and the rooms are the sort that make you think, do we _have_ to go sightseeing? Let's just stay in… While health-conscious guests slip into the wonderfully atmospheric swimming pool (in the style of an antique spa), the more decadent slope off to the Cigar Bar to savour some hand-rolled Havanas.

HOTEL HARMONY Map pp246-7 _Hotel_
☎ 222 319 807; www.hotelharmony.cz; Na poříčí 31; s/d 2400/3200Kč; metro Florenc

This is a 1930s, formerly state-owned hotel, now renovated and aimed mainly at the tour group and conference market. It offers spacious, spotless rooms (including five barrier-free doubles) from the 'forgettable modern' school of décor; the quieter ones face Biskupská.

HOTEL HILTON PRAGUE
Map pp258-9 _Hotel_
☎ 224 841 111; www.prague.hilton.com; Pobřežní 3; s/d from €195/205; metro Florenc; ⊠

The Hilton, beside the river just north of Florenc metro station, is Central Europe's biggest hotel with 788 rooms, a swimming pool (see p162 for details), four restaurants, and a vast, glass-roofed atrium. The only thing it hasn't got is atmosphere.

HOTEL OPERA Map pp246-7 _Hotel_
☎ 222 315 609; www.hotel-opera.cz; Těšnov 13; s/d 3650/4200Kč; metro Florenc

The Opera is a renovated, neo-Renaissance building (dating from 1890) with an unmissable pastel-pink façade near Florenc metro station. It has plush, olde-worlde rooms and it provides a sauna and fitness room.

JUNIOR HOTEL PRAHA
Map pp246-7 _Hotel_
☎ 224 231 754; www.euroagentur.cz; Senovážné náměstí 21; s/d €80/100; tram 5, 9, 26

This place has 14 smartly renovated hotel rooms with en suite bathroom, minibar and satellite TV, but also offers more basic rooms in a separate part of the building (s/d €25/34). The location is handy for the main train station, which is only one block away to the east.

RENAISSANCE PRAGUE HOTEL
Map pp246-7 _Hotel_
☎ 221 821 111; www.renaissancehotels.com; V celnici 1; d from €139; metro Náměstí Republiky; P ⊠ ⊡

The glitzy Renaissance (owned by Marriott) is a business traveller–friendly hotel, offering rooms with desk, broadband connection and voice mail, plus secretarial services and a business centre. There's also an indoor pool, sauna and solarium.

Wenceslas Square & Around
GRAND HOTEL EVROPA
Map pp252-3 _Hotel_
☎ 224 228 117; www.hotelevropa.cz; Václavské náměstí 25; s/d 1600/2600Kč, with private bathroom 3000/4000Kč; metro Můstek

The Evropa's famously gorgeous Art Nouveau façade conceals a musty warren of mostly shabby, run-down 1950s rooms. These days the place is trading solely on its fame. Considering its location it's reasonable value, but the rooms are genuinely rough. Some travellers, especially solo women, have found the atmosphere creepy.

HOTEL ADRIA Map pp252-3 _Hotel_
☎ 221 081 111; www.hoteladria.cz; Václavské náměstí 26; s/d from €160/175; metro Můstek

Conveniently located in the busiest part of town, the Adria's yellow baroque façade is Wenceslas Square's oldest surviving building (late-18th century). Its 88 rooms (including two barrier-free doubles), however, are entirely modern, and the hotel is popular with business travellers and tour groups. The hotel's restaurant (dating from 1912) is a bizarre but atmospheric blend of baroque stalactite grotto and Art Nouveau salon.

HOTEL ESPLANADE Map pp252-3 *Hotel*
☎ 224 501 172; www.esplanade.cz; Washingtonova 19; d from €149; metro Muzeum; Ⓟ

The Esplanade is one of the city's older luxury hotels, dating from 1927, with a classy location opposite the Státní opera Prague (State Opera Prague; p157) and close to Wenceslas Square. The soaring marble lobby gives the impression you're in for something special – those who can upgrade to an apartment get the full luxury treatment. Otherwise, expect clean and comfortable rooms that match fussily with the original neobaroque décor, all glitteringly lit by a mass of crystal chandeliers.

K+K HOTEL FENIX Map pp252-3 *Hotel*
☎ 225 012 222; www.kkhotels.cz; Ve Smečkách 30; s/d €238/258; metro Muzeum; Ⓟ ✕ ▣

With design elements contributed by Mies van der Rohe and Philippe Starck, among others, the Fenix provides a peaceful enclave of stylish and luxurious rooms just a few paces from Wenceslas Square.

PALACE HOTEL Map pp252-3 *Hotel*
☎ 224 093 111; www.palacehotel.cz; Panská 12; s/d from €240/255; metro Můstek; Ⓟ

The Palace, built in 1906, stands a block east of Wenceslas Square. The Art Nouveau façade is original, but the interior was completely rebuilt in the late 1980s; the luxurious rooms retain plenty of character, though, and have bathrooms lined with Carrara marble, no less.

PENSION MUSEUM Map pp252-3 *Pension*
☎ 296 325 186; www.pension-museum.cz; Mezibranská 15; s/d 2240/2650Kč, apt from 2750Kč; metro Muzeum; Ⓟ

Clean, bright, spacious and modern, the Pension Museum boasts a superb central location near the southern end of Wenceslas Square. All rooms have en suite bathroom, TV and fridge, and overlook a quiet courtyard. Try not to be put off by the occasionally grumpy reception staff.

RADISSON SAS ALCRON HOTEL
Map pp252-3 *Hotel*
☎ 222 820 000; www.radissonsas.com; Štěpánská 40; d from 6000Kč; metro Můstek; Ⓟ ▣

The Radisson Sas Alcron Hotel is the modern reincarnation of the 1930s Alcron Hotel, and has long been favoured by celebrities and diplomats. Much of the original Art Deco marble-and-glass fittings have been preserved, and the 211 rooms have been far more tastefully renovated than in many other refurbished Prague hotels.

Radisson Sas Alcron Hotel (see above), Nové Město

Karlovo Náměstí & Around

HOTEL 16 U SV KATEŘINY
Map pp252-3   *Boutique Hotel*
☎ 224 920 636; www.hotel16.cz; Kateřinská 16;
s/d from 2500/3400Kč; metro Karlovo Náměstí; P 🖳
Near the Botanic Gardens and about five minutes' walk from Karlovo náměstí metro station, this homely little hotel is quiet, clean and very comfortable. There's a peaceful terraced garden out the back (try to get a back room if you don't mind having twin beds) and a small bar.

HOTEL ANDANTE Map pp252-3   *Hotel*
☎ 222 211 616; www.andante.cz; Ve Smečkách 4;
s/d €110/135; metro Muzeum; 🖳
This converted apartment building (fully renovated in 2003) has 32 spacious, modern rooms with TV, minibar and a choice of shower or bath. The décor is bright and cheerful, as is the helpful and friendly staff. It's also in a great location not far from Wenceslas Square.

HOTEL GREEN GARDEN
Map pp260-1   *Hotel*
☎ 224 261 181; www.greengarden.cz in Czech;
Fügnerovo náměstí 4; s/d 3200/3700Kč, apt 4850Kč;
metro IP Pavlova; P
Although it's sandwiched between the raging traffic of Legerova and Sokolská, the 55-room (two of them barrier-free) Green Garden has friendly staff, bags of old-fashioned character, and a lovely glass-roofed 'winter garden' sitting area. Go for a room on the top floor – it's quieter, and there are great views towards the castle.

HOTEL IBIS PRAHA CITY
Map pp252-3   *Hotel*
☎ 224 941 212; www.hotelibis.cz; Kateřinská 36;
s/d €84/99; metro IP Pavlova; P ✗ 🖳
The Ibis is a comfortable modern chain hotel, right next door to the metro. There are four rooms adapted for wheelchair users. Though lacking in character, it offers good-value accommodation in a fairly central location.

HOTEL TCHAIKOVSKY
Map pp252-3   *Boutique Hotel*
☎ 224 912 121; www.hoteltchaikovsky.com;
Ke Karlovu 19; s/d €99/119; metro IP Pavlova
With 19 rooms ranged around a balcony overlooking a peaceful courtyard, the Tchaikovsky is one of the more appealing of Prague's new, small hotels. The spacious rooms have stylish Italian furniture, and reception is staffed 24 hours a day.

NOVOMĚSTSKÝ HOTEL
Map pp252-3   *Hotel*
☎ 222 231 498; www.novomestskyhotel.cz; Řeznická
4; s/d 2800/3500Kč; metro Karlovo Náměstí
Set on a quiet side street near Karlovo náměstí, the Novoměstský represents good value with its clean, bright, no-frills rooms (which include shower and TV). The hotel is close to a metro station and only 10 minutes' walk from Wenceslas Square.

Cheap Sleeps

HOTEL IMPERIAL Map pp246-7   *Hotel*
☎ 222 316 012; www.hotelimperial.cz; Na Poříčí 15;
s/d 1400/2400Kč; metro Náměstí Republiky
The Imperial is a grand old building dating from 1914, with an impressive Art Nouveau interior. The deep, dark corridors and air of intrigue offer a glimpse of a bygone Prague. The rooms are pretty basic (all have shared showers and toilets) and could do with a thorough overhaul, but this is still amazing value for the location.

PENSION BŘEZINA Map pp252-3   *Pension*
☎ 296 188 888; www.brezina.cz; Legerova 39-41;
s/d economy 1100/1300Kč, luxury 2000/2200Kč;
metro IP Pavlova; 🖳
The Březina is a welcoming pension in a converted Art Nouveau apartment block with a small garden out back, where you can sit and have a drink in summer. Ask for a room at the back as those facing the street can be pretty noisy. The economy rooms have shared bathrooms; luxury ones have private bathrooms, air-con and Ethernet sockets for your laptop (and free use of the Internet).

OUTER SUBURBS
You'll find a wide range of accommodation options in the outer suburbs, from the budget hostels and pensions of Žižkov and Holešovice (often more appealing than their city centre counterparts) to the boutique hotels of Vinohrady and Smíchov. These options offer the chance to save some money on accommodation in return for a 15- to 20-minute tram or metro trip from the centre.

Vyšehrad

HOTEL AMADEUS Map pp260-1   *Hotel*
☎ 224 937 569; www.dhotels.cz; Slavojova 8;
s/d/ste 3050/3250/4750Kč; metro Vyšehrad; P

Near the Airport

The following places all lie at the western edge of the city and make great options while staying within arm's reach of the airport.

Hotel Elegant (Map pp242-3; ☎ 235 300 521; www.hotelelegant.cz; Ruzyňská 197, Ruzyně; s/d 3100/3800Kč; bus 225; Ⓟ) The Elegant is a stylish, 1930s Functionalist building, which has been recently renovated and refurbished into a boutique hotel. It's only five minutes from the airport by car, or seven minutes on bus No 225; get off at the Ruzyňská škola stop.

Hotel Tranzit (Map pp242-3; ☎ 236 161 111; www.hoteltranzit.cz; Aviatická; d from 1750Kč; bus 100, 119, 179; Ⓟ ▣) Bright, modern hotel just five minutes' walk from the airport terminal, with some wheelchair-accessible rooms.

Pension Větrný Mlyn (Map pp242-3; ☎ 235 301 686; www.pensionmlyn.cz; Ruzyňská 3/96, Ruzyně; s/d 1000/1600Kč; bus 225; Ⓟ) The 'Windmill' is a friendly, family-run pension where all rooms have TV and en suite shower. It's just across the street from Hotel Elegant (above).

Ramada Airport Hotel (Map pp242-3; ☎ 220 111 250; www.euroagentur.cz; Terminal Jih, K letišti 25a, Ruzyně; s/d €130/150; Ⓟ) The brand-new Ramada is at the southern terminal of Ruzyně airport, four stops on bus No 100, 119, 179 or 225 from the main terminal.

You can just about smell the paint in this comfortable new hotel, which offers 29 en suite rooms with cable TV on a quiet street below the Vyšehrad citadel (p90). Rooms in the front block are spacious; those in back a little more cramped. One room has access for people with disabilities, and there are four two-storey suites that each provide accommodation for four people.

HOTEL CORINTHIA TOWERS
Map pp260-1   *Hotel*
☎ 261 191 111; www.corinthia.cz; Kongresová 1; d from €135; metro Vyšehrad; Ⓟ ⊠ ▣ ⬛

The Corinthia Towers is an ultramodern, 26-storey high-rise close to Vyšehrad and the Kongresové centrum (and not much else, the metro station is right beside the hotel). Recently refurbished, it has first-class service and a spectacular rooftop swimming pool. (Note: American citizens who stay here could, in theory, face criminal charges at home for 'engaging in commercial activity with a Specially Designated National of Libya – the Corinthia Group is partly Libyan-owned.)

HOTEL UNION Map pp260-1   *Hotel*
☎ 261 214 812; www.hotelunion.cz; Ostrčilovo náměstí 4; s/d from 2815/3380Kč; metro Vyšehrad; Ⓟ

The Union is a grand old family-run hotel that dates from 1906; nationalised by the communists in 1958, it was returned to the grandson of the former owner in 1991. Comfortably renovated, with a few period touches left intact, the deluxe rooms (4050Kč) are huge and have corner bay windows with a view towards the citadel.

Holešovice & Bubeneč

ART HOTEL Map pp256-7   *Boutique Hotel*
☎ 233 101 331; www.arthotel.cz; Nad Kralovskou oborou 53, Bubeneč; s/d from €85/95; tram 1, 8, 15, 25, 26; Ⓟ ⊠ ▣

There are lots of word-of-mouth recommendations for this small hotel hidden away in the peaceful embassy district. It has sleek modern styling and displays contemporary Czech art. It's only a few minutes' walk from a tram that will take you into the city centre, and you could stroll to the castle in less than 20 minutes.

HOTEL BELVEDERE Map pp256-7   *Hotel*
☎ 220 106 111; www.belvedere-hotel.com; Milady Horákové 19; s/d 2850/3850Kč; tram 1, 8, 15, 25, 26; Ⓟ

The Belvedere has posh three- and four-star rooms at very reasonable rates, including several adapted for wheelchair users. The 'executive' rooms (doubles 3300Kc) on the 2nd floor are very spacious, with huge, white, marble-lined bathrooms. There's a tram stop right outside the front door – it's only five minutes to Náměstí Republiky metro station on the No 8.

HOTEL SPLENDID Map pp256-7   *Hotel*
☎ 233 375 940; www.hotelsplendid.cz; Ovenecká 33; s/d 1820/2450Kč; tram 1, 8, 15, 25, 26; Ⓟ ⊠

Set on a quiet little side-street, this may be the only mid-range hotel in Prague that is apparently entirely free of IKEA-style furniture. It's a little worn around the edges, but the friendly, comfortable Splendid's mid-'80s décor has a certain charm. There are five rooms accessible to wheelchair users.

Cheap Sleeps
HOTEL EXTOL INN Map pp256-7 *Hotel*
☎ 220 876 541; www.extolinn.cz; Přístavní 2,
Holešovice; s/d from 700/1190Kč; tram 1, 3, 5, 25; ℗

Recently renovated and excellent value, the
bright, modern Extol Inn offers hefty discounts
on economy rooms for HI members. The more
expensive three-star rooms (singles/doubles
1290/1990Kč) have private bathroom, TV, minibar and free use of sauna and spa.

SIR TOBY'S HOSTEL Map pp256-7 *Hostel*
☎ 283 870 635; www.sirtobys.com; Dělnická 24,
Holešovice; dm 290-340Kč; s/d 900/1100Kč; tram 1, 3,
5, 25; ℗ 🖳

Set in a quiet, nicely refurbished apartment building with spacious kitchen and common room,
and run by friendly, cheerful staff, Sir Toby's is
only 10 minutes north of the city centre by tram.
If you want a private bathroom, add 50Kč to the
rate; for breakfast, add 60Kč. Travellers who are
wheelchair-bound should call ahead to check
whether a room can be prepared.

Žižkov & Karlín
HOTEL ČECHIE Map pp242-3 *Hotel*
☎ 266 194 111; www.hotelcechie.cz; U Sluncové 618,
Karlín; s/d 2200/2800Kč; business class 2700/3600Kč;
metro Invalidovna

The brisk and businesslike Čechie is part of a
modern sports complex; guests can use the
swimming pool for free, but all other facilities (tennis and squash courts, bowling alleys
and fitness centre) cost extra. There's at least
one barrier-free double among the newer and
more spacious business-class rooms; all rooms
have TV, shower and toilet.

HOTEL CITY CROWN Map pp258-9 *Hotel*
☎ 222 716 803; www.citycrown.cz; Bořivojova 94,
Žižkov; s/d €69/79; tram 5, 9 26; ℗

The newly renovated City Crown's candyfloss
pink façade conceals comfortable, modernised
rooms in a quiet street close to Žižkov's TV
Tower (p96). The tram line at the foot of the hill
is only a few stops from the city centre.

HOTEL IBIS PRAHA KARLÍN
Map pp258-9 *Hotel*
☎ 222 332 800; www.hotelibis.cz; Šaldova 54, Karlín;
s/d €59/74; metro Křižíkova; ℗

A comfortable and attractive chain hotel, the
Ibis Karlín is good value and only a couple of

metro stops away from the city centre. There's
one room specially adapted for wheelchair
users.

HOTEL OSTAŠ Map pp258-9 *Hotel*
☎ 226 279 386; fax 226 279 418; Orebitská 8, Žižkov;
s/d 1780/2560Kč; metro Florenc

This is a friendly, family-run hotel with just 30
rooms, set in a converted late-19th-century
apartment block with some surviving Art Nouveau touches discernible in the décor. It has plain
but pleasant rooms, both bright and comfortable, and is handy for Florenc bus station, which
is just five minutes' walk away to the north, and
Žižkov's many pubs and restaurants.

HOTEL U TŘÍ KORUNEK
Map pp258-9 *Hotel*
☎ 222 781 112; www.3korunky.cz; Cimburkova 28,
Žižkov; s/d 2200/3200Kč; bus 133, 207; ℗

The very pleasant, 58-room 'Three Crowns'
was recently renovated and sports comfortable, spotless rooms. Every room has phone,
satellite TV and separate toilet and bathroom.
Four of the rooms are accessible to people
with disabilities.

OLŠANKA HOTEL Map pp258-9 *Hotel*
☎ 267 092 202; www.hotelolsanka.cz in Czech;
Táboritská 23, Žižkov; s/d 2100/2700Kč; tram 5, 9, 26;
🖳 🖭

OK, so it's a 1970s concrete monstrosity, but
the Olšanka offers good-value, modern en
suite rooms with TV – some have balconies.
It's just a couple of tram stops from the city
centre, with the added attractions of a fitness
centre, sauna and a 25m-long indoor pool.

Cheap Sleeps
CLOWN & BARD HOSTEL
Map pp258-9 *Hostel*
☎ 222 716 453; www.clownandbard.com; Bořivojova
102, Žižkov; dm/d 250/900Kč; tram 5, 9, 26; ℗ 🖳

Set in the heart of Žižkov's pub district, the
Clown & Bard is a full-on party place – don't
come here looking for peace and quiet. The
ever-popular Clown has a café, a bar (with
regular guest DJ nights), friendly, knowledgeable staff and good tours. As well as dorms and
doubles, there are six-person self-catering flats
in the attic (2400Kč a night).

HOSTEL ELF Map pp258-9 *Hostel*
☎ 222 540 963; www.hostelelf.com; Husitská 11,
Žižkov; dm/s/d 290/700/840Kč; metro Florenc

Lots of readers have recommended this friendly and cheerful hostel, with its little beer-garden terrace, cosy lounge and comfortable, well laid-out dorms. Some doubles have their own bathrooms, but the shared bathrooms allow a lot of privacy. The Elf is less than 10 minutes' walk from Florenc bus station.

HOTEL GOLDEN CITY GARNI

Map pp258-9   *Hotel*

☎ 222 711 008; www.goldencity.cz; Táboritská 3, Žižkov; s/d/tr 1650/2450/2700Kč; tram 5, 9, 26; P ⊠ ▯

The Golden City is a converted 19th-century apartment block with crisp, clean, no-frills rooms, good buffet breakfasts and friendly, helpful staff. The owners have put a lot of money and effort into renovating the building over the last 10 years, with many period details on the exterior now lovingly restored, and in redesigning and redecorating the rooms to create comfortable, modern accommodation.

HOTEL KAFKA Map pp258-9   *Hotel*

☎ 222 781 333; www.ckvesta.cz; Cimburkova 24, Žižkov; s/d 1700/2300Kč; tram 5, 9, 26; P

The Kafka's quiet, simple rooms with phone and bath are very reasonably priced and can take up to five people (3100Kč). Self-contained apartments across the street go for 2500Kč to 3800Kč, depending on the number of occupants. Dogs can stay for 150Kč; call if you want to reserve parking.

HOTEL PROKOPKA Map pp258-9   *Hotel*

☎ 222 781 647; www.prokopka.cz; Prokopova 9, Žižkov; s/d 1150/1800Kč; tram 5, 9, 26; P ▯

Superfriendly and excellent value, the Prokopka's rooms have their own bath and kitchen, or shared facilities with one other room. The rooms on the top floor are smaller but have balconies. The rooms have phone but no TV (there's a lounge with a shared TV). There's also a laundry room and a backyard. Student guests – who should book ahead – can get rooms from 300Kč to 500Kč per person (four-person maximum per room).

PENSION 15 Map pp258-9   *Hostel/Pension*

☎ 222 719 768; www.pension15.cz; Vlkova 15, Žižkov; dm/s/d 350/600/700Kč; apt 1000-2600Kč; tram 5, 9, 26; P

One of our favourite budget options, No 15 has helpful staff, bright, modern rooms with shared cooking facilities, spotless bathrooms,

and self-catering apartments that sleep one to five people. There's private parking in the courtyard (100Kč extra).

PENSION PRAGUE CITY

Map pp258-9   *Pension*

☎ 222 782 483; www.praguecity.cz; Štítného 13, Žižkov; s/d 2000/2400Kč; tram 5, 9, 26

This is a shiny new place around the corner from Hotel Kafka, and only five tram stops away from Wenceslas Square. All 13 clean, comfortable rooms have en suite bathrooms and TV.

Vinohrady

APARTHOTEL LUBLAŇKA

Map pp252-3   *Apartments*

☎ 222 510 041; www.lublanka.cz; Lublaňska 59; s/d 3200/4600Kč, apt from 4100Kč; metro IP Pavlova

This is a friendly place offering a range of bright, simply decorated apartments, ranging from double rooms with en suite and kitchen corner, to two-bedroom and kitchen apartments that sleep four. All have fridge, satellite TV and phone, and rates include breakfast served in the downstairs bar.

HOTEL ABRI Map pp260-1   *Hotel*

☎ 222 515 124; www.abri.cz; Jana Masaryka 36; s/d 2800/3300Kč; metro Náměstí Míru; P

A pleasant, if somewhat anonymous, small hotel on a very quiet street, the Abri has 25 comfortable rooms, including one well fitted out for travellers with disabilities. There's a safe hotel car park and a decent restaurant serving traditional Czech dishes.

HOTEL ANNA Map pp260-1   *Hotel*

☎ 222 513 111; www.hotelanna.cz; Budečská 17; s/d €75/102; metro Náměstí Míru

The 22-room Hotel Anna is small and friendly, tucked away on a quiet back street but close to the metro and lots of good restaurants and bars. Rooms are bright and cheerful, and those on the top floor have a view towards the castle.

HOTEL SIEBER Map pp258-9   *Boutique Hotel*

☎ 224 250 025; www.sieber.cz; Slezská 55; s/d/ste 4480/4780/5480Kč; metro Jiřího z Poděbrad

Popular with business travellers, the Sieber is a small luxury hotel with 13 rooms and seven suites, set in a grand 19th-century apartment building. Stylish décor and attentive service are accompanied by thoughtful little touches, such as bathrobes and fresh flowers.

Cheap Sleeps
HOSTEL U MELOUNU
Map pp260-1   *Hostel*

☎ 224 918 322; www.hostelumelounu.cz; Ke Karlovu 7; dm 380Kč, s/d from 550/900Kč; metro IP Pavlova; **P** 🖥
One of the prettier hostels in town, 'At the Watermelon' is set in a historic building on a quiet back street, a short walk from Vinohrady's restaurants and bars. It has the added attraction of a peaceful, sunny garden complete with barbecue. It's a 10-minute walk south of IP Pavlova metro station.

HOTEL/PENSION CITY
Map pp260-1   *Pension*

☎ 222 521 606; www.hotelcity.cz; Belgická 10; s/d from 1160/1550Kč, with bathroom 1670/2320Kč; metro Náměstí Míru
A clean, family-friendly pension, the City offers plain, good-value rooms in a safe, peaceful neighbourhood. The main difference between the 'pension' and 'hotel' rooms is a private bathroom; mod cons such as phone and TV cost extra.

PENSION ARCO Map pp260-1   *Pension*

☎ 271 742 908; www.arco-guesthouse.cz; Voroněžská 21; d/apt from 1300/1900Kč; metro Náměstí Míru; 🖥
The Arco is a gay-owned pension and café-bar, offering clean and comfortably furnished pension rooms, as well as two- to four-person apartments in nearby buildings. Nicest of all is the little garden house in the backyard (1600Kč for two people), with private bathroom, TV, fridge and kettle (but no kitchen).

PENSION BEETLE Map pp260-1   *Pension*

☎ 222 515 093; www.beetle-tour.cz; Šmilovského 10; d from 1700Kč; tram 4, 22, 23
The Beetle occupies a lovely 1910 apartment building in a leafy back street, far from the tourist throng, but nearby trams (Nos 22 and 23) will whisk you all the way to the castle. Though basic, the rooms have en suite bathrooms and are equipped with bedside lamps, minibar, table and chairs.

Smíchov
ADMIRÁL BOTEL Map pp260-1   *Hotel*

☎ 257 321 302; www.admiral-botel.cz; Hořejší nábřeží 57; s/d 2710/2840Kč, ste 4910Kč; metro Anděl; **P**
The Admirál floating hotel has compact, well-designed rooms (perhaps a little overpriced for

what you get), a sunny terrace overlooking the river and a restaurant with more brass fittings than Nelson's fleet.

ANDĚL'S HOTEL PRAGUE
Map pp250-1   *Boutique Hotel*

☎ 296 889 688; www.andelshotel.com; Stroupežnického 21; s/d from €220/240; metro Anděl; **P** 🗙 🖥
Nowhere sums up the new Smíchov quite like Anděl's. This sleek, so-now-it's-almost-tomorrow boutique hotel, all stark designer chic in beige, black and red, has DVD and CD players, Internet access, and modern abstract art in every room. Bathrooms are a wonderland of polished chrome and frosted glass. There's a gym and a salon and rooms designed for wheelchair users. Kids under 12 stay free of charge. Go now before it gets dated.

HOTEL ARBES-MEPRO
Map pp250-1   *Hotel*

☎ 257 313 067; www.arbes-mepro.cz; Viktora Huga 3; s/d 2700/3300Kč; tram 6, 9, 12, 20; 🗙 **P**
The Arbes-Mepro has large, comfy rooms, big baths and a pleasantly old-fashioned feel. Rates are reasonable considering its location – strictly speaking it's in Smíchov, but right at the northern edge, and only 15 minutes' walk from Charles Bridge and central Malá Strana.

HOTEL KAVALÍR Map pp242-3   *Hotel*

☎ 257 216 565; www.europehotels.cz; Plzeňská 177; s/d 2100/2900Kč; tram 4, 7, 9, 10; **P**
This homely hotel is in western Smíchov, far from the madding crowds. All the rooms are comfortable and snug – there are five adapted for wheelchair users – but ask for one away from the main street, which is a pretty noisy thoroughfare. Take the tram four stops west from the Anděl metro station to the Kavalírka stop.

HOTEL U BLAŽENKY
Map pp242-3   *Boutique Hotel*

☎ 251 564 532; www.ublazenky.cz; U Blaženky 1; s/d/ste €105/130/140; bus 137; **P**
In the quiet streets above the Bertramka (p97) is this elegant villa, which hosts a collection of Czech modern art, including paintings by young Czech artist Markéta Výletalova. The nine rooms and four suites are stylishly decorated, and there's a good French restaurant with summer terrace. From Anděl metro take bus No 137 three stops to the Malvazinky stop, then walk five minutes downhill on U Mrázovky. Fresh

flowers in your room, champagne on request, and a cosy candlelit dining room make this place a favourite romantic retreat.

Cheap Sleeps

HOTEL BALKÁN Map pp250-1 _Hotel_
☎ 257 327 180; www.hotelbalkan.cz; Svornosti 28; s/d 1600/2200Kč; metro Anděl
Located at the grungier southern end of Smíchov, the Balkán's rooms are a bit on the sombre side – all grey carpet and fluorescent lights – but they're clean and have been tarted up with some new furniture and pine panelling. All have TV, phone and en suite bathroom.

Dejvice

HOTEL CROWNE PLAZA Map p255 _Hotel_
☎ 224 393 111; www.crowneplaza.cz; Koulova 15; d from €280; tram 8; Ⓟ Ⓧ ▣
Originally the Hotel International, this place was built in the 1950s in the style of Moscow University, complete with Soviet star atop the tower. Now modernised, it is comfortable and quiet, tucked away at the end of the tram line. Come for the décor rather than anything else – the rooms here are standard chain-hotel style, with all the necessities but not too many luxuries. The building itself is really something special, covered in bas reliefs and frescoes of the noble worker. The hotel has 24 rooms accessible to wheelchair users.

HOTEL PRAHA Map pp242-3 _Hotel_
☎ 224 341 111; www.htlpraha.cz; Sušická 20; s/d US$180/210; taxi; Ⓟ ⓡ
The Hotel Praha is one of Prague's more interesting hotels – hidden away on a hill in Dejvice, surrounded by several hectares of private grounds that were once protected by an electric fence, it's a luxury complex that was built in 1981 for the Communist Party elite.

The public areas are an intriguing mix of 1970s futuristic-style (sweeping curves and stainless steel) and 1950s Soviet-style splendour (polished marble and cut-glass chandeliers). The bedrooms are very spacious, with all the luxury you'd expect from a five-star establishment, and many are accessible to wheelchair users. But the hotel's big drawcard is the fact that each of its 124 rooms has its own private balcony. The entire southern face of the hotel is a sloping grandstand of stacked balconies, all draped with greenery and commanding a superb view of the castle.

Before 1989, such Soviet-era stalwarts as Nicolae Ceauşescu, Erich Honecker and Eduard Shevardnadze all hung their hats here; in recent years, the clientele has shifted from heads of state to Hollywood, with stars such as Johnny Depp, Alanis Morissette, Kris Kristofferson, Bryan Adams, Suzanne Vega and Paul Simon ringing room service in the small hours. Even Tom Cruise stayed here in 1995 during the filming of _Mission Impossible_.

There's no convenient public transport – it's a 10-minute uphill hike from the nearest tram stop, so taxi is your best bet.

OTHER SUBURBS

BOTEL RACEK Map pp242-3 _Hotel_
☎ 241 431 628; www.botelracek.cz; Na Dvorecké louce, Podolí; s/d €56/70; tram 3, 17; Ⓟ
The Botel Racek is a quiet, floating hotel offering dinky little wood-panelled cabins with shower and toilet. It's a five-minute walk from the Dvorce stop on tram line Nos 3 and 17.

HOTEL BRANÍK Map pp242-3 _Hotel_
☎ 244 462 844; www.hotelbranik.cz; Pikovická 199, Braník; s/d 1650/2500Kč; tram 3, 16, 17, 21; Ⓟ
The Braník is an attractive villa-type hotel set in a chestnut-shaded garden and five minutes' walk from the river. It's just 15 minutes from Wenceslas Square on tram No 3 (get off at the Nádranží Braník stop), and is handy for motorists arriving from the south as you can get there without having to drive into the city centre.

HOTEL GLOBUS Map pp242-3 _Hotel_
☎ 272 927 700; www.hotel-globus.cz; Gregorova 2115, Horní Roztyly; s/d €71/87; metro Roztyly; Ⓟ
The Globus is a quiet, modern hotel set at the edge of a forest, with eight barrier-free doubles and access to the nearby metro for wheelchair users. It's easily reached by car via Junction 1 on the D1 from Brno. On foot, it's five minutes from Roztyly metro station – turn right at the top of the stairs and follow the path uphill towards the woods; turn right, then fork left at the first junction – the hotel is 200m further, on the left.

HOTEL ILF Map pp242-3 _Hotel_
☎ 261 092 373; www.hotel-ilf.cz; Budějovická 15/743, Michle; s/d 2300/3200Kč; ste 4500Kč; metro Budějovická; Ⓟ ▣
The ILF is a smart business hotel aimed at the medical conference market, but it sells

surplus capacity (including seven barrier-free doubles, and seven family suites) to all-comers; kids aged 11 or under are charged 50%, those under three stay for free. It's only 10 minutes into the city centre from the neighbouring metro station.

SANS SOUCI HOTEL Map pp242-3 *Pension*
☎ 244 461 225; www.hotelsanssouci.cz; V podhájí 12, Podolí; s/d 2200/2600Kč; tram 3, 17; Ⓟ

The nine-room Sans Souci is a quiet and charming family-friendly pension in a restored 19th-century villa in the southern suburbs; the en suite rooms come with TV and breakfast. Take tram No 3 or 17 to the Dvorce stop, walk up Jeremenkova and turn through the underpass just beyond the shops at No 14. At the top of the stairs, walk right on Na Zvoničce for a few minutes until you see the hotel up on the right. By car, follow the signs from Jeremenkova.

VILLA VOYTA Map pp242-3 *Boutique Hotel*
☎ 261 711 307; www.villavoyta.cz; K Novému dvoru 124/54, Lhotka; s/d 4700/5300Kč; bus 113, 171, 189, 215; Ⓟ

The 20-room Villa Voyta is a beautiful Art Nouveau hotel dating from 1912. Rebuilt in the 1990s when a new 'wing' was added across the road, the Villa Voyta is now a small and executive-friendly hotel with elegant rooms, free parking and an excellent, gourmet French restaurant. Take bus No 113, 171, 189 or 215 south from Kačerov metro station to the Zálesí stop, and walk three blocks west along Na Větrově.

Cheap Sleeps

AV PENSION PRAHA Map pp242-3 *Pension*
☎ 272 951 726; www.pension-praha.cz; Malebna 75, Chodov; d with/without bathroom 2000/1500Kč; metro Chodov; Ⓟ Ⓩ

A readers' favourite, this garden villa in the southeastern suburbs offers bright, modern rooms, breakfast on the patio, and even a little pool for the kids. It's a five-minute walk east of Chodov metro station.

HOSTEL BOATHOUSE Map pp242-3 *Hostel*
☎ 241 770 051; www.aa.cz/boathouse; Lodnická 1, Braník; dm 360Kč; tram 3, 17, 21; Ⓟ ▢

Travellers rave about the Boathouse, a friendly and popular hostel with a peaceful riverbank setting, run by vivacious and unstinting crew Vera and Helena. Extras available include bike and boat hire, a mini shop and laundry service. Take tram No 3, 17 or 21 to the Černý kůň stop, and follow the hostel signs west to the river (it's a five-minute walk).

HOTEL OPATOV Map pp242-3 *Hotel*
☎ 271 196 222; www.horst.cz; U chodovského hřbitova 2141, Opatov; s/d 1740/2300Kč; metro Opatov; Ⓟ

The 20-storey Opatov is a grim-looking, communist-era tower block, but offers bargain three-star accommodation in mini-apartments with TV, phone and fridge. It's just 15 minutes from the city centre by metro. From Opatov metro station head east towards the park then bear right – it's the furthest away of the two big tower blocks.

Excursions

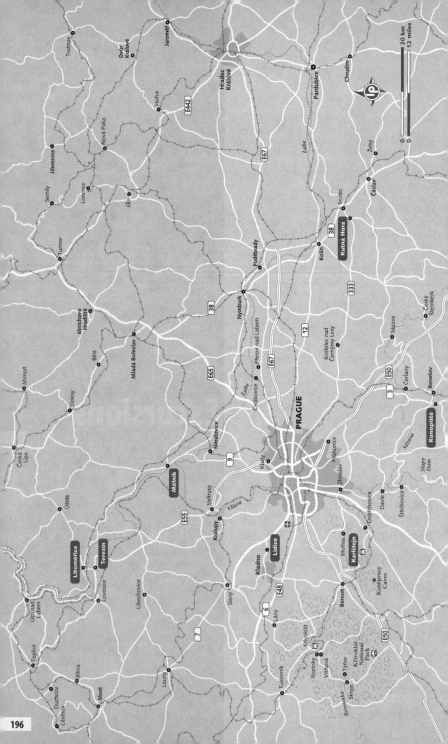

Excursions

The Central Bohemian countryside, most of it within an hour's train or bus ride from Prague, is rich in rural landscapes, attractive towns and historic sights. This chapter lists a selection of day trips and potential overnight visits that can easily be made using public transport.

Top of the list are photogenic Karlštejn Castle, the appealing silver-mining town of Kutná Hora and the harrowing former concentration camp, Terezín. Be prepared for huge summer crowds at Karlštejn and Konopiště castles.

CASTLES & CHATEAUX

Central Bohemia is rich in castles and chateaux, the former country seats of kings and aristocrats, within easy reach of the capital city. Popular castles include **Karlštejn** (p198), built to house the royal treasury; **Konopiště** (p199), the country retreat of the ill-fated Archduke Franz Ferdinand; and the Lobkowicz family's chateau at **Mělník** (p199), with its tiny but historic vineyard overlooking the confluence of the Labe and Vltava rivers.

MEDIEVAL TOWNS

There are many interesting medieval towns in the region surrounding Prague; they provide an escape from the crowds that churn though the capital's narrow streets. **Litoměřice** (p203) has a picture-postcard town square lined with lovely Gothic and Renaissance houses, while the tiny old town of **Mělník** (p199) has peaceful back streets and a stunning view over the Bohemian countryside. Most impressive of all is **Kutná Hora** (p204), with its lovely cathedral, Baroque statues and hilltop setting.

All Saints Church, Old Town Hall (p203), Litoměřice

WWII

The region to the north of Prague contains two deeply moving monuments to the suffering of the Czech people in WWII – the village of Lidice (p201), destroyed by the Nazis as an act of vengeance, and Terezín (p201), a former concentration camp through which 150,000 Czech Jews passed on their way to the gas chambers.

UNUSUAL SIGHTS

There're a number of tourist sites that are decidedly out of the ordinary. The Trophy Corridor and Chamois Room in Konopiště Chateau (p199), crammed with the antlers, skulls and stuffed heads of thousands of animals, stand as bizarre witness to the hunting obsession of Archduke Franz Ferdinand, while Kutná Hora's Czech Silver Museum (p206) offers the chance to don a miner's helmet and lamp and explore the claustrophobic tunnels of a medieval silver mine beneath the town. Most extraordinary of all is the Sedlec Ossuary (p204) at Kutná Hora, where the bones of 40,000 people have been fashioned into a series of weird and wonderful decorations.

KARLŠTEJN

Karlštejn, southwest of Prague, is in such good shape these days it wouldn't look out of place on Disney's Main St. The crowds come in theme-park proportions as well (it is best to book ahead for the guided tours), but the peaceful surrounding countryside offers views of Karlštejn's stunning exterior that rival anything you'll see on the inside.

Perched high on a crag that overlooks the Berounka river, and sporting a spotless new paint job, this cluster of turrets, high walls and looming towers is as immaculately maintained as it is powerfully evocative. Rightly one of the top attractions of the Czech Republic, the only drawback is its overwhelming popularity: in the summer months it is literally mobbed with visitors, ice-cream vendors and souvenir stalls.

Karlštejn was born of a grand pedigree, starting life in 1348, as a hideaway for the crown jewels and treasury of the Holy Roman Emperor, Charles IV. Run by an appointed Burgrave, the castle was surrounded by a network of landowning knight vassals, who came to the castle's aid whenever enemies moved against it.

Karlštejn again sheltered the Bohemian and Imperial crown jewels during the Hussite wars, but fell into disrepair as its defences became outmoded. Considerable restoration work, not least by Josef Mocker in the late 19th century, has returned the castle to its former glory.

There are two tours through the castle. Tour I passes through the Knight's Hall, still daubed with the coats-of-arms and names of the knight vassals, Charles IV's Bedchamber, the Audience Hall and the Jewel House, which includes treasures from the Chapel of the Holy Cross and a replica of the St Wenceslas Crown.

Tour II must be booked in advance and takes in the Great Tower, the highest point of the castle, which includes a museum on Mocker's restoration work, the Marian Tower and the exquisite Chapel of the Holy Cross, with its decorative ceiling.

Sights & Information

Karlštejn Castle (☎ 274 008 154; www.hradkarlstejn .cz; Karlštejn; ☿ 9am-6pm Tue-Sun Jul & Aug; 9am-5pm May, Jun & Sep; 9am-4pm Apr & Oct; 9am-3pm Nov-Mar) Tour I adult/concession 200/100Kč, Tour II adult/concession 300/100Kč.

Eating & Sleeping

Pension & Restaurant U Janů (☎ 311 681 210; info@ujana.cz; s/d incl breakfast 700/1000Kč) On the road up to the castle, this atmospheric place has dark wood décor and a decent dollop of authentic charm.

Penzión U královny Dagmar (☎ 311 681 614; d incl breakfast 1400Kč) Close to the castle and a rung – or two – up the price ladder, this slick place has all the creature comforts and a top-notch eatery.

Transport

Distance from Prague 30km
Direction Southwest
Travel time One hour
Train From Praha-Hlavní Nádraží and Praha-Smíchovské train stations, trains to Beroun stop at Karlštejn (46Kč, 45 minutes, hourly).

KONOPIŠTĚ

Archduke Franz Ferdinand d'Este, heir to the Austro-Hungarian throne, is famous for being dead – it was his assassination in 1914 that sparked off WWI. But the archduke was an enigmatic figure who avoided the intrigues of the Vienna court, and for the last 20 years of his life he hid away in what became his ideal country retreat, **Konopiště Chateau**.

The castle is a testament to the archduke's twin obsessions – hunting and St George. Having renovated the massive Gothic and Renaissance building in the 1890s, and installed all the latest technology – including electricity, central heating, flush toilets, showers and a luxurious lift – Franz Ferdinand decorated his home with his hunting trophies. His game books record that he shot about 300,000 creatures during his lifetime, from foxes and deer to elephants and tigers. About 100,000 of them adorn the walls, each marked with the date and place it met its end – the crowded **Trophy Corridor** (Tour I and III) and antler-clad **Chamois Room** (Tour III) are truly bizarre sights.

There are three guided tours available. Tour III is the most interesting, visiting the private apartments used by the archduke and his family, which have remained unchanged since the state took possession of the chateau in 1921. Tour II takes in the **Great Armoury**, one of the largest and most impressive collections in Europe.

The archduke's collection of art and artefacts relating to St George is no less impressive, amounting to 3750 items, many of which are on show in the **St George Museum** (Muzeum sv Jiří) beneath the terrace at the front of the castle.

Transport

Distance from Prague 50km
Direction South
Travel time 1¼ hours
Bus There are buses from Prague's Roztyly metro station to Benešov (36Kč, 40 minutes, twice hourly) – their final destination is usually Pelhřimov or Jihlava.
Train There are frequent direct trains from Prague's Hlavní Nádraží to Benešov u Prahy (64Kč, 1¼ hours, hourly). Konopiště is 2.5km west of Benešov. Local bus No 2 (7Kč, six minutes, hourly) runs from a stop on Dukelská, 400m north of the train station (turn left out of the station, then first right on Tyršova and first left) to the castle car park. Otherwise it's a 30-minute walk. Turn left out of the train station, go left across the bridge over the railway, and follow Konopištská street west for 2km.

Sights & Information

Konopiště Chateau (☎ 317 721 366; Benešov; ⏰ 9am-5pm Tue-Sun May-Aug; to 4pm Tue-Fri, to 5pm Sat & Sun Sep; to 3pm Tue-Fri, to 4pm Sat & Sun Apr & Oct; to 3pm Sat & Sun Nov, closed 12.30-1pm) Tour I or Tour II in English adult/child 145/75Kč; Tour III in English 250Kč, no conc.

St George Museum (Muzeum sv Jiří; adult/child 25/10Kč; ⏰ same hr as chateau)

Eating & Sleeping

Hostinec U zlaté hvězdy (☎ 317 723 921; Masarykovo náměstí, Benešov; mains 80-120Kč; ⏰ 11am-11pm)

Snug, inn-style Bohemian snacks can be had at this central *pivnice* (beer hall).

Hotel Atlas (☎ 317 724 771; hotelatlas@quo-reklama.cz; Tyršova 2063, Benešov; s/d 742/864Kč) This place is sterile and functional, but the rooms here are spotless and comfortable. Benešov is located just 2km east of the Konopiště Chateau.

Hotel Nová Myslivna (☎ 317 722 496; www.hotelmyslivna.zde.cz; Konopiště; d 500Kč; P) The sweeping angular roof of the chalet-style Hotel Nová Myslivna clashes somewhat with the softer lines of the castle, but the hotel's location by the Konopiště Chateau car park is unbeatable.

MĚLNÍK

Pretty Mělník, north of Prague, sprawls over a rocky promontory surrounded by the flat sweep of Bohemia's modest wine-growing region. Staunchly Hussite in its sympathies, the town was flattened by Swedish troops in the Thirty Years' War, but the castle was rebuilt as a prettier, less threatening chateau and the centre retains a strong historical

Transport

Distance from Prague 30km
Direction North
Travel time One hour
Bus On weekdays, buses run to Mělník (36Kč, 45 minutes) from Prague's Nádraží Holešovice metro station every 30 to 60 minutes, and less often from Florenc bus station. At weekends Florenc is your best bet.

kostel sv Petra a Pavla (see right), Mělník

identity. Modernity has caught up with the town's trailing edge, bringing a clutch of factories to its outskirts, but views from the castle side are untouched and Mělník remains a good bet for a spot of wine-tasting bacchanalia far from the bustle of the capital.

The Renaissance **zámek Mělník** (Mělník chateau) was acquired by the Lobkovic family in 1739. The family opened it to the public in 1990. You can wander through the former living quarters, which are crowded with a rich collection of Baroque furniture and 17th- and 18th-century paintings. Additional rooms have changing exhibits of modern works and a fabulous collection of 17th-century maps detailing Europe's great cities. A separate tour descends to the 14th-century wine cellars where you can taste the chateau's wines (70/110Kč for two/six wines); a shop in the courtyard sells the chateau's own label.

Next to the chateau is the 15th-century Gothic **kostel sv Petra a Pavla** (Church of SS Peter & Paul), with its Baroque furnishings and tower. Remnants of its Romanesque predecessor have been incorporated into the rear of the building. The old crypt is now an **ossuary**, packed with the bones of some 10,000 people dug up to make room for 16th-century plague victims, and arranged in macabre patterns.

The path between chateau and church leads to a **terrace** with superb views across the river and the central Bohemian countryside. The steep slopes below the terrace are planted with vines – supposedly descendants of the first vines to be introduced to Bohemia, by Charles IV, back in the 14th century.

Sights & Information

Ossuary (admission 30Kč; 9.30am-12.30pm & 1.15-4pm Tue-Sun)

Tourist Information Centre (☎ 315 627 503; infocentrum@melnik.cz; náměstí Míru 11; 9am-5pm May-Sep, Mon-Fri only Oct-Apr) Sells maps and historical guides, and can help with accommodation.

Zámek Mělník (Mělník Chateau; ☎ 315 622 121; adult/concession 60/30Kč; 10am-6pm)

Eating & Sleeping

Hotel U Rytířů (☎ 315 621 440; jansladecek@seznam.cz; Svatováclavská 17; mains 100-250Kč; d 1900-2500Kč; restaurant 8am-11pm) Located conveniently right next to the castle, this opulent little place has plush, apartment-style rooms with all the trimmings, and a garden restaurant.

Penzión V podzámčí (☎ 315 622 889; hrzi@post.cz; Seiferta 167; s/d incl breakfast 650/1300K č) This reasonably central place (three blocks from náměstí Míru, to the left as you face the chateau) has modest, modern rooms above a Bohemia crystal shop.

Restaurace sv Václav (☎ 315 622 126; Svatováclavská 22; mains 150Kč; 11am-11pm) Dark wood décor, cigar humidors, red leather seats and a lunchtime suntrapping outdoor terrace conspire to make this one of Mělník's most appealing restaurants.

LIDICE, TEREZÍN & LITOMĚŘICE

The Bohemian countryside to the north of Prague contains two villages that provide a sobering reminder of the horrors inflicted on the Czech people during WWII. If you're driving, Lidice and Terezín can be combined in one day; if you want to spend the night, head for the attractive town of Litoměřice, 3km north of Terezín. Using public transport, you'll have to choose; it's only practical to do one or the other on a day trip.

LIDICE

When British-trained, Czechoslovak para-troops assassinated Reichsprotektor Reinhard Heydrich in June 1942 (see the boxed text on p46), the Nazis took a savage revenge. Picking – apparently at random – the mining and foundry village of Lidice, 18km northwest of Prague, they proceeded on 10 June to obliterate it from the face of the earth. All its men were shot, all the women and the older children shipped to the Ravensbrück concentration camp, and the younger children farmed out to German foster homes. The village was systematically burned and bulldozed so that no trace remained. Of its 500 inhabitants, 192 men, 60 women and 88 children eventually died. The atrocity caused shock around the world and triggered a campaign to preserve the village's memory. The site is now a green field, eloquent in its silence, dotted with a few memorials and the reconstructed foundations of a farm where most of the men were murdered. The onsite Muzeum Lidice recreates the village in photographs and text, and also screens chilling SS film footage of its destruction.

Transport

Distance from Prague 60km (to Terezín)
Direction North
Travel time 1½ hours
Bus Direct buses from Prague to Litoměřice (61Kč, 1¼ hours, hourly), stopping at Terezín, depart from stance No 17 at Florenc bus station (final destination Ústí nad Labem). There are also frequent buses between Litoměřice bus station and Terezín (8Kč, 10 minutes, at least hourly). Buses from Prague to Lidice (18Kč, 30 minutes, hourly) depart from the bus stop on Evropa, opposite the Hotel Diplomat, just west of Dejvická metro station.

TEREZÍN

It is perhaps no coincidence that Terezín (Theresienstadt in German) and terror share the same first syllable. A massy bulwark of stone and earth, this immense fortress was built in 1780 by Emperor Joseph II with a single purpose in mind: to keep the enemy out. Ironically, when the Germans took control of Terezín during WWII, this role was reversed and the walls were employed as a grim holding pen for Jews bound for extermination camps. After the rich, gentrified structures of many Czech towns, Terezín is a stark, but profoundly evocative monument to a darker aspect of central Europe's past.

The bleakest phase of Terezín's history began in 1940 when the Gestapo established a prison in the Lesser Fortress. Evicting the inhabitant from the Main Fortress the following year, the Nazis transformed the town into a transit camp, through which some 150,000 Jews eventually passed en route to extermination camps. For most, conditions were appalling. Between April and September 1942 the ghetto's population increased from 12,968 to 58,491, leaving each prisoner with only 1.65 sq m of space and causing disease and starvation on a terrifying scale. In the same period, there was a 15-fold increase in the number of deaths within the prison walls.

Ironically, Terezín later became the centrepiece of one of Nazism's more extraordinary public-relations coups. Official visitors to the fortress, including representatives of the Red Cross, saw a town that was billed as a kind of Jewish 'refuge', with a Jewish administration, banks, shops, cafés, schools and a thriving cultural life – it even had a jazz band – a charade that twice completely fooled international observers. The reality was a relentlessly increasing concentration of prisoners, regular trains departing for the gas chambers of Auschwitz, and the death by starvation, disease or suicide of some 35,000 Jews.

From the ground, the sheer scale of the maze of walls and moats that surrounds the Main Fortress (hlavní pevnost) is impossible to fathom – mainly because the town is actually inside them. In fact, when you first arrive by bus or car, you may be left thinking that the central square looks no different to 101 other small town centres. Take a peek at the aerial photograph in the Museum of the Ghetto (Muzeum ghetta), or wander past the walls en route to the Lesser Fortress, however, and a very different picture begins to emerge. At the heart of the Main Fortress is the squared-off, boxy town of Terezín. There's little to look at except the chunky, 19th-century Church of the Resurrection, the arcaded commandant's office, the neoclassical administrative buildings on the square and the surrounding grid of houses with their awful secrets. South of the square are the anonymous remains of a railway siding, built by prisoners, on which loads of further prisoners arrived – and left.

Excursions – Terezín

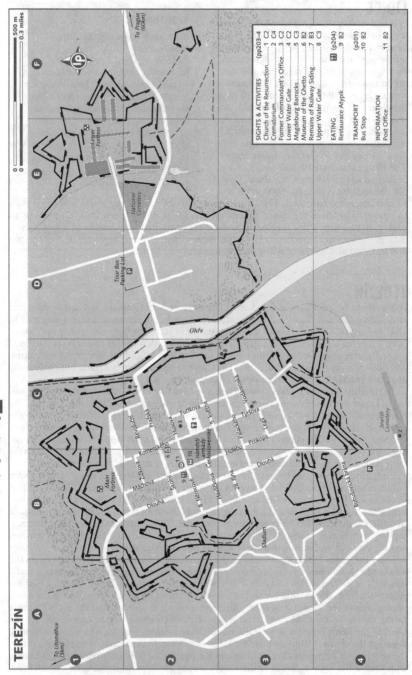

TEREZÍN

0   500 m
0   0.3 miles

SIGHTS & ACTIVITIES	(pp203-4)
Church of the Resurrection	1 C2
Crematorium	2 C4
Former Commandant's Office	3 C2
Lower Water Gate	4 C2
Magdeburg Barracks	5 C3
Museum of the Ghetto	6 B2
Remains of Railway Siding	7 B3
Upper Water Gate	8 C3

EATING	(p204)
Restaurace Atypik	9 B2

TRANSPORT	(p201)
Bus Stop	10 B2

INFORMATION	
Post Office	11 B2

To Litoměřice (3km)

To Prague (60km)

Lesser Fortress

National Cemetery

Tour Bus Parking Lot

Ohře

Main Fortress

Jewish Cemetery

Revoluční

Pražská

Husova

Fučíkova

Komenského

Žižkova

Máchova

Dlouhá

Školní

B. Němcové

Hlučíkova

náměstí Československé armády

5 května

Palackého

Tyršova

Legií

Vodárenská

Holého

Prokopa

28 října

Dlouhá

Bohušovická brána

Stadium

The main attraction here is the absorbing **Museum of the Ghetto**, which has two branches. The main branch explores the rise of Nazism and life in the Terezín ghetto, using the period bric-a-brac to startling and evocative effect. Erected in the 19th century to house the local school, the museum building was later used by the Nazis to accommodate the camp's 10- to 15-year-old boys. The haunting images painted by these children still decorate the walls. A newer branch is housed in the former **Magdeburg Barracks** (Magdeburská kasárna), which served as the seat of the Jewish 'town council'. Here you can visit a reconstructed dormitory for prisoners, and look at exhibits on the extraordinarily rich cultural life – music, theatre, fine arts and literature – that somehow flourished against this backdrop of fear. There is also a small exhibit in the grim **Crematorium** (Krematorium; ☉ 10am-5pm Sun-Fri Mar-Nov) in the Jewish Cemetery just off Bohušovická brána about 750m south of the main square.

You can take a self-guided tour of the **Lesser Fortress** (Malá pevnost) through the prison barracks, isolation cells, workshops and morgues, past execution grounds and former mass graves. It would be hard to invent a more menacing location, and it is only while wandering through the seemingly endless tunnels beneath the walls that you begin to appreciate fully the vast dimensions of the fort. The Nazis' mocking concentration-camp slogan, Arbeit Macht Frei (freedom through work) hangs above the gate. In front of the fortress is a National Cemetery, established in 1945 for those exhumed from the Nazis' mass graves.

LITOMĚŘICE

After contemplating the horrors of Terezín, **Litoměřice** is your chance to exhale. Although only a few kilometres to the north of the infamous fortress, this quaint riverside town is a million miles away in atmosphere. Pastel-hued façades and intricate gables jostle for dominance on the main square and the town's lively bars and restaurants play host to some vibrant, after-hours action. Once stridently Hussite, much of the Gothic face of Litoměřice was levelled during the Thirty Years' War and today the town's unassuming castle plays second fiddle to a clutch of effete Renaissance houses and impressive churches (many by esteemed 18th-century architect, Ottavio Broggio).

Dominating Mírové náměstí, the town's attractive main square, is the Gothic tower of **All Saints Church** (kostel Všech svatých), built in the 13th century and 'Broggio-ised' in 1718. Beside it, with multiple gables, pointy arches and a copper-topped tower, is the handsome, Gothic **Old Town Hall** (Stará radnice), with a small town museum. Most striking is the 1560 Renaissance **House at the Black Eagle** (dům U Černého orla), covered in sgraffito (mural technique in which the top layer of plaster is scraped away to reveal the layer underneath) biblical scenes and housing the Hotel Salva Guarda. A few doors down is the present town hall, in the 1539 **House at the Chalice** (dům U Kalicha), with a massive Hussite chalice on the roof. This building also houses the tourist information office. The thin slice of Baroque wedding cake at the uphill end of the square is the **House of Ottavio Broggio**.

Along Michalská at the southwest corner of the square you'll find another house where Broggio left his mark, the excellent **North Bohemia Fine Arts Gallery** with the priceless Renaissance panels of the Litoměřice Altarpiece.

Turn left at the end of Michalská and follow Domská towards grassy, tree-lined Domské náměstí on Cathedral Hill, passing pretty **St Wenceslas Church**, a true Baroque gem, along a side street to the right. At the top of the hill is the town's oldest church, **St Stephen Cathedral**, dating from the 11th century.

Go through the arch to the left of the cathedral and descend a steep cobbled lane called Máchova. At the foot of the hill turn left then first right, up the zigzag steps to the **old town walls**. You can follow the walls to the right as far as the next street, Jezuitská, where a left turn leads back to the square.

Sights & Information

Litoměřice Tourist Information Office (☎ 416 732 440; www.litomerice.cz; Mírové náměstí 15, Litoměřice;

☉ 8am-6pm Mon-Fri, 8am-5.30pm Sat, 9.30am-4pm Sun May-Sep; 8am-5pm Mon & Wed, 8am-4.15pm Tue & Thu, 8am-4pm Fri, 8-11am Sat Oct-Apr)

Muzeum ghetta (Museum of the Ghetto; ☎ 416 782 576; www.pamatnik-terezin.cz; Komenského, Terezín; adult/child 160/130Kč; ☺ 9am-6pm Apr-Oct, 9am-5.30pm Nov-Mar) Combined ticket for Muzeum Ghetta and Malá pevnost is 180/140Kč. The museum has good multilingual self-guide pamphlets, a large selection of books for sale, and guides (some of them ghetto survivors).

Malá pevnost (Lesser Fortress; ☎ 416 782 576; www.pamatnik-terezin.cz; Terezín; adult/child 160/130Kč; ☺ 8am-6pm Apr-Oct, 8am-4.30pm Nov-Mar) Combined ticket for Muzeum Ghetta and Malá pevnost is 180/140Kč.

Muzeum Lidice (www.lidice-memorial.cz; Lidice; adult/concession 50/20Kč; ☺ 9am-6pm Apr-Sep, 9am-4pm Oct-Mar)

North Bohemia Fine Arts Gallery (Severo česká galerie výtvarného umění; ☎ 416 732 382; Michalská 7, Litoměřice; adult/concession 32/18Kč; ☺ 9am-noon & 1-6pm Tue-Sun Apr-Sep, to 5pm Oct-Mar)

Eating

Music Café Viva (☎ 608 437 783; Mezibraní 5, Litoměřice; mains 80-200Kč) Housed in former bastion in the old city walls opposite the train station, this hip, music-oriented eatery has a cocktail bar below, a restaurant above and creaking wooden beams galore.

Restaurace Atypik (☎ 416 782 780; Máchova 91, Terezín; mains 60-100Kč; ☺ 11am-10pm) Atypik by name, but rather typical by nature, this bustling place offers all the predictable local favourites, with an emphasis on stodge and unapologetic meatiness.

Sleeping

Hotel Salva Guarda (☎ 416 732 506; www.salva-guarda.cz; Mírové náměstí 12, Litoměřice; s/d 920/1450Kč; Ⓟ) Litoměřice's top hotel is set in the lovely Renaissance House at the Black Eagle. It also has the best restaurant on the square.

Pension Prislin (☎ 416 735 833; pension@prislin.cz; Na Kocandě 12, Litoměřice; s/d 700/1100Kč; Ⓟ) A view across the river and breakfast in the garden are good reasons for choosing the family-friendly Prislin. It's five minutes' walk east of the town square, along the main road.

U Svatého Václava (☎ 416 737 500; usvateho vaclava@hotmail.com; Svatováclavská 12, Litoměřice; s/d 600/1000Kč) Tucked away in the shadow of St Wenceslas Church, this pretty villa houses a tip-top pension with sauna, well-equipped rooms and a homely apron-toting owner who whips up a fine breakfast.

KUTNÁ HORA

Now dwarfed by 21st-century Prague, Kutná Hora once marched in step with the capital and, with a little help from fate, might even have stolen its crown as the heart and soul of Bohemia. Enriched by the silver ore that ran in veins through the surrounding hills, the medieval city once enjoyed explosive growth, becoming the seat of Wenceslas II's royal mint in 1308 and the residence of Wenceslas IV just under 100 years later. The silver *groschen* that were minted here at that time represented the hard currency of Central Europe. But while boom-time Kutná Hora was Prague's undisputed understudy, the town tripped out of history when the silver mines began to splutter and run dry in the 16th century; a demise hastened by the Thirty Years' War and finally certified by a devastating fire in 1770. While the capital continued to expand, its sister city largely vanished from sight.

Which is not to say everyone has forgotten about it. Kutná Hora today is an A-list tourist attraction – it was added to Unesco's World Heritage List in 1996 – luring visitors with a smorgasbord of historic sights and more than a touch of nostalgic whimsy. Standing on the ramparts surrounding the mighty chrám sv Barbora (Cathedral of St Barbara), looking out across rooftops eerily reminiscent of Prague's Malá Strana, it's all too easy to indulge in spot of melancholic what-might-have-been.

If you arrive by train, a natural first stop is the remarkable **Sedlec Ossuary** (Kostnice), just a 10-minute walk south from Kutná Hora train station. When the Schwarzenberg family purchased Sedlec monastery in 1870 they allowed a local wood-carver to get creative with the bones that had been piled in the crypt for centuries. But this was no piddling little heap of bones; it was

---

Transport

Distance from Prague 65km
Direction East
Travel time 1½ hours
Bus To Kutná Hora from Prague (68Kč, 1¼ hours, hourly), departing from stance No 2 at Florenc bus station; services are less frequent at weekends.
Train There are direct trains from Prague's main train station to Kutná Hora Hlavní Nádraží (62Kč, 55 minutes, seven daily).

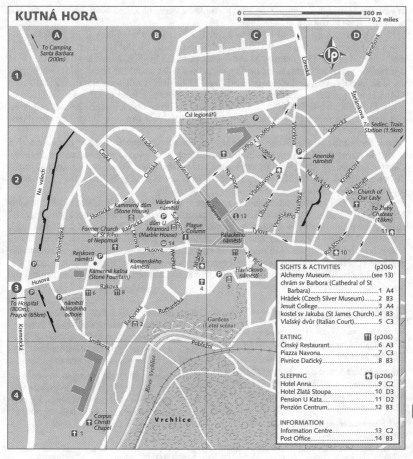

KUTNÁ HORA

SIGHTS & ACTIVITIES	(p206)
Alchemy Museum	(see 13)
chrám sv Barbora (Cathedral of St Barbara)	1 A4
Hrádek (Czech Silver Museum)	2 B3
Jesuit College	3 A4
kostel sv Jakuba (St James Church)	4 B3
Vlašský dvůr (Italian Court)	5 C3

EATING	(p206)
Čínský Restaurant	6 A3
Piazza Navona	7 C3
Pivnice Dačický	8 B3

SLEEPING	(p206)
Hotel Anna	9 C2
Hotel Zlatá Stoupa	10 D3
Pension U Kata	11 D2
Penzión Centrum	12 B3

INFORMATION	
Information Centre	13 C2
Post Office	14 B3

the remains of no fewer than 40,000 people. The result was spectacular: garlands of skulls and femurs are strung from the vaulted ceiling like Addams Family Christmas decorations, while in the centre dangles a vast chandelier containing at least one of each bone in the human body. Four giant pyramids of stacked bones squat in each of the corner chapels, and crosses, chalices and monstrances of bone adorn the altar. There's even a Schwarzenberg coat-of-arms made from bones.

From Sedlec it's another 20-minute walk (or five-minute bus ride) into central Kutná Hora. Palackého náměstí, the main square, is unremarkable; the most interesting part of the old town lies to its south. But first, take a look at the **Alchemy Museum**, in the same building as the information centre, complete with basement laboratory, Gothic chapel and mad-scientist curator.

From the upper end of the square a narrow lane called Jakubská leads directly to the huge **kostel sv Jakuba** (St James Church; 1330). Just east of the church lies the **Vlašský dvůr** (Italian Court), the former Royal Mint – it got its name from the master craftsmen from Florence brought in by Wenceslas II to kick-start the business, and who began stamping silver coins here in 1300. The oldest remaining part, the (now bricked-up) niches in the courtyard, were minters' workshops. The original treasury rooms now hold an exhibit on coins and minting. The guided tour (with translated text) is worth taking for a look at the few historical rooms open to the public, notably a 15th-century **Audience Hall** with two impressive 19th-century murals depicting the election of Vladislav Jagiello as king of Bohemia in 1471 (the angry man in white is Matthias Corvinus, the loser), and the Decree of Kutná Hora being proclaimed by Wenceslas IV and Jan Hus in 1409.

From the southern side of kostel sv Jakuba, a narrow cobbled lane (Ruthardská) leads down and then up to the **Hrádek** (Little Castle). Originally part of the town's fortifications, it was rebuilt in the 15th century as the residence of Jan Smíšek, administrator of the royal mines, who grew rich from silver he illegally mined right under the building. It now houses the **Czech Silver Museum** (České Muzeum Stříbra). The exhibits celebrate the mines that made Kutná Hora wealthy, including a huge wooden device once used to lift loads weighing as much as 1000kg from the 200m-deep shafts. You can even don a miner's helmet and lamp and join a 45-minute guided tour (adult/child 110/70Kč) through 500m of **medieval mine shafts** beneath the town.

Just beyond the Hrádek is the 17th-century former **Jesuit college**, fronted by a terrace with a row of 13 baroque sculptures of saints, an arrangement inspired by the statues on Prague's Charles Bridge. All are related to the Jesuits and/or the town; check out the second one – the woman holding a chalice, with a stone tower at her side, is St Barbara, the patron saint of miners and therefore of Kutná Hora.

At the far end of the terrace is Kutná Hora's greatest monument, the Gothic **chrám sv Barbora** (Cathedral of St Barbara). Rivalling Prague's St Vitus in size and magnificence, its soaring nave culminates in elegant, six-petalled ribbed vaulting. Work was started in 1380, interrupted during the Hussite Wars and abandoned in 1558 when the silver began to run out. It was finally completed in neo-Gothic style at the end of the 19th century. The **ambulatory chapels** preserve some original 15th-century frescoes, some of them showing miners at work. Take a walk around the outside of the church, too; the terrace at the east end enjoys the finest view in town.

Sights & Information

Alchemy Museum (☎ 327 511 259; Palackého náměstí 377; adult/concession 40/25Kč; ☼ 10am-5pm Apr-Oct, 10am-4pm Nov-Mar)

chrám sv Barbora (Cathedral of St Barbara; ☎ 776 393 938; adult/concession 30/15Kč; ☼ 9am-5.30pm Tue-Sun May-Sep, 10-11.30am & 1-4pm Apr & Oct, 10-11.30am & 2-3.30pm Nov-Mar)

Czech Silver Museum (České Muzeum Stříbra; ☎ 327 512 159; adult/concession 60/30Kč; ☼ 10am-6pm Jul & Aug; 9am-6pm May, Jun & Sep; 9am-5pm Apr & Oct; closed Mon)

Vlašský dvůr (Italian Court; ☎ 327 512 873; Havlíčkovo náměstí 552; adult/concession 70/50Kč; ☼ 9am-6pm Apr-Sep, 10am-5pm Mar & Oct, 10am-4pm Nov-Feb)

Sedlec Ossuary (Kostnice; ☎ 327 561 143; Zámecká 127; adult/concession 45/30Kč; ☼ 8am-6pm Apr-Sep, 9am-noon & 1-5pm Oct, to 4pm Nov-Mar)

Tourist Information Centre (☎ 327 512 378; www.kh.cz; Palackého náměstí 377; ☼ 9am-6pm Apr-Sep; 9am-5pm Mon-Fri, 10am-4pm Sat & Sun Oct-Mar) Books accommodation and has Internet access (1Kč per minute, 15Kč minimum).

Eating

Čínský Restaurant (☎ 327 514 151; náměstí Národního odboje 48; mains 90-200Kč; ☼ 11am-10pm Tue-Sat) Set in a plush old house with a garden out back, the imaginatively named 'Chinese' is a little heavy on the MSG but still manages a tasty chicken gung-po.

Piazza Navona (☎ 327 512 588; Palackého náměstí 90; mains 100-130Kč; ☼ 9am-midnight May-Sep, 9am-8pm Oct-Apr) Feed up on pizza at this homely Italian café-bar, plastered with Ferrari flags and Inter Milan pennants; tables spill onto the main square in summer.

Pivnice Dačický (☎ 327 512 248; Rakova 8; mains 60-100Kč; ☼ 11am-11pm) Get some froth on your moustache at this old-fashioned, wood-panelled Bohemian beer hall, where you can dine on dumplings while envying the folk who phoned ahead for the whole roast piglet.

Sleeping

Hotel Anna (☎ 327 516 315; hotel.anna@seznam.cz; Vladislavova 372; s/d 730/1050Kč; Ⓟ) Offers comfortable, modern rooms with shower, TV and breakfast in a lovely old building with an atmospheric stone-vaulted cellar restaurant.

Hotel Zlatá Stoupa (☎ 327 511 540; zlatastoupa@iol .cz; Tylova 426; s/d from 1070/1800Kč; Ⓟ) If you feel like spoiling yourself, the most luxurious place in town is the elegantly furnished 'Golden Mount'. We like a hotel room whose minibar contains full-size bottles of wine.

Penzión Centrum (☎ 327 514 218; penzioncentrum .kh@tiscali.cz; Jakubská 57; r per person 400-600Kč; Ⓟ) Tucked away in a quiet, flower-bedecked courtyard off the main drag, this place offers snug rooms and a sunny garden.

Penzión U Kata (☎ 327 515 096; www.volny.cz/ukata; Uhelná 596; s/d 300/400Kč; Ⓟ) This quiet, back-street pension offers basic but comfortable rooms, all with private shower and WC.

Directory

Directory

The practical information in this chapter is divided into two parts, Transport and Practicalities. Within each section information is presented in strictly alphabetical order.

TRANSPORT

AIR

The national carrier, **Czech Airlines** (ČSA; ☎ 220 104 310; www.csa.cz; V celnici 5, Nové Město), has direct flights to Prague from many European cities, including London, Edinburgh, Paris and Frankfurt, and from New York and Toronto.

Airlines

Main international airlines serving Prague:

Aer Lingus (EI; ☎ 221 667 407; www.aerlingus.ie)

Aeroflot (SU; ☎ 224 812 682; www.aeroflot.ru)

Air Baltic (BT; ☎ 257 532 829; www.airbaltic.lv)

Air France (AF; ☎ 221 662 662; www.airfrance.com)

Alitalia (AZ; ☎ 221 629 150; www.alitalia.com)

Austrian Airlines (OS; ☎ 220 116 272; www.austrianairlines.com)

British Airways (BA; ☎ 222 114 444; www.britishairways.com)

Croatia Airlines (OU; ☎ 222 222 235; www.croatiaairlines.hr)

ČSA (OK; ☎ 220 104 310; www.csa.cz)

EasyJet (EZY; www.easyjet.com)

El Al (LY; ☎ 224 226 624; www.elal.co.il)

JAT Airways (JU; ☎ 224 942 654; www.jat.com)

KLM (KL; ☎ 233 090 933; www.klm.com)

LOT (LO; ☎ 222 317 524; www.lot.com)

Lufthansa (LH; ☎ 220 114 456; www.lufthansa.com)

Malev (MA; ☎ 224 224 471; www.malev.com)

SAS (SK; ☎ 220 116 031; www.scandinavian.net)

SkyEurope (NE; www.skyeurope.com)

SN Brussels Airlines (SN; ☎ 220 114 323; www.flysn.com)

Turkish Airlines (TK; ☎ 221 518 386; www.turkishairlines.com)

Airport

Prague-Ruzyně Airport (Map pp242-3; ☎ 220 113 314; www.csl.cz/en; bus 100, 119, 179) is 17km west of the city centre. The arrivals hall and departure hall are next to each other, on the same level. The arrivals hall has exchange counters, ATMs, several accommodation and car-hire agencies, a public-transport information desk, taxi counters and a 24-hour left-luggage office. The 'Information' windows mainly dispense flight information.

The departure hall has a fast-food place and a bar (there are several more cafés and restaurants in the arrivals area), an airport information office, airline offices, an exchange counter, and travel agencies.

There's a **post office** (☺ 8am-6pm Mon-Fri, to 1pm Sat) in the Administrative Centre across the car park from the arrivals hall.

GETTING INTO TOWN

To get into town, buy a ticket from the public transport (Dopravní podnik; DPP) desk in arrivals and take bus No 119 (12Kč, 20 minutes, every 15 minutes) to the end of the line (Dejvická), then continue by metro into the city centre (another 10 minutes; no new ticket needed). Note that you'll need a half-fare (6Kč) ticket for your backpack or suitcase (anything larger than 25cm x 45cm x 70cm), too.

Alternatively, take a **Čedaz minibus** (☎ 220 114 296) from just outside arrivals – buy your ticket from the driver (90Kč, 20 minutes, every 30 minutes 5.30am to 9.30pm). There are city stops at metro Dejvická and at náměstí Republiky. You can also get a Čedaz minibus right to the door of your hotel or any other address (360Kč for one to four people, 720Kč for five to eight). You can phone to book a pick-up for the return trip.

Airport Cars (☎ 220 113 892) taxi service, whose prices are regulated by the airport administration, charges 650Kč (20% discount for the return trip) into the centre of Prague (a regular taxi fare *from* central Prague should be about 450Kč). Drivers usually speak some English and accept Visa credit cards.

Websites

As well as airline websites, there are a number of efficient online resources for buying good-value flight tickets. A couple of the best:

www.cheapflights.co.uk Lists discount flights to Prague from other parts of the UK and Ireland.

www.opodo.co.uk Site owned by consortium of European airlines; often cheaper than no-frills airlines for short-notice flights.

BICYCLE

Prague is not a brilliant place to ride a bike. Traffic is heavy, exhaust fumes can be choking and there are no bicycle lanes. The cobblestones will loosen your teeth, and tram tracks are treacherous, especially when wet.

You'll need a good lock for wheels and frame: bikes are a popular target. Spare parts are available in the city's many bike shops and in larger and smaller towns.

Bikes have to be equipped with a bell, front and rear brakes as well as mudguards, a front white reflector, a rear red reflector, a proper front white light, a flashing rear light, and reflectors on pedals – if not, a cyclist can be fined up to 1000Kč. Cyclists up to the age of 15 have to wear helmets.

If you're aged at least 12 you can take your bicycle on the metro. You must keep it near the last door of the rear carriage, and only two bikes are allowed in. You can't do it at any time when the carriage is full, nor if there's already a pram in the carriage.

Hire

Praha Bike (Map pp246-7; ☎ 732 388 880; www.prahabike.cz; Dlouhá 24, Staré Město; 2hr from 220Kč, 6hr 540Kč; ☯ 9am-7pm; tram 1, 5, 8) Good, new bikes with lock, helmet and map, plus free luggage storage. Also offers student discounts and group bike tours (also see p51).

City Bike (Map pp246-7; ☎ 776 180 284; Králodvorská 5, Staré Město; 4/9hr 500/900Kč; ☯ 9am-7pm; metro Náměstí Republiky) Rental includes helmet and padlock. Two-hour guided tours cost from 450Kc, departing at 11am, 2pm, 5pm and 7pm.

BUS

Long-distance companies include national carrier ČSAD (Czech Automobile Transport) and Čebus. All domestic long-distance buses and most regional services (such as those for excursions around Prague) use **Florenc bus station** (Map pp258-9; ☎ 12 999; www.jizdnirady .cz; Křižíkova 4, Karlín). **Eurolines-Sodeli CZ** (Map pp246-7; ☎ 224 239 318; www.eurolines.cz /english; Senovážné náměstí 6, Nové Město 6, Nové Město; ☯ 8am-6pm Mon-Fri) links Prague with points all over Western and Central Europe; it can book you seats and sell you tickets. There's also a Eurolines ticket office at Florenc bus station.

CAR & MOTORCYCLE

Driving in Prague is no fun, especially in the narrow, winding streets of the city centre. Trying to find your way around – or to park legally – while coping with trams, buses, other drivers, cyclists and pedestrians, can make you wish you'd left the car at home.

You can ease the trauma by avoiding weekday peak-traffic hours: in central Prague from 4pm onwards (on Friday from as early as 2pm). Try not to arrive in or leave the city on a Friday or Sunday afternoon or evening, when half the population seems to head to/from their *chaty* (weekend houses).

Central Prague has many pedestrian-only streets, including parts of Wenceslas Square, Na příkopě and 28.října, most of Old Town Square (Staroměstské náměstí) and some streets leading into it. Most are marked with *Pěší zóna* (Pedestrian zone) signs, and only service vehicles and taxis have special permits to drive in these areas.

Prague Information Service (Pražská informační služba; PIS) publishes a *Transport Guide* with much useful tips for drivers, including emergency breakdown services, where to find car-repair shops (by make) and all-important parking tips.

Car Hire

The main international car-hire chains all have airport pick-up points (where you may have to pay an extra 400Kč surcharge) as well as central offices, including:

A-Rent Car/Thrifty (Map pp252-3; ☎ 224 233 265; www.arentcar.cz; Washingtonova 9, Nové Město; metro Muzeum)

Avis (Map pp246-7; ☎ 221 851 225; www.avis.com; Klimentská 46, Nové Město; tram 5, 8, 14)

CS-Czechocar (Map pp246-7; ☎ 221 637 427; www .czechocar.cz; Rathova pasáž, Na příkopě 23, Nové Město; metro Náměstí Republiky)

Europcar (Map pp246-7; ☎ 224 810 515; www.europcar .cz; Pařížská 28, Staré Město; tram 17)

Hertz (Map pp252-3; ☎ 222 231 010; Karlovo náměstí 28, Nové Město; metro Karlovo náměstí)

A-Rent Car is the cheapest, charging from 1700/10,000Kč per day/week for a Škoda Felicia, including unlimited mileage, collision - damage waiver and value-added tax (VAT; or DPH in Czech). There's a 400Kč surcharge to pick up your vehicle from the airport, but delivery to hotels in central Prague is free. The other major companies are up to 10% more expensive.

Small local companies offer better prices, but are less likely to have fluent, English-speaking staff – it's often easier to book by email than by phone. Typical rates for a Škoda Felicia are around 700Kč a day, including unlimited kilometres, collision-damage waiver and VAT.

Reputable local companies:

Secco Car (Map pp242-3; ☎ 220 802 361; www.seccocar .cz; Přístavní 39, Holešovice; tram 1, 3, 12, 25)

Vecar (Map pp255; ☎ 224 314 361; www.vecar.cz; Svatovítská 7, Dejvice; metro Dejvická)

West Car Praha (Map pp242-3; ☎ 235 365 307; www .westcarpraha.cz in Czech; Veleslavínská 17, Veleslavín; tram 20, 26)

Car Theft

A Western car with foreign plates is a prime target for thieves, especially in central Prague, though the chances of theft are no higher than in the West. Older Czech cars are also getting popular, for the domestic spare-parts market, as are smaller items such as wind-screen wipers, antennae and car emblems. Of course, don't leave your possessions visible in the vehicle. Car alarms and steering-wheel locking devices are all the rage in Prague; if you're driving your own car in Prague, consider bringing a locking device.

Emergencies

In case of an accident the police should be contacted immediately if repairs are likely to cost over 20,000Kč or if there is an injury. Even if damage is slight, if you're driving your own car it's a good idea to report the accident, as the police can issue an insurance report that will help you avoid headaches when you take the car out of the country.

For emergency breakdowns, the **ÚAMK** (Central Automobile & Motorcycle Club; Map pp242-3; ☎ 1230, 261 104 111, 261 104 333; Na strži 9, Nusle) provides nationwide assistance; the 'Yellow Angels' (Žlutý andělé) operates 24 hours.

ÚAMK has agreements with numerous national motoring organisations across the world through its affiliation to the Alliance Internationale de Tourisme and the Fédération Internationale de l'Automobile. If you are a member of any of these, ÚAMK will help you on roughly the same terms as your own organisation would. If not, you must pay for all services.

Another outfit offering round-the-clock repair services nationwide is **Autoklub Bohemia Assistance** (Autoklub české republiky, ABA; Map pp252-3; ☎ 1240, 222 241 257; Opletalova 29, Nové Město).

Fuel

Leaded and unleaded fuel are available from all Prague petrol stations, and diesel at most of them. There is at least one round-the-clock station on every major highway and road in and out of Prague. LPG (liquefied petroleum gas, *autoplyn*) is mostly not available from petrol stations but only from LPG stations; there is at least one in each suburb.

Parking

Parking in most of Praha 1 is regulated with permit-only and parking-meter zones. Meter fees are 30Kč or 40Kč per hour, with time limits from two to six hours. Traffic inspectors willingly hand out fines, clamp wheels or tow away vehicles. Parking in one-way streets is normally only allowed on the right-hand side.

There are several car parks at the edges of Staré Město, and Park-and-Ride car parks around the outer city (most are marked on the 1:20,000 GeoClub SHOCart Praha and Žaket city maps), close to metro stations. Convenient underground car parks:

Hotel Inter-Continental (Map pp246-7; Pařížská, Staré Město)

Konstruktiva (Map pp246-7) Under náměstí Jana Palacha, Staré Město.

Kotva department store (Map pp246-7; náměstí Republiky, Nové Město)

Praha hlavní nádraží (Prague's main train station; Map pp252-3) Enter from Bolzanova or Wilsonova.

Státní opera Praha (Prague State Opera; Map pp252-3)
Enter from Wilsonova.

Tržnice Smíchov (Map pp250-1; Náměstí 14.října, Smíchov)

Guarded parking lots:

Hotel Opera (Map pp246-7; Těšnov 13)

Malostranské náměstí (Map pp244-5; Malá Strana)

Masarykovo nádraží (Map pp246-7; Na Florenci)

Náplavka (Map pp260-1) Corner of Řásnovka and Revoluční.

Národní divadlo (National Theatre; Map pp252-3; Divadelní)

Passing Trams

In Prague you may overtake a tram only on the right, and only if it's in motion. You must stop behind any tram taking on or letting off passengers where there's no passenger island. A tram has the right of way when making any signalled turn across your path.

Repairs

Spare parts (other than for Škodas) can be hard to find, but most well-known models can be repaired at a basic level by at least one garage in Prague. Repair shops for major foreign brands are listed in the PIS *Transport Guide*.

PUBLIC TRANSPORT

All public transport is operated by **Dopravní podnik hl. m. Prahy** (DPP; ☎ 296 191 817; www.dpp.cz), which has information desks (7am to 10pm) at Ruzyně airport and in five metro stations – at Muzeum (7am to 9pm), Můstek, Anděl and Nádraží Holešovice (all open 7am to 6pm) – where you can get tickets, directions, a multilingual transport system map, a map of night services *(noční provoz)* and a detailed English-language guide to the whole system.

You need to buy a ticket before you board a bus, tram or metro. Tickets are sold from machines at metro stations and major tram stops, at newsstands, Trafiky snack shops, PNS newspaper kiosks, hotels, all metro station ticket offices and DPP information offices.

A transfer ticket *(jízdenka)* valid on tram, metro, bus and the Petřín funicular (p66) costs 12/6Kč per adult/child aged six to 15 years; you'll need a 6Kč ticket for each

large suitcase or large backpack. Kids under six ride free. Validate (punch) your ticket by sticking it in the little yellow machine in the metro station lobby or on the bus or tram the first time you board; this stamps the time and date on it. Once validated, tickets remain valid for 60 minutes from the time of stamping, if validated between 5am and 8pm on weekdays, and for 90 minutes at all other times. Within this time period, you can make unlimited transfers between all types of public transport (you don't need to punch the ticket again).

There's also a short-hop 8Kč ticket, valid for 15 minutes on buses and trams, or for up to four metro stations or two zones. No transfers are allowed with these, and they're not valid on the Petřín funicular nor on night trams (Nos 51 to 58) or buses (Nos 501 to 512). Being caught without a valid ticket entails a 400Kč on-the-spot fine (50Kč for not having a luggage ticket). The plain-clothes inspectors travel incognito, but will show a badge when they ask for your ticket. A few may demand a higher fine from foreigners and pocket the difference, so insist on a receipt *(doklad)* before paying.

You can also buy tickets valid for 24 hours (70Kč) and three/seven/15 days (200/250/280Kč). Again, these must be validated on first use only; it a ticket is stamped twice, it becomes invalid.

On metro trains and newer trams and buses, an electronic display shows the route number and the name of the next stop, and a recorded voice announces each station or stop. As the train, tram or bus pulls away, the announcer says '*Příští stanice…*' (The next station is…) or '*Příští zastávka…*' (The next stop is…), perhaps noting that it's a *přestupní stanice* (transfer station). At metro stations, signs point you towards the *výstup* (exit) or to a *přestup* (transfer to another line).

The metro operates from 5am to midnight. There are three lines: Line A runs from the northwestern side of the city at Dejvická to the east at Skalka; line B runs from the southwest at Zličín to the northeast at Černý Most; and line C runs from the north at Nádraží Holešovice to the southeast at Háje. Line A intersects line C at Muzeum, line B intersects line C at Florenc and line A intersects line B at Můstek.

After the metro closes, night trams (Nos 51 to 58) and buses (Nos 501 to 512) still rumble across the city about every 40 minutes through the night. If you're planning a late evening, find out if one of these services passes near where you're staying.

TAXI

In 2002 Prague City Council finally cracked down on the city's notoriously dishonest taxi drivers by raising the maximum fine for overcharging to one million crowns (Kč).

However, hailing a taxi on the street – at least in a tourist zone – still holds the risk of an inflated fare. The taxi stands around Wenceslas Square, Národní třída, Na příkopě, Praha hlavní nádraží, Old Town Square and Malostranské náměstí are the most notorious rip-off spots; even the locals are not safe.

You're much better off calling a radio-taxi than flagging one down, as they're better regulated and more responsible. From our experience the following companies seem to have honest drivers (some of whom speak a little English) and offer 24-hour services.

AAA Radio Taxi (☎ 14 014)

Airport Cars (☎ 220 113 892)

Halo Taxi (☎ 244 114 411)

ProfiTaxi (☎ 261 314 151)

If you hail a taxi in the street, ask the approximate fare in advance and ask the driver to use the meter (*zapněte taximetr, prosím*). If it's 'broken', find someone else or establish a price before setting off. If you get the rare driver who willingly turns on the meter, they deserve a tip just for that (Czechs usually leave the change).

The official maximum rate for licensed cabs is 30Kč minimum plus 22Kč per kilometre, or 4Kč per minute while it's stalled in traffic or waits while you enjoy the view. On this basis, any trip within the city centre – say, from Wenceslas Square to Malá Strana – should cost around 100Kč to 150Kč. A trip to the suburbs should not exceed 250Kč, and to the airport 450Kč. Journeys outside Prague are not regulated.

Regulations note the meter must be at zero when you get in, and fares must be displayed. At the end of the journey the driver must give you a meter-printed receipt showing company name, taxi ID number, date and times of the journey, end points, rates, the total, the driver's name and their signature. Get one before you pay, and make sure it has all these things in case you want to make a claim. Complaints

about overcharging should be directed to **City Hall** (☎ 236 002 269; Office 405, 4th fl, Platnéřská 19, Staré Město; ◷ noon-5pm Mon, 8am-6pm Wed).

PRACTICALITIES

ACCOMMODATION

Accommodation listings in this book are broken down first by neighbourhood, then alphabetically within each neighbourhood heading with 'Cheap Sleeps' (places that cost less than 2500Kč for a double room) at the end. The average cost of a double room with en suite bathroom is in the 3000Kč to 5000Kč range, with seasonal variations – the highest rates are charged during May, June, September, October and the Christmas/New Year period.

Check out p178 for details of accommodation websites, longer-term rentals and self-catering.

BUSINESS

A free-market economy has been evolving, haphazardly, in the Czech Republic since 1989. Laws and regulations have been written from scratch; some have worked, some have failed and all are full of loopholes. It's not unusual for locals to take advantage of innocent newcomers, or to renege on agreements. Money laundering is also a big problem. It's essential that a reliable Czech partner be found for any venture: someone to deal with complex procedures and steer clear of crooked deals. Lawsuits can take years, and many judges have not yet grasped the meaning of a free society. Entrenched bureaucratic habits remain in place, and corruption is still a problem.

The expatriate business community in Prague is well informed by a glossy monthly magazine, the *Prague Tribune* (www.prague-tribune.cz), and a weekly newspaper, the *Prague Business Journal*, with business-oriented regional news plus a few entertainment and restaurant listings. The *Prague Post* (www.praguepost.cz; 65Kč) also has an extensive business section.

Business Hours

Shops tend to open from 8.30am or 9am to 5pm or 6pm Monday to Friday, and close between 11am and 1pm on Saturday. Department stores close at 8pm Monday to Friday, an hour or two earlier on Saturday, and at 6pm on Sunday. Touristy shops in central Prague are open later at night and on Saturday and Sunday.

Most museums and galleries open from 9am or 10am to 5pm or 6pm year-round. Many close on Monday and sometimes the first working day after a holiday. Some of Prague's bigger churches are open similar hours.

Castles, chateaux and other historical monuments outside the city are open May to September, from 8am or 9am to 5pm or 6pm, except for a lunch break, daily except Monday and the first working day after a holiday. Most shut down from November to March, with some limited to weekends in October and April. But Karlštejn Castle is open from at least 9am to 3pm year-round (except the day after any public holiday, and Christmas Eve and New Year's Day). If you plan to take a guided tour, remember that ticket offices close an hour or so before the official closing time, depending on the length of the tour. See p198 for more information on Karlštejn Castle.

Banks generally open 8am to 4.30pm Monday to Friday; the city's main post office opens 7am to 8pm every day, while other post offices open 8am to 6pm or 7pm Monday to Friday and until noon on Saturday. Restaurants tend to open between 10am and 11pm (cafés generally open around 8am), while bars usually open and close an hour or so later. You can start shopping at around 8.30am until 5pm or 6pm Monday to Friday, while you have till noon or 1pm on Saturday.

Useful Organisations

American Chamber of Commerce (Map p255; ☎ 222 329 430; www.amcham.cz; Dušní 10, Staré Město) Lots of useful resources, including info about work permits and other business matters.

Artlingua (Map pp260-1; ☎ 224 918 058; www.artlingua.cz; Myslíkova 6, Nové Město) Professional translation services.

CzechInvest (☎ 296 342 500; www.czechinvest.org; Štěpánská 15, Nové Město) Government agency that encourages inward investment in the Czech Republic.

Economic Chamber of the Czech Republic (Hospodářská komora ČR; Map pp244-5; ☎ 224 096 160; www.komora.cz; Freyova 27, Vysočany) Provides financial, legal

and organisational advice to small- and medium-sized businesses.

Trade Links (Map pp260-1; ☎ 224 241 535; www.tradelinks.cz; Opletalova 4, Nové Město) Publishes English translations of Czech commercial, accounting and bankruptcy laws, as well as information about living in Prague.

CHILDREN

Czechs are generally family-oriented and there are plenty of activities for children around the city. For some suggestions on where to keep kids entertained see the boxed text on p58.

Museums of possible interest to children include the muzeum hraček (Toy Museum; p59), though, frustratingly, its many displays are hands-off; the Národní Technické Muzeum (National Technology Museum; p93), especially the vast hall full of trains, cars and aeroplanes; the muzeum MHD (Public Transport Museum; p99), where kids will love climbing the vintage trams and buses; and the Letecké muzeum (Aircraft Museum), which offers children the chance to see up close Russian MiG fighter planes.

For outdoor activity, try Zoo Praha (p98) or Petřín (p66), a large park on a hill where parents and kids alike can take a break from sightseeing. In the park itself you can enjoy the funicular railway, the mirror maze, Petřínská rozhledna (Petřín Tower; with terrific views of Prague if the weather is clear), the Štefánikova Hvězdárna (Štefánik Observatory) and a playground. For the best views of all, go to the Televizní vysílač (TV Tower; p96) in Žižkov.

In summer there are rowing and paddle boats for hire along the Vltava river (also see p51), and there are safe, fenced playgrounds by the entrance to Petřín on náměstí Kinských (Map pp250-1); at the northern end of Kampa island (Map pp244-5); by the entrance to Kampa Park restaurant; on Dětský ostrov (Children's Island; see p65); and on Vlašská, just west of the German embassy. In winter there are plenty of ice rinks.

March is the time of the Matějská pouť (St Matthew Fair; p9), when the fairgrounds in Holešovice are full of rides, shooting galleries and candy floss. If there's a circus in town it will most likely be on Letná Plain, opposite the AC Sparta Praha Stadium (Map pp256-7).

At weekends and on holidays between April and mid-November, vintage tram cars trundle along a special sightseeing route, No 91, around the historical centre (see p52 for more information). And don't miss the changing of the guard at Prague Castle (see p55 for details) – but get in position before the crowds do, or the kids won't see a thing.

Several theatres cater for children, but nearly everything is in Czech. Two good ones are the divadlo Minor (p160) and the divadlo Spejbla a Hurvínka (p161). The latter is a marionette theatre named after Spejbl and Hurvínek, the Czech equivalent of Punch and Judy.

Few Prague restaurants cater specifically for children in the Western sense, with play areas and so on. Some restaurants have a children's menu (*dětský jídelníček*), but even if they don't, they can usually provide smaller portions for a lower price.

Baby-sitting

PIS (p222) usually has a list of baby-sitting (*hlídaní dětí*) agencies, and most top-end hotels provide a baby-sitting service; rates generally run from 80Kč to 120Kč per hour.

Agencies that can provide the services of English-speaking baby-sitters:

Babysitting Praha (☎ 602 885 074; blazinkk@centrum.cz)

Markéta Tomlová (☎ 608 082 8681; tomkovam@seznam.cz)

Tetty (☎ 233 340 766; www.tetty.cz)

CLIMATE

Prague lies in the transitional area between maritime and continental climates, characterised by hot, showery summers, cold, snowy winters and generally changeable conditions. A typical day in Prague from June to August sees the mercury range from about 12° to 22°C. Temperatures from December to February push below freezing. Wide vari-ations are common, sometimes surpassing 35°C in summer and -20°C in winter.

The closest thing to a 'dry season' is from January to March, when total precipitation (mostly as snow at that time) is less than a third of that during the wettest months, June to August. And yet January averages as many 'wet' days (about two out of five) as the summer months do. The summer's long, sunny, hot spells tend to be broken by sudden, heavy thunderstorms. May and September have the most pleasant weather.

Also see p8 for more information.

COURSES

The **Information-Advisory Centre of Charles University** (IPC; Map pp252-3; ☎ 224 491 896; ipc@ruk.cuni.cz; Školská 13a; Nové Město) is the place to go for general information on university courses.

Other courses include:

Institute for Language & Preparatory Studies (Ústav jazykové a odborné přípravy; Map pp260-1; ☎ 224 990 411; www.ujop.cuni.cz; Vratislavova 10, Vyšehrad; metro Vyšehrad) ÚJOP runs six-week Czech language courses for foreigners. No prior knowledge of the Czech language is required. The course fee is €585, not including accommodation. You can also opt for individual lessons (45 minutes) at €18 each. Further details and an application form are available on the website.

London School of Modern Languages (Map pp260-1; ☎ 222 515 018; www.londonschool.cz; Budečká 6, Vinohrady; tram 4, 22, 23) Czech courses for both individuals and companies, including specialised Czech language courses for business, law or IT.

Prague Center for Further Education & Professional Development (Map pp244-5; ☎ 257 534 013; www .prague-center.cz; Karmelitská 18, Malá Strana; tram 12, 20, 22, 23) Offers English-language courses on a whole range of subjects from screen-writing and jewellery design to wine-tasting and modern dance.

CUSTOMS

You can import a reasonable amount of personal effects and up to 6000Kč (around US$180) worth of gifts and other 'noncommercial' goods. If you're aged over 18, you can bring in 2L of wine, 1L of spirits and 200 cigarettes (or equivalent tobacco products).

Before you make a major purchase in Prague find out how much it will cost to get it out of the country. Duty of 22% must be paid on consumer goods exceeding 30,000Kč (US$1000) in value.

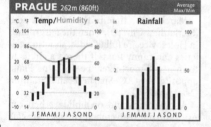

PRAGUE 262m (860ft)

Temp/Humidity   Rainfall

°C °F   %   in   mm

You can't export genuine antiques, and customs officials are a suspicious lot. If you are unsure about what you're taking out, ask at the Národní muzeum (National Museum; p84) or Umělecko-průmyslové muzeum (Museum of Decorative Arts; p74). Certification from them should satisfy airport or postal customs. For mailing any such items over 2kg, go to the **customs post office** (pobočka celního úřadu; Map pp242-3; ☎ 257 213 736; Plzeňská 139, Košiře; ☒ 7am-3pm Mon-Fri, to 6pm Wed). Take tram No 4, 7 or 9 to the Klamovka stop, three stops from Anděl metro station.

There is no limit to the amount of Czech or foreign currency that can be taken in or out of the country, but amounts exceeding 350,000Kč must be declared.

DISABLED TRAVELLERS

Increasing, but still limited, attention is being paid to facilities for people with disabilities in Prague. Wheelchair ramps are becoming more common, especially at major street intersections and in top-end hotels (in the text we identify hotels with facilities for the disabled). For people who are blind or vision-impaired, most pedestrian-crossing lights in central Prague have a sound signal to indicate when it's safe to cross. McDonald's and KFC entrances and toilets are wheelchair-friendly.

The Stavovské divadlo (Estates Theatre; p79) is equipped for the hearing-impaired; the Klášter sv Anežky (Convent of St Agnes; p73) has a ground-floor presentation of medieval sculptures with explanatory text in Braille – and this gallery and several other theatres are wheelchair-accessible. (The monthly what's-on booklet *Přehled* – which is published by PIS in Czech only – indicates venues with wheelchair access.) Prague Castle also has areas that are wheelchair-accessible (p54).

Few buses and no trams have wheelchair access; special wheelchair-accessible buses operate Monday to Friday on bus line Nos 1 and 3, including between Florenc bus station and náměstí Republiky, and between Holešovice train station and náměstí Republiky (visit the website at www.dpp.cz for more information).

Praha hlavní nádraží, Holešovice train station and a handful of metro stations (Hlavní Nádraží, Hůrka, Luka, Lužiny, Nádraží Holešovice, Stodůlky and Zličín) have self-operating lifts. Other metro stations (Chodov, Dejvická, Florenc C line, Háje, IP Pavlova, Opatov, Pankrác, Roztyly and Skalka) have modified lifts that can be used with the help of station staff. Czech Railways (ČD) claims that every large station in the country has wheelchair ramps and lifts, but in fact the service is poor.

When flying, travellers with special needs should inform the airline of their requirements when booking, and again when reconfirming, and again when checking in. Most international airports (including Prague's) have ramps, lifts, and wheelchair-accessible toilets and telephones. Aircraft toilets, on the other hand, present problems for wheelchair-users, who should discuss this early on with the airline and/or their doctor.

Organisations

Czech Blind United (Sjednocená organizace nevidomých a slabozrakých v ČR; Map pp252-3; ☎ 221 462 146; www .braillnet.cz; Krakovská 21, Nové Město) Represents the vision-impaired; provides information but no services.

Prague Wheelchair Users Organisation (Pražská organizace vozíčkářů; Map p255; ☎ 224 827 210; www.pov.cz in Czech; Benediktská 6, Staré Město) Can organise a guide and transportation at about half the cost of a taxi, and has an online guide to barrier-free Prague.

DISCOUNT CARDS

The Prague Card is a combined public transport pass and admission card that is valid for three days. It provides free entry to around 40 city sights, including Prague Castle, the Národní muzeum (National Museum) and many other museums and art galleries, and also allows unlimited travel on metro, trams and buses. It costs 790Kč for adults, 610Kč for students and children under 16, and can be purchased from PIS offices, Čedok travel agencies and Prague branches of American Express.

You can also buy a Prague Card without the public transport option; in this case the cost is 590/410Kč.

ELECTRICITY

Electricity in Prague is 220V, 50Hz AC, and is quite reliable. Nearly all the outlets have the standard European socket with two small round holes; some also have a protruding earth (ground) pin. If you have a different plug or want to use the earth pin, bring an adaptor, as they are difficult to find in the Czech Republic. North American 110V appliances will also need a transformer if they don't have built-in voltage adjustment.

EMBASSIES & CONSULATES

Australia (Map pp246-7; ☎ 296 578 350, fax 296 578 352; Klimentská 10, Nové Město) Honorary consulate for emergency assistance only (eg a stolen passport); nearest Australian embassy is in Vienna.

Austria (Map pp246-7; ☎ 257 090 511; www.austria.cz in Czech; Viktora Huga 10, Smíchov)

Canada (Map p255; ☎ 272 101 800; www.canada.cz; Muchova 6, Bubeneč)

France (Map pp244-5; ☎ 251 171 711; www.france.cz in Czech; Velkopřerovské náměstí 2, Malá Strana)

Germany (Map pp244-5; ☎ 257 113 111; www .deutschland.cz in Czech; Vlašská 19, Malá Strana)

Ireland (Map pp244-5; ☎ 257 530 061; www .irishembassy.cz; Tržiště 13, Malá Strana)

Netherlands (Map p255; ☎ 224 312 190; www.nether landsembassy.cz; Gotthardská 6/27, Bubeneč)

New Zealand (Map pp242-3; ☎ 222 514 672; egermayer@nzconsul.cz; Dykova 19, Vinohrady) Honorary consulate providing emergency assistance only (eg stolen passport); the nearest NZ embassy is in Berlin.

Poland (Map pp244-5; ☎ 257 530 388; www.ambpol.cz; Valdštejnská 8, Malá Strana) This is the embassy; go to the consular department for visas.

Poland (Map pp242-3; ☎ 224 228 722; konspol@mbox. vol.cz; V úžlabině 14, Strašnice) This is the consular department; come here for visas.

Russia (Map pp256-7; ☎ 233 374 100; rusembassy@cdnet.org; Pod Kaštany 1, Bubeneč)

Slovakia (Map p255; ☎ 233 113 051; www.slovakemb.cz in Czech; Pod Hradbami 1, Dejvice)

South Africa (Map pp242-3; ☎ 267 311 114; saprague@terminal.cz; Ruská 65, Vršovice)

UK (Map pp244-5; ☎ 257 402 111; www.britain.cz; Thunovská 14, Malá Strana)

USA (Map pp244-5; ☎ 257 530 663; www.usembassy.cz; Tržiště 15, Malá Strana)

EMERGENCY

Ambulance (☎ 155)

Autoklub Bohemia Assistance (ABA; ☎ 1240)

EU-wide emergency hotline (☎ 112)

Fire (☎ 150)

Municipal Police (☎ 156)

Police (☎ 158)

Ústřední auto-moto-klub (ÚAMK; ☎ 1230)

GAY & LESBIAN TRAVELLERS

Homosexuality is legal in the Czech Republic (the age of consent is 15), but Czechs are not accustomed to seeing same-sex couples showing affection to each other in public; it's best to be discreet.

The bimonthly gay guide and contact magazine *Amigo* has a few pages in English, and a useful English website (www.amigo .cz). The Gay Guide Prague (www.gayguide .net/europe/czech/prague) is another useful source of information. See also the boxed text on p156 for gay-friendly venues and accommodation options.

Gay Iniciativa (Gay Initiative; Map pp252-3; ☎ 224 223 811; www.gay.iniciativa.cz in Czech; Senovážné náměstí 2, Nové Město; tram 3, 9, 14, 24) is the national organisation for gays and lesbians; it can offer information on events, venues and resources.

HOLIDAYS

Banks, offices, department stores and some shops will be closed on public holidays. Restaurants, museums and tourist attractions tend to stay open.

New Year's Day 1 January

Easter Monday March/April

Labour Day 1 May

Liberation Day 8 May

SS Cyril & Methodius Day 5 July

Jan Hus Day 6 July

Czech Statehood Day 28 September

Republic Day 28 October

Struggle for Freedom & Democracy Day 17 November

Christmas Eve (Generous Day) 24 December

Christmas Day 25 December

St Stephen's Day 26 December

INTERNET ACCESS

Prague has dozens of Internet cafés. Here is a selection of conveniently located ones.

Bohemia Bagel (Map pp250-1; ☎ 257 310 694; www .bohemiabagel.cz; Újezd 16, Malá Strana; per min 1.50Kč; ☾ 7am-midnight Mon-Fri, 8am-midnight Sat & Sun;

tram 6, 9, 12, 20, 22, 23) This café is also a popular eatery, see p120 for details.

Bohemia Bagel (Map pp246-7; ☎ 224 812 560; www .bohemiabagel.cz; Masná 2, Staré Město; per min 1.50Kč; 🕑 7am-midnight Mon-Fri, 8am-midnight Sat & Sun; metro Náměstí Republiky) There's another branch in Malá Strana.

Globe Bookshop & Café (Map pp252-3; ☎ 224 934 203; Pštrossova 6, Nové Město; per min 1.50Kč; 🕑 10am-midnight; metro Karlovo Náměstí) No minimum time set. Also has Ethernet sockets where you can connect your own laptop (same price; cables provided, 50Kč deposit).

Internet Nescafe Live (Map pp246-7; ☎ 221 637 168; Rathova Pasáž, Na příkopě 23, Staré Město; per min 1.70Kč; 🕑 9am-10pm Mon-Fri, 10am-8pm Sat & Sun; metro Náměstí Republiky)

net k@fe (Map pp246-7; Na poříčí 8; Nové Město; per min 1Kč; 🕑 9am-11pm; metro Náměstí Republiky) Cheapest in the city centre.

Pl@neta (Map pp258-9; ☎ 267 311 182; Vinohradská 102, Vinohrady; per min 0.40-0.80Kč; 🕑 8am-11pm; metro Jiřího z Poděbrad) Cheapest rates before 10am and after 8pm Monday to Friday, all day Saturday and Sunday.

Spika (Map pp246-7; ☎ 224 211 521; www.spika.cz; Dlážděná 4, Nové Město; per 15 min 20Kč; 🕑 8am-midnight; metro Náměstí Republiky)

You should be able to log on from your hotel room for the cost of a local call by registering with an Internet roaming service such as **MaGlobe** (www.maglobe.com), which has access numbers for Prague. Most newer, midrange and top-end hotels have telephone jacks, usually US standard (RJ-11), which you can plug your modem cable into. Adaptors for the older, four-pin Czech phone jacks can be found in electronic supply shops.

Buy a line tester – a gadget that goes between your computer and the phone jack – so that you don't inadvertently fry your modem. Get on and off quickly; calls from hotels are expensive. An increasing number of Internet cafés in Prague now offer Ethernet sockets where you can connect a network-enabled laptop to the Internet. For more information on travelling with a laptop check out www .kropla.com.

Major Internet service providers such as **AOL** (www.aol.com), **CompuServe** (www.compuserve.com) and **AT&T** (www.attbusiness.net) have dial-in nodes in Prague. If you have an account with one of these, you can download a list of local dial-in numbers before you leave home.

If you access your account at home through a smaller ISP or your office or school network, your best option is to open a webmail account, such as Yahoo or Hotmail, before you leave, and either give your new webmail address to your friends and family, or use the account's 'Check Other Mail' option to download mail from your home account (this may not work for work-based accounts).

LEGAL MATTERS

If you find yourself under arrest for any reason whatsoever, you are entitled to call your embassy (see p216 for listings). Note that it is technically illegal not to carry some form of identification (normally your passport). If you can't prove your identity, police have the right to detain you for up to 48 hours.

Penalties for possession of drugs are harsh and it's unlikely that your embassy can do much to help if you are caught. In the Czech Republic it was, until recently, legal to possess and use cannabis (though it was illegal to sell it). However, a new law came into force on 1 January 1999 (despite a veto by President Havel) which made it illegal to possess 'more than a small amount' of drugs. Unfortunately the law does not define 'a small amount' or specify which drugs, giving the police a free hand to nick anyone in possession of any amount of any drug. It's simply not worth the risk to import, export or possess any illegal substances.

Many of the older police officers retain a communist-era mistrust of foreigners. Younger officers are easier to deal with, but almost none speak fluent English.

Drink-driving is strictly illegal; there is a zero blood-alcohol limit for drivers. Traffic fines are generally paid on the spot (ask for a receipt). The fine for littering is around 100Kč.

MAPS

Maps are available at newsagents, bookshops and travel agencies for 80Kč or less. An accurate and readable one of the city centre and inner suburbs is Kartografie Praha's *Praha – plán města* (1:10,000). It includes transport and parking information, an index, metro map, plans of the castle and Charles Bridge, and a brief description of the major historical sites.

Lonely Planet's plastic-coated *Prague city* map is tough and good value, and has sections covering central Prague, Prague Castle, greater Prague, the Prague metro, the area around Prague, and an index of streets and sights.

PIS (p222) stocks a free English-language pamphlet *Welcome to the Czech Republic*, which is produced by the Ministry of Interior. It features a map of the historical centre, transport routes in the centre, and information such as emergency phone numbers and embassy addresses.

If you are staying in Prague for a significant amount of time, Kartografie's pocket atlas *Praha – plán města* – standard (1:20,000), covering all of Prague, is invaluable.

A public transport map showing all day and night services (metro, tram and bus) is available from any of the public information offices of Dopravní podnik (DPP), the city transport department (for details see p211).

MEDICAL SERVICES

Emergency treatment and nonhospital first aid are free for all visitors to the Czech Republic. Citizens of EU countries may get cheap or free treatment under reciprocal health-care treaties (check before you leave home). Others must pay for treatment, normally in koruna, and at least some must be paid upfront. Everyone must pay for prescribed medications.

Some healthcare facilities:

American Dental Associates (Map pp246-7; ☎ 221 181 121; Stará Celnice Bldg, V celnici 4; Nové Město; metro Náměstí Republiky)

Canadian Medical Care (Map pp242-3; ☎ 235 360 133, after hr ☎ 724 300 301; www.cmc.praha.cz; Veleslavínská 1, Veleslavín; 8am-6pm Mon-Fri; tram 20 or 26 from metro Dejvická) A pricey but professional private clinic with English-speaking doctors; an initial consultation will cost from US$50 to US$200.

Na Homolce (Map pp242-3; ☎ 257 271 111, after hr 257 272 527; 5th fl, Foreign Pavilion, Roentgenova 2, Motol; bus 167 from metro Anděl) The best hospital in Prague, equipped and staffed to Western standards, with staff who speak English, French, German and Spanish.

Poliklinika na Národní (Polyclinic on Národní; Map pp252-3; ☎ 222 075 120, 24hr emergencies 777 942 270; www.poliklinika.narodni.cz; Národní 9, Nové Město; 8.30am-5pm Mon-Fri; metro Národní Třída) A central clinic with English-speaking staff. Expect to pay around 800Kč to 1200Kč for an initial consultation.

There are plenty of pharmacies *(lékárna)*, and most city districts have one that stays open 24 hours. In Nové Město it's at the **district clinic** (Map pp252-3; ☎ 224 946 982; Palackého 5, Nové Město; 7am-7pm Mon-Fri, 8am-noon Sat; metro Národní třída). Vinohrady's is **Lékárna U sv Ludmily** (Map pp260-1; ☎ 222 513 396; Belgická 37, Vinohrady; 7am-7pm Mon-Fri, 8am-noon Sat; metro Náměstí Míru).

For emergency service after hours, ring the bell – you'll see a red button with a sign *zvonek lékárna* (pharmacy bell) and/or *první pomoc* (first aid). Over-the-counter and prescription medicines are not always available, so it's wise to bring what you need.

METRIC SYSTEM

Czechs use the metric system. A comma is used instead of a decimal point, and full stops are used to indicate thousands, millions etc. A dash is used after prices rounded to the nearest koruna. For example, thirty thousand koruna would be written 30.000,- rather than 30,000.00. See the inside front cover of this guidebook for a conversion table.

MONEY

The Czech crown (Koruna česká, or Kč), is divided into 100 hellers or *haléřů* (h). Bank notes come in denominations of 20, 50, 100, 200, 500, 1000, 2000 and 5000Kč; coins are of 10, 20 and 50h and one, two, five, 10, 20 and 50Kč.

Keep small change handy for use in public toilets, telephones and tram-ticket machines, and try to keep some small denomination notes for shops, cafés and restaurants – getting change for the 2000Kč notes that ATMs spit out can be a problem.

See the inside front cover of this guidebook for the exchange rates table.

ATMs

There is a good network of ATMs, or *bankomaty*, throughout the city. Most accept Visa, MasterCard, Cirrus and Maestro cards.

Changing Money

The easiest, cheapest way to carry money is in the form of a debit card from your bank, with which you can withdraw cash either over the counter or from an ATM. Charges are minimal at major Prague banks (typically from zero to about 2%) and some home banks charge nothing at all for the use of these cards. Provided you make withdrawals of at least several thousand koruna at a time, you'll pay less than the assorted commissions on travellers cheques. Make sure you know your personal identification number (PIN), and check with your bank about transaction fees and withdrawal limits.

The main banks (see Map pp246–7) – Komerční banka, Česká spořitelna banka, Československá obchodní banka (ČSOB) and Živnostenská banka – are the best places to change cash. They charge 2% commission with a 50Kč minimum (but always check, as commissions can vary from branch to branch). They will also provide a cash advance on Visa or MasterCard without commission.

Hotels charge about 5% to 8% commission, while Čedok travel agencies and post offices charge 2% – similar rates to the banks.

Many private exchange offices in Prague charge exorbitant commissions (výlohy) of up to 10%. Some of these offices advertise higher rates and zero commission but don't mention their sky-high 'handling fee', or charge no commission but have very poor exchange rates.

Credit Cards

Many mid-range and top-end hotels and restaurants accept credit cards. You can use a card to get a cash advance in a bank or to withdraw money from ATMs, but charges will be higher than with a debit card.

You can report lost credit cards (or travellers cheques – see below) to:

Amex (☎ 222 800 111)

Diners Club (☎ 267 314 485)

MasterCard/Eurocard (☎ 261 354 650)

Visa (☎ 224 125 353)

Travellers Cheques

Banks charge 2% with a 50Kč minimum for changing travellers cheques. Amex and Thomas Cook/Travelex offices change their own-brand cheques without commission, but charge 2% or 3% for other brands, 3% or 4% for credit-card cash advances, and 5% for changing cash.

Lost travellers cheques can also be reported to the same telephone numbers listed for lost credit cards (see above).

NEWSPAPERS & MAGAZINES

The kiosks on Wenceslas Square and Na příkopě sell a wide range of international newspapers and magazines, including British papers, such as the *Times, Independent* and *Guardian* (international edition), which are available on the day of publication (85Kč to 110Kč). You'll also find newspapers and magazines in English-language bookshops (see p127).

See p18 for general information on the Czech press.

POST

The **main post office** (Map pp252-3; ☎ 221 131 111; www.ceskaposta.cz; Jindřišská 14, Nové Město; ☯ 7am-8pm; metro Můstek) is just off Wenceslas Square. There's an information desk just inside the main hall to the left.

In Prague's main post office you must use the automatic queuing system. Take a ticket from one of the machines in the entrance corridors – press button No 1 for single-item stamps, letters and parcels, and No 4 for Express Mail Service (EMS). Then watch the display boards in the main hall – when your ticket number appears (flashing), go to the desk number shown.

Most of the city's other post offices open from 8am to 6pm or 7pm Monday to Friday, and until noon Saturday. There's also a **nonstop post office** (Map pp246-7; ☎ 224 219 714; Hybernská 15, Nové Město; ☯ 12.30am-11.30pm; tram 5, 9, 26) near Masarykovo nádraží.

Postal Rates

The Czech postal service is fairly efficient. Anything you can't afford to lose, however, should go by registered mail (doporučený dopis) or by EMS.

An aerogram costs 8Kč; letters up to 20g cost 9Kč to other European countries, 14Kč elsewhere. A 2kg parcel (by airmail) costs 490Kč to anywhere in Europe, and 830Kč to elsewhere. You can send parcels of books (or printed matter such as magazines, newspapers etc) up to 15kg at lower rates.

Receiving Mail

You can pick up poste-restante mail (výdej listovních zásilek) at desk Nos 1 and 2 (at the far left) of the main post office from

Directory – Practicalities

7am to 8pm Monday to Friday and until noon Saturday. Mail should be addressed to Poste Restante, Hlavní pošta, Jindřišská 14, 110 00 Praha 1, Czech Republic. You must present your passport to claim mail (check under your first name, too). Mail is held for one month.

Holders of Amex cards or travellers cheques can have letters and faxes held for up to one month at the central Prague **Amex office** (Map pp252-3; ☎ 222 800 258 Václavské náměstí 56, Nové Město). The British and Canadian embassies will hold only letters for their citizens for a few months. None of these offices will accept registered letters or parcels.

Sending Mail

You can buy stamps from street vendors and PNS newspaper kiosks as well as from post offices. Letters go in the orange boxes found outside post offices and around the city.

Small-packet services and EMS close at noon on Saturday, and are closed Sunday. Always get a receipt *(potvrzení)* when sending anything larger than a letter by airmail, or when using a more expensive service, to ensure it goes by the service you have paid for.

See p214 for details on posting antiques (though it's best to carry anything of value out of the country yourself). In principle, anything else can be posted internationally from any major post office (though parcels containing glass or crystal will not be accepted by the postal systems in the USA, Australia or New Zealand). In practice, many postal employees still suffer from communist-era anxieties about 'regulations', and may send you off to the customs post office if you want to send anything over 2kg (see p214 for details), no matter what it is.

If you need a professional courier service, **DHL** (Map pp252-3; ☎ 800 103 000; www .dhl.cz; Václavské náměstí 47, Nové Město; ☯ 8am-6.30pm Mon-Fri, 9am-3pm Sat) has a convenient office just off Wenceslas Square, with English-speaking staff.

RADIO

Český rozhlas (Czech Radio) channel 7 (92.6MHz FM) broadcasts 15-minute-long programmes in English covering Czech news, culture and current affairs at 7.07pm Monday to Thursday.

The **BBC World Service** (www.bbc.cz) broadcasts both English-language and Czech news and cultural programmes locally on 101.1MHz FM, 24 hours a day. The programme is available on its website (in Czech).

SAFETY

Tourism and heady commercialism have spawned an epidemic of petty (and not-so-petty) crime. Where tourists are concerned, this mainly means pickpockets. Naturally, the prime trouble spots are where tourists gather in crowds. These include Prague Castle (especially at the changing of the guard), Charles Bridge, Old Town Square (especially in the crowd watching the Astronomical Clock mark the hour), the entrance to Starý židovský hřbitov (the Old Jewish Cemetery), Wenceslas Square, Ruzyně airport, Praha hlavní nádraží, in the metro and on trams (especially getting on and off the crowded Nos 9 and 22). Be aware that people who lean over to look at your menu may be more interested in your wallet.

It's common sense to keep valuables well out of reach, such as inside your clothing. Be alert in crowds and on public transport. A classic ruse involves someone asking directions and thrusting a map under your nose, or a woman with baby hassling you for money – anything to attract your attention – while accomplices delve into your bags and pockets. If anything like this happens, immediately check your bags and look around you.

Lost or Stolen Belongings

Try your embassy first. The staff should give you a letter to take to the police, preferably in Czech, asking for a police report, without which you cannot collect on insurance. Try to get the embassy to provide its own report in your language, too.

The British embassy has this down to an art and will also help you get in touch with a relative or the bank to get more money. For British and unrepresented Commonwealth citizens, it may even arrange an emergency passport to get you home.

For a police report, go to the **police station** (Map pp252-3; ☎ 261 451 760; Jungmannovo náměstí 9, Nové Město) near the northwestern end of Wenceslas Square, as this is the only station that can organise an interpreter. If the theft occurred in another district, the interpreter will take you to that district's police station to make a report. Unless you speak Czech, forget about telephoning the police, as they rarely speak English.

If your passport has been stolen and it contained a visa, apply for a replacement visa at the Foreigners' Police & Passport Office in Žižkov (see p223 for details).

For advice on dealing with lost or stolen credit cards or travellers cheques, see p219.

For anything except travel documents, you might get lucky at the city's **lost & found office** (ztráty a nálezy; Map pp252-3; ☎ 224 235 085; Karoliny Světlé 5; ☾ 8am-noon & 12.30-5.30pm Mon & Wed, to 4pm Tue & Thu, to 2pm Fri; tram 6, 9, 18, 22, 23), east of Národní divadlo (National Theatre). There's another **lost & found office** (☎ 220 114 283; ☾ 24hr) at the airport.

Racism
You may be surprised at the level of casual prejudice directed against the Roma, whom people are quick to blame for the city's problems. Overt hostility towards visitors is rare, though there have been some assaults by skinheads on dark-skinned people.

Scams
Over the last few years there have been reports from foreigners being robbed by bogus police. Men who claim that they are plain-clothes police investigating counterfeiting or illegal money-changing approach tourists and ask to see their money, which is returned after being examined. The unsuspecting tourist finds out later when they check their wallet that a substantial amount of money has been taken.

Another ploy involves a 'lost tourist' asking for directions (usually in halting English). Once you have been in conversation for a few minutes, two of the tourist's 'friends' interrupt, claiming to be plain-clothes policemen and accusing you of changing money illegally. They will demand to see your wallet and passport, but if you hand them over they are likely to run off with them. If in doubt, insist on accompanying them to a police station.

TELEPHONE
All Czech phone numbers have nine digits – you have to dial all nine for any call, local or long distance (ie there is no separate city area code). You can make international calls at main post offices or directly from card-phone booths.

There are payphones all over the place – blue coin-phones only accept 2Kč, 5Kč, 10Kč and 20Kč coins, and can be used to make local, long-distance and international calls. A more common and convenient alternative is a *telekart* (telephone card), which is good for local, long-distance and international calls. You can buy phonecards from post offices, hotels, newsstands and department stores for 175Kč or 320Kč.

There is also Karta X, a pre-paid calling card which allows you to make domestic and international calls from any phone or payphone in the Czech Republic; international rates are cheaper than using an ordinary phonecard (8.40Kc a minute to Australia, UK and USA, as opposed to 11.80Kc a minute). You can buy them in the same place as ordinary phone cards, at prices ranging from 300Kc to 1000Kc. To use Karta X, you do not insert it into the phonecard slot. Instead, you dial the access number (☎ 822 160 161 for English language instructions), then the 14-digit number written on the card, then the number you want to call.

The simplest option (25% less than coin or card phones) is to pay a deposit at the main telephone bureau (to the left inside the main post office's right-hand entrance)

Country-Direct Numbers
The Country-Direct service is available in the Czech Republic (you can get a full list of countries and numbers from any telephone office or directory). Use the following numbers, preceded by 00420, to make a charge-card or reverse-charge call to your home country.

Australia Direct (☎ 06101)

Canada (AT&T; ☎ 00152)

Canada Direct (☎ 00151)

Deutschland Direct (☎ 04949)

France Direct (☎ 03301)

Netherlands (☎ 03101)

UK Direct (BT; ☎ 04401)

USA (AT&T; ☎ 00101)

USA (MCI; ☎ 00112)

USA (Sprint; ☎ 87187)

and make your call in a soundproof booth, where a little meter ticks off your money.

Calls from hotel or restaurant telephones tend to cost at least twice as much as those from a public telephone. Calls to mobile telephones are more expensive than those to landlines.

Mobile Phones

The Czech Republic uses GSM 900, which is compatible with the rest of Europe, Australia and New Zealand but not with the North American GSM 1900 or the totally different system in Japan. Some North Americans, however, have GSM 1900/900 phones that do in fact work here. If you do have a GSM phone, check with your service provider about using it in Prague, and beware of calls being routed internationally (which is very expensive for a 'local' call). You can rent a mobile from **EuroTel** (☎ 224 948 467; www.eurotel.cz; Národní třída 32, Nové Město; ☺ 9am-7pm Mon-Fri, to 1pm Sat) for approximately 1800Kč per week (plus a 5000Kč deposit). In this case, however, you can't use your existing mobile number.

Useful Numbers & Codes

The telephone bureau at the post office has directories for Prague and other major cities.

Useful numbers and codes include:

Czech Republic country code (☎ 420)

Directory inquiries – domestic/international (☎ 1180/1)

Domestic operator (☎ 133 002)

International access code (☎ 00)

Operator assisted international or reverse-charge (collect) calls – English/French/German (☎ 133 004/3/5)

TELEVISION

The only regular English-language programming on the two state-run TV channels is the 45-minute 'Euronews' bulletin on ČT 2, which goes to air at noon Monday to Thursday and 7.15pm Friday to Sunday. There are two independent commercial channels: TV Nova and Prima TV. Nova shows lots of old American and European flicks and dubbed sitcoms. Anyone with a satellite dish can choose from an extensive menu of European stations.

TIME

The Czech Republic is on Central European Time, ie GMT/UTC plus one hour. Clocks are set to daylight-saving time in summer, that is, forward one hour on the last weekend in March and back one hour on the last weekend in October.

Czechs use the 24-hour clock and there's no equivalent of am and pm, though they can commonly add *ráno* (morning), *dopoledne* (before noon), *odpoledne* (afternoon) or *večer* (evening).

TIPPING

After fair service it's normal practice in pubs, cafés and mid-range restaurants to round up the bill to the next 10Kč (or the next 20Kč if it's over about 150Kč); for more information on tipping in restaurants see p116. The same applies to tipping taxi drivers. If your driver is honest and turns on the meter then you should round up the fare at the end of your journey.

TOILETS

Public toilets are free in state-run museums, galleries and concert halls. Most cafés and restaurants don't seem to mind nonguests using theirs – ask for *záchod*, *vé cé* (WC) or *toalet* – note many in tourist areas cost 2Kč or 5Kč.

Elsewhere, such as in train, bus and metro stations, toilets are staffed by mostly burly attendants who ask for 2Kč for use of the toilet (their only pay) and may sell a few sheets of toilet paper *(toaletní papír)* if you need it. Most places are fairly clean. Men's are marked *muži* or *páni*, and women's *ženy* or *dámy*.

TOURIST INFORMATION

The **Prague Information Service** (Pražská informační služba, PIS; ☎ 12 444; www.prague-info.cz; Betlémské náměstí 2, 116 98 Praha 1) is the main provider of tourist information: good maps and detailed brochures (including accommodation options and historical monuments), all free. PIS also publishes the detailed what's-on guide *Přehled* (in Czech only) and other general material.

There are four main PIS branches (the Betlémské náměstí address is for postal inquiries only). See the list opposite.

Malostranská mostecká věž (Malá Strana Bridge Tower; Map pp244-5; Charles Bridge; ⊙ 10am-6pm Apr-Oct)

Nové Město (Map pp246-7; Na příkopě 20, Nové Město; ⊙ 9am-7pm Mon-Fri, to 5pm Sat & Sun)

Praha hlavní nádraží (Main train station; Map pp252-3; Wilsonova 2, Nové Město ⊙ 9am-7pm Mon-Fri, to 4pm Sat & Sun Apr-Oct; 9am-6pm Mon-Fri, to 3pm Sat Nov-Mar)

Staroměstská radnice (Old Town Hall; Map pp246-7; Staroměstské náměstí 5, Staré Město; ⊙ 9am-7pm Mon-Fri, to 6pm Sat & Sun)

The following Czech Tourism (www.czech tourism.com) international offices provide information about tourism, culture and business in the Czech Republic.

Austria (☎ 01-533 21933; Herrengasse 17, 1010 Vienna)

Canada (☎ 416-363 9928; Czech Airlines Office, 401 Bay St, Suite 1510, Toronto, Ontario M5H 2Y4)

France (rue Bonaparte 18, 75006 Paris) No phone inquiries.

Germany (Friedrichstrasse 206, Kreuzberg, 10969 Berlin) No phone inquiries.

Poland (☎ 022-629 29 16; Al. Róż 16, 00-555 Warsaw)

UK (information line ☎ 09063-640641) Office not open to callers.

USA (☎ 212-288 0830; 1109 Madison Ave, New York, NY 10028)

VISAS

Everyone requires a valid passport (or ID card for EU citizens) to enter the Czech Republic. Citizens of EU and EEA (Europe Economic Area) countries do not need a visa for any type of visit. Citizens of Australia, Canada, Israel, Japan, New Zealand, Switzerland and the USA can stay for up to 90 days without a visa; other nationalities do need a visa. Visas are not available at border crossings or at Prague's Ruzyně airport; you'll be refused entry if you need one and arrive without one.

Visa regulations change from time to time, so check www.czech.cz, or one of the Czech embassy or consulate websites listed on p216.

Extensions

Visa extensions are granted once only for a maximum of 90 days. Apply at entrance B of the drab **Foreigners' Police & Passport Office** (Úřadovna cizinecké policie a pasové služby; Map pp258-9; Olšanská 2, Žižkov; ⊙ 7.30-11.45am & 12.30-2.30pm Mon, Tue & Thu, 7.30-11.30am & 12.30-5pm Wed, 7.30am-noon Fri). Take tram No 9 or 26 to the Olšanská stop (opposite the bright yellow Telepoint sign). An extension costs 1000Kč, and is payable with special stamps (kolky) sold at the passport office or at any post office. The paperwork takes about four working days. See below if you intend to stay longer than the statutory tourist period.

WOMEN TRAVELLERS

To many Westerners the Czech Republic seems to have picked up, in terms of sexual equality, where it left off in 1948. Some newsstands stock dozens of porno titles, and even mainstream advertising has no qualms about using the occasional naked breast to sell products. The city has developed a burgeoning sex industry, with strip clubs, lap-dancing clubs, brothels and street workers all in evidence.

Attacks on local women have happened in all parts of Prague, though women are far safer walking alone on the street here than in most large Western cities. The most dangerous area for women at night is the park in front of Praha hlavní nádraží, but be aware that the area at the intersection of Wenceslas Square and Na příkopě, and Perlová, a block west, are effectively red-light districts after dark.

Women (especially solo travellers) may find the atmosphere in some traditional Czech pubs a bit raw, as they tend to be exclusively male territory.

There are very few services for women such as helplines and refuge or rape crisis centres. The main organisation in Prague is the **White Circle of Safety** (Map pp242-3; Bílý kruh bezpečí; ☎ 257 317 110; www.bkb .cz; Duškova 20, Smíchov), which provides help and counselling to victims of criminal offences of all kinds.

WORK

Unemployment in Prague is low – less than 2% – and although there are job opportunities for foreigners in English teaching, IT, finance, real estate and management firms, competition for jobs is fierce and finding one increasingly difficult.

EU citizens do not need a work permit to work in the Czech Republic. You can find short- or long-term employment teaching

English (or other languages) at the numerous language schools in Prague.

You might find employment in the many expat-run restaurants, hostels and bars springing up like mushrooms around Prague. Possibilities also exist in many foreign-owned businesses. Investment, banking, real estate, IT and management firms need experienced staff and often employ non-Czech speakers, but the odds of getting such a job are better from home than in Prague. You can also look for jobs on the Internet at www.jobs.cz and in the classified-ad sections in *Prague Post* (www .praguepost.cz) and *Prague Business Journal* (www.pjb.cz).

Language

Language

It's true – anyone can speak another language. Don't worry if you haven't studied languages before or that you studied a language at school for years and can't remember any of it. It doesn't even matter if you failed English grammar. After all, that's never affected your ability to speak English! And this is the key to picking up a language in another country. You just need to start speaking.

Learn a few key phrases before you go. Write them on pieces of paper and stick them on the fridge, by the bed or even on the computer – anywhere that you'll see them often.

You'll find that locals appreciate travellers trying their language, no matter how muddled you may think you sound. So don't just stand there, say something! If you want to learn more Czech than we've included here, pick up a copy of Lonely Planet's comprehensive but user-friendly *Czech Phrasebook*.

PRONUNCIATION

It's not easy to learn Czech pronunciation, and you may have to learn a few new linguistic tricks to do so. It is, however, spelt the way it's spoken, and once you become familiar with the sounds, it's easy to read. Stress is usually on the first syllable.

Vowels

Vowels have long and short variants; they have the same pronunciation, but long vowels are simply held for longer. Long vowels are indicated by an acute accent. The following approximations reflect British pronunciation:

a	as the 'u' in 'cut'
á	as the 'a' in 'father'
e	as in 'bet'
é	as the word 'air'
ě	as the 'ye' in 'yet'
i/y	as the 'i' in 'bit'
í/ý	as the 'i' in 'marine'
o	as in 'pot'
ó	as the 'aw' in 'saw'
u	as in 'pull'
ú/ů	as the 'oo' in 'zoo'

Diphthongs

aj	as the 'i' in 'ice'
áj	as the word 'eye'
au	as the 'ow' in 'how'
ej	as the 'ay' in 'day'
ij/yj	short; as 'iy'
íj/ýj	longer version of ij/yj
oj	as the 'oi' in 'void'
ou	as the 'o' in 'note', though each vowel is more strongly pronounced than in English
uj	as the 'u' in 'pull', followed by the 'y' in 'year'
ůj	longer version of uj

Consonants

c	as the 'ts' in 'lets'
č	as the 'ch' in 'chew'
ch	like 'ch' in Scottish *loch*
f	as in 'fever', never as in 'of'
g	as in 'get', never as in 'age'
h	as in 'hand'
j	as the 'y' in 'year'
r	a rolled 'r' (at the tip of the tongue)
ř	no English equivalent; a rolled 'rzh' sound, as in the composer, Dvořák
s	as in 'sit', never as in 'rose'
š	as the 'sh' in 'ship'
ž	a 'zh' sound, as the 's' in 'treasure'
ď, ľ, ť	very soft palatal sounds, ie consonants followed by a momentary contact between the tongue and the hard palate, as if followed by 'y' (like the 'ny' in canyon). The same applies to **d**, **n** and **t** when followed by **i**, **í** or **ě**.

All other consonants are similar to their English counterparts, although the letters **k**, **p** and **t** are unaspirated, meaning they are pronounced with no audible puff of breath after them.

SOCIAL
Greetings & Civilities
Hello/Good day.
Dobrý den.
Ahoj. (informal)
Goodbye.
Na shledanou.
Ahoj/Čau. (informal)
Yes.
Ano/Jo. (polite/informal)
No.
Ne.
May I? (asking permission)
Dovolte mi?
Sorry/Excuse me. (apologising or seeking assistance)
Promiňte.
Could you help me, please?
Prosím, můžete mi pomoci?
Please.
Prosím.
Thank you (very much).
(Mockrát) děkuji.
You're welcome.
Není zač.
Good morning.
Dobré jitro/ráno.
Good afternoon.
Dobré odpoledne.
Good evening.
Dobrý večer.
How are you?
Jak se máte?
Well, thanks.
Děkuji, dobře.

Going Out
What's there to do in the evenings?
Kam se tady dá večer jít?
What's on tonight?
Co je dnes večer na programu?
In the entertainment guide.
V kulturním programu.

I feel like going to a/an/the ...
Mám chuť jít ...

bar	do baru
café	do kavárny
cinema	do kina
disco	na diskotéku
opera	na operu
restaurant	do restaurace
theatre	do divadla

Do you know a good restaurant?
Znáš nejakou dobrou restauraci?

Are there any good nightclubs?
Jsou tady nějaké dobré noční podniky?

Language Difficulties
Do you speak English?
Mluvíte anglicky?
I understand.
Rozumím.
I don't understand.
Nerozumím.
Could you write it down, please?
Můžete mi to napsat, prosím?

PRACTICAL
Directions
Do you have a local map?	Máte mapu okolí?
Where is ...?	Kde je ...?
Go straight ahead.	Jděte přímo.
Turn left.	Zatočte vlevo.
Turn right.	Zatočte vpravo.
behind	za
in front of	před
far	daleko
near	blízko
opposite	naproti

Numbers
It's quite common for Czechs to say the numbers 21 to 99 in reverse; for example, *dvacet jedna* (21) becomes *jedna dvacet*.

0	nula
1	jedna
2	dva
3	tři
4	čtyři
5	pět
6	šest
7	sedm
8	osm
9	devět
10	deset
11	jedenáct
12	dvanáct
13	třináct
14	čtrnáct
15	patnáct
16	šestnáct
17	sedmnáct
18	osmnáct
19	devatenáct
20	dvacet
21	dvacet jedna

22	dvacet dva
23	dvacet tři
30	třicet
40	čtyřicet
50	padesát
60	šedesát
70	sedmdesát
80	osmdesát
90	devadesát
100	sto
1000	tisíc

Banking

Where's a/the ...?
Kde je ...?

ATM	bankomat
bank	banka
exchange office	směnárna

I want to change (a) ...
Chtěl/a bych vyměnit ... (m/f)

cash/money	peníze
(travellers) cheque	(cestovní) šek

What time does the bank open?
V kolik hodin otevírá banka?

Post Office

Where's a/the post office?
Kde je pošta?

I want to buy ...
Rád/a bych koupil/a ... (m/f)

postcards	pohlednice
stamps	známky

I want to send a ...
Chtěl/a bych poslat ... (m/f)

fax	fax
letter	dopis
parcel	balík
postcard	pohled

Phones & Mobiles

Where's the nearest public phone?
Kde je nejbližší veřejný telefon?
Could I please use the telephone?
Mohu si zatelefonovat?
I want to call ...
Chci zavolat ...
I want to make a long-distance call to ...
Chtěl/a bych volat do ... (m/f)
I want to make a reverse-charge/collect call.
Chtěl/a bych zavolat na účet volaného. (m/f)
I want to buy a phonecard.
Chtěl/a bych koupit telefonní karta. (m/f)

Internet

Is there a local Internet café?
Je tady Internet kavárna? (m/f)
I'd like to get Internet access.
Chtěl/a bych se připojit na Internet. (m/f)
I'd like to check my email.
Chtěl/a bych si skontrolovat můj email. (m/f)

Paperwork

name	jméno
address	adresa
date of birth	datum narození
place of birth	místo narození
age	věk
sex	pohlaví
nationality	národnost
passport number	číslo pasu
visa	vizum
driver's licence	řidičský průkaz

Question Words

Who?	Kdo?
What?	Co?
When?	Kdy?
Where?	Kde?
How?	Jak?

Shopping & Services

Where's (a/the) ...?
Kde je ...?
I'm looking for (a/the) ...
Hledám ...

art gallery	uměleckou galérii
city centre	centrum
embassy	velvyslanectví
main square	hlavní náměstí
market	tržiště
museum	muzeum
public toilet	veřejné záchody
tourist office	turistická informační kancelář

What time does it open/close?
V kolik hodin otevírají/zavírají?

Signs

Kouření Zakázáno	No Smoking
Otevřeno	Open
Umývárny/Toalety	Toilets
Dámy/Ženy	Men
Páni/Muži	Women
Vchod	Entrance
Vstup Zakázán	No Entry
Východ	Exit

Zákaz	Prohibited
Zavřeno	Closed

Time & Dates

What time is it?	Kolik je hodin?
in the morning	ráno
in the afternoon	odpoledne
in the evening	večer
today	dnes
now	teď
yesterday	včera
tomorrow	zítra
next week	příští týden
Monday	pondělí
Tuesday	úterý
Wednesday	steda
Thursday	čtvrtek
Friday	pátek
Saturday	sobota
Sunday	neděle
January	leden
February	únor
March	březen
April	duben
May	květen
June	červen
July	červenec
August	srpen
September	září
October	říjen
November	listopad
December	prosinec

Dates in Museums

year	rok
century	století
millennia	milénium/tisíciletí
beginning of ...	začátek ...
first half of ...	první polovina ...
middle of ...	polovina ...
second half of ...	druhá polovina ...
end of ...	konec ...

Transport

What time does the train/bus leave?
V kolik hodin odjíždí vlak/autobus?
What time does the train/bus arrive?
V kolik hodin přijíždí vlak/autobus?
Excuse me, where is the ticket office?
Prosím, kde je pokladna?
I want to go to ...
Chci jet do ...

I'd like ...
Rád/a bych ... (m/f)

a one-way ticket	jednosměrnou jízdenku
a return ticket	zpáteční jízdenku
two tickets	dvě jízdenky

FOOD

breakfast	snídaně
lunch	oběd
dinner	večeře

Is service included in the bill?
Je to včetně obsluhy?

For more detailed information on food and dining out, see p12.

EMERGENCIES

Help!
Pomoc!
It's an emergency!
To je naléhavý případ!
Could you please help me?
Prosím, můžete mi pomoci?
Call an ambulance/a doctor/the police!
Zavolejte sanitku/doktora/policii!
Where's the police station?
Kde je policejní stanice?

HEALTH

Where's the ...?
Kde je ...?

chemist	lékárna
dentist	zubař
doctor	doktor
hospital	nemocnice

I need a doctor who speaks English.
Potřebuji lékaře, který mluví anglicky.
I'm sick.
Jsem nemocný/nemocná. (m/f)
My friend is sick.
Můj přítel je nemocný. (m)
Moje přítelkyně je nemocná. (f)

Symptoms

I have (a) ...
Mám ...

diarrhoea	průjem
fever	horečku

I have headache
Bolí mě hlava.
It hurts here.
Bolí mě zde.

Glossary

You may encounter the following terms and abbreviations while in Prague. For more on food terms see p12.

bankomat(y) – ATM(s)

čajovná – tea house
ČD – Czech Railways, the state railway company
Čedok – the former state tour operator and travel agency, now privatised
chrám – cathedral
ČSA – Czech Airlines, the national carrier
ČSAD – Czech Automobile Transport, the state bus company
ČSSD – Social Democratic Party
cukrárna – cake shop

divadlo – theatre
doklad – receipt or document; see also *potvrzení*
dům – house or building

galérie – gallery, arcade

hlavní nádraží (hl nád) – main train station
hora – hill, mountain
hospoda – pub
hostinec – pub
hrad – castle
hřbitov – cemetery

jízdenka – ticket

kaple – chapel
kavárna – café or coffee shop
Kč (Koruna česká) – Czech crown
kino – cinema
knihkupectví – bookshop
kolky – duty stamps, for payment at certain government offices, such as for a visa extension; sold at post offices and elsewhere
kostel – church
kreditní karta – credit card

lékárna – pharmacy

město – town
most – bridge

nábřeží (nábř) – embankment
nádraží – station
náměstí (nám) – square

ODS – Civic Democratic Party
ostrov – island

palác – palace
pekárna – bakery
penzión – pension
pěší zóna – pedestrian zone
pivnice – small beer hall
pivo – beer
pivovar – brewery
potraviny – grocery or food shop
potvrzení – receipt or confirmation; see also *doklad*
Praha – Prague
provozní doba – business hours, opening times
přestup – transfer or connection

restaurace – restaurant

sad(y) – garden(s), park(s), orchard(s)
samoobsluha – self-service, minimarket
stanice – train stop or station
sv (svatý) – Saint

třída (tř) – avenue

ulice (ul) – street

Velvet Divorce – separation of Czechoslovakia into fully independent Czech and Slovak republics in 1993
Velvet Revolution (Sametová revoluce) – bloodless overthrow of Czechoslovakia's communist regime in 1989
věž – tower
vinárna – wine bar
vlak – train
výdej listovních zásilek – poste restante mail

zahrada – gardens, park
zámek – chateau
zastávka – bus, tram or train stop

Behind the Scenes

THE LONELY PLANET STORY

The story begins with a classic travel adventure: Tony and Maureen Wheeler's 1972 journey across Europe and Asia to Australia. There was no useful information about the overland trail then, so Tony and Maureen published the first Lonely Planet guidebook to meet a growing need.

From a kitchen table, Lonely Planet has grown to become the largest independent travel publisher in the world, with offices in Melbourne (Australia), Oakland (USA) and London (UK). Today Lonely Planet guidebooks cover the globe. There is an ever-growing list of books and information in a variety of media. Some things haven't changed. The main aim is still to make it possible for adventurous travellers to get out there – to explore and better understand the world.

At Lonely Planet we believe travellers can make a positive contribution to the countries they visit – if they respect their host communities and spend their money wisely. Every year 5% of company profit is donated to charities around the world.

THIS BOOK

This 6th edition of *Prague* was researched and written by Neil Wilson. Neil also wrote the 5th edition of *Prague* and was a contributing author to the 4th edition. This guide was commissioned in Lonely Planet's UK office, and produced by:

Commissioning Editor Judith Bamber
Coordinating Editor Gina Tsarouhas
Coordinating Cartographers Greg Tooth/Jolyon Philcox
Coordinating Layout Designer Margie Jung
Editors Helen Christinis, Kyla Gillzan, Nancy Ianni, Kate McLeod, Lucy Monie, Elizabeth Swan
Cartographers Kim McDonald, Marion Byass
Prelayout Designer Margie Jung
Layout Designers Adam Bexstream, Jacqueline McLeod, Jacqui Saunders, Wibowo Rusli
Index Gina Tsarouhas, Helen Christinis
Cover Designer Pepi Bluck, Wendy Wright
Managing Cartographer Mark Griffiths
Project Managers Eoin Dunlevy, Celia Wood
Language Editor Quentin Frayne

Cover photographs Bridge Tower from Charles Bridge at dawn, Walter Bibikow/Photolibrary (top); Front façade known as Fred and Ginger, eye35.com/Alamy (bottom); Cobblestoned Thunovská at night, Richard Nebeský/LPI (back)

Internal photographs by Richard Nebeský except for the following: p2 (#1) Jan Stromme/LPI; p2 (#3) Cheryl Conlon/LPI; p50 Brent Winebrenner/LPI; p197 and p200 Witold Skrypczak

All images are the copyright of the photographers unless otherwise indicated. Many of the images in this guide are available for licensing from Lonely Planet Images: www.lonelyplanetimages.com.

ACKNOWLEDGMENTS

Many thanks to the following for the use of their content:
Prague Transit Map © DP Praha, akciová společnost

THANKS
NEIL WILSON

Mockrat děkuji to tourist office staff around the Czech Republic, and to Richard Nebeský and Tomaš Harabís for their insights into Czech

SEND US YOUR FEEDBACK

We love to hear from travellers – your comments keep us on our toes and help make our books better. Our well-travelled team reads every word on what you loved or loathed about this book. Although we cannot reply individually to postal submissions, we always guarantee that your feedback goes straight to the appropriate authors, in time for the next edition. Each person who sends us information is thanked in the next edition – and the most useful submissions are rewarded with a free book.

To send us your updates – and find out about Lonely Planet events, newsletters and travel news – visit our award-winning website: www.lonelyplanet.com/feedback

Note: We may edit, reproduce and incorporate your comments in Lonely Planet products such as guide-books, websites and digital products, so let us know if you don't want your comments reproduced or your name acknowledged. For a copy of our privacy policy visit www.lonelyplanet.com/privacy.

society. And as always, a big thank you to Carol for helping out with research on Prague's restaurants and shops.

OUR READERS

Many thanks to the following travellers who used the last edition and wrote to us with helpful hints, useful advice and interesting anecdotes.

A Olga Akimova-Farrand, Karen Alaway, Madhu Anhes **B** Elena Bonny, Michelle Brazier, Anna Byk **C** Paul Chidgey, George Clark, Merle Cooke **D** Kate Darwent, Lisa Dolton, Richard Drapes **E** Catherine Ebbels **F** Kate Fletcher **G** Denise Gomez, Lona Gray **H** Geoff Hall, Sara Hamilton, Arthur Hook, Jan Hruza, Lynn Hurton **K** Wing lok Kam, Edward Kellow, David Kvapil **L** Pasquale Liguori, Phil Linz **M** John Macaulay, John L Martin, Val McCarthy, Helene Mercier, Don Munro, Joanne Murphy **N** Emma Newton **P** Gautam Patel, Emma Payne, Carl Pickerill, Marcia Popper **R** Karen Rayner, Jamie Reid, Johan Reyneke, Marvin Richmann, Achalavira Rose, Glenn Rounding **S** Synnøve Seglem, Tobias Slordahl, Fraser Stephenson, Bill & Ann Stoughton, Jenna Stroud **W** Richard & Sasti Watson, D Wickes **Y** Nazan Yuksel

Index

See also separate indexes for Eating (p239), Shopping (p240) and Sleeping (p240).

Index

Index

Index

000 map pages
000 photographs

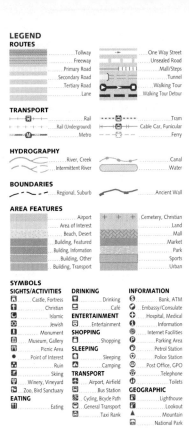

LEGEND

ROUTES

Tollway	One Way Street
Freeway	Unsealed Road
Primary Road	Mall/Steps
Secondary Road	Tunnel
Tertiary Road	Walking Tour
Lane	Walking Tour Detour

TRANSPORT

Rail	Tram
Rail (Underground)	Cable Car, Funicular
Metro	Ferry

HYDROGRAPHY

River, Creek	Canal
Intermittent River	Water

BOUNDARIES

Regional, Suburb	Ancient Wall

AREA FEATURES

Airport	Cemetery, Christian
Area of Interest	Land
Beach, Desert	Mall
Building, Featured	Market
Building, Information	Park
Building, Other	Sports
Building, Transport	Urban

SYMBOLS

SIGHTS/ACTIVITIES
- Castle, Fortress
- Christian
- Islamic
- Jewish
- Monument
- Museum, Gallery
- Picnic Area
- Point of Interest
- Ruin
- Skiing
- Winery, Vineyard
- Zoo, Bird Sanctuary

EATING
- Eating

DRINKING
- Drinking
- Café

ENTERTAINMENT
- Entertainment

SHOPPING
- Shopping

SLEEPING
- Sleeping
- Camping

TRANSPORT
- Airport, Airfield
- Bus Station
- Cycling, Bicycle Path
- General Transport
- Taxi Rank

INFORMATION
- Bank, ATM
- Embassy/Consulate
- Hospital, Medical
- Information
- Internet Facilities
- Parking Area
- Petrol Station
- Police Station
- Post Office, GPO
- Telephone
- Toilets

GEOGRAPHIC
- Lighthouse
- Lookout
- Mountain
- National Park

NOTE: Not all symbols displayed above appear in this guide.

Map Section

GREATER PRAGUE

A   B   C   D

1

Lysolaje

Dolní Šárka

Podbaba   Podhoř

Ve Višničkách

15   12

See Dejvice Map (p255)

Troja

Baba

Nebušice

Císařský ostrov   Vltava River

Stromovka

Hanspaulka   1

Horní Šárka

Sárecký Potok

Divoká Šárka

PRAHA 6

Dejvice   29

jug partyzánů

Roosveltova   Bub enecká

Bubeneč   PRAHA 7

Horoměřická

2

To Pension Větrný
Mlyn; Hotel Elegant;
Hotel Radegast (1.5km);
Prague-Ruzyně Airport (3km);
Hotel Tranzit (3km);
Ramada Airport Hotel (3km)

Vokovice

Staré
Dejvice

Dželun
Reservoir

Evropská

6

Ořechovka

Veletržní

Milady Horákové   Letná

Letenské
sady

See Hradčany & Northern
Malá Strana Map (pp244–5)

See Staré Město &
Josefov Map (pp246–7)

36

Veleslavín

34

Střešovičky

8

Hradčany

Prague Castle
(Pražský hrad)

Josefov

Staré
Město

Střešovice

Střešovice

To
Klub
Delta

3

To Letohrádek
Hvězda

Vypich

Obora
Hvězda

Břevnov

Patočkova

19

Bělohorská

PRAHA 1

Malá Strana

Semínářská
zahrada

Národní   Wenceslas Square

Strahov   11

Kinského
zahrada

Nové Město

PRAHA 2

Žitná

Bělohorská

To Bílá Hora (800m);
Kladno; Karlovy Vary

Podbělohorská

38

See Southern Malá
Strana Map (pp250–1)

See Nové Město Map (pp252–3)

42   14   16

28   37   Vrchlického

30   Anděl   18   17

Vltava River

PRAHA 2

Motol

Plzeňská   5

4

To Zličín; Plzeň;
Kemp Eva

Košíře

Jinonická

Smíchov

Strakonická

Vyšehrad   Jaromírova

U Waltrovky

Radlická   M

Radlická

See Vyšehrad & Vinohrady
Map (pp260–1)

Vyšehradský
ostrov

Radlice

5

To
Jezdecké
Středisko
Zmizlík
(4km)

PRAHA 5

Strakonická

Podolské nábřeží

10

Podolí

31

Zlichov

Jeremenkova

Na Dobešce

Hlubočepy

To Velká Chuchle
Závodiště Praha
(2km);
Zbraslav
(7.5km)

Modřanská

6

Pražského

K Barrandovu

Lamačova

To Karlštejn;
Křivoklát

Barrandov   2   Braník

25

To Hostel
Boathouse (600m);
Golf & Country Club
(1km)

Jižní spojka

Císařská
louka

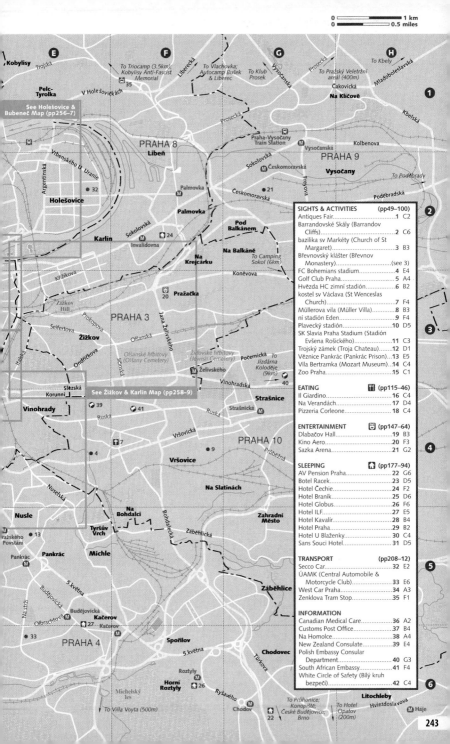

0	1 km
0	0.5 miles

SIGHTS & ACTIVITIES (pp49–100)

Antiques Fair	1 C2
Barrandovské Skály (Barrandov Cliffs)	2 C6
bazilika sv Markéty (Church of St Margaret)	3 B3
Břevnovský klášter (Břevnov Monastery)	(see 3)
FC Bohemians stadium	4 E4
Golf Club Praha	5 A4
Hvězda HC zimní stadión	6 B2
kostel sv Václava (St Wenceslas Church)	7 F4
Müllerova vila (Müller Villa)	8 B3
ní stadión Eden	9 F4
Plavecký stadión	10 D5
SK Slavia Praha Stadium (Stadión Evžena Rošického)	11 C3
Trojský zámek (Troja Chateau)	12 D1
Věznice Pankrác (Pankrác Prison)	13 E5
Vila Bertramka (Mozart Museum)	14 C4
Zoo Praha	15 C1

EATING 🍽 (pp115–46)

Il Giardino	16 C4
Na Verandách	17 D4
Pizzeria Corleone	18 C4

ENTERTAINMENT 🎭 (pp147–64)

Dlabačov Hall	19 B3
Kino Aero	20 F3
Sazka Arena	21 G2

SLEEPING 🛏 (pp177–94)

AV Pension Praha	22 G6
Botel Racek	23 D5
Hotel Čechie	24 F2
Hotel Braník	25 D6
Hotel Globus	26 F6
Hotel ILF	27 E5
Hotel Kavalír	28 B4
Hotel Praha	29 B2
Hotel U Blaženky	30 C4
Sans Souci Hotel	31 D5

TRANSPORT (pp208–12)

Secco Car	32 E2
ÚAMK (Central Automobile & Motorcycle Club)	33 E6
West Car Praha	34 A3
Zenklova Tram Stop	35 F1

INFORMATION

Canadian Medical Care	36 A2
Customs Post Office	37 B4
Na Homolce	38 B3
New Zealand Consulate	39 E4
Polish Embassy Consular Department	40 G3
South African Embassy	41 F4
White Circle of Safety (Bílý kruh bezpečí)	42 C4

243

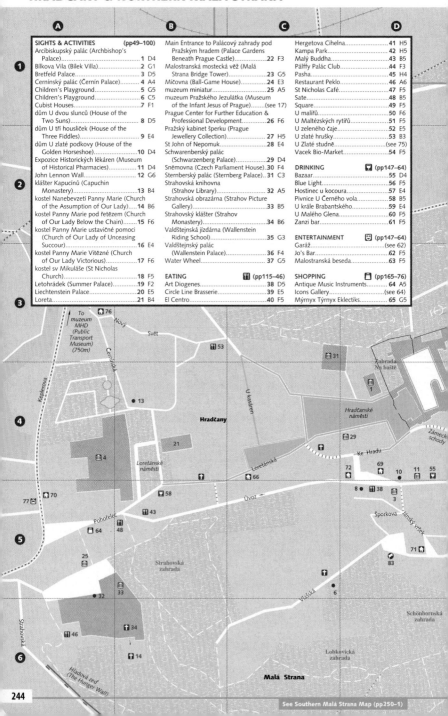

A

SIGHTS & ACTIVITIES (pp49–100)
Arcibiskupský palác (Archbishop's
Palace)..1 D4
Bílkova Vila (Bílek Villa).........................2 G1
Bretfeld Palace.....................................3 D5
Černínský palác (Černín Palace)..............4 A4
Children's Playground............................5 G5
Children's Playground............................6 C5
Cubist Houses.......................................7 F1
dům U dvou slunců (House of the
Two Suns)...8 D5
dům U tří housliček (House of the
Three Fiddles)....................................9 E4
dům U zlaté podkovy (House of the
Golden Horseshoe)............................10 D5
Expozice Historických lékáren (Museum
of Historical Pharmacies)...................11 D4
John Lennon Wall................................12 G6
klášter Kapucínů (Capuchin
Monastery)......................................13 B4
kostel Nanebevzetí Panny Marie (Church
of the Assumption of Our Lady).....14 B6
kostel Panny Marie pod řetězem (Church
of Our Lady Below the Chain)...........15 F6
kostel Panny Marie ustavičné pomoci
(Church of Our Lady of Unceasing
Succour)..16 E4
kostel Panny Marie Vítězné (Church
of Our Lady Victorious)....................17 F6
kostel sv Mikuláše (St Nicholas
Church)...18 F5
Letohrádek (Summer Palace)................19 F2
Liechtenstein Palace............................20 D5
Loreta..21 B4

B

Main Entrance to Palácový zahrady pod
Pražským hradem (Palace Gardens
Beneath Prague Castle)....................22 F3
Malostranská mostecká věž (Malá
Strana Bridge Tower)........................23 G5
Míčovna (Ball-Game House).................24 E3
muzeum miniatur.............................25 A5
muzeum Pražského Jezulátka (Museum
of the Infant Jesus of Prague)........(see 17)
Prague Center for Further Education &
Professional Development................26 F6
Pražský kabinet šperku (Prague
Jewellery Collection).........................27 H5
St John of Nepomuk..........................28 E4
Schwarzenberský palác
(Schwarzenberg Palace)...................29 D4
Sněmovna (Czech Parliament House)....30 F4
Sternberský palác (Sternberg Palace)..31 C3
Strahovská knihovna
(Strahov Library)............................32 A5
Strahovská obrazárna (Strahov Picture
Gallery)...33 B5
Strahovský klášter (Strahov
Monastery)......................................34 B6
Valdštejnská jízdárna (Wallenstein
Riding School).................................35 G3
Valdštejnský palác
(Wallenstein Palace)..........................36 F4
Water Wheel.....................................37 G5

EATING 🍴 (pp115–46)
Art Diogenes....................................38 D5
Circle Line Brasserie..........................39 F5
El Centro..40 F5

C

Hergetova Cihelna.............................41 H5
Kampa Park......................................42 H5
Malý Buddha.....................................43 B5
Pálffy Palác Club................................44 F3
Pasha...45 H4
Restaurant Peklo...............................46 A6
St Nicholas Café................................47 F5
Sate...48 B5
Square..49 F5
U malířů...50 F6
U Maltézských rytířů..........................51 F5
U zeleného čaje................................52 E5
U zlaté hrušky...................................53 B3
U Zlaté studně................................(see 75)
Vacek Bio-Market..............................54 F5

DRINKING 🍷 (pp147–64)
Bazaar..55 D4
Blue Light...56 F5
Hostinec u kocoura............................57 E4
Pivnice U Černého vola.......................58 B5
U krále Brabantského.........................59 E4
U Malého Glena.................................60 F5
Zanzi bar..61 F5

ENTERTAINMENT 🎭 (pp147–64)
Garáž..(see 62)
Jo's Bar..62 F5
Malostranská beseda.........................63 F5

SHOPPING 🛍 (pp165–76)
Antique Music Instruments...............64 A5
Icons Gallery..................................(see 64)
Mýrnyx Týrnyx Eklectiks....................65 G5

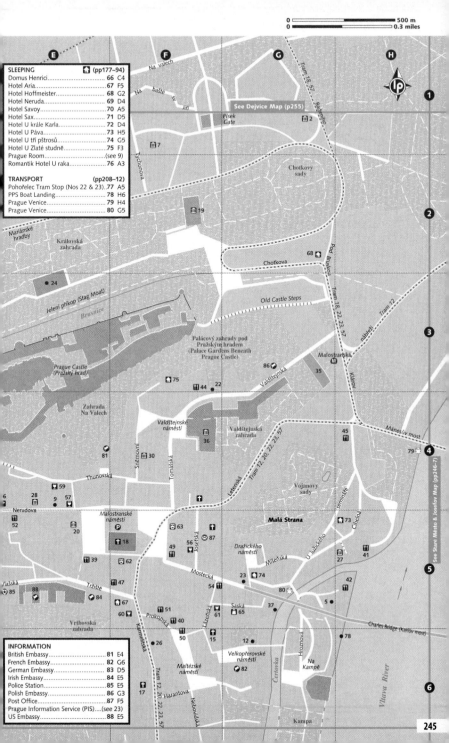

SLEEPING (pp177–94)

Domus Henrici	**66** C4
Hotel Aria	**67** F5
Hotel Hoffmeister	**68** G2
Hotel Neruda	**69** D4
Hotel Savoy	**70** A5
Hotel Sax	**71** D5
Hotel U krále Karla	**72** D4
Hotel U Páva	**73** H5
Hotel U tří pštrosů	**74** G5
Hotel U Zlaté studně	**75** F3
Prague Room	(see 9)
Romantik Hotel U raka	**76** A3

TRANSPORT (pp208–12)

Pohořelec Tram Stop (Nos 22 & 23)	**77** A5
PPS Boat Landing	**78** H6
Prague Venice	**79** H4
Prague Venice	**80** G5

INFORMATION

British Embassy	**81** E4
French Embassy	**82** G6
German Embassy	**83** D5
Irish Embassy	**84** E5
Police Station	**85** E5
Polish Embassy	**86** C3
Post Office	**87** F5
Prague Information Service (PIS)	(see 23)
US Embassy	**88** E5

See Dejvice Map (p255)

Na valech

Na baště sv. Jiří

Písek Gate

Tychonova

Chotkovy sady

Pod Bruskou

Chotkova

Old Castle Steps

Mariánské hradby

Královská zahrada

Jelení příkop (Stag Moat)

Brusnice

Prague Castle (Pražský hrad)

Palácový zahrady pod Pražským hradem (Palace Gardens Beneath Prague Castle)

Malostranská

Zahrada Na Valech

Valdštejnská

Valdštejnské náměstí

Valdštejnská zahrada

Mánesův most

Šnemovní

Thunovská

Tomášská

Letenská

Vojanovy sady

Malá Strana

Nerudova

Malostranské náměstí

Josefská

Dražického náměstí

Míšeňská

U lužického

Cihelná

Vlašská

Tržiště

Mostecká

Lázeňská

Saská

Vrtbovská zahrada

Prokopská

Harantová

Nebovidská

Maltézské náměstí

Velkopřevorské náměstí

Na Kampě

Karmelitská

Čertovka

Hroznová

Kampa

Vltava River

Charles Bridge (Karlův most)

Tram 18, 5Z

Badeniho

Tram 18, 22, 23, 57

Tram 12

nábřeží

Klárov

Tram 12, 20, 22, 23, 57

Tram 12, 20, 22, 23, 57

See Staré Město & Josefov Map (pp246–7)

0 — 500 m
0 — 0.3 miles

245

Ⓐ   Ⓑ   Ⓒ   Ⓓ

1

See Holešovice & Bubeneč Map (pp258–9)

Letenské sady

Metronome

Letná terása

nábřeží Edvarda Beneše

Tram 12, 17, 51, 54

Tram 12

80

2

Čechův most   Tram 17, 53

197

Dvořákovo nábřeží

Dušní

U milosrdných

Josefov

Kozí

U obecního dvora

104

Bílkova

See Hradčany & Northern Malá Strana Map (pp244–5)

Vltava River

Dvořákovo nábřeží

3

P 223

8

Elišky Krásnohorské

Dušní

Rámová

89

92

167

Dlouhá

Kozí

Vězeňská

87

196

43

U starého hřbitova   Červená

25

56

100

52

101

84

103

70

V kolkovně

91

62

143

5

Maiselova

Široká

63

134

127

Masná

72

Starý židovský hřbitov (Old Jewish Cemetery)

59

51

17. listopadu

48

220

149

Pařížská

141

4

Dlouhá

69

165

náměstí Jana Palacha

Široká

38

2

Salvátorská

88

120

Týnská u.

130

139

129

4

Mánesův most   Tram 18

190

P 224

Jáchymova

36

112

135

203

44

166

13

Týnský dvů

79

121

Štupartsk

Kaprova

Staroměstská Ⓜ

71

125

81

154

114

Žatecká

7

18

11

29

Old Town Square (Staroměstské náměstí)

57

22

67

Staré Město

5

Alšovo nábřeží

Křížovnická

Valentinská

U radnice

Linhartská

180

12

55

95

21

Železná

Kamzíková

23

117

Velešavínova

163

75

155

Platnéřská

Mariánské náměstí

Malé náměstí

60

159

181

Husova

26

65

108

144

Jilská

123

150

76

31

119

153

Křížovnické náměstí

30

198

Tram 17, 18, 53

28

61

34

Karlova

17

172

187

118

58

94

106

3

146

98

Michalská

Valentinská

157

205

124

Havelská

Rytířská

131

Charles Bridge (Karlův most)

191

54

183

40

Liliová

186

78

Řetězová

182

V kotcích

148

Provaznická

6

39

113

Novotného lávka

Anenská

Anenské náměstí

105

162

Husova

33

Zlatá

Karolíny Světlé

109

Smetanovo nábřeží

0 — 500 m
0 — 0.3 miles

E **F** **G** **H**

Tram 5, 8, 12, 14, 17, 51, 53, 54

Ostrov Štvanice
(Chase Island) **1**

Tram 12, 17, 51 ,54

● 64

2

🏠 161

nábřeží Ludvíka Svobody

Na Františku

225

🏠 24

Rásnovka

47 ● 🏛 49
Novomlýnská
Nové mlýny

Klimentská **Klimentská**

● 189

178
P

Tram 5, 8, 14, 51, 54

Klášterská

Hradební

Benediktská

Barvířská

Šamcová

Mlynářská

Těšnov

🏠 170

⚘ 204

97
🏛

● 15
Lodecká

Petrské
náměstí

Petrská

🏠 46

🏠 3

Haštalské
náměstí
🏛

Haštalská

77

116
🏠

Dlouhá

Soukenická

Biskupská

● 37

● 211

66
🏛

173
🏠 Tram 8, 24, 26, 52, 56

133
🏠
Rybná

96 🏛
99

Revoluční

Truhlářská

Zlatnická

Na poříčí Tram

🏠 168

137
🏠

151

126

174

$ 206

Nové Město **4**

🏠 175
⚘ 219

217

160
🏛

14

Havlíčkova

Tram 3, 8, 14, 24, 26, 51, 53, 54, 56

138 🏠

Na Florenci

142
P

192

Tram 5, 8, 14, 51, 54

53
@ 215

188 🏠

P

Masná

Rybná

171
🏠

176
🏠 93

náměstí
Republiky

209
V celnici

**Náměstí
Republiky**

177
🏠 32

Jakubská

86
Templová

184
🏠 102
🏠 85

90

🏛

U Obecního domu

179
111
122

164

M
Náměstí
Republiky

● 201

Masarykovo nádraží **5**

🏠 110

Celetná ul

202
158
9 🏛

42

82 🏛

Hybernská

● 16

😊 216

Ovocný trh
(Former Fruit
Market)

194

213 $
50

● 200

207 Na příkopě

Dlážděná

@ 221

Pasáž

212 @

218

115
🏠

152
🏠

Senovážná

Nové Město

🏠 195

● 210

🏠 169

41

145
147

1
107

222

83
🏛

Senovážné
náměstí

🏠 185

35
🏠

Tram 5, 9, 26, 55, 58

Opletalova

Wilsonova

See Žižkov & Karlín Map (pp258–9)

132

$ 208

10

214

Panská

Nekázanka ul

156 🏠

● 19

Jeruzalémská

🏛 45

🏠 128

Jindřišská ul

🏛 20

Tram
3, 9, 14, 24, 51, 52, 54, 55, 56

247

See Nové Město Map (pp252–3)

STARÉ MĚSTO & JOSEFOV (pp246–7)

SOUTHERN MALÁ STRANA

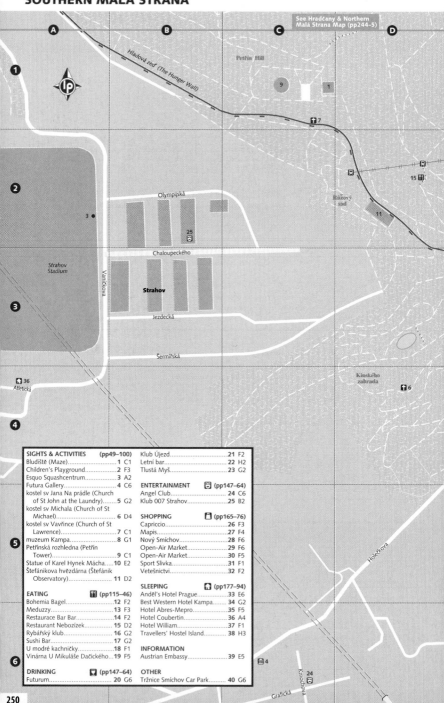

See Hradčany & Northern Malá Strana Map (pp244–5)

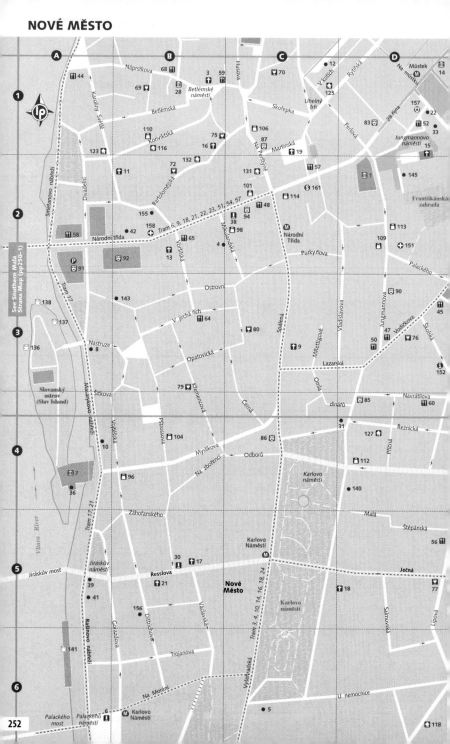

A • **B** • **C** • **D**

Náprstkova • 68 • 3 • 59 • Husova • 70 • 12 • Rytířská • Na můstku • Můstek • 14

44 • 69 • 28 • Betlémské náměstí • Skořepka • V kotích • 125 • Uhelný trh • 157 • 22 • 52 • 33

110 • Konviktská • 106 • 83 • 28 října • Jungmannovo náměstí • 15

Betlémská • 123 • 116 • 75 • 16 • Na Perštýně • Martinská • 19 • 145 • 1 • Františkánská zahrada

72 • 132 • 11 • 131 • 57 • 161 • 114 • 113

Bartolomějská • 155 • 158 • 101 • 48 • 94 • 109 • 151

42 • Tram 6, 9, 18, 21, 22, 23, 51, 54, 57 • 38 • 98 • Národní Třída • Palackého

58 • Národní třída • 65 • Mikulandská • 4 • Purkyňova • 90

13 • 92 • Ostrovní • Vladislavova • 45

138 • 143 • V jirchářích • 64 • 80 • Spálená • 47 • Vodičkova • 76

137 • Nástrčné • 8 • Opatovická • 9 • M.Rettigové • Lazarská • 50 • Školská • 152

136 • Slovanský ostrov (Slav Island) • 79 • Křemencová • Černá • Ostrní • dinářů • 85 • Návrátilova • 60

Sítková • Voršilská • Pštrossova • 104 • Myslíkova • Na zbořenci • Odborů • 31 • 127 • Řeznická • Příčná • 112

10 • 7 • 36 • 96 • 86 • Karlovo náměstí • 140

Záhořanského • Malá • Štěpánská • 56

Jiráskův most • Jiráskovo náměstí • 30 • 17 • Karlovo Náměstí • Nové Město • 18 • Ječná • 77

39 • Resslova • 21 • Karlovo náměstí

41 • 156 • Dittrichova • Vladislav • Salmovská • Lípová

141 • Gorazdova • Trojanova • Vyšehradská • Na Moráni

Palackého most • Palackého náměstí • 6 • Karlovo Náměstí • 5 • U nemocnice • 118

See Southern Malá Strana Map (pp250–1)

Smetanovo nábřeží • Divadelní • Karoliny Světlé • Tram 17 • Makarovovo nábřeží • Vltava River • Tram 17, 21 • Rašínovo nábřeží

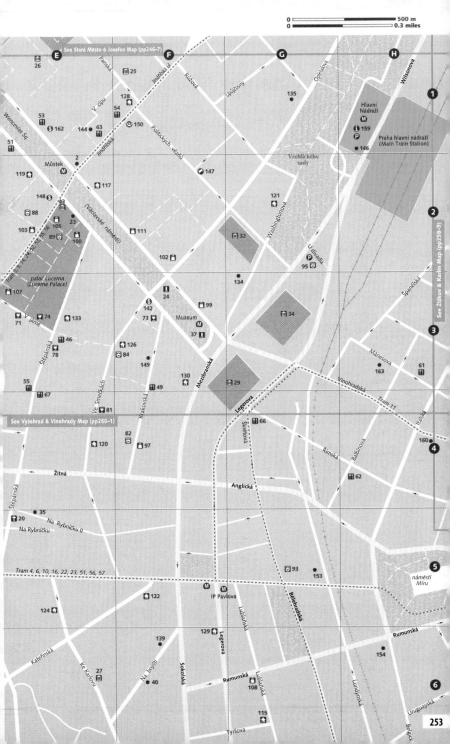

See Staré Město & Josefov Map (pp246–7)

See Žižkov & Karlín Map (pp258–9)

See Vyšehrad & Vinohrady Map (pp260–1)

0 ——— 500 m
0 ——— 0.3 miles

Panská
Jindřišská ul.
Růžová
Opletalova
Wilsonova

V cípu
Upytory
135

Wenceslas Sq.
53
162
144 63
150
Policických vězňů
Hlavní Nádraží
159
146
Praha hlavní nádraží (Main Train Station)

51
Müstek
2
Jindřišská
147
Vrchlického sady

119
148
117
Washingtonova
121

88
43
23
105
89 100
111
102
U divadla
95

103
107
palác Lucerna (Lucerne Palace)
134

71 V jámě 74
133
24
142 73
99
Muzeum
37
32

46
78
126
84
149
130
49
Mezibranská
34

55
67
81
Krakovská
Ve Smečkách
Legerova
29
Měnesova
163
61

82
97
66
Škrétova
Římská
Balbínova
Vinohradská Tram 11
Haliská
160

120

Žitná
Anglická
62

Štěpánská
20 35
Na Rybníčku II
Na Rybníčku

Tram 4, 6, 10, 16, 22, 23, 51, 56, 57
93
153
náměstí Míru

Bělehradská

122
IP Pavlova

124

139
129
Legerova
Rumunská

Kateřinská
Ke Karlovu
27
Na bojišti
40
Sokolská
Rumunská
108
Lublaňská
154

Londýnská

115
Tyršova

Bělgick

253

DEJVICE

0 ━━━━━━━━━ 1 km
0 ━━━━━━━━━ 0.5 miles

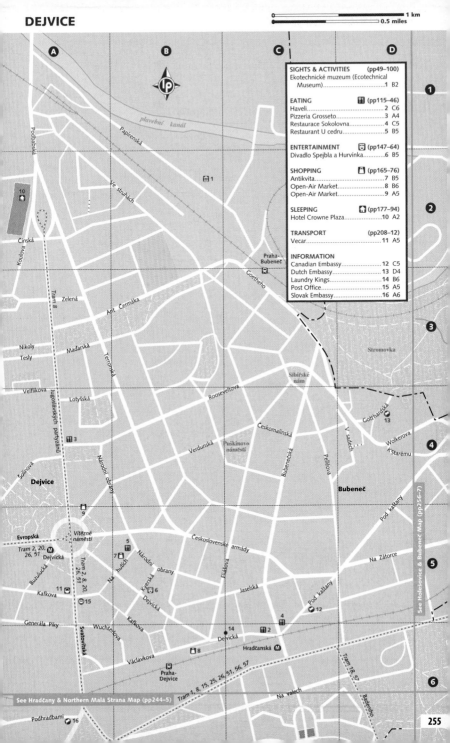

See Holešovice & Bubeneč Map (pp256–7)

See Hradčany & Northern Malá Strana Map (pp244–5)

255

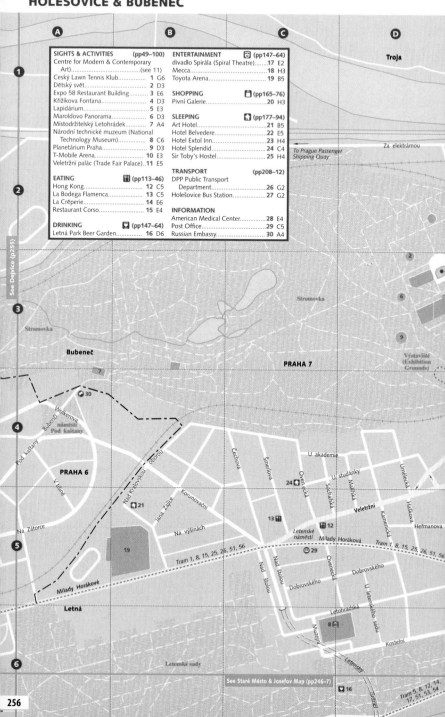

A   **B**   **C**   **D**

SIGHTS & ACTIVITIES	(pp49–100)
Centre for Modern & Contemporary Art)..(see 11)	
Český Lawn Tennis Klub.............. **1**	G6
Dětský svět.................................. **2**	D3
Expo 58 Restaurant Building........ **3**	E6
Křižíkova Fontána........................ **4**	D3
Lapidárium.................................. **5**	E3
Maroldovo Panorama.................. **6**	D3
Místodržitelský Letohrádek........ **7**	A4
Národní technické muzeum (National Technology Museum)................. **8**	C6
Planetárium Praha....................... **9**	D3
T-Mobile Arena........................... **10**	E3
Veletržní palác (Trade Fair Palace)..**11**	E5

EATING	(pp113–46)
Hong Kong.................................. **12**	C5
La Bodega Flamenca.................... **13**	C5
La Crêperie.................................. **14**	E6
Restaurant Corso......................... **15**	E4

DRINKING	(pp147–64)
Letná Park Beer Garden.............. **16**	D6

ENTERTAINMENT	(pp147–64)
divadlo Spirála (Spiral Theatre).......**17**	E2
Mecca... **18**	H3
Toyota Arena.............................. **19**	B5

SHOPPING	(pp165–76)
Pivní Galerie............................... **20**	H3

SLEEPING	(pp177–94)
Art Hotel.................................... **21**	B5
Hotel Belvedere.......................... **22**	E5
Hotel Extol Inn............................ **23**	H4
Hotel Splendid............................ **24**	C4
Sir Toby's Hostel......................... **25**	H4

TRANSPORT	(pp208–12)
DPP Public Transport Department.............................. **26**	G2
Holešovice Bus Station................ **27**	G2

INFORMATION	
American Medical Center............. **28**	E4
Post Office.................................. **29**	C5
Russian Embassy.......................... **30**	A4

Troja

See Dejvice (p255)

Za elektrárnou

To Prague Passenger Shipping Quay

Stromovka

Stromovka

Bubeneč

PRAHA 7

Výstaviště (Exhibition Grounds)

Wolkerova
Bubeneč
náměstí
Pod kaštany

PRAHA 6

V tůně

Na Zátorce

Nad Královskou oborou

Jana Zajíce

Korunovační

Na výšinách

U akademie

Čechova

Šmeralova

Ovenecká

Schnirchova

Malířská

U studánky

Umělecká

Haškova

Hefmanova

Kamenická

Veletržní

Letenské náměstí   Milady Horáková

Tram 1, 8, 15, 25, 26, 51, 56

Dobrovského

Nad Štolou

Ovenecká

Dobrovského

U letenského sadu

Milady Horákové

Letná

Letohradská

Muzejní

Letenské sady

Kostelní

Nad Štolou

Letenský

Tunel

See Staré Město & Josefov Map (pp246–7)

Tram 5, 8, 12, 14, 17, 51, 53, 54

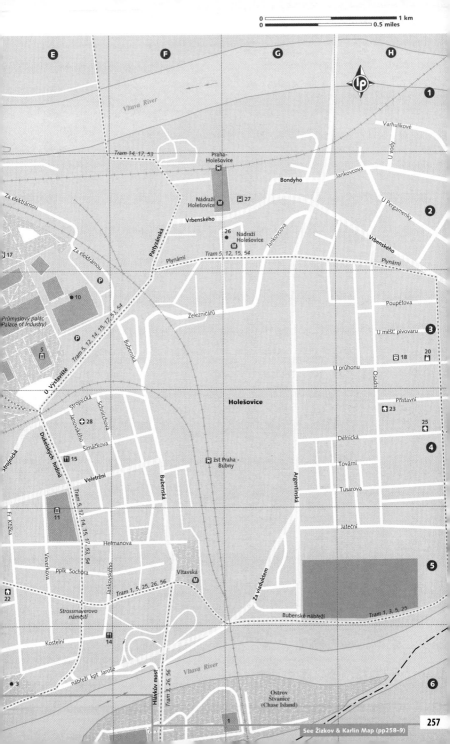

0 ▭▭▭▭▭ 1 km
0 ▬▬▬▬▬ 0.5 miles

E **F** **G** **H**

1

Vltava River

Varhulíkové

Tram 14, 17, 53

Praha-
Holešovice

U vody

Bondyho

Jankovcova

2

Nádraží
Holešovice ⓂＭ 🚇 27

Vrbenského

Za elektrárnou

Vrbenského

Za elektrárnou

Partyzánská

26
● Nádraží
Holešovice

Jankovcova

Plynární

🚇 17

Plynární

Tram 5, 12, 15, 54

Průmyslový palác
(Palace of Industry)

P

● 10

Železničářů

Poupětova

U měšť. pivovaru **3**

🚇 18 20

P

5
🏛

P

Tram 5, 12, 14, 15, 17, 53, 54

Bubenská

U průhonu

Osadní

U Výstaviště

Holešovice

Přístavní

🏠 23

Strojnická

Schnirchova

Janovského

✚ 28

25
🏠

Šimáčkova

Dělnická

4

Strojnická

Dukelských hrdinů

🏛 15

Veletržní

Tovární

Tram 5, 12, 14, 15, 17, 53, 54

Bubenská

žst Praha -
Bubny

Tusarova

Argentinská

Fr. Křížka

🏛
11

Jatečni

Heřmanova

5

Veverkova

Pplk. Sochora

Janovského

Vltavská
Ⓜ

Za viaduktem

22
🏠

Tram 1, 5, 25, 26, 56

Strossmayerovo
náměstí

Bubenské nábřeží
Tram 1, 3, 5, 25

Kostelní

14
🏛

Vltava River

● 3

nábřeží kpt Jaroše

Hlávkův most

Tram 3, 26, 56

Ostrov
Štvanice
(Chase Island)

6

1

257

See Žižkov & Karlín Map (pp258–9)

ŽIŽKOV & KARLÍN

Vltava River

A **B** **C** **D**

See Holešovice & Bubeneč Map (pp256–7)

1

Tram 3, 26, 56

P

📍 32

Pobřežní

Tram 8, 24, 52

M Křižíkova

P Pobřežní

Sokolovská

Karlín

Tram 8, 24, 52

Karlínské náměstí

Křižíkova

Thámova

Sokolovská

Na poříčí

M Florenc

Ke Štvanici

📍 43

Kollárova

Těšnov

P

Vltkova

Peckova

🛈

Za Poříčskou bránou

2

🏛 6

Křižíkova

Prvního pluku

Malého

Pernerova

See Staré Město & Josefov (pp246–7)

Nové Město

M Florenc

📍 42

Trocnovská

7 🏛

🏛 9

Žižkov Hill (Vítkov)

Tachovské náměstí

3

Husitská

🏛 1

U pam átníku

21 📍

Husitská

29 🛈

38 🛈

Prokopovo náměstí

Řehořova

34 🛈

Prokopova

See Nové Město Map (pp252–3)

Wilsonova

35 🛈

Orebitská

Cimburkova

Milíčova

Chlumova

36 🛈

Havlíčkovo náměstí

Seifertova

Husinecká

41 🛈

Štítného

14 🛈

Tram 5, 9, 26, 55

Seifertova

Tram 5, 9, 26, 55

Lipanská

Lupáčova

4

Italská

Havelkova

22

8 🛈

13 📍

31 🛈

Praha hlavní nádraží (Main Train Station)

U Rajské zahrady

25 📍

40 🛈

Vlkova

Krásova

Žižkov

30 📍

Vita Nejedlého

Lipanská

Táboritská

Španělská

28 🛈

Bořivojova

24 📍

Kubelíkova

Kubelíkova

5

Italská

Rajská zahrada

Vlkova

Krkonošská

Křížkovského

Fibichova

● 2

10 📍

Žižkovo náměstí

Helénská

Riegrovy sady

18 🛈

Chopinova

Štítkova

12 🛈

Mahlerovy sady

Onřičkova

46 ●

Krkonošská

Čerkovská

Polská

19 📍

Jagellonská

Velehradská

Bořivojova

15 🛈

Polská

Rípská

Máchová

16 🛈

See Vyšehrad & Vinohrady Map (pp260–1)

11 🛈

44 ●

5 🛈

Tram 11

Vinohradská

Máchová

Blanická

Budečská

Třebízského

náměstí Jiřího z Poděbrad

Tram 11

Vinohradská

6

48 ●

23 🛈

26 🛈

Sázavská

Slavíkova

U Kanálky

Jiřího z Poděbrad M

U vodárny

37 🛈

47

Římská

Slezská

Lucemburská

258

SIGHTS & ACTIVITIES	(pp49–100)
Armádní Muzeum	
(Army Museum)................1	B3
Cybex Health Club & Spa.........(see 32)	
Former Jewish Cemetery.............2	D5
Jan Palach's Grave.....................3	G6
kaple sv Rocha	
(St Roch Chapel)...................4	E5
kostel Nejsvětějšího Srdce Páni	
(Church of the Most Sacred	
Heart of Our Lord)................5	D6
Muzeum hlavního města Prahy	
(Prague City Museum)...........6	A2
Národní Památník (Monument to	
National Liberation).............7	C3
St Procopius Church....................8	C4
Statue of Jan Žižka....................9	C3
Televizní vysílač	
(TV Tower)..........................10	D5

EATING	🍴 (pp115–46)
Ambiente....................................11	B6
Hanil...12	C5
Mailsi..13	D4
Restaurace Televizní věž......(see 10)	
U radnice....................................14	D4

DRINKING	🖥🍸 (pp147–64)
Bond's Cocktail Bar....................15	C6
Caffé Kaaba................................16	A6
Hapu..17	D6
Park Café...................................18	B5
Piano Bar...................................19	D5
Potrefena Husa...........................20	E6
U Vystřeleného oka....................21	C3

ENTERTAINMENT	🎫 (pp147–64)
FK Viktoria Žižkov stadium..........22	B4
Gejzee..r....................................23	A6
Palác Akropolis...........................24	C5
Sedm Vlků.................................25	B4

SHOPPING	🛍 (pp165–76)
Orientalni Koberce Palácka..........26	A6
Palác Flóra................................27	F6

SLEEPING	🛏 (pp177–94)
Clown & Bard Hostel..................28	C4
Hostel Elf...................................29	C3
Hotel City Crown........................30	C4
Hotel Golden City Garni.............31	D4
Hotel Hilton Prague...................32	A1
Hotel Ibis Praha Karlín...............33	D1

Hotel Kafka...............................34	D3
Hotel Ostaš................................35	C3
Hotel Prokopka..........................36	D3
Hotel Sieber..............................37	D6
Hotel U tří korunek....................38	D3
Olšanka Hotel............................39	E4
Pension 15.................................40	B4
Pension Prague City...................41	D4

TRANSPORT	(pp208–12)
Bohemia Euroexpress	
International......................(see 42)	
Eurolines Ticket Office..........(see 42)	
Florenc Bus Station....................42	A2
Kingscourt Express Coach	
Stand.................................43	A2
Tourbus...............................(see 42)	

INFORMATION	
CKM Travel Centre.....................44	C6
Foreigners' Police & Passport	
Office.................................45	G4
Mary's Travel & Tourist	
Service................................46	A5
Pl@neta...................................47	D6
Stop City Accommodation.........48	A6

0 |———————————| 1 km
0 |———————————| 0.5 miles

E F G H

Rohácova

Domažlická

Hájkova

Tram 10, 16, 19

Koněvova

Rohácova

Osíkomecká

Žerotínova

Jeseniová

Žižkov

Malešická

Jeseniová

Parukárka

PRAHA 3

Pitterova

Jana Želivského

Chelčického

Tram 9, 26, 55

Olšanská

● 45

Olšanské
náměstí

🏨 39

U nákladového nádraží

🍴 4

Křešanová

Jičínská

Baranova

Sudoměřská

Radhošťská

Olšanské
hřbitovy
(Olšany
Cemetery)

Jewish
Cemetery

Lucemburská

Tram 5, 9, 26

Izraelská

Želivského Ⓜ

Přemyslovská

🛍 27

Flóra
Ⓜ

Tram 5, 10, 11, 16, 51, 58 Vinohradská

🅿 3

● 20

Kolínská

Lužická

Tram 10, 16

Hradecká

Písecká

Tram 5

Koufimská

Koufimská

A · B · C · D

1 · 2 · 3 · 4 · 5 · 6

Slovanský ostrov (Žofín)

Vojtěšská

Petrossova

Myslíkova

Na zbořenci

Odborů

Řeznická

Pštrossova

Karlovo náměstí

Žitná

Záhořanského

Malá

Štěpánská

Na Rybníčku II

Na příkopě

Karlovo Náměstí

M

Štěpánská

Tram 17, 21

See Southern Malá Strana Map (pp250–1)

Resslova

Nové Město

Ječná

Tram 4, 6, 10, 16, 22, 23, 51, 56, 57

Jiráskův most

25

Corazzova

Dittrichova

Václavská

Karlovo náměstí

Salmovská

Lípová

Kateřinská

Na bojišti

Rašínovo nábřeží

Trojanova

Vyšehradská

Tram 3, 4, 10, 16, 18, 24

Na Moráni

M

Karlovo Náměstí

U nemocnice

See Nové Město Map (pp252–3)

Viničná

Palackého most

Palackého náměstí

Pod Slovany

Na Slovanech

To Káva.Káva.Káva

Ke Karlovu

📛 9

📛 12

Benátská

Botanická zahrada Univerzity Karlovy

Apolinářská

Vltava River

📛 45

Trojická

Podskalská

Tram 18, 24, 53, 55

Vyšehradská

📛 46

Plavecká

Na slupi

Albertov

Studničkova

Horská

11 📛

Holešší nábřeží

📛 30

Tram 3, 7, 16, 17, 21, 54

Svobodova

Tram 7

Vnislavova

Horská

Na slupi

Sekaninova

📛 26

Libušina

7 📛

Vratislavova

Hošťířova

Neklanova

Vnislavova

Nezamyslova

Oldřichova

2 📛

Ostrčilovo náměstí

📛 28

Štulcovy sady

1

51 📛

Tram 7, 18, 24, 53, 5

40

Tram 3, 16, 17, 21, 54

20 📛

V pevnosti

Jaromírova

📛 3

Vyšehrad

📛 23

Karlachovy sady

Slavojova

Čiklova

📛 14

K rotundě

8 📛

📛 48

Strakonická

📛 18

5

📛 22

Lumírova

Krokova

Vyšehradské sady

33 📛

📛 16

4

📛 6

15

Na Bučánce

louky

Vyšehradské skála (Vyšehrad Rock)

Podolské nábřeží

57 📛 21

10

24

Na Pankráci

Císařská louka (Imperial Meadow)

Pankrácké náměstí

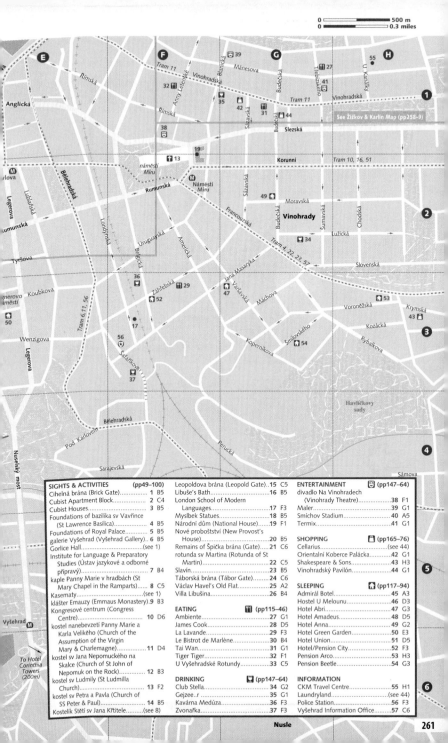

0 ▬▬▬▬▬ **500 m**
0 ▬▬▬▬▬ **0.3 miles**

See Žižkov & Karlin Map (pp258–9)

Nusle

METRO & TRAM MAP

Orientační plán · Metro

Dopravní podnik hl. m. Prahy, akciová společnost

STANICE METRA
METRO STATION

STANICE PŘESTUPNÍ
POINT OF CHANGE

TRATĚ METRA
METRO ROUTES

BEZBARIÉROVÝ PŘÍSTUP
BARRIERLESS ACCESS

ZÁCHYTNÁ PARKOVIŠTĚ
PARKING FACILITIES

Černý Most

Rajská zahrada

Hloubětín
Kolbenova
Vysočanská
Hloubětín
LEHOVEC
HLOUBĚTÍN
HRDLOŘEZY
MALEŠICE
STRAŠNICE
HORNÍ MĚCHOLUPY
JIŽNÍ MĚSTO

Hostivař
Skalka
Strašnická
Želivského
Flora
Jiřího z Poděbrad
Náměstí Míru

Opatov
Chodov
Roztyly
Kačerov
Háje
SPOŘILOV
ZÁBĚHLICE
LHOTKA
KUNRATICE

KBELY
LETŇANY
PROSEK
STŘÍŽKOV
ĎÁBLICE
KOBYLISY
Ládví
Kobylisy
TRÓJA
BOHNICE
ZOO

Vysočanská
VYSOČANY
Českomoravská
Palmovka
Invalidovna
Křižíkova
Florenc
LIBEŇ
KARLÍN
ŽIŽKOV
VINOHRADY
VRŠOVICE
MICHLE
PANKRÁC

Náměstí Republiky
Hlavní nádraží
Muzeum
Vltavská
Nádraží Holešovice
HOLEŠOVICE

Staroměstská
Můstek
Národní třída
Karlovo náměstí

I.P.Pavlova
Vyšehrad
Pražského povstání
Pankrác
Budějovická
Kačerov
NUSLE
KRČ
PODOLÍ
BRANÍK
MODŘANY

Hradčanská
BUBENEČ
DEJVICE
Dejvická
Malostranská
HRADČANY
STRAHOV
MOTOL
BŘEVNOV
PETŘINY
BÍLÁ HORA
DIVOKÁ ŠÁRKA
NEBUŠICE
LIBOC
ŘEPY

Anděl
SMÍCHOV
Smíchovské nádraží
Radlická
Jinonice
Nové Butovice
Luka
Lužiny
Hůrka
Stodůlky
Zličín
HLUBOČEPY
VELKÁ CHUCHLE
SÍDLIŠTĚ BARRANDOV
RADOTÍN
ŘEPORYJE
HOSTIVICE

X-14

262